The History and Archaeology of the Iroquois du Nord

The History and Archaeology of the Iroquois du Nord

**Edited by Robert von Bitter
and Ronald F. Williamson**

MERCURY SERIES
ARCHAEOLOGY PAPER 182
CANADIAN MUSEUM OF HISTORY
AND UNIVERSITY OF OTTAWA PRESS

© 2023 Canadian Museum of History

All rights reserved. No part of this book may be reproduced or transmitted in any form or by any means electronic or mechanical, including photocopying, recording, or any retrieval system, without the written permission of the publisher.

Co-published by the **Canadian Museum of History** and the **University of Ottawa Press**

The University of Ottawa Press gratefully acknowledges the support extended to its publishing list by the Government of Canada, the Canada Council for the Arts, the Ontario Council for the Arts, the Federation for the Humanities and Social Sciences through the Awards to Scholarly Publications Program, and the University of Ottawa.

Copy editing Tanina Drvar
Proofreading Crystal Chan, Robbie McCaw, Michael Waldin
Typesetting Édiscript enr.
Indexing Édiscript enr.
Cover design Lefrançois, agence marketing B2B
Cover image Map of the Great Lakes drawn by Jacques Nicolas Bellin, 1755. *Atlas Homannianus Mathematic-Historice Delineatus*, Nuremberg, Germany, Homann Heirs. Image provided by Geographicus Rare Antique Maps through Wikimedia Commons.

Legal Deposit: First Quarter 2023
Library and Archives Canada
Printed in Canada

Library and Archives Canada Cataloguing in Publication

Title: The history and archaeology of the Iroquois du Nord / edited by Robert von Bitter and Ronald F. Williamson.
Names: Bitter, Robert von, editor. | Williamson, R. F. (Ronald F.), editor.
Series: Mercury series. | Archaeology paper (Canadian Museum of History) ; 182.
Description: Series statement: Mercury series | Archaeology paper ; 182 | Includes bibliographical references.
Identifiers: Canadiana (print) 20220417180 | Canadiana (ebook) 20220420173 | ISBN 9780776639833 (hardcover) | ISBN 9780776639802 (softcover) | ISBN 9780776639819 (PDF) | ISBN 9780776639826 (EPUB)
Subjects: LCSH: Ontario, Lake, Region (N.Y. and Ont.)—History. | LCSH: Ontario, Lake, Region (N.Y. and Ont.)—Antiquities. | CSH: First Nations—Ontario, Lake, Region (N.Y. and Ont.)—History. | CSH: First Nations—Ontario, Lake, Region (N.Y. and Ont.)—Antiquities.
Classification: LCC E78.O5 H57 2023 | DDC 971.3/50049755—dc23

The Mercury Series

The best resource on the history, archaeology, and culture of Canada is proudly published by the Canadian Museum of History and the University of Ottawa Press.

La collection Mercure

Le Musée canadien de l'histoire et les Presses de l'Université d'Ottawa publient avec fierté la meilleure ressource en ce qui a trait à l'histoire, à l'archéologie et à la culture canadiennes.

For this book/Pour ce livre

Series Editor/Direction de la collection
  Pierre M. Desrosiers

Editorial Committee/Comité éditorial
  Laura Sanchini, Janet Young, Matthew Betts

Managing Editor/Responsable de l'édition
  Robyn Jeffrey

Coordination
  Lee Wyndham, Shannon Moore, Pascal Scallon-Chouinard

How to Order

All trade orders must be directed to the University of Ottawa Press:
  Web: www.press.uOttawa.ca
  Email: PUO-UOP@uOttawa.ca
  Phone: 613-562-5246

All other orders may be directed to either the University of Ottawa Press (as above) or to the Canadian Museum of History:

  Web: www.historymuseum.ca/shop
  Email: publications@historymuseum.ca
  Phone: 1-800-555-5621 (toll-free) or
    819-776-8387 (National Capital Region)
  Mail: Mail Order Services
    Canadian Museum of History
    100 Laurier Street
    Gatineau, QC, K1A 0M8

Pour commander

Les libraires et les autres détaillants doivent adresser leurs commandes aux Presses de l'Université d'Ottawa :
  Web : www.presses.uOttawa.ca
  Courriel : PUO-UOP@uOttawa.ca
  Téléphone : 613-562-5246

Les particuliers doivent adresser leurs commandes soit aux Presses de l'Université d'Ottawa (voir plus haut), soit au Musée canadien de l'histoire :

  Web : www.museedelhistoire.ca/magasiner
  Courriel : publications@museedelhistoire.ca
  Téléphone : 1-800-555-5621 (numéro sans frais)
    ou 819-776-8387 (région de la capitale nationale)
  Poste : Service des commandes postales
    Musée canadien de l'histoire
    100, rue Laurier
    Gatineau (Québec) K1A 0M8

Land Acknowledgement
Reconnaissance territoriale

The Canadian Museum of History and the University of Ottawa Press are located on the traditional, unceded territory of the Algonquin Anishinabeg. This land has held, and continues to hold, great historical, spiritual, and sacred significance. We recognize and honour the enduring presence of the Algonquin people. We also know that you, our readers, are joining us from many places near and far, and we acknowledge the traditional owners and caretakers of those lands.

Le Musée canadien de l'histoire et Les Presses de l'Université d'Ottawa sont situés sur le territoire traditionnel non cédé des Anishinabeg (Algonquins). Ce territoire a eu, et continue d'avoir, une grande importance historique, spirituelle et sacrée. Nous reconnaissons et honorons la présence pérenne du peuple algonquin. Nous avons aussi conscience que notre lectorat provient de nombreux endroits, proches et lointains, et nous reconnaissons les gens qui sont les propriétaires et les gardiens traditionnels de ces terres.

Abstract

In the mid- to late 1660s and early 1670s, the Haudenosaunee established a series of settlements at strategic locations along the trade routes inland at short distances from the north shore of Lake Ontario. From east to west, these Iroquois villages consisted of Ganneious, on Napanee or Hay Bay, on the Bay of Quinte; Kenté, near the isthmus of the Quinte Peninsula; Ganaraské, at the mouth of the Ganaraska River; Quintio, on Rice Lake; Ganatsekwyagon, near the mouth of the Rouge River; Teiaiagon, near the mouth of the Humber River; and Outinaouatoua, on the portage between the western end of Lake Ontario and the Grand River. While Outinaouatoua appears not to have had a primary affiliation, Ganatsekwyagon and Teiaiagon were mostly Seneca; Ganaraské, Kenté, and Quintio were likely Cayuga; and Ganneious was Oneida. Judging from documentary accounts, however, all the villages might have contained people from several Haudenosaunee constituencies as well as former Ontario Iroquoians who had been adopted by the Haudenosaunee.

These self-sufficient villages acted as bases for their own inhabitants, as well as shelter for south-shore Haudenosaunee on their way to and from the beaver hunt beyond the lower Great Lakes. They may also have acted as "tollgates" for Anishinaabe fur brigades by which the Haudenosaunee could control the flow of furs to Albany. It has further been suggested that the continual harassment by the Andastes/Susquehannock on the south side of Lake Ontario was another reason some Cayuga, and probably some Seneca and Oneida as well, moved north. One of these villages was also the site of a Sulpician mission, better known as the Kenté or Quinte mission for where it was based. Beginning with the abbés Claude Trouvé and François de Salignac de la Mothe-Fénelon at Kenté in 1668, various Sulpicians visited the north-shore villages over the next decade. In 1676, Abbé Mariet set up a subsidiary mission at Teiaiagon. It appears that most of the north-shore villages were abandoned by 1688. While they were likely due for relocation after twenty years, their depopulation seems to have been accelerated by hostilities with Anishinaabe and Denonville's campaign against the homelands in 1687.

This volume brings together Indigenous knowledge as well as documentary and recent archaeological evidence of this period to focus on describing the historical context, efforts to find the villages, and examinations of the unique material culture discovered there and at similar settlements in the Haudenosaunee homeland.

Résumé

À la fin des années 1660 et au début des années 1670, les Haudenosaunee ont peuplé des lieux stratégiques le long de routes commerciales à l'intérieur des terres, non loin de la rive nord du lac Ontario. D'est en ouest, il s'agissait de Ganneious, à l'emplacement de Napanee ou de la baie Hay, sur la baie de Quinte; de Kenté, près de l'isthme de la péninsule de Quinte; de Ganaraské, à l'embouchure de la rivière Ganaraska; de Quintio, sur le lac Rice; de Ganatsekwyagon, près de l'embouchure de la rivière Rouge; de Teiaiagon, près de l'embouchure de la rivière Humber; et de Outinaouatoua, devant la pointe ouest du lac Ontario et de la rivière Grande. Si les membres de la communauté d'Outinaouatoua ne semblent pas avoir fait partie d'un groupe précis, ceux de Ganatsekwyagon et de Teiaiagon étaient des Sénécas; ceux de Ganaraské, de Kenté et de Quintio des Cayugas; et ceux de Ganneious des Onéidas. Toutefois, selon des récits documentés, des personnes de territoires haudenosaunee ainsi que d'anciens Iroquoiens du Saint-Laurent adoptés par les Haudenosaunee y étaient établis.

Ces peuplements autosuffisants servaient de bases pour leurs habitants, mais aussi de halte lors du passage des Haudenosaunee de la rive sud chassant le castor au-delà des Grands Lacs inférieurs. Ils pourraient aussi avoir agi comme des « postes de péage » pour les brigades des fourrures des Anishinabés permettant aux Haudenosaunee de contrôler le flux de ce produit vers Albany. Il a été suggéré en outre que le harcèlement continu des Andastes/Susquehannock sur la rive sud du lac Ontario aurait poussé des Cayugas et, peut-être, des Sénécas et Onéidas, à se déplacer au nord. En raison de son emplacement, un de ces villages abritait la mission sulpicienne Kenté, ou Quinte. Fondée par les abbés Claude Trouvé et François de Salignac de la Mothe-Fénelon en 1668, celle-ci a accueilli plusieurs sulpiciens visitant les villages de la côte nord pendant la décennie suivante. En 1676, l'abbé Mariet a établi une filiale à Teiaiagon. En 1688, la plupart des villages de la rive nord auraient été abandonnés. Bien qu'une relocalisation ait sans doute été requise après 20 ans, leur dépopulation aurait été accélérée par les conflits avec les Anishinabés et par la campagne de Denonville contre leurs territoires ancestraux en 1687.

Cet ouvrage réunit le savoir autochtone et des données documentaires et archéologiques récentes sur cette période. Les autrices et les auteurs se penchent sur le contexte historique de ces peuplements et les efforts déployés pour les trouver, ainsi que sur la culture matérielle unique liée à ces lieux et à des communautés similaires sur le territoire ancestral des Haudenosaunee.

Land Acknowledgment for this Volume

We acknowledge the land as our mother who continues to provide for our health and wellbeing. She supports us as we go about doing the work that we do. She holds the memory of countless generations of ancestors who were also supported by her. Those ancestors tell us that no one owns the land, as the land holds us. We are of this land. We all have a responsibility to be grateful and treat the earth as our mother.

Dedication

This volume is dedicated to the memory of two Haudenosaunee women—Councillor Barbara Harris and Joanne Thomas.

Barb Harris was a councillor for Six Nations Elected Council for District 6 from 2001 until 2010 and worked diligently with Elders and traditionalists to rebury ancestors' remains promptly and normally in the same place that they were found. Barb oversaw the reburial of the Seneca women from Teiaiagon.

Barb was a mentor for Joanne Thomas who was equally dedicated at her positions as land-use officer and later consultation supervisor for Six Nations Lands and Resources. Joanne was a warm, caring person and became a friend of many archaeologists in Ontario. She was central in securing her Council's support for establishing a Heritage Conservation District for Teiaiagon as an additional layer of protection for the site and the ancestors buried there.

These women were instrumental in protecting Haudenosaunee interests in Ontario. We miss them both.

Figure D.1. Celebration at the opening of the permanent exhibit entitled *Uncovering Our Early Past: First Nations in Toronto*, May 2012. Department of Anthropology, University of Toronto. *Left to right*: Susan Pfeiffer, Barb Harris, Luc Lainé, Joanne Thomas.
Source: Jon Horvatin.

Table of Contents

Land Acknowledgement / Reconnaissance territoriale v

Abstract vi

Résumé vii

Land Acknowledgment for this Volume viii

Dedication ix

List of Figures xvii

List of Tables xxiii

Chapter 1
Introduction
RONALD F. WILLIAMSON 1
  1. Who Were the Iroquois du Nord? 1
  2. The Iroquois Wars 8
    2.1. Pre-Dispersal Period (1609–1648) 11
    2.2. Dispersal Period (1648–1651) 17
    2.3. Post-Dispersal Period (1651–1666) 21
    2.4. Occupation of the Iroquois du Nord Settlements and their Abandonment 23
  3. Volume Organization 26
  Acknowledgements 29

SECTION 1 – HISTORY OF THE PERIOD

Chapter 2
Departing and Returning: Haudenosaunee Homeland Contexts for the Iroquois du Nord Villages
KURT A. JORDAN 33
  1. Peak Power, 1650–1680 35
    1.1. Incorporation 39
    1.2. Colonization 40
    1.3. Regional Settlement Intensification 41
    1.4. Settler Forts and Missionaries 42

  1.5. Material Culture, 1650–1680 43
 2. The Twenty Years' War and French Invasions, 1680–1696.......... 44
 3. After the Invasions, 1696–1713 46
  3.1. Contraction and Consolidation 46
  3.2. Material Culture, 1696–1713 49
 4. Conclusion: After Uncertainty 50
 Acknowledgements 51

SECTION 2 – THE SETTLEMENT LOCATIONS AND HISTORY OF INVESTIGATIONS

Chapter 3
The Search for Kenté: A Review
Robert von Bitter, Chris Menary, and Nick Gromoff 55
 1. The Search for Kenté 60
  1.1. The Reverend Phillip Bowen Squire 63
 2. Spatial Analysis 70
 3. Conclusion 76
 Acknowledgements 76

Chapter 4
Clues in the Landscape: The Search for Ganaraské, Quintio, and Ganneious
Chris Menary and Robert von Bitter 77
 1. Documentary Record: Accounts 78
  1.1. Ganaraské and Quintio 78
  1.2. Ganneious 81
 2. Documentary Record: Historical Maps 81
 3. Relocating the Villages: Landscape Analysis 86
  3.1. Quintio 86
  3.2. Ganaraské 89
  3.3. Ganneious 89
 4. Relocating the Villages: LiDAR and Remote Sensing 91
  4.1. Ganaraské and Quintio 91
  4.2. Ganneious 96
 5. Conclusion 97

Chapter 5
The Bead Hill Site: A Late Seventeenth-Century Seneca Village on the Lower Rouge River
Dana R. Poulton 99
 1. The Lower Rouge River Valley, ca. 1665–1687 102
 2. Archaeological Investigations 104

3. Site Description 105
　　4. Material Culture Remains... 107
　　5. Discussion 116
　　6. Historical Identity 118
　　　　6.1. Abandonment.. 119
　　7. Conclusion 122
　　Acknowledgements.. 122

Chapter 6
Teiaiagon: A Village on the West Branch of the Toronto Carrying Place
DAVID ROBERTSON 125
　　1. The Toronto Carrying Place... 125
　　2. The Historical Context of the Site of Teiaiagon................. 126
　　3. The Archaeology of Teiaiagon.. 131
　　Acknowledgements.. 139

Chapter 7
Changing Continuities of Home: Outinaouatoua in the Context of Seventeenth-Century Indigenous Heritage Landscapes
NEAL FERRIS 141
　　1. The Galinée and Dollier Expedition in the Context of 1669 145
　　2. The Context of Outinaouatoua in 1669............................. 147
　　3. Outinaouatoua Within the Context of an Indigenous Heritage Landscape 150
　　4. Conclusion 155

SECTION 3 – THE MATERIAL CULTURE OF THE IROQUOIS DU NORD SITES

Chapter 8
Drawing a Bead on the Iroquois du Nord Narrative
WILLIAM A. FOX, APRIL HAWKINS, AND DAVID HARRIS 159
　　1. Evidence from the Haudenosaunee Homeland..................... 161
　　2. Glass Beads 163
　　3. Marine Shell Beads 175
　　4. Bone Beads 178
　　5. Stone Beads 180
　　6. Discussion.. 183
　　7. Conclusion 186
　　Acknowledgements.. 186

Chapter 9
Come from the Shadows: Metals on the Iroquois Frontier
MARTIN S. COOPER 187
- 1. Kettles 189
    - 1.1. Teiaiagon 189
    - 1.2. Ganatsekwyagon 192
    - 1.3. Chadd Collection 193
- 2. Projectile Points 193
    - 2.1. Teiaiagon 193
    - 2.2. Ganatsekwyagon 194
    - 2.3. Chadd Collection 194
- 3. Axes 195
    - 3.1. Teiaiagon 195
    - 3.2. Chadd Collection 196
- 4. Hoes 196
    - 4.1. Teiaiagon 196
- 5. Knives 197
    - 5.1. Teiaiagon 197
    - 5.2. Ganatsekwyagon 198
- 6. Firearms 198
    - 6.1. Teiaiagon 199
    - 6.2. Ganatsekwyagon 199
- 7. Gunflints 200
- 8. Iconographic Rings 201
    - 8.1. Teiaiagon 202
    - 8.2. Ganatsekwyagon 202
    - 8.3. Chadd Collection 203
- 9. Religious Medallions 205
    - 9.1. Teiaiagon 205
    - 9.2. Chadd Collection 206
- 10. Coins 207
    - 10.1. Ganatsekwyagon 208
- 11. Is the Van Son Cemetery an Iroquois du Nord Site? ... 208
- 12. Conclusion 211
- Acknowledgements 212

Chapter 10
Iroquois du Nord Decorated Antler Combs: Reflections of Ideology
RONALD F. WILLIAMSON AND ROBERT VON BITTER 213
- 1. Iroquois du Nord Antler Combs 223
    - 1.1. Teiaiagon 223

    1.2. Ganatsekwyagon-Bead Hill 228
    1.3. Kenté 228
2. Discussion 234
Acknowledgements 237

Chapter 11
Iroquois du Nord Ceramic Vessels and Pipes
WILLIAM E. ENGELBRECHT AND RONALD F. WILLIAMSON 239
1. Late Ceramic Vessel Trends Among Northern Iroquoians............ 240
2. Timing of the Decline of Indigenous-Made Ceramic Vessels
    and Pipes on Haudenosaunee Sites... 241
    2.1. Seneca 241
    2.2. Cayuga 243
    2.3. Onondaga 244
    2.4. Oneida 244
    2.5. Mohawk 244
    2.6. Susquehannock 245
3. Significance, Persistence and Eventual Cessation of Indigenous
    Ceramic and Pipe Manufacture 245
4. The Iroquois du Nord Sample 247
    4.1. Kenté 249
    4.2. Ganatsekwyagon 256
    4.3. Teiaiagon 257
5. Discussion and Conclusion 259
Acknowledgements 260

SECTION 4 – THE ANISHINAABE OCCUPATION

Chapter 12
After the Haudenosaunee: The Mississauga Occupation of the North Shore of Lake Ontario
GARY WARRICK AND RONALD F. WILLIAMSON 263
1. History of the Mississauga Occupation 265
2. Archaeology of the Mississauga Occupation 274
3. Conclusion 281
Acknowledgements 281

SECTION 5 – DISCUSSION AND CONCLUSIONS AND THE HAUDENOSAUNEE VIEW

Chapter 13
The "Iroquois du Nord" of the Late Seventeenth Century: Revisiting the Haudenosaunee on the North Shore of Lake Ontario
Victor Konrad 285
   1. Archaeology, Geography, History, and Memory 285
   2. Confirmations of Site Locations 287
   3. East–West Regionalization and South–North Expansion of the Settlement System 289
   4. Iroquois du Nord Territory as Borderlands and the Advancement of Border Theory 291
   5. A Re-populated North Shore: Transformation, Prosperity, Precarity, and Becoming Iroquois du Nord 293
   6. An Anishinaabe North Shore 297
   7. Prospective 298

Chapter 14
View from the North Shore: Indigenous Imaginations, Then and Now
Rick Hill 301

References Cited 307

Index 347

List of Figures

Figure D.1. Celebration at the opening of the permanent exhibit entitled *Uncovering Our Early Past: First Nations in Toronto*, May 2012. Department of Anthropology, University of Toronto.. vii

Figure 1.1. Map published in 1688 by Jesuit Father Pierre Raffeix, titled "Le lac Ontario avec les lieux circonvoisins & particulièrement les cinq nations Iroquoises".................. 2

Figure 1.2. Map showing the possible locations of the eastern Iroquois du Nord villages and find locations as well as Fort Frontenac... 3

Figure 1.3. Map showing the location of the western Iroquois du Nord villages and the Van Son cemetery................... 4

Figure 1.4. Map published in 1680 by Abbé Claude Bernou, showing "LAC DE TARONTO" (current-day Lake Simcoe) and the villages of "Teyoyagon" (Teiaiagon) and "Ganatchakiagon" (Ganatsekwyagon)... 6

Figure 1.5. Map showing the locations of the Haudenosaunee and Ontario Iroquoian nations at the time of contact, as well as the ancestral territory of the Wendat............... 7

Figure 1.6. Graphs showing the distribution of scattered human bone and human bone artifacts using data from sixty Ontario Iroquoian villages 10

Figure 1.7. Engraving of the Battle of Lake Champlain, 1609, published by Samuel de Champlain................................ 12

Figure 1.8. Map showing the locations of Wendat villages mentioned in the text 14

Figure 2.1. Haudenosaunee principal town sites likely to have been visited by New York official Wentworth Greenhalgh in 1677 36

Figure 2.2. Haudenosaunee principal town sites occupied after the French invasions of 1687–1696. Mohawk-area sites include both those identified by the Snow model and those identified by the Lenig model 47

Figure 3.1. Late seventeenth- and early eighteenth-century French mission and fort site plans... 57

Figure 3.2. Comparative analysis of detail from 1675 Jolliet map and a modern map (2020) of Wellers Bay 61

Figure 3.3. Contemporary map centred on Wellers Bay.................. 62

Figure 3.4.	Ontario Heritage Foundation plaque relating to the Kenté mission	**64**
Figure 3.5.	Fake birdstone from the Squire Collection	**67**
Figure 3.6.	Example of metal cross possibly manufactured by Squire	**68**
Figure 3.7.	Metal projectile points	**69**
Figure 3.8.	First option for spatial analysis of the Chadd Collection	**71**
Figure 3.9.	Second option for spatial analysis of the Chadd Collection	**73**
Figure 3.10.	Detail from the 1688 Raffeix map showing a barque; map published in 1688 by Jesuit Father Pierre Raffeix, titled "Le lac Ontario avec les lieux circonvoisins & particulièrement les cinq nations Iroquoises"	**75**
Figure 4.1.	Detail of François Vachon de Belmont's "Carte du cours du fleuve Saint-Laurent depuis son embouchure jusques et y compris le Lac supérieur," 1680	**80**
Figure 4.2.	Detail of Jean-Baptiste-Louis Franquelin's "Carte pour servir a l'éclaircissement du papier terrier de la Nouvelle-France," 1678	**80**
Figure 4.3.	Detail of René Bréhant de Galinée's "Carte du lac Ontario et des habitations qui l'environnent. Ensemble le pays que M.M. Dollier et Galinée, missionnaires du Séminaire de St-Sulpice ont parcouru, 1670"	**83**
Figure 4.4.	Detail of Jean-Baptiste-Louis Franquelin's "Carte de la Louisiane en l'Amérique septentrionale, depuis la Nouvelle France jusqu'au golfe du Mexique"	**85**
Figure 4.5.	The portage routes from Rice Lake to Lake Ontario and the probable locations of IDN villages and possible location options for Quintio on the Trent Waterway	**87**
Figure 4.6.	Topographical map of Hay Bay and comparison with Belmont 1680	**90**
Figure 4.7.	The topography of the Rice Lake-Lake Ontario portage	**92**
Figure 4.8.	Potential locations of Ganaraské and least cost path analysis of portage routes	**93**
Figure 4.9.	Potential location of Quintio and portage, least cost path analysis	**95**
Figure 5.1.	Location of the Rouge National Urban Park	**100**
Figure 5.2.	The lower Rouge River, Joseph Adamson Blakely, 1908	**101**

Figure 5.3.	Bead Hill site plan showing 1987 and 1991 archaeological investigations	106
Figure 5.4.	Bead Hill site, Trench 1 plan showing settlement patterns	107
Figure 5.5.	Bead Hill site, distribution of selected artifacts in the 1991 investigations sample	108
Figure 5.6.	Partially reconstructed Middle Woodland ceramic vessel	114
Figure 6.1.	Map showing the location of the village of Teiaiagon on the lower Humber River and the southern terminus of the west branch of the Toronto Carrying Place	127
Figure 6.2.	Andrew Hunter's and A. J. Clark's sketches of the principal areas of archaeological finds at Baby Point, Toronto, overlaid on a map of the modern neighbourhood	134
Figure 7.1.	Speculative route of Galinée's 1669–1670 journey based on Coyne (1903) and the area in which Outinaouatoua is likely located	146
Figure 8.1.	Glass Bead Period 3 beads from the Lake Medad site	160
Figure 8.2.	Map showing locations of Haudenosaunee sites mentioned in the text	161
Figure 8.3.	Glass beads from the Dann site	163
Figure 8.4.	Glass beads from the Boughton Hill and Rochester Junction sites	164
Figure 8.5.	Glass beads from the Wellers Bay localities	173
Figure 8.6.	Glass beads from Ganatsekwyagon	174
Figure 8.7.	Glass beads from Teiaiagon	174
Figure 8.8.	Marine shell wampum belt from Ganatsekwyagon	175
Figure 8.9.	Marine shell loon effigy pendants from the Picton and Bloomfield localities	176
Figure 8.10.	Classic late seventeenth-century marine shell runtee beads and catlinite tubes, assumed to be from King Township, York County, in the John R. Mortimer Collection at the Hull and East Riding Museum, England	177
Figure 8.11.	Marine shell pipe beads from Ganatsekwyagon	178
Figure 8.12.	Marine shell wampum beads from Teiaiagon	178
Figure 8.13.	A string of glass and bone beads from the Wellers Bay locality with close-ups of round and oval bone rosary beads	179
Figure 8.14.	Tubular bone crucifix beads from the Wellers Bay locality	180

Figure 8.15.	Glass beads from Trent River Mouth, including a red siltstone tubular bead	182
Figure 8.16.	Red siltstone beads from Teiaiagon	183
Figure 9.1.	Brass kettle from Teiaiagon	190
Figure 9.2.	Brass kettle from Teiaiagon	191
Figure 9.3.	Omega lug from brass kettle from Ganatsekwyagon	192
Figure 9.4.	Three triangular brass projectile points from Teiaiagon	194
Figure 9.5.	Conserved iron axe from Teiaiagon	195
Figure 9.6.	Iron axe from Teiaiagon	196
Figure 9.7.	Conserved hoe from Teiaiagon	197
Figure 9.8.	Bone-handled knife from Teiaiagon	198
Figure 9.9.	Lead bar from Teiaiagon	199
Figure 9.10.	Portion of a reworked iron musket barrel from Ganatsekwyagon	200
Figure 9.11.	Three European gunflints from Ganatsekwyagon	201
Figure 9.12.	Pieta-type iconographic ring from Ganatsekwyagon	203
Figure 9.13.	L-heart-type iconographic ring from Bald Head Island/Kenté	204
Figure 9.14.	IHS-type iconographic ring from Bald Head Island/Kenté	204
Figure 9.15.	Unique portrait ring from Bald Head Island/Kenté	205
Figure 9.16.	Unique religious medallion from Teiaiagon	206
Figure 9.17.	Unique religious medallion from Bald Head Island/Kenté	207
Figure 9.18.	French 1655 *liard* coin from Ganatsekwyagon	208
Figure 9.19.	Brass projectile points from the Van Son cemetery site	210
Figure 10.1.	Comb from the Late Archaic Frontenac Island site, New York, collection of Rochester Museum & Science Center	216
Figure 10.2.	Combs from the Middle Woodland period	217
Figure 10.3.	Comb from the Late Woodland Lawson site	218
Figure 10.4.	Comb from the Neutral Grimsby site	219
Figure 10.5.	Two combs illustrating hourglasses, from Ganondagan and the Grimsby site	221
Figure 10.6.	"Doorkeeper" comb from the Seneca Rochester Junction site, New York	222
Figure 10.7.	Comb from the Teiaiagon site, found by Archaeological Services Inc.	224
Figure 10.8.	Comb from the Teiaiagon site, found by Historic Horizon Inc.	226
Figure 10.9.	Combs from the Teiaiagon site	227
Figure 10.10.	Comb from Ganatsekwyagon	229

Figure 10.11.	Comb from Smokes Point	230
Figure 10.12.	Combs from Bald Head Island and Smokes Point	232
Figure 10.13.	Three combs with asymmetrical panther, from the Dann site	233
Figure 10.14.	Two combs illustrating use of dots, from Boughton Hill site	234
Figure 10.15.	Comb from Carrying Place, and comb with unknown provenience	235
Figure 10.16.	Sun reflected in water	236
Figure 11.1.	Map showing locations of select mid- to late seventeenth-century Seneca, Cayuga, Onondaga, Oneida, and Mohawk sites	242
Figure 11.2.	Map showing locations of select mid- to late seventeenth-century Susquehannock sites	243
Figure 11.3.	Effigy castellation, Hocker type pipe, G. J. Chadd Collection	249
Figure 11.4.	Ceramic vessel rim sherds from Bald Head Island, G. J. Chadd Collection	250
Figure 11.5.	Ceramic vessel sherds from Wellers Bay	251
Figure 11.6.	Effigy pipes found in Ameliasburgh Township, G. J. Chadd Collection	254
Figure 11.7.	Three complete pipes, G. J. Chadd Collection	256
Figure 11.8.	Two pipe bowl fragments from Ganatsekwyagon	257
Figure 11.9.	Three pipes from Teiaiagon	258
Figure 12.1.	Davisville 2 (AgHb-242), East Locus, artifacts from 299E 300N 20–25 cm DBS	277
Figure 12.2.	Davisville 3 (AgHb-243) artifacts	278
Figure 12.3.	Size distribution of calcined bone from an excavation unit of Davisville 3 (AgHb-243)	280

List of Tables

Table 2.1.	Names and sources for Haudenosaunee principal town sites likely to have been visited by New York official Wentworth Greenhalgh in 1677	37
Table 2.2.	Names and sources for Haudenosaunee principal town sites occupied after the French invasions of 1687–1696	47
Table 5.1.	Artifact samples from the Bead Hill site	110
Table 5.2.	Glass trade beads from the Bead Hill site	112
Table 8.1.	Glass beads from the Sandbanks locality	165
Table 8.2.	Glass beads from Indian Island locality	166
Table 8.3.	Glass beads from the Ameliasburgh Township	166
Table 8.4.	Glass beads from Bloomfield locality	167
Table 8.5.	Glass beads from the Carrying Place area	168
Table 8.6.	Glass beads from the Coe Hill area	168
Table 8.7.	Glass beads from the Picton area	169
Table 8.8.	Glass beads from Sugar Point	169
Table 8.9.	Glass beads from the Trent River mouth (Murray Township)	170
Table 8.10.	Glass beads from the Wellers Bay locality	171
Table 8.11.	Glass beads from Ganatsekwyagon	171
Table 8.12.	Glass beads from Teiaiagon	172
Table 9.1.	Metal artifacts from Iroquois du Nord sites	188
Table 9.2.	Iconographic finger rings from Iroquois du Nord sites	189
Table 11.1.	Ceramic vessel fragments from the Kenté region	252

1

INTRODUCTION

RONALD F. WILLIAMSON

1. Who Were the Iroquois du Nord?

Between the mid to late 1660s and early 1670s, the Haudenosaunee (Five Nations Iroquois) established a series of settlements at strategic locations along the trade routes inland, a short distance from the north shore of Lake Ontario. Collectively, these sites have become known as Iroquois du Nord (IDN) settlements (Konrad 1981:130). This is a period of Great Lakes Indigenous and early colonial-period history about which little has been written, with the exception of publications by Percy Robinson (1933); Preston and Lamontagne (1958); James Pritchard (1973a, b); Victor Konrad (1981); and Nick Adams (1986); there are no published articles on the archaeology of these sites. We hope to remedy that with this volume, which is based on the presentations given at a session held on November 2 at the 2019 Ontario Archaeological Society Annual Symposium, entitled "The Seventeenth Century Iroquois du Nord: History, Archaeology, and the Search for the Villages."

From east to west, these Haudenosaunee settlements consisted of Ganneious, on Napanee or Hay Bay, an arm of the Bay of Quinte; Kenté, near the isthmus of the Quinte Peninsula; Ganaraské, near the mouth of the Ganaraska River; Quintio, on Rice Lake; Ganatsekwyagon, near the mouth of the Rouge River; Teiaiagon, near the mouth of the Humber River; and Outinaouatoua, on the portage between the western end of Lake Ontario and the Grand River (Figures 1.1–1.4).[1] While Outinaouatoua appears not

---

1. The Iroquois du Nord settlements appear with different spellings on various maps and documents of the period. We chose, for the sake of consistency with previous scholarship, to use the spellings of the sites based on both Konrad (1981) and Robinson (1933), who relied on J. N. Hewitt for advice. While Haudenosaunee is used throughout the volume to refer to the Iroquois, we chose to retain the terms "Iroquois du Nord" and "Iroquois Wars," to be consistent with previous scholarship. While we have chosen to use the common English names of the

Figure 1.1. Map published in 1688 by Jesuit Father Pierre Raffeix, titled "Le lac Ontario avec les lieux circonvoisins & particulièrement les cinq nations Iroquoises." The map shows Lake Ontario, also known as the Lake of Saint Louis, with the surrounding area marked as including territory belonging to the five Iroquois nations. Current-day Lake Simcoe is marked as "Lac Taronthe." The villages of "theyagon" (Teiaigon) and "Ganestikagon" (Ganatsekwyagon) are also marked. Source: Map and Data Library, University of Toronto.

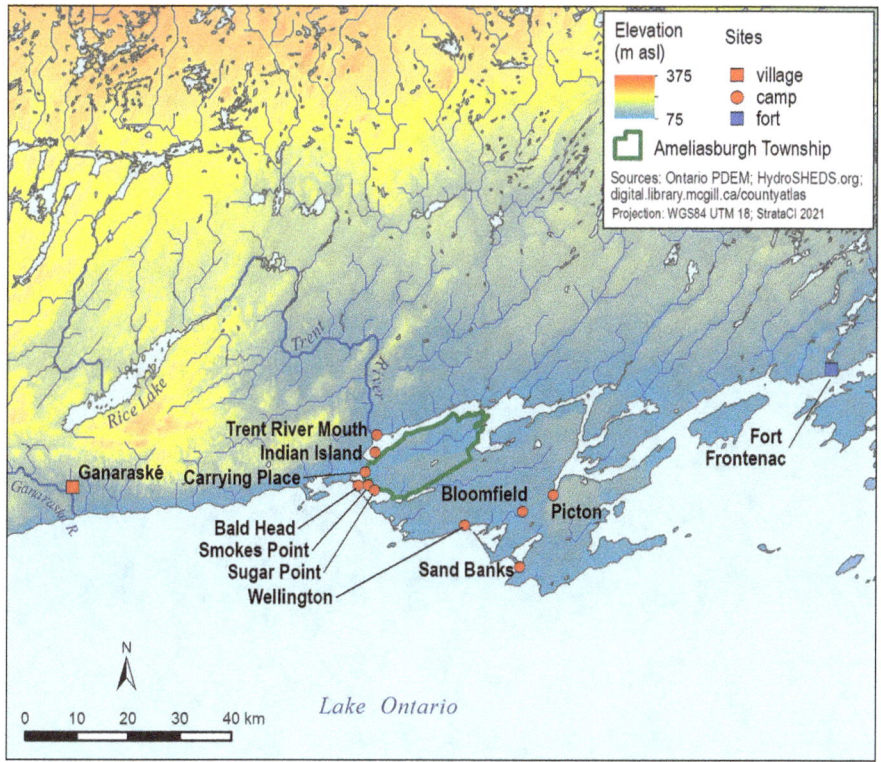

Figure 1.2. Map showing the possible locations of the eastern Iroquois du Nord villages and find locations as well as Fort Frontenac.
Source: Map by Ron Williamson.

to have had a primary affiliation (Ferris, this volume), Ganatsekwyagon and Teiaiagon were primarily Seneca; Ganaraské, Kenté, and Quintio were likely Cayuga; and Ganneious was Oneida (Konrad 1981:136). Judging from accounts of Teiaiagon, however, all these places may have hosted people from several Haudenosaunee constituencies. Konrad (1981) suggested that these villages probably contained about twenty to thirty structures with populations of approximately five hundred to eight hundred people, though Quintio may have been smaller.

According to Kurt Jordan (2013), Haudenosaunee satellite communities were originally situated near principal settlements, but after the 1660s, the Seneca and other Haudenosaunee nations also established extra-regional satellites, or "colonies" (2013:37). The documentary record suggests that, by 1687, in addition to being present in satellites on the north shore of Lake Ontario,

nations of the Haudenosaunee, their endonyms are presented in Jordan, this volume.

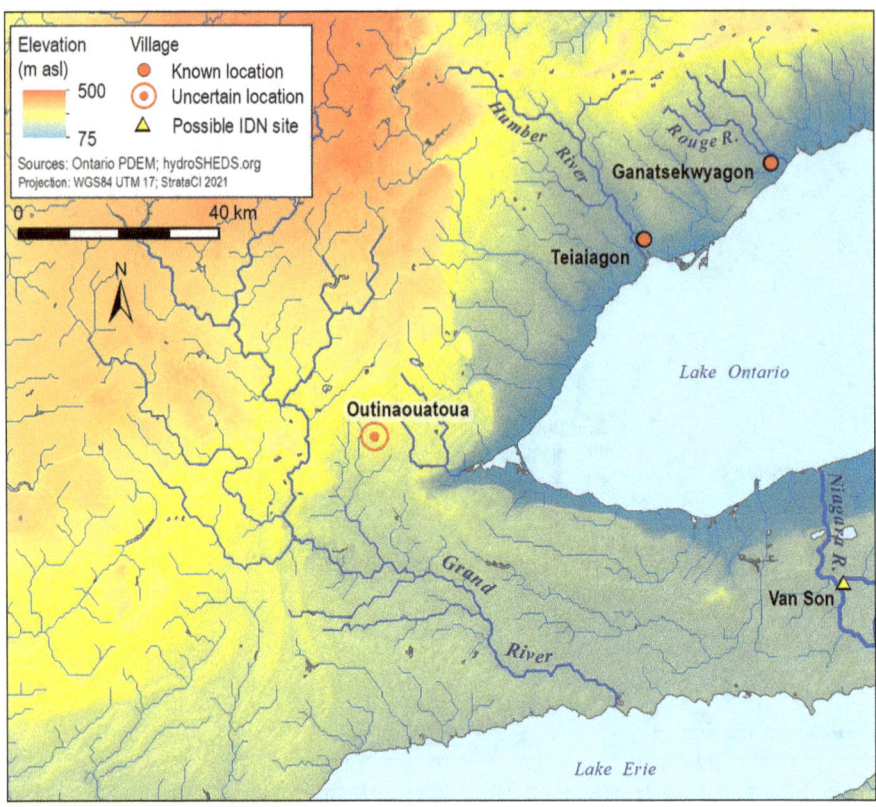

Figure 1.3. Map showing the location of the western Iroquois du Nord villages and the Van Son cemetery. *Source:* Map by Ron Williamson.

Seneca, for example, were also present near the Niagara portage and contributed to multinational populations at sites in the St. Lawrence and Susquehanna valleys (Jordan 2013:37).

The establishment of the north shore of Lake Ontario and other distant satellites occurred during the expansion of Haudenosaunee hegemony in the second half of the seventeenth century (Jordan and Gerard-Little 2019:45; Jordan, this volume). Their forays in the 1680s, however, against French-allied western Indigenous groups, had increasingly mixed results and occasioned a French response. The French launched several invasions of the Haudenosaunee homelands, first in the 1660s, then in the 1680s and 1690s, including an abortive expedition into Seneca Territory in 1684 and the destructive 1687 Denonville expedition. This latter campaign resulted in the movement of Seneca communities in the homeland to the south and east to distance themselves from possible additional French incursions originating from Lake Ontario and to be closer to their Cayuga allies to the east (Jordan and Gerard-Little 2019:45) (see Figure 2.2). Other satellites were also abandoned at this time, and according to Jordan and Gerrard-Little (2019:45), "there is no trace of any Seneca satellite whatsoever from 1688 to 1704."

Konrad (1981) noted that these villages not only acted as self-sufficient bases for their own inhabitants, but also served as shelter for south shore of Lake Ontario Haudenosaunee on their way to and from the beaver hunt beyond the lower Great Lakes, at distances of up to two hundred leagues. They could further act as tollgates or terminal points for Anishinaabe[2] fur brigades, by which, during times of peace, the Haudenosaunee could control the flow of furs to Albany. It is possible that the continual harassment by the Andaste (Susquehannock) on the south side of Lake Ontario pushed some Cayuga, and probably some Seneca and Oneida as well, to move north. Jordan and Gerrard-Little (2019:45) note that these settlements also functioned generally to monitor the activities of European and Indigenous allies and foes.

It is likely that some people who occupied the IDN satellites were former members of Wendat (Huron), Tionontaté (Petun), and Neutral (known to the Wendat as the Attawandaron) nations who had been incorporated into Haudenosaunee communities during the Iroquois Wars. It has been suggested that some of these individuals, at least the former Huron-Wendat, may have had first-hand familiarity with the north shore of Lake Ontario region. In my opinion, this is not likely to have been the case since that region was considered a dangerous area by the Huron-Wendat for fear of enemies at that time. Indeed, early Europeans were aware of the risks of travelling along the north shore of Lake Ontario to get to Quebec. In describing his journey from Quebec to Wendake, Father Jean de Brébeuf wrote in 1635, "It is true the way is shorter by the Saut de St. Louys and Lake of the Hiroquois [Ontario]; but the fear of enemies, and the few conveniences to be met with, cause that route to be unfrequented" (Thwaites 1896–1901:8:75), a sentiment also echoed by the Jesuit Paul Ragueneau in the Relation of 1648, when he states, "fear of the enemies who dwell along the shores of this Lake compels our Hurons, and us with them, to make a long detour […]" (Thwaites 1896–1901:33:65–66). The boundaries of Wendake in the historic period (1615–1650) have been marked using Jesuit accounts and the locations of known villages (Heidenreich 1971:22–53, Map 17). Conrad Heidenreich defined the southern frontier as extending from just north of Spratt Point; through Cranberry, Orr, and Bass lakes; to the narrows between Lake Couchiching and Lake Simcoe. There is no archaeological evidence of post-1615 Wendat use of lands south of the southern boundary. In addition, the Haudenosaunee had no lack of information about the region north of the north shore of Lake Ontario, having been conducting raids in southern Ontario and camping there for generations.

---

2. In keeping with common Indigenous practice, we have chosen to use Anishinaabe as an adjective and Anishinaabeg when referring to groups of people.

Heidi Bohaker (2006) suggests an alternate explanation: that a desire on the part of Wendat and Tionontaté adoptees to re-establish their symbiotic relationships with Anishinaabe hunters may have played a role in the establishment of the north shore of Lake Ontario Haudenosaunee villages. Wendat and Tionontaté families would have been able to access their old Anishinaabe allies and trading partners aiding the Haudenosaunee, and for the Anishinaabeg, the re-established trading partnerships would have "helped to reshape the political landscape of this area along familiar lines" (Bohaker 2006:247). It is also possible that there was a desire to more frequently visit distant ancestral landscapes and exercise responsibilities to their ancestors (see Birch and Williamson 2015).

There are several maps that provide details of the locations of the IDN settlements and nations in the Great Lakes region during this period (see Konrad 1981:Table 1). These include the map by the Jesuit Pierre Raffeix (Figure 1.1) dating to 1688, and a map ascribed to Abbé Claude Bernou, created circa 1680 (Figure 1.4). The Bernou map shows a route between "Ganatsekyagon" and "Lac de Taronto" (now known as Lake Simcoe), which is described as the route the Haudenosaunee take to the Ottawa, whom they would have brought to trade in New Holland had Fort Frontenac not been built. It also indicates that the area north of Lake Ontario served as beaver hunting grounds for the "Loups" (wolves; perhaps Mohegans of Taracton) and the Haudenosaunee, and

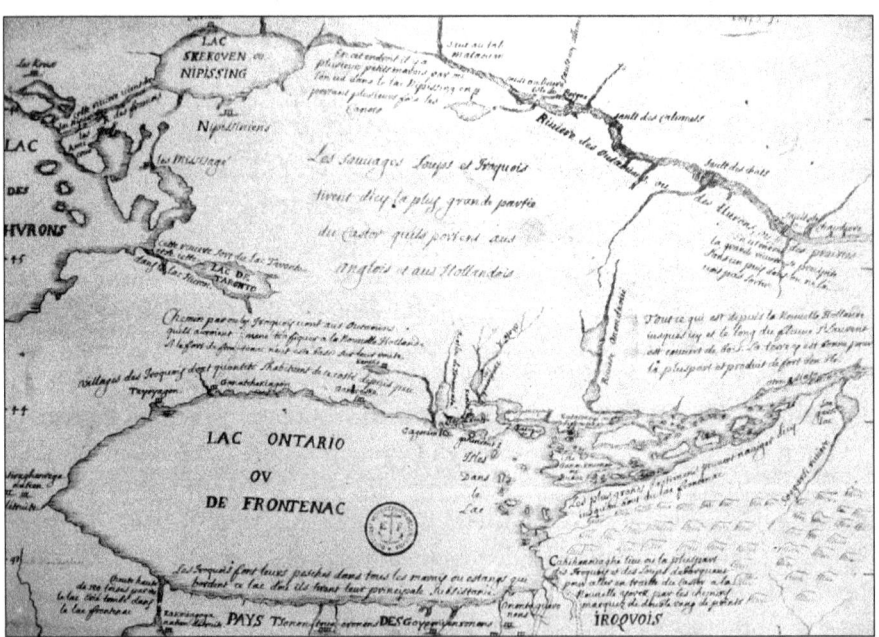

Figure 1.4. Map published in 1680 by Abbé Claude Bernou, showing "LAC DE TARONTO" (current-day Lake Simcoe) and the villages of "Teyoyagon" (Teiaiagon) and "Ganatchakiagon" (Ganatsekwyagon).
Source: Library and Archives Canada; image available from the Map and Data Library, University of Toronto.

that they traded the peltries with the English and the Dutch. Between the late 1660s and the late 1670s, the north shore of Lake Ontario was the site of a Sulpician mission, better known as the Kenté, or Quinte, mission, for where it was based. Beginning with Abbé Claude Trouvé and Abbé François de Salignac de La Mothe-Fénelon, who visited Kenté in 1668, various Sulpicians visited the north-shore villages over the next decade. Fénelon spent the winter of 1669–1670 with the Seneca at Ganatsekwyagon, and in 1676, Abbé Joseph Mariet set up a subsidiary mission at Teiaiagon. René de Bréhant de Galinée created a map of his 1669–1670 travels, which provides the location of populations, individual villages, missions, and forts, as well as interesting landscape features.

How did the Haudenosaunee come to have familiarity with, and sovereignty over, the north shore of Lake Ontario region? Figure 1.5 illustrates the locations of the Haudenosaunee and Ontario Iroquoian nations at the time of contact, as well as the ancestral territory of the Wendat. Between 1580 and 1610, those ancestral Wendat populations who had lived along the north shore of Lake Ontario and in the Trent valley moved north, amalgamating with other populations in Wendake (present day Simcoe County), who had also migrated

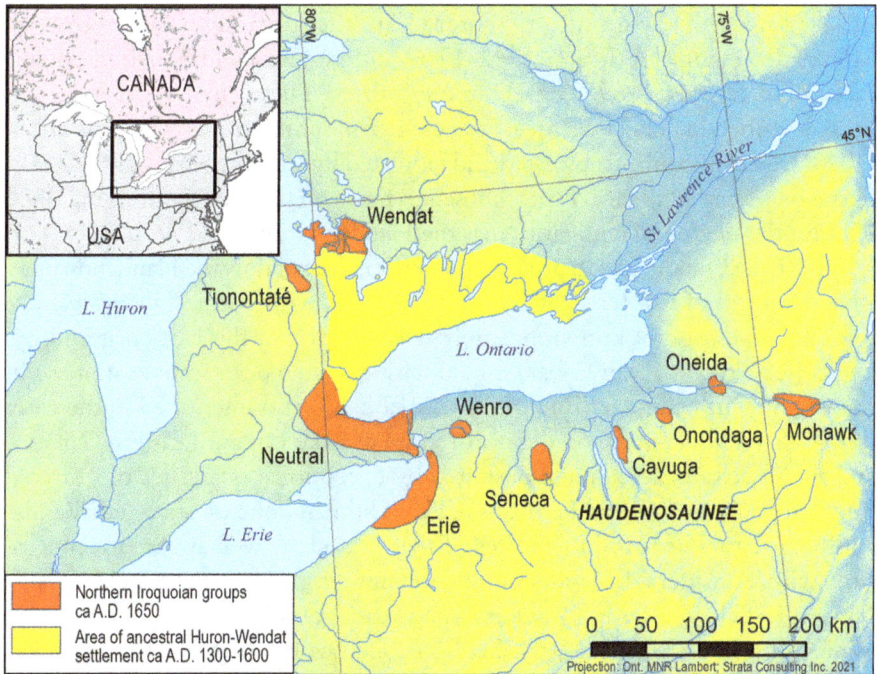

Figure 1.5. Map showing the locations of the Haudenosaunee and Ontario Iroquoian nations at the time of contact, as well as the ancestral territory of the Wendat.
Source: Map by Ron Williamson.

northward from the north shore of Lake Ontario, beginning at the end of the thirteenth century, to complete the formation of the Wendat Confederacy known from the documentary record (Thwaites 1896–1901:16:227; Warrick 2008:204–207; Williamson 2014:15). No permanent Wendat villages are known in the documentary record to have existed along the north shore of Lake Ontario after the first decade of the seventeenth century, as the region became part of a large buffer zone between the Wendat, the Tionontaté, and their Algonquian allies, on the one hand, and the Haudenosaunee Confederacy, on the other. The Tionontaté were situated advantageously for trade with the upper Great Lakes nations via their Odawa trade partners. The reasons for that movement northward and the consolidation of the Wendat Confederacy seems to lie in the traditional hostility between the Haudenosaunee and the Wendat and the heightening of that conflict in the seventeenth century, known as the Iroquois Wars.

2. The Iroquois Wars

By the mid-seventeenth century, the Haudenosaunee had defeated the Ontario Iroquoian Confederacies and some of their Algonquian allies, during which many lives were lost. Survivors fled to Quebec and the upper Great Lakes, and the remainder were absorbed by the Haudenosaunee. The numerous encounters that led to this outcome are entered in the documentary record by Samuel de Champlain (Biggar 1922–1936) and by various authors in the Jesuit Relations (Thwaites 1896–1901), among others. These encounters have also been described in detail by Bruce Trigger (1976), summarized by Gary Warrick (2008:236–243), and encapsulated and tabulated by José Brandão (1997, 2020). In the following summary, I have chosen to focus on those encounters that shed light on the degree of familiarity that the Haudenosaunee had with the region north of Lake Ontario and to provide a general outline of how the Haudenosaunee gained control of that territory by the 1650s and held it for half a century.

Although it is not known precisely why warfare, or this particular enmity, began (see Trigger 1985:96–100 for a discussion), it appears to have done so in the late fifteenth century (Birch et al. 2021:82–83) and intensified in the early to mid-sixteenth century on the north shore of Lake Ontario, eastern Ontario, and the Ottawa valley, as demonstrated by exceptional quantities of scattered butchered human bone and artifacts made of human bone on ancestral Wendat and Saint Lawrence Iroquoian sites of that period, as well as the presence of sites with considerable evidence of violence (e.g., Lite, Roebuck, Alhart, Draper, Keffer, Van Ordt, Quackenbush, Uxbridge) (Figure 1.6) (Jenkins 2015; Williamson 2007; Lesage and Williamson 2020; see Birch et al. 2021; Manning et al. 2019 for the revised chronological placement of the sites to this period; see also Abel 2019 for a chronology of the abandonment of northern New York). This is about the same time that Haudenosaunee national identities were emerging with larger fortified village entities and village clusters (e.g., Snow 1994; Wonderley and Sempowski 2019:19–21). The initial appearance of Haudenosaunee ceramics in the first half of the sixteenth century on many ancestral Wendat sites along the north shore of Lake Ontario (Trigger 1976:158–162; Williamson and Ramsden 2019) supports the notion that violence more broadly and community coalescence in Ontario occurred in response to hostilities with the Haudenosaunee.

The hostilities abated toward the end of the sixteenth century, as evidenced by the near-absence of scattered human bone and fewer artifacts made of human bone on such sites as Mantle (Jean-Baptiste Lainé), Aurora, McKenzie-Woodbridge, Seed-Barker, Skandatut, and Ball (e.g., Birch and Williamson 2013:39; Jenkins 2016:153). It is interesting to note that Wonderley and Sempowski (2019) comment that late sixteenth-century Haudenosaunee villages have also decreased signs of hostility. Although it is clear from the documentary record that hostility and trophy taking between the Wendat and the Haudenosaunee was a regular feature of Iroquoian life in the early to mid-seventeenth century (Williamson 2007:195–198), the manufacture of artifacts from human bone does seem to wane, perhaps due to the increasing importance of prisoner adoption (Richter 1983:530–531; Williamson 2007:215–216). Too few historic Wendat sites have been excavated, however, for us to know with certainty whether there are any trends regarding the quantities of altered scattered human bone on sites. What is known from the documentary record is that hostilities escalated throughout the early to mid-seventeenth century, as Europeans and Indigenous groups were all drawn into a complex web of global geopolitics and economics locally fuelled by competition for the trade in beaver pelts.

Several causes have been suggested for the Haudenosaunee invasion of historic Wendake, which forced the Wendat and their neighbours to flee, and the subsequent incursions against Anishinaabe groups to the north and west. Economic theories of the war as presented by various scholars include growing dependence on European trade goods, a desire to replace the Wendat as middlemen, and a related series of factors regarding the growing and lucrative fur trade. With respect to the latter, apparent depletion of beaver pelts in the Haudenosaunee homeland combined with the fact that northern pelts were more abundant and of higher quality, were advanced as reasons for Haudenosaunee intention to achieve access to and control of the beaver hunting and trapping territories as well as trade routes, and to provide the Seneca and the other western Haudenosaunee tribes with a northern territory in which to hunt and secure furs like the Mohawk had farther east (e.g., Cleland 1992:90; Hunt 1940; Landon 1944:34; Lytwyn 1997:214; Starna 1994:4; Surtees 1985:16; Trelease 1962; Trigger 1976:729). Karl Schleiser (1976:131–133) dismissed the theory that the Haudenosaunee wanted to become middlemen in the fur trade

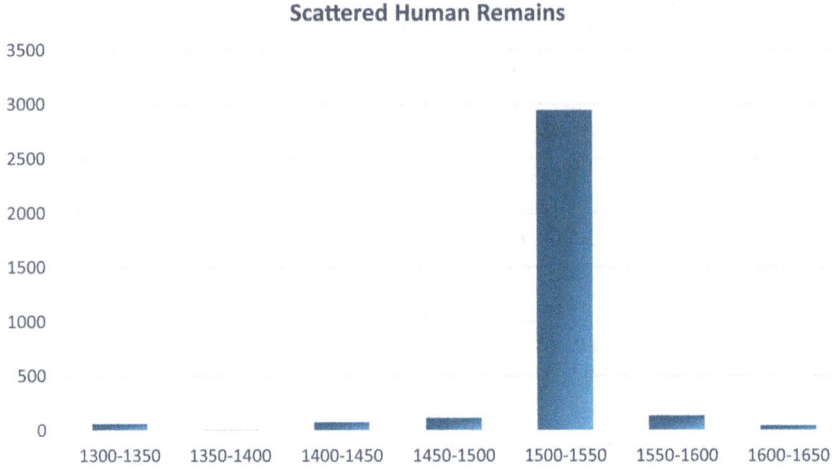

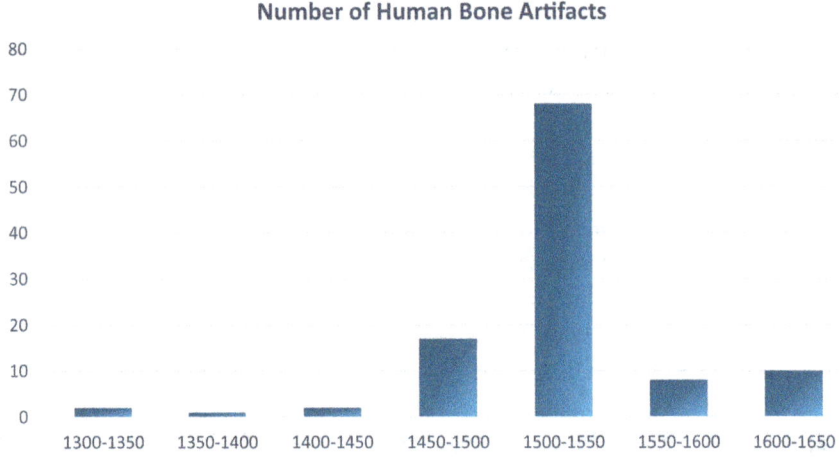

Figure 1.6. Graphs showing the distribution of scattered human bone and human bone artifacts using data from sixty Ontario Iroquoian villages.
Source: Based on Williamson 2007; Jenkins 2015 and updated February 2021.

and argued that the real middlemen were in fact the French *coureurs de bois* (see also Trelease 1962).

Other scholars stressed reasons beyond the economic for the severity of the war, suggesting that "longstanding intertribal animosities were aggravated by the appearance of Europeans who, in turn, provided the means of one protagonist to destroy the other" (Cleland 1992:90). Daniel Richter (1992:62–64) argued that, in addition to their long-standing feud with the Wendat, the Haudenosaunee conducted these wars within the context of their traditional mourning wars and that the taking of captives (or scalps) was more important than the taking of furs. This is evident in the great number of Iroquoian-speaking captives (Wendat, Tionontaté, Neutral, Erie, Susquehannock) caught during their wars since, as Richter explained, "each of these nations shared with the Haudenosaunee mixed horticultural and hunting and fishing economies, related languages, and similar beliefs, making their people ideal candidates for adoption." By the mid-1650s, the Haudenosaunee had adopted so many captives that missionary Paul Le Jeune believed that there were "more Foreigners than natives of the country" in Iroquoia (Thwaites 1896–1901:43:265). Brandão (1997:36–37; also 2020) agrees that, although there often were material rewards for fighting, "more powerful and enduring reasons for the almost constant warfare by the Haudenosaunee were the pursuit of glory, honor and the taking of prisoners," as well as the need to avenge an injury, whether an insult or a death, that occurred during a previous fight. Yet as the violence heightened, so, too, did mortality, creating a constant cycle of loss and recovery through adoption (Hunt 1940:33–25; Richter 1992:50, 57; Trigger 1976:626–627, 1985:260).

Still others, such as Richard White (1991:1), argue correctly, in my opinion, that the reasons for Haudenosaunee attacks were a combination of both economic and cultural factors, but I would add that they shift over time. Certainly, in the beginning, the hostilities can likely be characterized as feuding with revenge and adoption playing the most important roles. Eventually, this cycle of violence becomes more intense and involves clear economic motives, such as attacks on fur brigades and, eventually in the 1640s, culminates in focused attacks on villages and fields with the intent of the full-scale removal of competitors from the region north of Lake Ontario (including Algonquian allies). Yet throughout this time and the decades following, the replacement of population lost by both epidemics and warfare remains a significant objective (e.g., Bradley 2020:123, 166, 282, 397). While the Wendat population had been reduced by 60 percent due to European-introduced diseases in 1634 and subsequent years, which left them more vulnerable to attack by the Haudenosaunee (Warrick 2008:222–227), the Haudenosaunee had also suffered dramatic losses, underpinning the notion of population replacement being an important element of the wars (Jones and DeWitte 2012; Snow and Lanphear 1988). These epidemics also dramatically affected the Tionontaté, the Algonquin, and the Nipissing, and likely other Algonquian nations as well (Heidenreich 1987: Plate 34; Trigger 1976:588–589; Warrick 2008:223, 224, 227).

2.1. Pre-Dispersal Period (1609–1648)
Before the dispersal of the Wendat and their allies, trading in Quebec annually yielded two or three hundred thousand livres worth of beaver skins, from animals that had been hunted largely by Algonquians. This trade was soon

disrupted by a period of sustained hostility between the Wendat and their allies on the one hand, and the Haudenosaunee, on the other. The invitation by Champlain in 1608 to the Ottawa valley Algonquin leader Iroquet to have the Onontchataronon nation join the French in an attack on the Mohawk on the Richelieu River the following year led to Iroquet asking the Arendarhonon (Wendat Rock Nation) to join them in this endeavour. The ensuing Battle on Lake Champlain of July 30, 1609, marks an important departure point in the lower Great Lakes for Europeans participating in that traditional enmity. Figure 1.7 shows Champlain and two French musketeers assisting the Algonquin and the Wendat in a skirmish with the Haudenosaunee. In June of 1610, Champlain again participated in an attack on the Mohawk, which appears to have also marked the time of new trade by the Mohawk with the Dutch and the beginning of a period of absence on the part of the Mohawk from the St. Lawrence valley (Trigger 1976:246–261).

Around this time, however, the Oneida and Onondaga had begun attacking the Ottawa valley region in an attempt to gain access to European trade goods. This had led to a 1613 retaliative raid involving more than one thousand Algonquian and Wendat warriors (Trigger 1976:292–293). Champlain wrote after his 1615–1616 visit to Wendake that very few Wendat arrived to trade with the French in 1617, as warriors were required at home to protect their villages from the western Haudenosaunee nations. He also noted that the

Figure 1.7. Engraving of the Battle of Lake Champlain, 1609, published by Samuel de Champlain. The canoes that look like French riverboats, the nudity of the Indians, and their erroneous hairstyles undermine the credibility of the picture. The hammocks and palm trees are borrowed from scenes of Latin America. *Source:* Bibliothèque nationale de France.

Wendat were worried about visiting the St. Lawrence valley that year because of conflict with the Oneida. By 1618, the Wendat were urging Champlain to again come to Wendat country with Frenchmen because they wanted assistance to rebuff the harassment from their enemies, the Seneca. While this may have been concomitant with their desire to strengthen their alliance with the French, Trigger argues the presence of armed Frenchmen living in their villages alongside fur traders seemed to have resulted in fewer raids by the Haudenosaunee (Trigger 1976:339).

The entire region was indeed not safe for the Wendat or their Algonquian allies, as Haudenosaunee raiding parties were present. In 1621, on the way to Nipissing Country, Recollect missionary Guillaume Poulain and his companions were captured by the Haudenosaunee, who thereby challenged French hegemony over the St. Lawrence River valley (Trigger 1976:349). By the summer and autumn of 1623, raids between the Wendat and the Haudenosaunee became more frequent. In one encounter, the Wendat captured sixty Haudenosaunee. They killed most of them and took some to various villages, including Ossossané and Toanche (Trigger 1976:416–417).

England and France were at war between 1628 and 1633. Quebec was seized by an English merchant family named the Kirkes, who were welcomed by the Montagnais as independent traders. Champlain and most of the remaining French eventually returned home. This also resulted in renewed militancy on the part of the Mohawk in the St. Lawrence valley, who had in 1624 made peace with the French and the Algonquin in order to focus on the Mahican of the upper Hudson River valley. With the dispersal of the Mahican in 1628, the Mohawk turned their attention back to the northern Algonquin, preventing them from trading with the Dutch and feuding with them. Quebec was restored to France in 1632 (Trigger 1976:455–467).

In spring of 1634, a party of five hundred Wendat left their territory to attack the Seneca, who had heard of the intended attack and organized a larger group to meet the Wendat on their way south. The Seneca were successful in the encounter and killed two hundred individuals and took another one hundred prisoner. It is not certain where this encounter occurred, but it was likely south of Wendat country, somewhere along the north shore of Lake Ontario, perhaps on the Toronto passage (see also Brandão 2020). The Seneca chose not to attack further, keeping some of the most important Wendat prisoners as leverage for negotiating a lasting peace. The Wendat accepted the peace discussions, and in 1635, a group of Wendat travelled to Seneca country to confirm peace (Thwaites 1896–1901:6:145, 7:213–215, 8:69, 115, 149; Trigger 1976:489).

Yet, others of the Haudenosaunee nations carried on with raids into Wendat Territory that summer, one of which took place at Ihonatiria, in the interior of Wendat country (see Figure 1.8 for location of Wendat villages). It was noted that a considerable number of Haudenosaunee raiders were present in Wendat

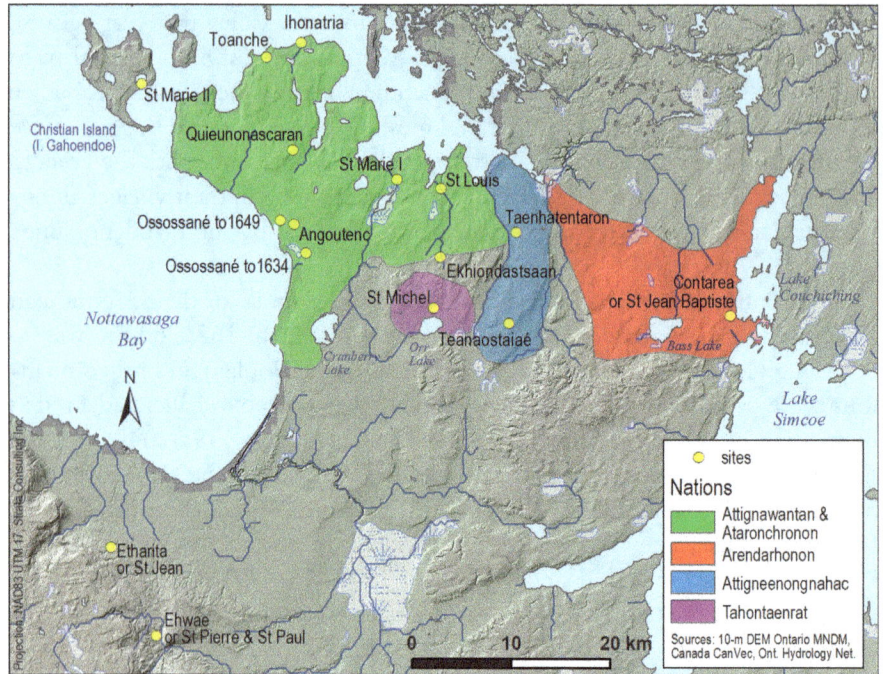

Figure 1.8. Map showing the locations of Wendat villages mentioned in the text. The Huron-Wendat endonyms for their various nations include Hatindiawanten (Attignawantan – Bear), Hatingënnoniahahk (Attigneenongnahac – Cord), Yärendahrönon (Arendarhonon – Rock), and Tahonhtayenrat (Tahontaenrat – Deer).
Source: Site locations based on Heidenreich 1971 (Maps 16 and 17) and Trigger 1976 (Maps 20 and 23).

country that June, resulting in general alarm (Trigger 1976:513). The following winter, entire villages were placed on alert and were prepared to disperse into the woods or to the nearest fortified settlement. Men were required to build palisades around villages. Ihonatiria men went to help build a palisade at the village of Angoutenc, for example, which was the principal village of the northern Attignawantan (Bear), which supplanted both Quieunonascaran and Toanche. The French advised the Wendat to build square palisades around their villages so they could protect the villages with muskets from towers erected at the four corners. When the village of Ossossané was moved north, the palisades were square and with taller and wider posts, as may have been the case with other village fortifications constructed after 1635 (Trigger 1976:513–515).

By the spring of 1636, Aenons, who aspired to be a principal headman, lobbied the Jesuits to live with them at a settlement formed by five smaller villages in the Penetanguishene Peninsula. This would form one well-supplied and fortified village that could protect the occupants from the Haudenosaunee (Trigger 1976:517). That same spring, a group of Haudenosaunee was discovered four leagues from a Wendat village, waiting to ambush people passing by that area (Thwaites 1896–1901:10:95). Outside the village of Contarea, a Wendat war party that had left their village were attacked by Haudenosaunee while they slept; twelve of the Wendat were killed, and the rest escaped (Thwaites 1896–1901:10:83, 95). In the summer of 1636, ongoing talk of the Haudenosaunee engaging in raids and of the Wendat engaging in heightened hostilities caused the French to worry that the Wendat might not travel to trade with the French that year (Trigger 1976:520).

Thus, although the truce with the Seneca seems to have held until 1638, the Wendat were still at war with the other Haudenosaunee nations. In September 1637, members of three Wendat nations met twenty-five to thirty Haudenosaunee fishing on Lake Ontario. One Haudenosaunee person was killed during the encounter, and seven others were brought to Wendat villages as prisoners (Trigger 1976:552). In the summer of 1639, a similar encounter occurred near the southern Bear Wendat village of St. Xavier. A group of Wendat was on a fishing expedition when Haudenosaunee attacked them while they were in their canoes. One Wendat died while shielding his younger brother from the arrows, and the others seem to have escaped (Thwaites 1896–1901:18:27, 19:223–227).

For the Wendat, protecting their home territory and their trade routes were two separate objectives. The homeland had to be protected from renewed attack by Haudenosaunee raiders, who were mainly from the western Haudenosaunee nations. But when they were travelling along the Ottawa and St. Lawrence Rivers for trade with the French, they were in danger from the Mohawk and the Oneida. One response to this was to send larger groups of men on trading expeditions; however, this left villages vulnerable to Haudenosaunee attacks within Wendat country (Trigger 1976:607–608). By the 1640s, there were many reports of Haudenosaunee present in Wendat country. Women and children were afraid to leave their villages. The Haudenosaunee seemed to be hiding everywhere; they would sometimes come into the villages undetected in the middle of the night and kill Wendat while they were sleeping; and attacks were taking place during all seasons of the year (Trigger 1976:660; Thwaites 1896–1901:22:305).

In the spring of 1640, the attacks spread to the Wendat's westerly neighbours, the Tionontaté, at a village called Ehwae. Although the attackers are not named in the documentary record, they were most likely Haudenosaunee (for an analysis of this attack and the identity of the raiders, see Garrad 2014:221–224, 463; for a contrary view, see Warrick 2008:236). It is the earliest recorded raid by the Haudenosaunee on the Tionontaté.

The Jesuits recorded that by later that summer, the paths that led to Wendat villages were "infested" with Haudenosaunee (Thwaites 1896–1901:21:169) and that in August, a Wendat man was killed as he was working in his fields (Thwaites 1896–1901:20:79–81, 21:211).

During the following two years, the general climate of the region was very violent. Haudenosaunee warriors hid in the fields and forests from winter to late summer to attack and kill Wendat, Algonquin, and French. Many individuals were killed or taken prisoner. Reports indicate that the Haudenosaunee had moved farther inland within Algonquian Territory and may have reached as far as Manitoulin Island (Thwaites 1896–1901:22:41–43, 51, 129, 249, 251, 253, 265). In June of 1642, Haudenosaunee attacked a Wendat frontier village and set it on fire, killing everyone, including women and children. Only the strongest were spared, in order for them to carry Wendat goods taken from the village back to Haudenosaunee country. The village name was not recorded, but it is thought to have been Contarea or a smaller Wendat village nearby. Fear spread throughout Wendat country after word got out about the destruction of one of their villages, which seemed to signify an escalation in warfare techniques and motives (Thwaites 1896–1901:26:175). All that summer, there was nothing but talk of Haudenosaunee attacks throughout Wendat country (Thwaites 1896–1901:26:179), and in the later part of the summer, a Wendat woman working in her field was killed by two Haudenosaunee (Thwaites 1896–1901:26:225).

In 1643, near the Wendat village of Teanaostaiaé, several Wendat from the village were killed by Haudenosaunee while gathering hemp. About forty people had left the village to go to the harvesting area, and in the middle of the night, around twenty Haudenosaunee attacked the group while they were sleeping. Some Wendat were killed, some were taken prisoner, and a few were able to escape (Thwaites 1896–1901:23:241, 26:203–205). Throughout the year, there were devastating raids and attacks on Wendat communities, with hundreds of people being taken prisoner and reports of women being killed while working in their fields. Records during this time describe Wendat bands trying to track the Haudenosaunee within Wendat country and then being attacked themselves. It was also a year of famine, perhaps caused by weather or the fact that women were unable to harvest crops safely (Trigger 1976:661).

In 1644, three Wendat trading parties travelling to or from Quebec were attacked by the Haudenosaunee (Trigger 1976:604), and the following spring, the Haudenosaunee were back in Wendat country. A group of Haudenosaunee hid outside a village overnight and captured a group of women as they were leaving to go out to the fields. Two hundred armed Wendat went after them, but the Haudenosaunee escaped (Trigger 1976:662). Later that summer, the Wendat encountered a group of Haudenosaunee hiding in the forest. When they seized the group, the Haudenosaunee asked to discuss peace, which ended in the Haudenosaunee killing Wendat headmen and either killing or capturing those Wendat who did not escape (Trigger 1976:663).

In 1645, the Wendat at the village of St. Joseph were expecting a Haudenosaunee attack and were on guard throughout the night, singing war songs, which echoed throughout the fields and forest. The nearby Haudenosaunee could tell that the Wendat were getting tired, as the war cries became more silent toward dawn. They attacked, overpowering one of the watch towers and killing two sleeping Wendat. They then fled before the Wendat could rise and catch them (Thwaites 1896–1901:29:253, 255). The following spring, a Wendat village was nearly destroyed (Thwaites 1896–1901:29:147–149), and subsequently a series of attacks and raids were carried out with the objective of destroying the Wendat. By 1646, the western Haudenosaunee nations were better armed with European weapons; the Mohawk—with the help of the Oneida and the Onondaga—and the Seneca were coordinating their attacks against the Wendat and the French (Trigger 1976:725–726).

Early in 1647, a Wendat war party captured an important Onondaga headman, named Annenraes, within Wendat country. Most of the Onondaga were killed, but this man was kept as a prisoner due to his importance. This event took place while the Wendat were collaborating with the Susquehannock to join forces and attempt to make peace with the eastern Haudenosaunee nations. At the time, it seemed that the Onondaga might be interested in negotiating with them for a truce (Trigger 1976:730–732).

Later that summer, though, Haudenosaunee carried out an attack on a Wendat fishing cabin on Lake Simcoe, during which four or five Wendat were killed and seven were taken prisoner. One of the Wendat was able to escape and thereafter organized a group of Wendat to rescue the prisoners. They cut the Haudenosaunee off approximately twenty to twenty-five miles to the south of the camp (somewhere in southern York Region, perhaps on the Toronto passage) and rescued the Wendat and killed the leader of the Haudenosaunee raiding party. Although the Haudenosaunee were less of a threat during 1647, they still continued to harass the Wendat (Trigger 1976:736).

In 1647, a band of three hundred Seneca attacked a Neutral village, killing many within, purportedly as revenge for the death of a kinsman the previous winter, when a Seneca was caught by a Wendat just outside that Neutral village and was killed. The Haudenosaunee man who had been captured by the Wendat just outside the village gates was fleeing from Wendat country near Tionontaté Territory, and for that reason it was considered a fair capture (Thwaites 1896–1901:33:81–83).

2.2. Dispersal Period (1648–1651)

In 1648, the Mohawk temporarily stopped attacking the French and focused on helping the Seneca raid the Wendat. Their goal was to start destroying the Wendat villages on the eastern frontier, that is, the Arendarhonon (Rock) villages, and to then press westward toward the Attigneenongnahac (Cord) settlements and then the Tahontaenrat (Deer) settlements. Lastly, they would attack the Attignawantan (Bear), the largest Wendat nation (Trigger 1976:730).

In early January 1648, a group of Wendat was travelling to present the Onondaga with beaver furs to reaffirm peace between their nations. The group consisted of six Wendat warriors and one of the three Onondaga men who had stayed in Wendat country as an act of peace. Near the village of Taenhatentaron, they were attacked by a group of one hundred Mohawk. Two Wendat escaped and may have continued on to the Onondaga. The Onondaga man who was part of the group was taken by the Mohawk, likely to be returned to his nation. It had become evident that the other Haudenosaunee nations (Mohawk and Seneca) had no interest in peace negotiations with the Wendat, and the Onondaga and the Cayuga abandoned peace talks after this event (Trigger 1976:740).

In the winter of 1648, a group of Seneca attacked part of a group of three hundred Wendat who were hunting two days' travel south of Taenhatentaron. That would place the event in modern-day Halton, Peel, or York Region, the latter two of which had always been considered by the Wendat to be unsafe because of the risk of attack. Perhaps they thought their number was sufficient to preclude attack. Seven Wendat were killed immediately, and twenty-four were taken prisoner. Several days later, the Mohawk, who had learned of the attack, confronted the rest of the hunting party while they were returning to Taenhatentaron; many more Wendat were killed, and another forty were taken prisoner. These events led the Wendat to conclude that the Seneca and the Mohawk intended to destroy Taenhatentaron, and the village inhabitants dispersed to villages nearer to Sainte-Marie (Trigger 1976:742–743).

Later that summer, before the Wendat departed for trade, several hundred Haudenosaunee attacked and destroyed Teanaostaiaé, which was the largest and best protected Wendat village located in the upper Sturgeon valley. They also attacked a smaller, neighbouring community, possibly Ekhiondastsaan or Tiondatsae (also known as La Chaudière). Both communities were Attigneenongnahac, and these events sparked fear throughout Wendat country. It is estimated that seven hundred Wendat were killed or taken prisoner. The destruction of Teanaostaiaé cost the Wendat one tenth of their remaining population and displaced about one thousand people. Having occurred in mid-summer, the attack and destruction of fields precluded the planting of new crops and resulted in famine the following winter (Trigger 1976:751–753).

In the fall of that year, more than one thousand Haudenosaunee (mainly Seneca and Mohawk) gathered and spent the winter north of Lake Ontario. To my knowledge, the location of the Haudenosaunee winter camp(s) has never been identified. It may be surmised, however, given the discovery of 1640s-period beads at Teiaiagon (see Fox et al., this volume) and similar aged material in the vicinity of Kenté (see Engelbrecht and Williamson, this volume), that the Seneca camped at the former location and the Mohawk at the latter. The goal was to surprise the Wendat in the early spring. The dispersal of the

Arendarhonon and the Attigneenongnahac meant that the Wendat were not safe to use their regular hunting territory east of Lake Simcoe. As a result, the Haudenosaunee were able to travel as far as the Sturgeon River valley without being seen.

In the spring of 1649, the Haudenosaunee acted quickly to attack and capture the village of Taenhatentaron, as the gates were not being watched so early in the year. Of the four hundred people there, only three men escaped. Some Haudenosaunee went on to attack St. Louis, which had been warned of the attack and had evacuated five hundred people to Sainte-Marie. Eighty Wendat warriors stayed and succumbed to the Haudenosaunee, who then sent scouts to Sainte-Marie, where they planned to attack next. Further fighting over St. Louis and the Wendat's success at recapturing the village discouraged the Haudenosaunee from pursuing their attack on Sainte-Marie. The Haudenosaunee started retreating from Wendat country, taking their prisoners and goods. After these events, the Wendat abandoned their villages, burning them down as they left. This was the beginning of the permanent dispersal of the Wendat (Trigger 1976:762–763).

By the winter of 1649–1650, all the villages within Wendake had been abandoned (Trigger 1976:768–769). A great number of Wendat decided to seek refuge with the Tionontaté, their trading partners situated west of the Nottawasaga River (Thwaites 1896–1901:34:203, 223, 35:81). A shortage of food, along with a severe drought in the summer of 1649, however, led to a serious famine among the Tionontaté and the Wendat refugees by the following winter (Thwaites 1896–1901:35:147, 127; Trigger 1976:767).

In December of 1649, the Tionontaté were warned of a possible upcoming Haudenosaunee attack. Warriors from Etharita decided to go to surprise them along the route they were expected to follow. The Haudenosaunee followed another route, and in the warriors' absence, attacked and plundered the village. Some Tionontaté managed to escape to other villages, but many were slain or taken prisoner (Thwaites 1896–1901:35, 107–119). Soon after, the Tionontaté abandoned their lands and retreated northwest, accompanied by the Wendat who had joined them earlier (Trigger 1976:778, 789), some probably going to Ekaentoton (now known as Manitoulin Island), taking refuge with the Odawa there (Bohaker 2006:246; Hunt 1940:95; Schlesier 1976:143; Tanner 1987:30), and others going southward, to join the Neutral, and eventually westward (Garrad 2014:503–506).

A number of Wendat had already fled to Gahoendoe, or Christian Island, which lies within sight of the mainland off the western tip of the Penetanguishene Peninsula. The Jesuits, who decided to join the Wendat at that location, called it St. Joseph Island (Thwaites 1896–1901:34, 203, 209–211, 223). Father Paul Ragueneau also refers to it as the Island of Sainte-Marie (Thwaites 1896–1901:35:179–181), probably due to the construction of Sainte-Marie II on the island. The Wendat population on the island grew as scattered refugees learned of the gathering, leading to a shortage of food. In the fall of 1649, the Jesuits sent canoes to buy food from the Algonquian nations "sixty, eighty, or a hundred leagues away" (Thwaites 1896–1901:35:99). In the spring of 1650, a number of Wendat left the island in search of food, despite the constant threat of Haudenosaunee attacks once they arrived on the mainland. Despite splitting up into small groups for safety, most did not escape the Haudenosaunee, who were waiting for them. Some were taken captive, but most were killed on the spot (Thwaites 1896–1901:35:181–191). In the spring of 1650, approximately three hundred Wendat Christians, along with the Jesuits at Sainte-Marie II (and other French), left Gahoendoe to seek refuge in Quebec (Thwaites 1896–1901:35:195–205). A number of Wendat remained behind.

Despite the attempts of the Haudenosaunee to kill or capture any of the remaining Wendat over the course of that year, in the spring of 1651, a group of Wendat managed to flee Gahoendoe. They travelled over the ice and in canoes when it was possible to do so and made their way to Ekaentoton, possibly joining other Wendat who had fled there earlier. The few Wendat who were left behind on Gahoendoe due to a lack of canoes were soon killed. That summer, a fleet of about forty canoes, the occupants of which were all said to be Christian Wendat, left Ekaentoton and safely made their way to the Wendat colony in Quebec (Thwaites 1896–1901:36:179–189). There were still Indigenous people on Ekaentoton in July of 1652, where a band of Haudenosaunee "made a capture" (Thwaites 1896–1901:37:111).

The Wendat on Gahoendoe were not the only ones attacked by the Haudenosaunee. In addition to the shortage of food, intermittent Haudenosaunee raids in the Georgian Bay area added to the precarious situation of Algonquians over the winter of 1649–1650 and throughout 1650. The Haudenosaunee attacked the Nipissing. Some of them managed to escape to Lake Nipigon, but many were killed or taken prisoner. In the spring of 1650, two Haudenosaunee forts were discovered east of Lake Nipissing by the Christian Wendat and Jesuits moving to Quebec. Another group of Algonquians, who had gathered to fish, was attacked at Lake Nipissing in the spring or summer of 1651, and the Tangwaonronnon, Wendat who had moved there as early as 1646, were also defeated at that location around the same time (Tailhan 1864:81; Thwaites 1896–1901:34:181, 35:181, 201, 36:31, 181, 189; Trigger 1976:779).

When the Wendat were dispersed from their homeland, some decided to join the Neutral (Thwaites 1896–1901:35:81). In the fall of 1650 and the following spring, however, the Haudenosaunee also attacked the Neutral, many of whom were taken captive, although some managed to escape. Those who could not make the journey to the country of the Haudenosaunee, such as the very young or the old, were killed. The Wendat and Neutral individuals who managed to escape split up, with some heading south to New Sweden (lower reaches of the Delaware River); some heading west, and others joining the Wendat in Quebec (Thwaites 1896–1901:36:177). As mentioned above, a great number of people who had been displaced by the Haudenosaunee were adopted and integrated into the Haudenosaunee nations. It should be noted that some Wendat, such as those who lived in the villages of Saint Michel and Saint Jean-Baptiste, voluntarily and peacefully relocated and joined the Haudenosaunee in their country, rather than fight or flee (Thwaites 1896–1901:36:179). Many of those who went with the Tionontaté joined Odawa groups, who became dominant in the fur trade. Over the next century, Odawa and Wendat–Tionontaté (Wyandot) villages were often located side by side (as they had been since ca. 1580), such as in Chequamegon Bay, Mackinac, and Detroit (Stone and Chaput 1978:603; see also White 1991).

2.3. Post-Dispersal Period (1651–1666)

The immediate post-dispersal period can be described generally as one of intermittent periods of hostility and precarious peace throughout the Great Lakes region. Some semblance of peace, for example, was established around 1653, and by 1654, trading in the French colonies was resumed. Making the long journey east to trade, however, could only be justified in the years when the threat of Haudenosaunee attacks was low and food supplies were high. The Anishinaabeg and the Wyandot gave priority to safety and security and, during the 1650s and 1660s, often chose to stay home or abandon their journey in the face of a heightened Haudenosaunee threat. During the years when the western trade routes were not blocked, large convoys of Odawa and other Anishinaabe groups and Wyandot came to trade (White 1991:24, 105).

A number of peace talks were held during this time, including the following attempts:

- In 1652, between the Haudenosaunee and the French, with ratification of the treaty made the following spring. All the Five Nations joined in this peace. Presents were exchanged during the negotiations, which "asked that the hunting might be shared by all the confederated nations, and that there might be no more war except on Elks, Beavers, Bears, and Deer—in order that all might enjoy together the dainty dishes that are obtained from these good animals" (Thwaites 1896–1901:40:185) All parties involved agreed that peace could only be confirmed by the return of hostages on all sides (Thwaites 1896–1901:40:156–191).
- In 1661, when the Onondaga and two other Haudenosaunee nations were again seeking peace with the French, as a result of the escalating tensions with non-specified "new and very warlike enemy" who had recently declared war against them (Thwaites 1896–1901:46:155).

- In 1663, when the Cayuga, speaking for all the Haudenosaunee nations except for the Oneida, visited Quebec with presents for the French as well as the "Algonquins, their old Enemies, with whom they testify their desire to form a friendship which shall never be broken" (Thwaites 1896–1901:49:149–151).

Moments of peace, however, could be precarious, and a number of Jesuits commented that they were uncertain whether the Haudenosaunee had either the ability or the desire to actually keep the peace (Thwaites 1896–1901:40:157, 45:211, 49:151, 52:203). Additionally, peace with the French did not necessarily translate into peace with French allies. According to Nicolas Perrot, who recorded accounts that he did not witness first-hand but later "learned from the lips of the old men among the Outaouas tribes," the Haudenosaunee sent a party of eight hundred warriors to attack the Outaouas around 1653, around the same time the Haudenosaunee were agreeing to peace with the French. The Outaouas moved farther north due to fear of continued Haudenosaunee pressure, and the Saulteur and Mississauga moved north due to lack of game, eventually settling on the Keweenaw Peninsula, on Lake Superior (Blair 1911:1:151–153, 159).

Peace with the French and the Anishinaabeg, or at least a temporary cessation of hostilities, seems to have coincided with an elevation in tensions between the Haudenosaunee and other Indigenous groups. This includes the war with the Ehriehronnon, called the Cat Nation by the Jesuits, around 1653–1655 (Thwaites 1896–1901:41:81–83). Similarly, as one Jesuit explained in the late 1660s, "the Haudenosaunee [...] will be delighted to continue the peace with the Outaouacs, having on their hands the war with the nation of the Loups [Mohegans] and that with the Andastogués" (Thwaites 1896–1901:52:203).

Thus, although this period did see some moments of peace, the Jesuit Relations contain numerous examples of Haudenosaunee ambushes and attacks and of a general fear of the Haudenosaunee, especially in the early 1660s. During this time, the Jesuits note that Haudenosaunee access to Dutch firearms had allowed them to conquer their neighbours and be "victorious over all the Nations with whom they have been at war" (Thwaites 1896–1901:45:207).

In some instances, Haudenosaunee attacks were thwarted. In the spring of 1662, a group of one hundred Mohawk and Oneida men formed an expedition to hunt north of Lake Ontario, as well as to ambush the Outaouas along their canoe route. Their planned attack was frustrated by Saulteur in a surprise attack of their own, which spared few Haudenosaunee, as Gabriel Lalemant wrote in his Relation of 1662–1663 (Thwaites 1896–1901:48:75–77).

In December 1667, ambassadors of the Onondaga, Cayuga, Seneca, and Oneida nations presented articles of peace, requesting that "the divisions and enmities which have existed between the said Algonquians and Wendat and between the Haudenosaunee ceasing by the present treaty, there will be a friendship and mutual help between the said nations [...]" The Algonquians in question were described as those living on the north side of the St. Lawrence, up to Lake Huron and north of Lake Ontario (Jaenen 1996:59–62; O'Callaghan 1856–1887:9:786). At the beginning of 1666, Alexandre de Tracy and his troops had attacked the Mohawk, burning four of their villages and the surrounding corn fields. In 1667, "news came from Montreal that the five nations manifest favourable inclinations for peace" (O'Callaghan 1856–1887:9:785; Thwaites 1896–1901:50:203–211). The Jesuits received word in 1668–1669 that the Onondaga were planning on sending a delegation to the Sault to confirm the peace with the Outaouas by presents (Thwaites 1896–1901:52:203).

Following the 1666–1667 peace made with the Haudenosaunee and the establishment of the Iroquois du Nord settlements, French trade was mostly conducted at forts, Indigenous villages, including the IDN settlements, and hunting camps in the west (White 1991:108).

2.4. Occupation of the Iroquois du Nord Settlements and their Abandonment

Relatively little is known of the activities carried out in and around the IDN villages, as there is a paucity of historical documents dealing with this area. The Jesuit Relations deal with the settlements south of the lake, where the Haudenosaunee were ministered by the Jesuits themselves. They ignore the north shore, which was the responsibility of the Sulpicians. As the Sulpician mission was brief and unsuccessful, a comparatively small written record was produced by the Sulpicians (Konrad 1981:144; see von Bitter et al., this volume).

In addition to being mission locations, the villages on the north shore of Lake Ontario served as trading sites. In 1673, Louis de Buade, Comte de Frontenac, learned of a treaty negotiated between the Haudenosaunee and Outaouas. Under the terms of the treaty, the Haudenosaunee would provide all the merchandise that the Outaouas needed in exchange for all their peltries; this exchange would happen on Lake Ontario. The only way for the French to stop the communication between the two groups was to establish a French post on the north shore of the lake (Margry 1879:1:195; O'Callaghan 1856–1887:9:95–96).

Such a post would give protection to the French allies coming to trade their peltries, who would otherwise be robbed by the Haudenosaunee (Margry 1879:1:86; O'Callaghan 1856–1887:9:63–65), and it would prevent the Haudenosaunee who hunted on the north side of Lake Ontario from taking their peltries to New Holland (Margry 1879:1:180–181; O'Callaghan 1856–1887:9:80, 91). Following peace talks between Frontenac and representatives of the five Haudenosaunee nations in the spring of 1673 (Margry 1879:1:211–217), Fort Frontenac was established, at the mouth of the Cataraqui River, where the St. Lawrence River leaves Lake Ontario (present-day Kingston). According to Frontenac, the Haudenosaunee travelled to Montréal in the summer of 1674 to ratify the peace treaty they had made the year before. As a sign of good faith, they brought a number of children from the main families of their villages and promised to stop the "Loups de Taracton" (the English version identifies them as the Mohegans of Taracton), located near New Holland, from attacking the Outaouas. They also promised to stop the trade they had started at Ganatsekwyagon with the Outaouas, which would have ruined French trade by supplying all peltries to the Dutch (Margry 1879:1:273–274; O'Callaghan 1856–1887:9:117).

Peace with the Haudenosaunee also meant that the use of the beaver hunting grounds in Ontario could occur without fear of harassment. In 1673, Father Henri Nouvel reported that the Haudenosaunee and the Mississauga were hunting together (Thwaites 1896–1901:57:21). In 1676, he wrote that the Amikwa (or Beaver nation) spent the winter hunting near Lake Erie (Thwaites 1896–1901:60:215–229). On his way to meet them at their hunting grounds from Michilimackinac, and over the course of the winter, Father Nouvel encountered several other groups, including two different groups of "pennengous" (Openangoes) married to Algonquian and Nipissing women, a group of Nipissing, and a group of Mississauga. Peace also meant much safer travelling for the Anishinaabeg as well as French traders. The Belmont map, dated around 1680, reveals that the French could take a different, and much easier, route to the Ottawa when they were at peace with the Haudenosaunee. Rather than taking the Ottawa River route, with its many rapids and portages, the French could travel along the north shore of Lake Ontario to "Gandatsekiagon," where they followed the overland route to "Lake Taronteau" (Lake Simcoe) and on to the upper Great Lakes.

In a letter dated May 29, 1673, Father Nouvel reported that the Haudenosaunee had sent peace-presents to the inland groups who visit Lake Superior, as well as the groups of the Green Bay area. Although the Haudenosaunee said that these presents were to confirm the peace made by Onontio, the Jesuits suspected an ulterior motive: these presents were either to get peltries, to entice them to trade with the Dutch, or "to beguile them into a renewal of the war if they succeed with the Andastogue" (Thwaites 1896–1901:57:21–23). By the mid-1670s, the Seneca had defeated the Andastogues, and, according to the Jesuits living among them, "they talk of nothing but renewing the war against our allies, and even against the French, and of beginning by the destruction of fort Catarokoui" (Thwaites 1896–1901:59:251).

The murder of a leading Seneca Haudenosaunee by an Illinois within the Kiskakon (a band of the Odawa) section of the village at Michilimackinac reignited tensions between the Haudenosaunee and the Ottawa. In August 1682, Ottawa from Michilimackinac recounted the event to Frontenac. They urged Frontenac to permit them to conduct their trade so they could go back to their village as soon as possible, in case there was a Haudenosaunee attack. Frontenac, although permitting the Ottawa to defend themselves in their own villages, urged them not to go on an attack in Haudenosaunee country (O'Callaghan 1856–1887:9:163–165, 176–177, 181–182). A month later, an Onondaga chief related to Frontenac that the Haudenosaunee did not wish to make war on "the Kiskakons nor the Wendats, neither on the Miamis" but would defend themselves if attacked. They were, however, on their way to attack the Illinois (O'Callaghan 1856–1887:9:183–184).

In 1682, it was reported that more than three hundred "Nepiseriniens, one of the Outaouois tribes the most devoted to the French" went to Montréal with a Jesuit father asking for safe lands that would provide some security against the Haudenosaunee. It was also reported that the plan of the Haudenosaunee was to destroy all nations found at the Baie des Puants [Green Bay], as well as the Kiskakons at Michilimackinac, in order to "rob the Outaouois of the trade" (O'Callaghan 1856–1887:9:798).

Following the successful repulsion of a Haudenosaunee attack on the Illinois by a coalition of the French and the Anishinaabeg in 1684, Governor Joseph-Antoine Le Febvre de La Barre decided to gather western warriors for an assault on Iroquoia. The attack failed miserably, however, due to a variety of factors, which ultimately led to his being replaced by Jacques-René de Brisay de Denonville (White 1991:31–32). Two years after La Barre's failed attack, the Marquis de Denonville wrote to Jean-Baptiste Antoine Colbert, Marquis de Seignelay, about the state of affairs in Canada, explaining why war still needed to be waged against the Haudenosaunee. Backed by the English, they had gone on an expedition against the Wendat and Ottawa of "Missilimackinac." Denonville was certain that the English were also encouraging the Haudenosaunee to attack the French whenever they could. He also learned that the Haudenosaunee were forming a large war party against the nations of the Baie des Puants, whom they had already attacked at the beginning of the year, and that they had destroyed a large number of Illinois settlements in the past few years. If they did not attack the Haudenosaunee within the next year, the colony would be lost. In the same letter, Denonville suggested keeping the post at Cataraqui and erecting one at Niagara in order to control the Haudenosaunee, and to gain advantages in the trade with the Illinois and the Ottawa. Denonville also recommended that posts be constructed at Detroit and at the portage of Toronto in order to fortify two of the passes to Michilimackinac. In addition to blocking access to Michilimackinac from the enemy, these posts would serve as retreats for their allies while hunting or marching against the Haudenosaunee (O'Callaghan 1856–1887:9:296–303).

More than three hundred "Indians of all nations" engaged in this war on the side of the French, including the Ottawa, the Wendat of Michilimackinac, "our Christian Indians," and the Illinois (O'Callaghan 1856–1887:9:336–341). Nicolas Perrot, who was at the Baie des Puants, received orders to gather all available men, French, and allies, to take part in this war. In the spring of 1687, they made their way to Niagara, stopping by Michilimackinac on their way. After several days at Niagara, the Wendat and Outaouas they had met at Michilimackinac, and who had initially refused to join them, arrived. They had "reached us by land from Thehegagon, and left their canoes opposite, in Lake Huron" (Blair 1911:1:249–251).

The French and their allies wounded and killed a number of Seneca and managed to destroy four villages and their associated corn fields and stores. According to Denonville, had they not attacked the Seneca, the Wendat and the Ottawa would have submitted to the Haudenosaunee and placed themselves under the protection of the English. Around that same time, the Haudenosaunee living in the villages on the north shore of Lake Ontario began to move back south, and Denonville determined it would be in the French interest to repopulate these villages with allies (O'Callaghan 1856–1887:9:336–341). Many of the villages were reoccupied by Mississauga peoples by the beginning of the eighteenth century (Konrad 1981:138–142; Tanner 1987:31–35; von Gernet 2002:7; see Warrick and Williamson, this volume).

This summary of the Iroquois Wars and the historical context for the establishment of the IDN settlements demonstrates that there was no shortage of familiarity with southern Ontario on the part of the Haudenosaunee or, obviously, the refugees who had joined them. It is clear that the Haudenosaunee had been familiar with Wendat Territory and the lands to the south along the north shore of Lake Ontario since the mid-sixteenth century and perhaps earlier. During the relatively peaceful period between 1666 and the early 1680s, the IDN settlements would have provided both economically strategic advantages and distance from their enemies to the south. It is also clear that archaeological materials dating from the 1620s to the dispersal period found south of Wendake along the north shore of Lake Ontario are more likely to be Haudenosaunee in origin than Wendat, an observation noted in a number of the chapters in this volume.

3. Volume Organization

The volume has been organized into five parts, the first being the historical context of the period, some of which, however, has been provided in this introduction. In Part I, Kurt Jordan (Chapter 2) outlines the historical and archaeological contexts for the Haudenosaunee and describes their homeland in what is now New York State. He explains the decisions on the part of the Haudenosaunee to establish settlements north of Lake Ontario within the broader framework of Haudenosaunee settlement trends of the period, their desire to incorporate individuals and groups from other nations, and influences from the ever-expanding European presence.

Part II of the volume explores what is known about the locations of the IDN settlements and provides histories of the search for their locations or their investigations. In Chapter 3, Robert von Bitter, Chris Menary, and Nick Gromoff examine numerous maps that position Kenté in the northwestern corner of Prince Edward County, and they review the work of Rev. Bowen Squire, who claimed to have found the mission site on his property on the north shore of Lake Consecon. The authors debunk Squire's claim and reveal that Kenté is likely situated on Wellers Bay rather than Lake Consecon. Chris Menary and Robert von Bitter explain in Chapter 4 their efforts and advances in finding the locations of Ganaraské, Quintio, and Ganneious using leading-edge technology (including light detection and ranging [LiDAR]). They believe that these sites were situated strategically to control the flow of furs to the north shore of Lake Ontario, as demonstrated by Quintio at the head of the portage from Rice Lake to the Ganaraska River. Dana Poulton, in Chapter 5, describes the Bead Hill site, situated on the lower Rouge River, in the east end of the city of Toronto, concluding that it is the best candidate for the historically documented village of Ganatsekwyagon. Poulton reviews the historical documentary record concerning the village and details the long but episodic history of archaeological investigations of the site. David Robertson examines the tony Toronto neighbourhood of Baby Point, in Chapter 6, on which the settlement of Teiaiagon is located. The site, situated on the Humber River, near the limit of upstream travel by canoe, was the terminus for the western branch of the Toronto Carrying Place, which overtook the eastern arm along the Rouge River as the more heavily used route to the interior. Robertson examines the surviving archaeological record of the settlement and the efforts by the City of Toronto to preserve those remnants beneath the pavements and lawns of Baby Point, as well as the remnants of Ganatsekwyagon. Finally, Neal Ferris, in Chapter 7, examines what is known about the westernmost Iroquois du Nord community, Outinaouatoua, through the recorded observations of René-Robert Cavelier de La Salle, Galinée, and a handful of other Europeans who visited the region and settlement. Ferris views this place within a broader cultural landscape, connecting the Haudenosaunee to the Neutral of earlier years and noting the deeper continuity of Indigenous heritage across that landscape.

In Part III, the material culture of the IDN settlements is examined. In Chapter 8, William Fox, David Harris, and April Hawkins examine the glass, stone, shell, and bone bead assemblages from the IDN sites, in a critical comparison with contemporary assemblages recovered from sites in the Haudenosaunee homeland in north-central New York State. They describe the evolving Indigenous and European bead manufacturing industries of the late seventeenth century as they reflect on international trade systems spanning eastern North America from the Atlantic Coast to the Midwest.

In Chapter 9, Martin Cooper examines the metal assemblages of the villages from chronological, technological, and cultural perspectives and contrasts them to the metal assemblages of contemporary Haudenosaunee sites to the south of Lake Ontario. Ronald Williamson and Robert von Bitter (Chapter 10) then describe the antler combs that have been recovered from Kenté, Bead Hill, and Teiaiagon and show how their designs are similar to those found in the Haudenosaunee homeland, and how they all convey aspects of Haudenosaunee ideology. In Chapter 11, William Engelbrecht and Ronald Williamson examine fragments of Indigenous ceramic vessels and pipes found in the collections made by avocational and professional archaeologists from and in the vicinity of Iroquois du Nord sites. Although European-made kettles had largely replaced ceramic pots by the end of this period, the use of European-made pipes expands but does not replace Indigenous-made pipes; it is clear that Indigenous ceramic pipes and vessels were still being used well into the second half of the seventeenth century, the reasons for which are explored by Engelbrecht and Williamson.

Most of the material culture representing the Iroquois du Nord occupation of southern Ontario derives from nineteenth-century collections of artifacts with little or no provenience information beyond a site of origin. Some sites had been cleared for settler farming and had been under cultivation since the latter half of the nineteenth century, such as those on the Humber and Rouge Rivers, as noted by David Boyle (e.g., 1888). In the case of Kenté and environs, much of the examined material includes the artifacts collected by G. J. Chadd, a Trenton-based avocational collector, who had collected for a half-century in Prince Edward County (see Harris 2020). In 1921, when this collection was accessioned by the provincial museum (now the Royal Ontario Museum), it was described by Rowland Orr as "the finest private archaeological collection in Canada" (Orr 1922:102). It includes a wide range of artifacts representing most of the Woodland period (and many earlier periods) in Great Lakes pre-contact history (Orr 1922:123–132). It is evident from the material in the Chadd Collection that Bald Head Island was the location of a cemetery, a component of which related to Kenté, as evidenced by many graves and by unmistakable mid- to late seventeenth-century artifacts, such as glass beads and Jesuit rings (see Fox et al., this volume; Cooper, this volume). Boyle (1897:48) also describes collecting a small number of shell and glass beads at Bald Head, on Wellers Bay, in the company of Mr. Chadd Jr., noting that "On account of the constant changes that take place on the surface of Bald Head owing to the shifting of the sand, it is impossible to select places for examination, otherwise than as these may come to light after a gale."

Part IV of the volume consists of a single chapter, Chapter 12, authored by Gary Warrick and Ronald Williamson. Drawn from oral tradition and the documentary record, as well as archaeological data from other Mississauga settlements that have been investigated, the chapter addresses the Anishinaabe occupation of the villages after their abandonment by the Haudenosaunee. The "western Mississauga," later known as the Mississaugas of the Credit, settled at Ganatsekwyagon and at or adjacent to Teiaiagon, near the mouth of the Humber River. The "eastern Mississauga," today the Williams Treaties Mississauga communities of Alderville, Hiawatha, Curve Lake, and Scugog, on the other hand, used other IDN village sites, in eastern Ontario.

Part V comprises two chapters, which discuss the volume and provide concluding statements. Chapter 13 is by Victor Konrad, one of the pioneer scholars to examine the settlements, and the eminent Haudenosaunee scholar Rick Hill, in Chapter 14, provides his view of this endeavour to shed light on a period of Haudenosaunee history poorly known by the northeastern North American public and academic community.

Acknowledgements

I would like to thank Annie Veilleux and Sarah Proulx for their research assistance, as well as Kurt Jordan, Bill Fox, Suzanne Needs-Howarth, Robert von Bitter, and Gary Warrick for their useful comments on an earlier draft of this chapter. I would also like to take this opportunity to thank, on behalf of both Robert and myself, the efforts of Suzanne Needs-Howarth in copyediting early drafts of these chapters, the expertise and attention to detail by John Howarth in the digital enhancement of images throughout the volume, and the efforts of Andrew Stewart of Strata Consulting Inc. in the creation of many of the maps throughout the volume (as noted in legends). We are also thankful for the assistance of Andrea Carnevale in preparation of the volume.

All the authors would like to acknowledge Carl Benn and Jennifer Birch for reviewing the volume for publication and for offering insights and helpful suggestions for its improvement. We acknowledge that their efforts far exceed that for reviewing a single paper and we are very grateful for their time and expertise.

SECTION 1
HISTORY OF THE PERIOD

2

DEPARTING AND RETURNING
Haudenosaunee Homeland Contexts for the Iroquois du Nord Villages

KURT A. JORDAN

This chapter discusses the Haudenosaunee, or Five Nations Iroquois, contexts in what is now New York State—from which the Iroquois du Nord settlers departed in the 1660s and to which they returned by the 1680s—from an archaeological perspective. I assert that the basic cycle is that the du Nord settlements were established during a peak period of Haudenosaunee political, economic, and military power and that they were abandoned when Five Nations fortunes took a turn for the worse. This downturn was particularly the result of French military invasions of their homeland, accompanied by settlement burnings, in 1687, 1693, and 1696, but also due to military defeats north of Lake Ontario (Warrick and Williamson, this volume). While peace was negotiated with the French and their Indigenous allies in 1701, overall uncertainty and violence continued until about 1713. Thereafter, I posit that the Haudenosaunee enjoyed a new period of prosperity that lasted at least into the 1740s. My intention is to provide some of the details from archaeology and history that act as the foundation for this overall framework.

During the seventeenth century, the Haudenosaunee were an alliance of the Seneca (self-name Onöndowa'ga:'), Cayuga (Gayogo̱hó:nǫ'), Onondaga (Onoñda'gega'), Oneida (Onʌyota'a:ka), and Mohawk (Kanyen'kehá:ka) nations. They were village- and town-dwelling agriculturalists with a subsistence base centred on the cultivation of maize, bean, squash, and sunflower, supplemented by hunting, fishing, and the gathering of wild plants (for archaeological overviews, see Engelbrecht 2003; Snow 1994; for Haudenosaunee history, see Parmenter 2010; Richter 1992). New programs of accelerator mass spectrometry (AMS) dating, coupled with Bayesian modelling, suggest that materials originating in Europe (such as iron and brass) circulated in the Haudenosaunee region as early as 1500 (Manning and Hart 2019). The first documented face-to-face encounter between the Haudenosaunee and Europeans took place in 1609, when Samuel de Champlain and Wendat and Algonquian allies battled a Haudenosaunee force near what is now known as Lake Champlain. Subsequently, Haudenosaunee-European interactions—economic, military, diplomatic, and epidemiological—became routine. This did not result in decline or conquest: the Haudenosaunee nations remained politically autonomous, and sizeable populations of European settlers remained no farther west than Schenectady and Montréal by 1650, with the arguable exception of the period French settlements of Sainte-Marie and Sainte-Marie II, in Wendake in the period 1639–1650.

The archaeological excavation, analysis, and publication of the Haudenosaunee sites I discuss in this chapter are of very uneven quality, in many ways paralleling the situation for the Iroquois du Nord sites. Many New York Haudenosaunee sites have not seen formal investigation, and there is quite a bit of information from museum collections that has never been fully reported. I use a "catch-as-catch-can" approach, incorporating information new and old, from both formal and informal investigations, and from both domestic and mortuary contexts. Toward the end of the chapter, I briefly discuss data from domestic-context excavations I directed at the Seneca White Springs and Townley-Read sites. I also incorporate evidence from primary source documents written by English, French, and Dutch diplomats, missionaries, and traders, although at times the archaeology and documentary sources are not easy to reconcile.

My own knowledge is strongest in the Seneca region. To understand the archaeology of the other Haudenosaunee nations, I rely on regional experts who have spent most of their careers concentrating on a single nation. For the most part, there is consensus in dating the sites discussed in this chapter. The main exception is in the Mohawk Valley, where Dean Snow (1995a) and Wayne Lenig (2020) have constructed divergent site chronologies based on interpretations of different datasets. It is beyond the scope of this chapter to re-examine the Mohawk details, so I present both the Snow and Lenig models and encourage interested readers to delve into the issue on their own.

I make use of a scheme for the Haudenosaunee use of space that simultaneously serves as a shorthand way to determine the ease of social interaction between communities (see Jordan 2013). Each site is surrounded by a zone of *local space* 20 km in diameter. Local space could have been easily accessed on foot within a single day; people would have had enough time to travel to the edge of the zone, conduct activities or interactions there, and travel home. Haudenosaunee principal towns often had associated smaller satellite villages within local space, indicating that these communities would have been in very regular contact. I term the zone between 20 km and 80 km away from a community *regional space*. This zone could have been visited with two days of foot travel, making it slightly less accessible than local spaces but still regularly used given the Haudenosaunee emphasis on mobility for hunting, fishing, diplomacy, and social connection. *Extra-regional space* was that beyond 80 km from a given site. This scheme certainly could be refined by geographical information systems (GIS)–based analysis of the ease of moving through the specific terrain around particular sites, although the frequent Haudenosaunee use of canoe travel certainly complicates mobility models. But I have found that the scheme provides a useful shorthand, and I deploy it throughout this chapter.

My interpretation of the historical context is divided into four eras: a period that was positive for the Haudenosaunee, from about 1650 to 1680; a difficult time of war, between 1680 and 1701; a stage of political, military, and economic uncertainty, from 1701 to 1713; and a renewed period of prosperity, from 1713 to 1744 (see Jordan 2008). However, it is important to recognize the vicissitudes of particular historical eras. There were years or seasons of setbacks during positive periods; similarly, victories and moments of surety emerged within times of distress. It is also key to remember that evidence from documents can reflect the goals and biases of their writers, varying levels of care in recording details (especially regarding seemingly precise house counts or town populations), and even intentional misinformation that Indigenous actors passed along to European agents. So while we have the oft-quoted 1668 Jesuit statement that "because the fear of the enemy has obliged some of that [Cayuga] Nation to separate from the rest, and go and settle on the North Shore of the great Lake Ontario" (Thwaites 1896–1901: 51:257), in 1670, the Jesuit Étienne de Carheil said of the same Cayuga "there is nothing more inimical to our Missions than the victories that these peoples gain over their enemies, because by these victories they are made insolent" (Thwaites 1896–1901:54:75). Similarly, there were peace negotiations in 1689 and 1690 between Seneca and several western Indigenous groups who typically were French allies (Parmenter 2010:208–215) during the height of a period of warfare in 1680–1701. An overall assessment needs to account for these fluctuations, but at the same time must keep an eye on the picture that emerges from an accumulation of details.

1. Peak Power, 1650–1680

During the period 1650–1680, despite occasional downturns, the Haudenosaunee either had defeated or were in the process of defeating or dispersing from their homelands many rival Indigenous groups on or near their borders, including the Mahican, Wenro, Wendat, Tionontaté, Nipissing, Algonquin, Odawa, Neutral (Attawandaron), Erie, and Susquehannock. Documentary evidence indicates thriving trade with European colonists, centred on the exchange of beaver pelts for trade goods. Archaeologically, this prosperity is reflected in the enormous quantities of gun parts and marine shell wampum beads on Haudenosaunee sites of this period, such as the Seneca Dann site (Ryan and Dewbury 2010; Wray 1985).

The task of describing any sort of archaeological homeland "baseline" for the Iroquois du Nord communities is complicated by the fact of Haudenosaunee settlement relocation, which principally took place due to depletion of firewood and other local resources. On occasion, resettlement also took place for geopolitical reasons, either positive or negative. The 1677 account of New York official Wentworth Greenhalgh (Snow et al. 1996:188–192) provides a convenient reference because he visited and described most of the settlements of all Five Nations, and because archaeologists have spilled much ink trying to determine which specific sites he frequented (Figure 2.1, Table 2.1).

Greenhalgh described two Seneca principal towns and two smaller satellites totalling 324 houses; none were fortified. The Cayuga were reported to have three unfortified settlements totalling one hundred houses; the Onondaga, a large, unfortified 140-house town with a smaller village nearby; and the Oneida, a town of one hundred houses with a double palisade. The Mohawk were said to have five communities of ten to thirty houses each, all with single or double palisades, except for the smallest village, which was unfortified.

Despite the seeming precision of Greenhalgh's descriptions, scholars have had some difficulty aligning his account with known archaeological sites. Previously, I have questioned Greenhalgh's house counts (Jordan 2004); for example, Greenhalgh asserted there were 150 houses at the Seneca town of "Canagorah" (likely the Ganondagan site, also known as Boughton Hill), whereas house-lot area figures from comparable sites suggest only 75–119 houses could have fit in a site of 3.7 ha. Bradley (2020:292) also questions

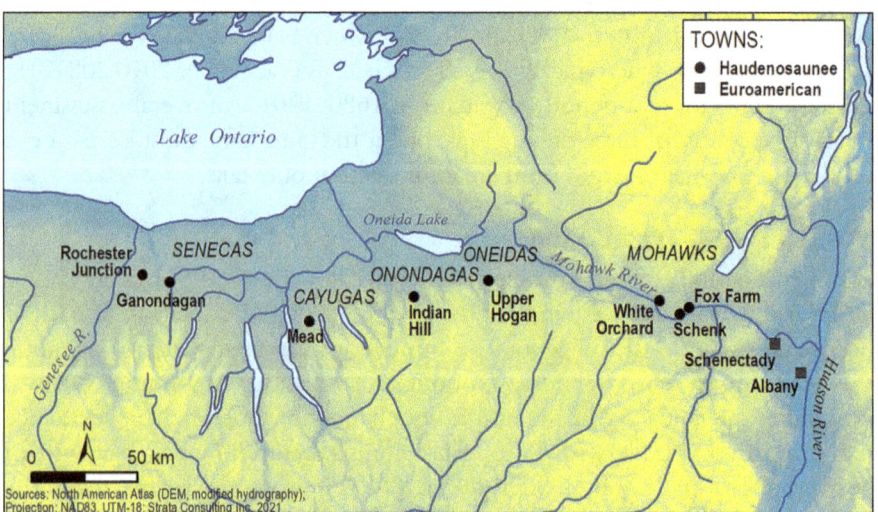

Figure 2.1. Haudenosaunee principal town sites likely to have been visited by New York official Wentworth Greenhalgh in 1677.
Source: Kurt Jordan.

Table 2.1. Names and sources for Haudenosaunee principal town sites likely to have been visited by New York official Wentworth Greenhalgh in 1677

Nation	Site Names	Source
Seneca	Ganondagan/Boughton Hill*; Rochester Junction*; Beal; Kirkwood	Dean 1984; Houghton 1912; Jordan 2013, 2018a; Schoff 1949; Wray and Graham 1985; Wray and Schoff 1953
Cayuga	Mead*; Crane Brook; Young Farm *or* Lamb	DeOrio 1978; Mandzy 1992
Onondaga	Indian Hill*; Weston	Bradley 2005, 2020; Tuck 1971
Oneida	Upper Hogan*	Bennett and Cole 1974
Mohawk (Snow model)	White Orchard*; Schenck*; Fox Farm*; Jackson-Everson; unknown site	Snow 1995
Mohawk (Lenig model)	White Orchard*; Schenck*; Fox Farm*; Turtle Pond; Nestle/Sanfield; J. Y. Edwards	Lenig n.d.

* = principal towns (shown in Figure 2.1.); unmarked = satellites (not shown)
Source: Kurt Jordan.

Greenhalgh's house count for the Onondaga Indian Hill site. Further, archaeologists have questioned why Greenhalgh did not discuss the low-lying Cayuga satellite sites at René Ménard Bridge Hilltop (RMBH) and Rogers Farm, which contained Jesuit chapels at the time (Robert DeOrio, personal communication 2006). It is possible that Greenhalgh's visit was heavily stage-managed, and that his guides made sure that the New York official did not see any more evidence of French Jesuit presence than was necessary. Greenhalgh, therefore, is unlikely to have mentioned all the Haudenosaunee sites occupied at that time.

Nonetheless, there is a wealth of information in Greenhalgh's brief account. He notes that the Oneida town (likely the Upper Hogan site) was "newly settled" and that the Seneca town of Tiotohatton (likely Rochester Junction) "has nott [sic] much cleared ground" (Snow et al. 1996:189–191), likely reflecting the recent construction of both communities. Archaeologists further have argued that Greenhalgh caught two other communities in mid-move. DeOrio (1978) asserts one of the three Cayuga sites was Young Farm, under construction to be the new principal town site to replace Mead. Similarly, Bradley (2020:289) posits that the Onondaga at the large town at Indian Hill were constructing their next town site at Weston in 1677. This may mean that some of the smaller communities reported by Greenhalgh were only temporarily of that size, rather than being durable small satellites.

The principal Haudenosaunee settlements in 1677 ranged in size from the large Seneca, Oneida, and Onondaga principal towns to smaller Cayuga and

Mohawk principals, to satellite villages. Very few sites have precise area estimates, and there are significant discrepancies with the Greenhalgh account. A Shovel test survey at the Seneca Ganondagan site found the domestic portion of the site to be 3.7 ha (Hayes et al. 1978). Bradley reports an initial palisaded settlement of 2.4 ha at the Onondaga Indian Hill site, which was subsequently expanded beyond the palisade to 4.0 ha (2020:290–293). Bennett and Cole (1974) estimate that the Oneida Upper Hogan site is only 0.8 ha in size, even though Greenhalgh reported one hundred houses. Snow (1995a:415, 428) estimates the Mohawk Fox Farm and White Orchard sites to be 0.7 ha and 1.4 ha, respectively. The Cayuga satellite community at Rogers Farm is estimated to be 0.4 ha in size (Williams-Shuker 2009:196).

The east-west division in the presence of palisades in Greenhalgh's descriptions is interesting: perhaps the memory of the 1666 French burning of Mohawk settlements was freshest for the Mohawks and Oneidas. That the three western nations lacked defences presumably relates to the level of comfort they had with the military situation in 1677. This appears to have been a change: the immediately preceding Seneca towns, occupied during active periods of warfare with the Erie and Susquehannock (among others) *had* been fortified (Jordan 2018a:178). The Onondaga Indian Hill site, erected around 1663, was built on a "steep-sided promontory" (Bradley 2020:260), and there is archaeological evidence for a trapezoidal fortification 2.6 ha in size at the site. Bradley (2020:290–292) suggests the fortification followed Indigenous precedent by following topographic lines. The presence of refuse middens atop former palisade lines at Indian Hill suggests that the Onondagas dismantled a pre-existing fortification (or let it decay) by 1677, when Greenhalgh did not see defences, while undertaking a major expansion of the site late in the occupation (Bradley 2020:290; Tuck 1971:178–182).

These communities appear to have been nucleated settlements of longhouse dwellings (cf. Tuck 1971:182). Greenhalgh only describes houses at the Seneca town of Tiotohatton (Rochester Junction), noting that what he called "the ordinary" house was 15–18 m long and the longest was 40–43 m (Snow et al. 1996:91). This corresponds to approximately three to four hearths in the ordinary houses and seven to ten hearths in the longest (Jordan 2008:247–248). A single dwelling of 15.2 × 6.1 m was excavated at the Onondaga town at Indian Hill (Bradley 2020:292). Excavations at the Cayuga-region Rogers Farm satellite (occupied in 1677 but apparently not visited by Greenhalgh) recovered a portion of a longhouse 6.7 m wide; topographic limitations suggest it could have been no more than 25 m long, holding at maximum three to four hearths (Williams-Shuker 2009:197, 199). A dwelling interpreted as a "short longhouse" of 11 × 6 m, excavated at the Seneca Ganondagan site (Dean 1984), further demonstrates the diversity in Haudenosaunee house forms. All these structures appear to have been built using Iroquoian architectural principles and covered with bark.

1.1. Incorporation

Documentary and archaeological sources suggest that large numbers of non-Haudenosaunee individuals had been incorporated into both principal communities and nearby smaller satellites. Jesuits noted in 1657 that Haudenosaunee communities "now contain more Foreigners than natives of the country" and that persons from seven Indigenous nations lived among the Onondaga and persons from eleven nations lived among the Seneca (Thwaites 1896–1901:43:265). Incorporated persons are identified in historical documents as Wendat, Susquehannock, Attawandaron, probable Shawnee, and others. While some outsiders were incorporated as individuals, whole groups were also brought in (Lynch 1985). Some smaller local satellite communities appear to have consisted entirely of individuals of non-local origin. Of those incorporated, Wendat likely were the most numerous; Parmenter (2010:80) estimates that between 1,600 and 2,800 Wendat were brought in by the Haudenosaunee in the years after their 1649 defeat, and we know from other sources that hundreds were brought in even before that (see Williamson, this volume). Many incorporated individuals would have spent much of their lives in other regions and would have spoken different languages and practised different customs than their Haudenosaunee hosts. Some, particularly Wendat, were identified as having converted to Christianity prior to their incorporation. Documentary sources also identify members of other Haudenosaunee nations as long-term residents in some communities (Waterman 2008), which I suspect was likely a long-standing practice. Haudenosaunee communities at this time thus would have featured significant diversity along many lines.

Notable archaeological examples of circa 1677 satellites, likely to have contained large proportions of incorporated individuals, include the Seneca Beal and the Cayuga Rogers Farm sites. At these sites and at the Bunce cemetery (associated with the Beal site), secondary burials and small, multi-person ossuaries with commingled remains reminiscent of Wendat tradition have been excavated (Houghton 1912; Mandzy 1992; Schoff 1949; Williams-Shuker 2009; Wray and Graham 1960). Domestic ceramics and a smoking pipe rendered in what Robert Kuhn (1986) identifies as Wendat styles but manufactured from local clays were recovered from the Mohawk Jackson-Everson site (which may have been abandoned slightly prior to Greenhalgh's visit). My review of the scanty published archaeological evidence from satellite villages purported to have housed non-Haudenosaunee outsiders and from principal towns suggests that differences in mortuary practices may have accelerated over time; there are no known ossuary-style burials at the earliest alleged Wendat satellites from the 1650s, but they appear at sites occupied in the 1670s (Jordan 2018b).

The status of these incorporated persons remains a major scholarly question. Some have declared that incorporated individuals were "slaves" of the Haudenosaunee (e.g., Starna and Watkins 1991), while others have shown how some incorporated persons eventually became valued leaders in Haudenosaunee communities (e.g., Parmenter 2010). My review of the archaeological evidence (Jordan 2018b) suggests that satellite villages of outsiders generally appear to have the same range of material culture forms as principal towns, including valued objects, such as firearms and wampum. But this subject undoubtedly is in need of additional attention.

Incorporated outsiders provided a critical demographic boost needed to reverse Haudenosaunee losses from European-borne diseases and warfare. The process of incorporation certainly has helped the Haudenosaunee perpetuate themselves to the present. Neal Ferris (2009:118), William Fox (2009:70), and others have suggested that, additionally, outsiders incorporated into Haudenosaunee Territory for a time may have returned to their homelands as du Nord settlers. This could have been motivated by a desire to return to well-known places, a response to friction with Haudenosaunee hosts, or some combination of both. I leave this contention to the other authors in this volume to evaluate.

1.2. Colonization

This period of prosperity witnessed the Haudenosaunee establishment of a number of settlements in extra-regional spaces distant from their homeland towns. The du Nord settlements are, of course, a primary example of this process. I have, perhaps cheekily, referred to extra-regional Haudenosaunee settlements as "colonies" (Jordan 2013), as they provided opportunities to capture resources (especially furs), protect transportation routes, surveil territory, funnel population movements (including persons and groups intended for incorporation), and make new social connections in ways similar to European colonies.

There are indications that placement of distant settlements in key locations was a long-standing Haudenosaunee practice (Jordan 2013), but the scope and intensity of colonization definitely increased during this period of prosperity. Victor Konrad (1981) has eloquently demonstrated how the du Nord communities were firmly connected to the Haudenosaunee homeland. Historian Jon Parmenter (2010) has made a similar case for the continued association between the homeland and the so-called mission Iroquois in the St. Lawrence Valley, raising the possibility that we could consider these communities the "Mohawks du Nord." While standard accounts typically portray the predominantly Mohawk St. Lawrence settlements as fleeing from factionalism, hostility to Christianity, social disintegration, and alcohol abuse, these sources may uncritically take Jesuit accounts at face value. As Parmenter (2010:142) notes:

> the larger story of Iroquois movements to the St. Lawrence valley settlements may only be discerned by reading between the lines of missionary

sources. On the one hand, the Laurentian communities represented secure spaces for Iroquois individuals pursuing conversion to Catholicism as a response to changing conditions in their homelands. On the other hand, the majority of Iroquois people came to view relocation to these settlements not as flights to spiritual refuge from their pagan kinfolk, but rather as an effort to expand League homelands. The Laurentian communities developed from seasonal bases incorporated into Iroquois peoples' annual subsistence cycle into centres of trade and strategic nodes of League diplomacy and communications.

Later Haudenosaunee expansions into Pennsylvania and Ohio appear to have followed similar principles.

1.3. Regional Settlement Intensification

The intensified use of extra-regional space during the 1650–1680 period appears to have a parallel at the regional level. I have recently made the case (Jordan 2022) that Haudenosaunee people intensified their use of regional space through expanded use of small-scale settlement at locations distant from principal towns and satellites. Clusters of diagnostic artifacts from this period appear at some small, poorly understood sites, several of which have been completely destroyed by residential development and are known only from documentation by non-archaeologists one hundred or more years ago.

Cayuga-region examples include a site in downtown Ithaca that contained a distinctive marine shell "arc rosette" disk runtee, a form that Duane Esarey (2013) has dated to between 1670 and 1710. This site may be associated with a cemetery nearby of about fifty buried individuals that contained brass kettles and likely iron knives. The Ithaca area previously had been considered to have been relatively sparsely occupied by Indigenous peoples, and no seventeenth-century sites had formally been identified. Additionally, an AMS date on a maize kernel from the predominantly sixteenth-century Indian Fort Road site, west of Cayuga Lake, yielded a most likely date of 1640–1680 (Sanft 2013), an occupation date also supported by the find of a long tubular white glass bead. A Christian-themed brass ring and possibly other seventeenth-century brass items were found at the Seneca-region Eugene Frost site, located south of Seneca Lake, on Catherine Creek. This indicates that the pattern may extend across the territories of multiple nations.

These data suggest that Haudenosaunee people intensified use of their home regions but that these settlements were short-lived. The Ithaca sites and Indian Fort Road are at least 44 km from contemporaneous Cayuga principal towns, and the Eugene Frost site is almost 80 km from the Seneca principal towns of the period. These sites were "exposed" in a military sense, suggesting that their occupants were confident enough in the diplomatic climate to live in isolated locations. These small sites are a further indication that the spatial coverage of Wentworth Greenhalgh's travels was limited.

1.4. Settler Forts and Missionaries

It would be remiss in any discussion of late seventeenth-century Haudenosaunee history to leave out an account of the European soldiers, settlers, and missionaries present in Five Nations Territory. I purport that during this period of prosperity, the Haudenosaunee remained even less impacted by Europeans than had the Wendat before their defeat and expulsion from their home territory.

Substantial settler populations, as mentioned earlier, were no closer than Schenectady and Montréal. While Mohawks were relatively close to what Dutch settlements were at the beginning of this period, other Haudenosaunee nations were quite distant. The most substantial European endeavours directly within Haudenosaunee Territory did not last long. The 1,300-man French expedition led by the Marquis de Tracy in 1666 resulted in the destruction of three to six Mohawk settlements, burned by the Mohawk themselves in advance of the French army (Parmenter 2010:122). But the French departed Haudenosaunee Territory quickly: "in their haste they neither destroyed food that they could not carry nor burned the Mohawk's outlying fields" (2010:124). The army was back in Quebec within three weeks.

In terms of installations, Sainte Marie de Gannentaha, a fortified French Jesuit/secular centre in Onondaga Territory, was modelled along the lines of Sainte-Marie among the Hurons. While it had a fairly substantial footprint, the centre was abandoned in the middle of the night less than two years after its founding in 1656 (Bradley 2020; Connors et al. 1980). The earliest French forts in the Niagara area, including Fort LaSalle, founded in 1669, Fort Hennepin, built in 1678, and Fort Conti, founded in 1679, were not durable either (NYS Division of Military and Naval Affairs 2012; Scott 1998:46).

Jesuit missionaries provided a more regular presence, although even they were not consistent fixtures in Haudenosaunee Territory. Jesuit endeavours started in 1656; beside Sainte Marie de Gannentaha they were small in scale. In most instances, Jesuit outposts were manned by only one to two priests, housed in one Native-built structure or even only a single compartment in a longhouse (French-built chapels at Onondaga [Bradley 2020:148, 517] are an exception). Accounts published in the *Jesuit Relations* (Thwaites 1896–1901) state that missionaries were often under threat, although no Jesuits were killed by the Haudenosaunee after 1649. Many of the archaeological sites discussed in this section contained Jesuit chapels, and Christian-themed artifacts are relatively plentiful in this era. It should be noted that Christian-themed artifacts do not necessarily indicate Christian conversion or missionary activity (see Mason 2003, 2010). In the Seneca region, Christian-themed materials at Seneca sites both pre- and post-date the presence of Jesuits (Eastly 2012). Roughly during this era, there was a widespread change in Haudenosaunee burial practices, from predominantly flexed interments to extended burials (DeOrio 1978; Wray 1973:28), which occasionally has been interpreted to reflect European influence (e.g., Wray and Schoff 1953, 59 term extended burials "European style"). This interpretation may not be warranted, as the proportions of Christian converts among the Haudenosaunee did not approach the proportion of extended burials. There may have been different motivations for this change in funerary custom. I have asserted elsewhere (Jordan 2016:66) that Christian Wendat converts probably contributed more to Haudenosaunee notions of spirituality than did the Jesuit missionaries, whom they vastly outnumbered.

Another consequence of the settler presence in the Northeast was the circulation of epidemic diseases of European origin. Using Mohawk evidence, Snow and Lanphear (1988) asserted that the first major impact of European disease in the interior Northeast took place in 1633 and that further outbreaks took place regularly thereafter. Modelling by Jones and DeWitte (2012) suggests that the level of disease impact was quite variable among the Haudenosaunee nations. Scholarship on disease in recent years has placed greater emphasis on social factors and power relations, going beyond biological elements (see Cameron et al. 2016). However, the new approaches do not seem to have been entirely accepted within Iroquoian studies. Losses from epidemics certainly were a major motivation for the taking of captives and the incorporation of outsiders into Haudenosaunee Territory.

1.5. Material Culture, 1650–1680

It is beyond the scope of this chapter to include a comprehensive discussion of the material culture forms found at Haudenosaunee sites of this era; some individual chapters in this volume make detailed comparisons with homeland Haudenosaunee sites. Nonetheless, it is worth pointing out that assemblages from these sites show a fascinating combination of Indigenously produced goods and European imports. For almost every function or task one can conceive, there were both Indigenous and European-derived forms. There are firearms (in some cases, lots of them—see Wray 1985) and arrowheads. Some projectile points are brass, others are stone. Sites contain Indigenous-made and imported European smoking pipes and gunflints. There are red glass beads and red brass beads, and there are white and blue glass beads alongside white and purple shell. Iron cutting tools were used at the same sites as at least some stone tools. The "trade good" or "exotic good" category was not limited to European imports, as many materials produced by Indigenous trade partners (such as shell beads and pendants and red pipestone forms) show up on Haudenosaunee sites. Vectors of trade and alliance and supply chains extended in many directions, continentally and globally (for detailed treatments of the material culture forms at Ganondagan, see Dean [1984] and Wray and Graham [1985]).

The Haudenosaunee appear to have incorporated European-derived plants and animals very selectively. Pig bones have been found in secure Haudenosaunee contexts at the circa 1655–1675 Seneca Dann site (Morton 2010:91) and the circa 1663–1682 Onondaga Indian Hill site (Bradley 2020:296). Very few plant remains have been recovered or studied from sites of this era, which is a significant weakness in the research carried out to date.

Since most assemblages from Haudenosaunee sites contain numerous goods acquired from Europeans or made from European materials, earlier archaeologists often claimed that Haudenosaunee culture was in decline (e.g., Wray and Schoff 1953). While European objects and materials are ubiquitous, it is important to consider the use of space (settlement structure and house forms) and the use of plants and animals in subsistence alongside material culture. When one looks at the whole picture, any notions of "Europeanization" are much harder to sustain (Jordan 2008:348–352).

2. The Twenty Years' War and French Invasions, 1680–1696

The window of Haudenosaunee political, economic, and diplomatic success began to close when they directed military efforts to the west in about 1680. This initiated what historian Richard Aquila (1983) has termed the "Twenty Years' War," in which Haudenosaunee forces overextended themselves in battling (among others) Illinois, Ottawa, Fox, Miami, Ojibwe, Wyandot, and their French allies. French forces under Governor La Barre attempted to invade Seneca Territory in retaliation in 1684. Given the pending hostilities, many Jesuit missionaries left Haudenosaunee Territory (O'Callaghan 1969:9:229).

Several of the sites described in the previous section continued to be occupied into the Twenty Years' War period: the Seneca principal towns at Ganondagan and Rochester Junction and satellites at Beal and Kirkwood; the Oneida principal town at Upper Hogan; and possibly the Mohawk principal town at White Orchard. But several new sites were established during the war. The downturn in Haudenosaunee fortunes appears to have had a quick effect on settlement choices, particularly the degree of fortification.

The new Onondaga town at the Weston site, fully occupied by circa 1682, included a 2.6 ha palisaded area and other structures outside the fort (Bradley 2020; Sohrweide 2001). The newly built 0.6 ha Mohawk settlement at the Caughnawaga (or Veeder) site, constructed either circa 1683 (Snow 1995a:442) or circa 1689 (Lenig 2020), was also fortified. Rumours preceding the La Barre expedition encouraged the Seneca to build a palisaded enclosure of about 3.2–4.0 ha at what is known as the Fort Hill site (Jordan 2018a:179–180). La Barre ended up returning to New France after disease swept through his forces. The Seneca never occupied Fort Hill, but the fact of its construction indicates a change in mindset. The western Seneca satellite village had also been fortified by 1687.

Then, three subsequent (and more consequential) French invasions resulted in the burning of the homeland settlements of all the Haudenosaunee nations except the Cayuga (Parmenter 2010:190–195, 224–226, 246–247). In several instances, Haudenosaunee forces burned their communities themselves, perhaps to prevent the French armies and their allies from spending time in the area and finding people, hidden caches of food, and even other settlements. The Seneca were attacked first by a force led by the Marquis de Denonville in 1687, resulting in the destruction of the Ganondagan, Rochester Junction, Kirkwood, and Beal sites (Jordan 2018a:180–181). A second invasion force in 1693, led by the Comte de Frontenac, destroyed several Mohawk settlements. In Snow's (1995a) model, these likely were the Caughnawaga, White Orchard, and Lipe sites, whereas Lenig (2020) asserts that the destroyed sites were Caughnawaga, Leichner, Allen, and Crouse. Another force led by Frontenac resulted in the destruction of the Onondaga Weston and Oneida Upper Hogan sites in 1696. Cayuga settlements were the only ones not affected by the French invasions of this period. In each instance, French troops made sure that settlements and stored and growing food were destroyed, and then the main force returned to New France, leaving behind only small garrisons at forts (such as Fort Denonville, near Niagara Falls, and a temporary fort in Onondaga Territory) that were abandoned in relatively short order (Bradley 2020:21; Scott 1998).

Of the burned settlements, the Onondaga Weston and Mohawk Caughnawaga sites have been the most thoroughly studied. Greg Sohrweide (2001) observed many similarities between a 1696 French map and the architectural features he excavated at Weston. This town consisted primarily of longhouses, the largest of which was 27 m long, with most 15–24 m in length (likely indicating two to three hearths). A variety of non-residential structures and a plaza also appear to have been present. At Caughnawaga, excavations conducted in the 1940s and 1950s resulted in the complete clearance of the town plan (Snow 1995a). Snow (1995a:443) has argued that the seeming uniformity of the three to four hearth longhouses represents repackaging of disrupted social units into "standardized" architecture. This, however, appears to be an aberration: it contrasts with the diverse forms seen at the contemporaneous Weston site, as well as to later Mohawk towns (O'Callaghan 1969:4:345). The regular house size at Caughnawaga may be a product of the truncated use life of the settlement: since it was burned well prior to the planned end of its occupation span, there had been less time for the size of the households to have changed (Jordan 2008:321–323).

Fortifications at sites of this era exhibit a mix of Indigenous- and European-derived characteristics. The palisade line at Seneca Fort Hill appears to have followed natural topography (Jordan 2018a:Figure 11.2). In contrast, defences at Weston included a three-row palisade with straight walls and protruding bastions (a European innovation) at each corner of the fort; these details are evident both in the 1696 French map of the site and in the archaeologically recovered site plan (Bradley 2020; Sohrweide 2001). At Caughnawaga, a very regular, rectangular palisade two rows deep was built (Snow 1995a), following the European pattern but using Haudenosaunee methods, with spaces between upright posts that would have been filled with horizontal elements. There is textual evidence that English officials lent their support for the Onondaga fortification, but Sohrweide concludes, due to the Indigenous nature of the construction itself, that "the English probably just supervised the construction or at best provided a small work detail to assist the Onondaga" (2001:22).

The sites built during the Twenty Years' War—Weston, Caughnawaga, and Fort Hill—provide a very concrete indication of the new military reality that Haudenosaunee nations faced. Archaeologically, these relatively short-lived settlements provide a clear snapshot of material culture almost to the decade level (see Bradley [2020] for a thorough description of material culture at Weston). More details on the impact of the French invasions are presented in the next section.

3. After the Invasions, 1696–1713

The Haudenosaunee communities re-established after the French-led attacks of the 1680s and 1690s were in a very uncertain situation. A "hot" war continued to take place until 1701, and the military situation remained fraught until around 1713 (Jordan 2008). All Haudenosaunee nations except the Cayuga had to rebuild their communities in adverse wartime conditions, and this process appears to have been accompanied by significant population reorganization and movement (Figure 2.2, Table 2.2).

3.1. Contraction and Consolidation

Within this troubled setting, the spatial extent of Haudenosaunee settlements contracted dramatically. It is likely that many outlying Haudenosaunee satellite communities—extra-regional, regional, and even local ones—that had been established during the period of prosperity were abandoned due to military danger as the war progressed. As Konrad (1981) notes, the du Nord settlements were all but vacated by the time of the 1687 Denonville expedition; this was probably due to a combination of setbacks in the homeland and direct pressure by Algonquian groups on the north shore (Warrick and Williamson, this volume). It is also possible, as both Carl Benn and Jennifer Birch suggested in their comments for the volume, that the du Nord settlements may have been close to the end of their use-lives and that the labour costs of upcoming reconstruction were another factor that encouraged abandonment. While most of the new, post-invasion towns were built close to the locations of the burned sites, the Senecas moved southeast to an unimproved area, effectively moving the exterior border of their settlements southeast by about 32–35 km (Jordan 2018a).

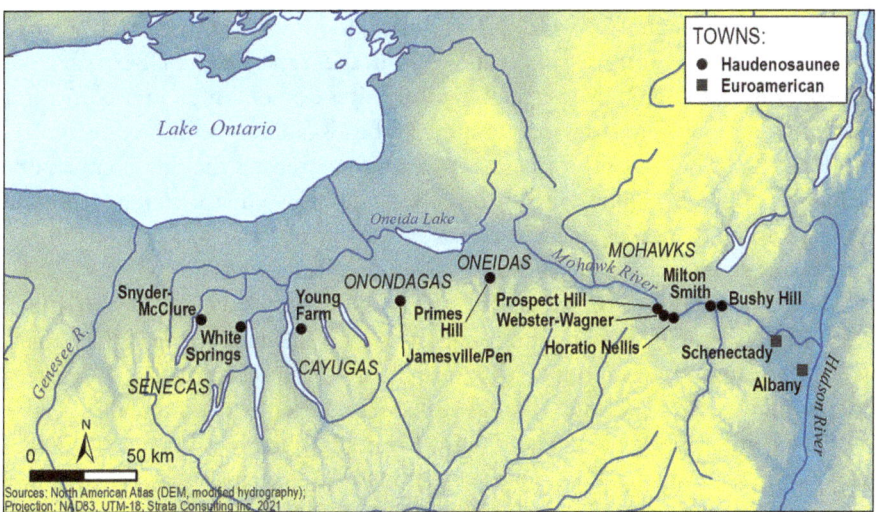

Figure 2.2. Haudenosaunee principal town sites occupied after the French invasions of 1687–1696. Mohawk-area sites include both those identified by the Snow model and those identified by the Lenig model. Source: Kurt Jordan.

Table 2.2. Names and sources for Haudenosaunee principal town sites occupied after the French invasions of 1687–1696

Nation	Site Names	Source
Seneca	Snyder-McClure*; White Springs*	Jordan 2008; Jordan and Gerard-Little 2019; Schoff 1949
Cayuga	Young Farm*	DeOrio 1978; Mandzy 1992
Onondaga	Jamesville*	Bradley 2005, 2020
Oneida	Primes Hill*	Bennett 1988
Mohawk (Snow model)	Prospect Hill/Fort Plain*; Dekanohage; Allen; Milton Smith*; Auriesville; Bushy Hill*	Snow 1995
Mohawk (Lenig model)	Empire Lock; Milton Smith*; Horatio Nellis*; Webster-Wagner/Reinhart*	Lenig n.d.

* = principal towns (shown in Figure 2.2.); unmarked = satellites (not shown)
Source: Kurt Jordan.

Mohawks continued to build numerous smaller settlements that may have followed principal-local satellite organization (Lenig 2020; Snow 1995a:450), but there is no evidence for year-round satellite settlements in Seneca, Onondaga, or Oneida Territory after the burnings. These three nations are represented by four large towns in total. The Cayuga, who Greenhalgh reported were considering joining populations in a single town in 1677, appear to have done so by the 1690s at the Young Farm site. There is no evidence for Seneca satellite settlements between 1687 and 1704, when documents suggest that a small satellite had been founded at Kendaia, on the east shore of Seneca Lake (Jordan 2008:181–182). Most small, regional sites do not contain post-invasion diagnostic artifacts, such as wire-wound glass beads (amber "truncated teardrop" beads appear to be the only wire-wound form that predates the French invasions [LaGrasta 2021:85]). This contraction of settlements is a major change from the extra-regional "colonies" and regional expansion of the 1660s, and from the much longer-standing pattern of local satellite villages.

Site size is largely consistent with the pre-invasion towns. Shovel test pits, test units, and surface investigation suggest that the habitation area at the Seneca White Springs site was about 3.4 ha (Jordan and Gerard-Little 2019:47); a very coarse estimate for the contemporaneous Seneca settlement at Snyder-McClure is 2.0 ha (Jordan 2008:173). The Oneida Primes Hill site is estimated to be only 1.0 ha in size, despite a 1714 account that says the principal Oneida town had 1,100–1,200 residents (Wonderley 2020). Snow (1995a:459) puts the Mohawk Milton Smith site at 0.4 ha.

All post-invasion sites where substantial domestic-context excavation has taken place show evidence for palisade construction. It is likely that these fortifications (and also houses) initially were constructed in great haste, without having the advantage of several years of materials stockpiling that typically preceded a Haudenosaunee community move. Probable palisade segments have been recovered at the Oneida Primes Hill and Seneca White Springs sites (Bennett 1988; Bridges 2020). A fortification of unclear date has been uncovered at the Onondaga Jamesville site; historic plan maps of the site provide divergent interpretations of the size and shape of the town (Bradley 2020:741, n11.7; Tuck 1971). Snow (1995a:456) asserts that Milton Smith was palisaded, although this has not been substantiated archaeologically. It is interesting to note that relatively small posts appear to have been used in all the excavated post-invasion palisades (cf. Tuck 1971:119).

Excavations have not been extensive enough at any of these sites to determine whether fortification lines followed the natural topography (i.e., using Indigenous precedents) or were laid out in straight lines across elevation changes (i.e., following European models, such as at Weston). At White Springs, several large, fire-related features were found in one zone of the site, possibly representing an outdoor work area within the bounds of the fortified area. This indicates that the site's residents did not feel entirely safe outside the town and placed features and activities that normally would have been located outside the palisade inside for protection.

Alongside the contraction in the number of settlements and attention to defence and safety came consolidation of formerly separated groups. Incorporated populations previously distributed across principal towns, local and regional satellites, and distant colonies, presumably all now had to live together with "homeland" Haudenosaunee within the principal towns. This was likely to have been a difficult and contentious process.

Evidence for consolidation can be seen in mortuary practices. Whereas burials at pre-invasion principal settlements like the Seneca Ganondagan site predominantly consisted of extended burials, those post-invasion sites where large-scale burial excavations have taken place (mostly prior to 1990) show a variety of different mortuary practices. The Cayuga Young Farm site contains flexed, extended, primary, secondary, and multiple burials (Mandzy 1992; Skinner 1921). Daniel Weiskotten (2000: Section 3.3.2.3) documented "30 single burials, 12 multiple graves with 31 individuals (seven double, four triple, and one with five), 10 apparently empty graves, and two apparent bundle burials with four and eight individuals" at the Onondaga Pen cemetery, associated with the post-invasion town at Jamesville (see Bradley 2020).

While settlement contraction and population consolidation contrasted greatly with patterns seen prior to 1680, many other lifeways remained quite consistent across the divide established by the settlement burnings. The new, post-invasion communities appear to have been nucleated villages where longhouses continued to be built. Cornell University–sponsored excavations under my direction at White Springs uncovered the traces of segments of four apparent longhouses, including a 51 m^2 area enclosed by an arc of posts, about 6 m wide at maximum, which we have interpreted as a storage compartment or vestibule at the end of a longhouse. While no house patterns could be determined at the Oneida Primes Hill site, traces of post-in-ground architecture were common. A 1698 document mentions diverse house sizes at a Mohawk settlement, stating that some "contain one family, some two, and some four" (O'Callaghan 1969:4:345).

While the overall situation certainly was fraught, the newly founded communities appear to have come together socially. That widely varying mortuary practices could co-exist even within the same cemetery suggests a certain acceptance of plural practices in the post-invasion towns. Thomas Jamison's study of Pen site mortuary practices concludes that the Onondaga were "a fairly well integrated community" (1998:2). My recent paper, with Dusti Bridges (2019) found distinct redundancy in the material culture from the four Seneca houses excavated at White Springs, suggesting that consolidation and the adversity faced at the newly established communities did not produce a division between "have" and "have-nots."

3.2. Material Culture, 1696–1713

It is difficult to compare material culture across the sites due to the varied standards in place when investigations were undertaken; the differing recovery methods used in excavation, surface collection, and metal detection; and whether domestic, midden, or mortuary contexts were emphasized. Nonetheless, a few observations can be made.

While brass kettles had dramatically increased in popularity throughout the 1600s, the invasions do seem to mark the last gasp of local Haudenosaunee pottery production. Although some potsherds are present in domestic contexts at pre-invasion sites, at the Seneca Ganondagan site they are outnumbered by Indigenous-made ceramic pipe fragments (Dean 1984:55). Numbers from post-invasion sites are even more stark: only one Indigenous-made potsherd was found at the Onondaga Jamesville site (Bradley 2020:758 n11.96), and none have been found in the fairly extensive excavations my project has conducted at White Springs. Increased prevalence of wire-wound glass beads is a notable change in post-invasion assemblages. Wire-wound beads make up over five percent of the Seneca White Springs (LaGrasta 2021), approximately nine percent of the Onondaga Jamesville (Bradley 2020:Table 11.2), and 40 percent of the Oneida Primes Hill (Bennett 1988) bead assemblages, although these figures are highly conditioned by the precision of the recovery methods used.

That said, most material forms show some consistency across the invasion break. Haudenosaunee communities appear to have maintained access to guns and wampum despite wartime conditions. Rapprochement with the French in the years following 1701 resulted in the reintroduction of Jesuit missions and renewed ties with French officials and traders, though the largely unsuccessful missions ended in 1713 and were very poorly documented compared to the seventeenth-century endeavours (Jordan 2008:36).

Low-level use of European domesticated animals appears consistent at sites occupied between the 1660s and 1710, including the Seneca Dann (Morton 2010) and White Springs (Disotell 2021) sites and the Onondaga Weston and Jamesville sites (Bradley 2020). Archaeological specimens are mainly pig remains, although Bradley notes finds of limited numbers of cattle and sheep bones at Weston (2020:433). Botanical analysis has been incredibly rare in this era as well: emerging work from White Springs shows very, very low use of some European plants, including three wheat kernel fragments and one possible piece of barley (Turkon 2010). We also recovered probable peach tree wood charcoal, possibly indicating that peaches were grown on-site (Gerard-Little 2017).

4. Conclusion: After Uncertainty

I argue in my 2008 book, *The Seneca Restoration*, that conditions for the Seneca, and likely most other Haudenosaunee nations, improved after the 1713 Treaty of Utrecht ended French-English warfare and Indigenous entanglement as allies. This marked the start of a lengthy period of relative regional peace. The Mohawk, however, faced significant encroachment from European settlers and increased Protestant missionary activity, particularly after the English construction of Fort Hunter at the eastern Mohawk town in 1711. This presented the Mohawk with significantly different and more constrained social and economic options (Jordan 2009). The other Haudenosaunee nations would not encounter substantial numbers of European farmers until the 1760s or even after the American Revolution.

After 1710, major changes in settlement and housing are visible. Presumably related to the improved military climate, regional networks of smaller sites at key locations began to replace the nucleated principal towns of earlier days (Jordan 2018a). Haudenosaunee communities also segmented into multiple, spatially separate neighbourhoods. At the circa 1715–1754 Seneca Townley-Read site, where I conducted excavations from 1996 to 2000, dispersed houses were built 60–80 m apart along a watercourse (Jordan 2008). Finally, there is documentary and archaeological evidence that two-family "short longhouse" dwellings constructed with a mix of Haudenosaunee and European techniques and tools became the most common residential form across the Confederacy (Jordan 2008). Beyond Townley-Read, other examples of dispersed Haudenosaunee communities likely include the Seneca Huntoon (Jordan 2008:181), the Cayuga Pattington (DeOrio 1978), the Onondaga Coye (Tuck 1971:193), and the Oneida Lanz-Hogan (Bennett 1982) sites. Although Mohawk communities also dispersed, some of their motivation may have been to protect their lands in the face of competition from European settlers (Jordan 2009).

These changes took place alongside significant continuities in Haudenosaunee subsistence—which remained focused on the three sisters, gathered plants, white-tailed deer, furbearers, birds, and fish. Extra-regionally, new Haudenosaunee "colonies" were established, especially in what is now Pennsylvania and Ohio (Jordan 2013). Certainly, there would have been homeland interaction with the Mississauga residents of the north shore during this era.

Thus, the French incursions of the 1680s and 1690s, although they ended village-scale Haudenosaunee settlement in the du Nord area, did not mark the onset of permanent decline. The second decade of the eighteenth century brought a new form of prosperity to Haudenosaunee communities.

Acknowledgements

I am grateful to Ron Williamson and Rob von Bitter for the invitation to present at the 2019 Ontario Archaeological Society Annual Symposium in Toronto, and to contribute to this volume. I benefited from Ron Williamson's and Suzanne Needs-Howarth's careful editorial reading, the comments of the volume reviewers, Carl Benn and Jennifer Birch, and from du Nord–related exchanges with Bill Fox and Dana Poulton. I have been helped immeasurably over the years by conversations with Haudenosaunee regional experts Jim Bradley, Bob DeOrio, Wayne Lenig, Martha Sempowski, Greg Sohrweide, and Tony Wonderley. I also acknowledge the important research contributions made to this chapter by current and former students Dusti Bridges,

Brian Broadrose, Adam Dewbury, Sam Disotell, Sarah Eastly, Perri Gerard-Little, Matthew Krohn, Kaitlin LaGrasta, Beth Ryan, Sam Sanft, Alex Walton, Adam Watson, and Alice Wolff. Research design and field methods for the Townley-Read and White Springs projects were developed in consultation with Onöndowa'ga:' (Seneca Nation) cultural leaders. Townley-Read fieldwork was supported by Columbia University, Hobart and William Smith Colleges, the National Science Foundation, and the Early American Industries Association. Cornell University has supported field and lab work, analysis, and scholarships for Indigenous participants for the White Springs project.

SECTION 2
THE SETTLEMENT LOCATIONS AND HISTORY OF INVESTIGATIONS

3

THE SEARCH FOR KENTÉ
A Review

Robert von Bitter, Chris Menary, and Nick Gromoff

In 1668, the French mission of Kenté was established on the north shore of Lake Ontario, on what was then the frontier of New France. It was established at the Cayuga village of Kenté, which was one of the first permanent Haudenosaunee villages in Ontario following the dispersal of Ontario Iroquoians and their Algonquian allies in 1650–1651 (see Williamson, this volume). The mission lasted for twelve years before it was abandoned, and its exact location is lost to history. There have been many episodes in the search to discover where the mission had been situated. This chapter provides an overview of the history of Kenté and outlines past and current efforts to relocate it.

Missionary work in the Great Lakes region had seemingly ended in 1650 with the dispersal of the Wendat and the abandonment of the French missions in Wendake. Peace between the French and the Haudenosaunee was eventually reached in 1654, and two years later the Jesuits (missionaries of the Society of Jesus, also referred to as the "black robes") were invited to open a new mission, called Sainte Marie de Gannentaha, on Lake Onondaga, in what is now the state of New York. Rising tensions resulted in the abandonment of the mission in 1658, and the subsequent hostilities lasted until 1667. King Louis XIV, crowned in 1661, saw the precarious situation of the colony and sent reinforcements that subsequently attacked Mohawk Territory. The peace treaty of 1667 allowed the Jesuits to return to Mohawk and Oneida Territory.

In 1666, emissaries from the north-shore Cayuga village of Kenté travelled upriver to Montréal to ask for "black robes" to be sent to their village. The Cayuga had been familiar with Jesuit missionaries in their homeland and perhaps saw them as a form of protection against their enemies. Receiving no reply to their initial request, the Cayuga returned in 1667 to again ask for missionaries, this time led by their chief, Roharío. The colonial government agreed, and preparations were made to dispatch missionaries the following year.

The Society of Jesus was a Roman Catholic evangelizing religious order founded in 1540 by Saint Ignatius Loyola, who became the champion of the Counter-Reformation (Wright 2004:10). These "new athletes to combat God's enemies" took vows of poverty, chastity, and obedience to the Pope and were independent of the local bishop. They viewed missionary work as cleansing to the soul and preferred to live in isolation and among Indigenous groups, where they used local stories and beliefs in their evangelization efforts (Wright 2004:111).

The policy of the Intendant of New France, Jean Talon, and the colonial government in the 1660s was cultural assimilation; rather than merely saving souls, missionary work was to Europeanize Indigenous Peoples. This policy was meant to influence how the Kenté mission was operated and led to the hindering of future missions. Because most of the colony's Jesuit missionaries had been sent to work with the Haudenosaunee, there was a lack of Jesuit priests to undertake this task. Jean Talon disliked the Jesuits and saw this lack of Jesuit priests as an opportunity to break the hold of that order and to centralize French contact with Indigenous people under royal control. The colonial government and Bishop François de Laval turned to the Society of the Priests of Saint Sulpice—known as the Sulpicians. This Roman Catholic Society of Apostolic Life was founded in Paris in 1641, primarily for the training of secular (parish) priests. One was first ordained to the priesthood, and then joined the Society thereafter. Sulpicians took the ordinary vows (poverty, chastity, obedience) when ordained, but Societies of Apostolic Life did not require religious vows to the Pope like those taken by members of the Society of Jesus. As such, the Sulpicians, unlike the Jesuits, could own property and were directly under the purview of the local bishop. When New France was placed under direct royal control in 1663, the Sulpicians succeeded the Société de Notre-Dame, who had founded Ville-Marie twenty-one years earlier, and they were granted the Seigneury of Montréal. This gave the order both secular and religious power. As a relatively new order, the Sulpicians were eventually drawn to missionary work in New France, after witnessing the work of the Jesuits and the Recollects. When Bishop Laval asked if they would go work with the Cayuga, they agreed.

Two recently ordained Sulpician priests were chosen to establish the mission: Claude Trouvé, 24, and François de Salignac de La Mothe-Fénelon, 27. Both were new to the colony and had been ordained only six months prior to their leaving to establish the mission. Trouvé would lead the mission, having been ordained one day before Fénelon (Pritchard 1973a:133). Both required training before leaving for Kenté, as neither had any missionary experience nor knew the local languages. Before they left, in the fall of 1668, Bishop Laval gave Trouvé a letter of instruction, which included contacting the Jesuits south of the lake in order to further their learning (Hawley 1879:95). A land grant may have been given to the mission with rights to build, farm, and fish. The missionaries left Montréal by canoe on October 2, 1668, accompanied by Chief Rohario and other Cayuga. The journey to Kenté took twenty-six days.

The mission was financed through wealthy benefactors both in the colony and in France, including Bishop Laval and the head of the Sulpicians in France. The first winter was spent with the Cayuga in their lodgings, but the following year lay workers were sent to Kenté from Montréal. They constructed a wooden mission house and a farm equipped with a grindstone, furniture, agricultural implements, and other necessities (Lamontagne 1958:9). Cattle and swine were also transported upriver, and the mission supplemented the products of their agriculture with fish and berries. The letters sent back from the missionaries contain little to no description of the physical form, layout, or geographic location of the mission. There is a mention of "buildings" in one letter, which must include the mission house and any farm buildings, but that is all. The original Jesuit missions in Wendake were cabins located within or outside of a village; only later was Sainte-Marie I built as a central administrative centre to support them. Sulpician missions post-Kenté consisted of buildings (fortified post-1687) separated from the nearby Indigenous village. This was in line with Sainte-Marie showing an example of a model European community for the

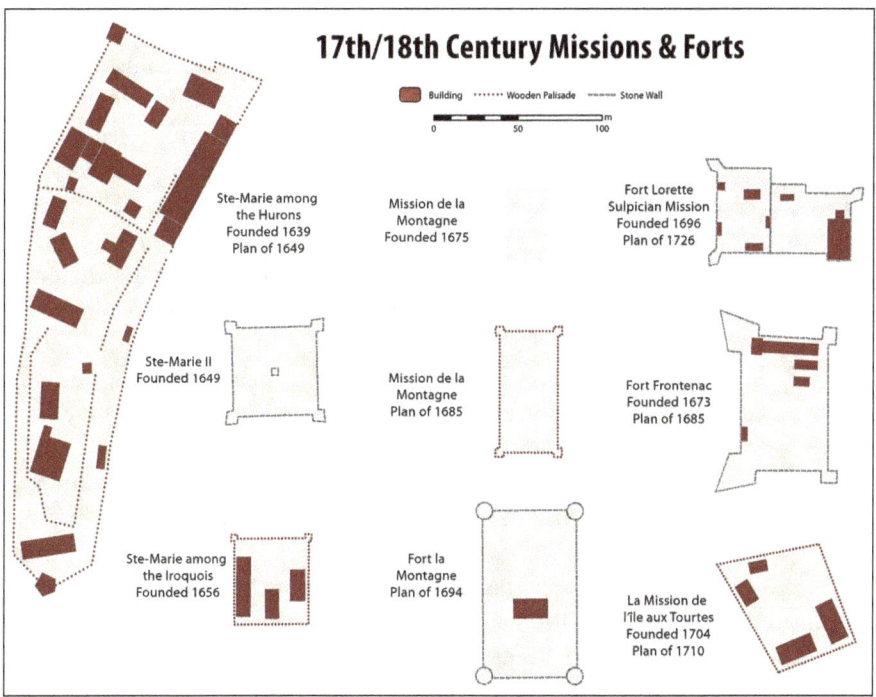

Figure 3.1. Late seventeenth- and early eighteenth-century French mission and fort site plans. *Source:* Prepared by Chris Menary.

purpose of cultural assimilation. An examination of contemporary late seventeenth- to early eighteenth-century missions and forts (Figure 3.1) shows the wide range of possible forms during this period. As the Kenté mission was built during a time of peace, it is unlikely to have been fortified, unlike later Sulpician missions around Montréal.

Kenté's successor, the mission at La Montagne in Montréal, began as a mission house and chapel in 1675. Only after hostilities with the Haudenosaunee started again, in the 1680s, was it enclosed by a wooden palisade and corner bastions. It was rebuilt in stone in 1685 and thereafter functioned as both a spiritual and a military structure—now named Fort de la Montagne—and was able to repulse a Haudenosaunee raid in 1694.

The mission on l'Île-aux-Tourtes in Lake of Two Mountains presents a form that may be analogous to Kenté. Founded by the Sulpicians in 1704, after peace with the Haudenosaunee in 1701, this complex consisted of a mission house, church, and other buildings adjacent to a Nipissing village (Archéotec 2007). The first building erected was the house that served as both residence and chapel, which parallels the founding of Kenté with a similar structure. The church was built six years later, yet Kenté never built one in all its twelve years. The complex on l'Île-aux-Tourtes was separate but close (less than 100 m distant) to the neighbouring Nipissing village, which may give an indication of how close Kenté's mission was to the Cayuga village. Although it appears that l'Île-aux-Tourtes was surrounded by a wooden palisade during a time of peace, it is not comparable with the stone-built mission-forts of the 1680s. Kenté is not likely to have been fortified, but as the missionaries kept livestock, a fenced enclosure probably existed. This mission at l'Île-aux-Tourtes was also a commercial centre, and Kenté, likewise, was involved in the fur trade.

Although Fénelon and Trouvé were the primary missionaries, other Sulpicians, including François-Saturnin Lascaris d'Urfé, Michel Barthélemy, Louis-Armand Champion de Cicé, Joseph Mariet, Isidore Mercadier, and Mathieu Ranuyer spent time at the mission. Kenté missionaries visited other Iroquois du Nord villages; Trouvé is said to have travelled to Teiaiagon and d'Urfé to Ganaraské, and Fénelon is said to have overwintered at Ganatsekwyagon. Kenté became the hub of a multi-settlement pattern.

The decline and eventual abandonment of Kenté cannot be attributed to a single cause, but, rather, to a series of events and misfortunes both internal and external. The Kenté missionaries wished to accompany the Cayuga into the interior during the winters (as had been done in 1669–1670). They felt that the spiritual needs of the Cayuga could best be served in this manner, rather than waiting for their return at the mission. Sulpician superiors, however, were not in favour of this practice, as it was believed missionaries would lose their faith if they lived in solitude, and it was imperative to maintain a sedentary life in order to present the appearance of a model community into which the Cayuga would assimilate. Eventually, the practice of accompanying the Cayuga during the winter was forbidden, and the missionaries had to remain at Kenté. As many of the Cayuga left during the winter, the ability to teach and convert was curtailed. The Sulpician superiors also forbade the mission from commercial ventures in the fur trade, which meant that one of their sources of revenue was eliminated. Kenté was expensive to maintain and was financed through donations from wealthy benefactors and family. But the missionaries also managed to raise their own funds. With the death of the mission's main benefactor, Sulpician Superior Alexandre Le Ragois de Bretonvilliers, in 1676, the financial situation became untenable, and the mission began to falter (Pritchard 1973a:144).

The year 1673 was pivotal for Kenté; the previous year had seen a change in leadership within the colony with the appointment of Louis de Buade, Comte de Frontenac, as the new governor. He wished to extend French influence farther westward and envisioned doing so with the building of forts and permanent garrisons on the shores of Lake Ontario. As he wanted to avoid provoking the Haudenosaunee with this expansion, he arranged for a meeting of both north- and south-shore Haudenosaunee with himself. He dispatched Robert Cavelier, Sieur de La Salle to invite representatives from the Onondaga and the other Iroquois nations as well as the north-shore villages, to a meeting at Kenté towards the end of June (Lamontagne 1958:10). La Salle replied that two hundred Haudenosaunee had agreed to meet, but that the south-shore contingent felt that it was unfair that the meeting was closer for the north-shore group, being at Kenté. As the south-shore Haudenosaunee were eminently more powerful and could threaten the colony, Frontenac then changed the location of the meeting to the mouth of the Cataraqui River, where Lake Ontario empties into the St. Lawrence River. The French delegation built a palisaded enclosure for Frontenac and this structure became the foundation for Fort Frontenac. This decision moved the centre of French influence in the region from Kenté to Cataraqui, and a new mission under the Recollects was built at the latter. As Fort Frontenac became the centre of French commercial and military power on Lake Ontario, some of the Cayuga left Kenté and migrated there. Because Kenté had been eclipsed and then drained of funds, Trouvé commented on the state of the Mission in 1676 indicating "ruined buildings, the lack of order seen there, the frequent journeys, the dissipation of individuals, and the instability of the Indians" (Pritchard, 1973:145). In 1677, he was instructed by his superiors in France to maintain the status quo at Kenté and begin nothing new. It was reported that only seven or eight Cayuga lived in their village by 1679, and the order to abandon Kenté came in 1680. The remaining missionaries and lay workers returned to Montréal, and some continued their work at the mission of La Montagne. Some of the Cayuga followed, and some returned to the Haudenosaunee homelands south of the lake. The

Cayuga village continued on until it was destroyed during Governor Jacques-René Brisay de Denonville's 1687 campaign against the Haudenosaunee, a military action ordered by King Louis XIV.

The Sulpicians did not want to see their work abandoned in vain, so they looked to other groups, including the Jesuits, to run the mission. In the end, Kenté was leased for a term of three years (with hunting and fishing rights from what is now Presqu'ile to the mouth of the Trent River) for 150 livres to some traders. An extremely early land deed at the Archives du Séminaire de Saint-Sulpice records that the land had to be worked and the houses had to be maintained, and what tools (axes, pans) and supplies (wheat, maize seed) were left behind.

1. The Search for Kenté

In July 2016, Robert von Bitter, in his role as provincial archaeological data coordinator, responded to a request for site information related to the French mission of Kenté from Brianna Logan and François Paré from the University of Waterloo. The data von Bitter provided in his response included information about the Squire site (BaGi-8), located north of Lake Consecon, which had an alternate site name of "Kenté Mission." This was a site Ken Swayze reported in 1976 using information provided by the Reverend Bowen Squire twenty years earlier. Logan's and Paré's skepticism concerning the Squire site representing the correct location of Kenté led to subsequent research presented here.

A second query of the Provincial Sites Database encompassed most of Prince Edward County but did not reveal any obvious matches. An attempt was, therefore, made to employ a GIS function called "rubber sheeting," which uses common reference points between historic and modern mapping to overlay one to the other. The rubber sheeting operation was a failure because there was a complete lack of alignment between the historical and the modern maps. The landmass that appeared to represent what is now Prince Edward County on the historical map resulted in the modern vector data appearing scrambled over the seventeenth-century map.

Louis Jolliet's 1675 map (left in Figure 3.2) seemed more detailed than other seventeenth-century maps for this particular section of Lake Ontario. It was only when it was observed that a body of water that dominated the landmass on the map represented a small fraction of Prince Edward County (Figure 3.2A and B) that the maps could be oriented to one another. Rotating Jolliet's map forty-five degrees in a clockwise direction revealed two distinctive peninsulas flanking each side of Wellers Bay (Figure 3.2C and D). This low-tech identification of common features on maps 350 years apart led to the delineation of a two-square-kilometre search area around Wellers Bay (Figure 3.2E), a distance of eight kilometres northwest from Consecon.

The Search for Kenté 61

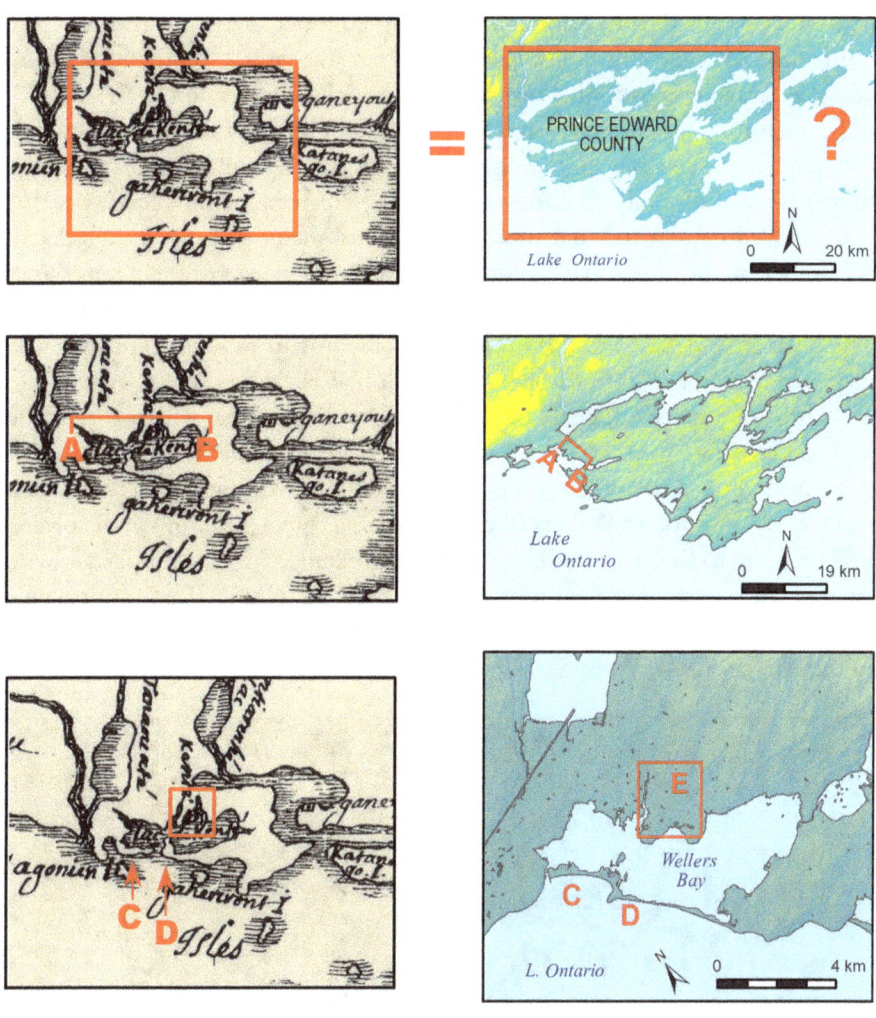

Figure 3.2. Comparative analysis of detail from 1675 Jolliet map and a modern map (2020) of Wellers Bay.
Source: Jolliet Carte du Lac Ontario ou de Frontenac, Bibliothèque nationale de France.

It was noted that Abbé Claude Bernou's map of 1680 (Figure 1.4) exactly matches the details in the Jolliet map in the vicinity of Wellers Bay. Heidenreich (1978) reminds readers that many cartographers of the era relied on information from third parties to inform their own mapmaking and provides a detailed analysis of the relationship between maps attributed to Jolliet and Bernou and records that Jolliet may have only jotted down notes for particular areas. He also suspects that some maps signed as Jolliet may have been produced by Bernou. This seems supported by the depictions of Wellers Bay on both the Jolliet map and the Bernou map. The bay being flanked by such distinctive peninsulas points to the cartographer having considerable familiarity with the immediate area, and since Jolliet is recorded to have visited Kenté in the spring of 1669, it is likely that Jolliet was the source of the information in the vicinity of Kenté found on these maps and that Bernou reused the information. Jolliet's map depicts Wellers Bay 800% larger than it actually is on modern maps, which suggests it was a highly detailed section of a map referencing a landmass that was less well known and that was exaggerated to include all the known detail. A number of prominent but fictional waterways to the east of the Trent River indicate that cartographic details were sporadic on the Jolliet/Bernou maps. The distinctive detailed features found on Jolliet's map are what initially led to the realization that Kenté had been located on Wellers Bay, not Consecon.

Other evidence supports the Wellers Bay target area as being the true location of Kenté. In the seventeenth century, for example, Kenté is recorded as being twenty leagues from the Cataraqui River (Coyne 1903:15), which matches the location of Wellers Bay. Moreover, Trouvé (1871:87), in recording his initial trip to Kenté in 1668, noted they travelled down a beautiful river with an island in it to shorten their journey, and there is a solitary island immediately adjacent to the east entry point of the Carrying Place (Figure 3.3F). Also, prior to the arrival of Asa Weller in 1791, Wellers Bay had gone by the name of Lac

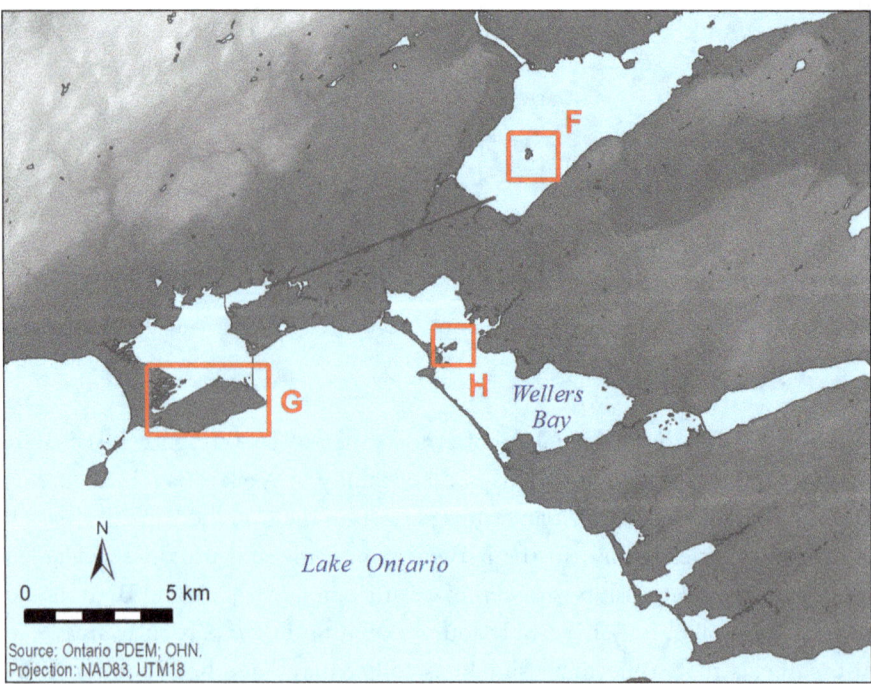

Figure 3.3. Contemporary map centred on Wellers Bay.
Source: Map by Chris Menary.

du Kenté, and this label appears on seventeenth-century maps thus "it is likely that Wellers Bay was the original Baye de Quinte" (Taylor 1968:17). Only after comparing the maps was it observed that when Ken Swayze had completed an archaeological inventory of Prince Edward County in 1976, he registered a number of sites in Wellers Bay that had contact-era material and that most of these were based on the G. J. Chadd Collection, which is discussed below.

After the mission was abandoned and before its location was lost, there was one subsequent known European visitor to Kenté. In 1751, Abbé François Picquet, a Sulpician priest, traversed the perimeter of Lake Ontario looking for Indigenous people to move to his new mission of La Présentation, at what is now Ogdensburg, New York. In his travel journal covering his time on the north shore of Lake Ontario, Picquet records that he visited Kenté and provides the following description: "The place is charming, but the soil is not good. I then made the crossing with considerable trouble because of all the bad weather and camped at the rise of the first headland" (Jezierski 1970:369). Related to Picquet's reference to soils, it is worth noting that another clue to the village's location comes from the words Kenté, Keinthe, Kendae, and Kentucky, all being cognates that describe fields and meadows (George Hamell, personal communication with William Fox, 2019). Picquet's account of the mission being between the portage and prior to the paddle to Presqu'ile (Figure 3.3G) also accords with a Wellers Bay location.

A survey of published material revealed that a number of researchers prior to the late 1950s had also considered Wellers Bay for the location of Kenté. Canniff (1869:251), for example, wrote: "From the nature of relics found in the Indian burying ground, near the Carrying Place, at Bald Bluff, by Wellers Bay, it [Kenté] might have been situated there. Silver crosses and other evidence of Roman Catholic Christianity have been found in this place." He also wrote: "An old graveyard here, upon being plowed, has yielded rich and important relics, showing that the Indians were Christianized, and that valuable French gifts had been bestowed" (Canniff 1869:133). Bald Head is an island in Wellers Bay (Figure 3.3H). James H. Coyne interpreted maps and distances to place Kenté between the Murray Canal and Wellers Bay (1904:22). The Bulletin of the College of Montréal manuscript on Kenté also includes a map which marks the location of Kenté within the 2 km^2 target area on Wellers Bay.

Our research to find Kenté thus refocused the search from Lake Consecon to Wellers Bay, almost 8 km to the northwest. An important question is how the Reverend Squire was able to influence our archaeological understanding of the area and mislead provincial authorities as to the location of Kenté.

1.1. The Reverend Phillip Bowen Squire

In the Village of Consecon, in the northwest corner of Prince Edward County, is a historical plaque erected in 1969 by the Ontario Heritage Foundation to commemorate the Kenté mission (see Figure 3.4). The plaque states that the mission was likely in the Consecon area. Historically, this can be traced to the efforts and dogged insistence of one man, the Reverend Phillip Bowen Squire, a local Baptist minister, commercial illustrator, artist, and amateur archaeologist, who was born in Hendon, England in 1901, and immigrated with his family to Canada as a youth. In about 1948, Squire began searching for archaeological sites near Lake Consecon, where he lived (Upper 1956).

Articles on Squire and his finds appeared in the local *Belleville Intelligencer* and *Trentonian* newspapers in the mid-1950s. In 1956, *The Globe and Mail* ran

Figure 3.4. Ontario Heritage Foundation plaque relating to the Kenté mission.
Source: Richard Tong.

an article it had acquired from the Belleville paper on Squire and the important archaeological site he had found. In the article, Squire claimed to have discovered a "Laurentian Archaic" site on his property on the north shore of Lake Consecon, in about 1952 (Upper 1956). He also stated that part of the collection he had recovered was from the more recent "moundbuilder" phase (Upper 1956). The article featured photographs of the artifacts mounted on board, as well as several hand-drawings Squire had made in the style of contemporary articles in *Ontario Archaeology*, the then-nascent journal of the Ontario Archaeological Society.

The article relates that Squire had found about seven hundred artifacts from his excavations at the site. The artifact collection included bannerstones, large spear points, carved pipes, human and animal effigies, stone pendants, and many bone tools (Upper 1956). Squire also claimed to have recovered "bushel baskets full of Indian pottery" (Upper 1956).

In 1958, a short article by Squire was published in *Ontario Archaeology* about the same "Squire Site," with nine plates of his artifact drawings. He related that he first found a midden ten inches (25 cm) below the surface, with "broken pottery, bone awls and clay pipes" (Squire 1958a:5) and that a little farther away, by a dried-up spring, he found an aceramic deposit six inches (15 cm) under the surface that included two "banner" stones, a catlinite "birdstone," a slate gorget, flint (chert) pieces, and a hexagonal celt, as well as pendants and beads of red, green, and black slate (Squire 1958a:5).

The article included a crude site plan showing areas where artifact and ash concentrations were found, along with topographic features of the site. The plates illustrate 112 artifacts, mostly decorated Iroquoian ceramic vessel rims and castellations ($n = 52$), pipe fragments ($n = 23$), bone tools ($n = 14$), chert bifaces ($n = 5$), and stone pendants ($n = 15$). There are also two stone bird effigies, one said to be catlinite, although neither resemble what are termed birdstones in other Ontario archaeological collections.

That same year Squire published an article in *Historic Kingston*, the journal of the Kingston Historical Society. It had much the same information but also dwelt on the French and early British history of the region, mentioning the "Lost Mission of Kenté," but not associating it with the Squire site (Squire 1958b:54). The site was described as at least three acres in size, with a "Laurentian Archaic" component alongside a fortified village with stratified deposits of "Lalonde" ceramics below historic "Huron" pottery (Squire 1958b). Squire also bemoaned the lack of funding to protect his important site (Squire 1958b:54).

In 1959, Squire authored a piece in the journal of the Ontario Historical Society in which he began to associate the site on his property with the "Lost Mission of Kenté," an assertion he made more frequently with time. Squire related that he knew of five other village sites within a "5-mile radius" of Lake Consecon, as well as an Archaic burial ground and four campsites (Squire 1959:58–59).

In 1973, Ken Swayze conducted a research project on the archaeology of Prince Edward County, compiling an annotated bibliography and a preliminary list of known or potential sites and local informants, including Bowen Squire. At the time, Swayze noted that Squire's collection was not catalogued, that there were no field notes, and that Squire claimed that the site was completely exhausted by excavation (Swayze 1976:54). By then, Squire had sold most of his collection (approximately two hundred artifacts), along with his paintings, to the Ameliasburgh Museum, for two thousand dollars, although he retained some of his favourite pieces (Swayze 1973:12).

In the fall of 1976, Swayze visited Bowen Squire at his property, where he was shown the location of both components of the Squire site. Swayze walked the field where Bowen Squire said the Kenté site was and found no artifacts (Swayze 1976). Swayze followed up by visiting James Pendergast in Ottawa, as well as James V. Wright. Neither thought the Squire site was Kenté, and Wright believed it was a fraud (Ken Swayze, personal communication 2020).

Over the years, Thomas Lee, T. F. McIlwraith, W. A. Ritchie, Norman Emerson, J. V. Wright, and James Pendergast had all visited the site and viewed Squire's collection, but none felt compelled to further investigate it (Squire 1958a, 1959; Swayze 1973, 1976).

Swayze learned that Squire had excavated the Melville Snackbar Burial (BaGi-18). This was described as a red-ochre burial with copper grave goods (Swayze 1976). Squire was also known to have recovered artifacts from the Finlan site (BaGk-1), a Glacial Kame burial site north of Trenton (Donaldson and Wortner 1995).

In 1999, Nick Gromoff examined the Squire Collection at the Ameliasburgh Museum and Glanmore House National Historic Site in Belleville, which was holding some of Squire's artifacts on loan. In particular, Gromoff was looking for historic-period artifacts that might provide evidence that the Squire site was the Kenté mission. The Squire Collection consisted of about two hundred artifacts, almost all without any supporting documentation. The museum had accessioned Squire's collection under the number prefix 968.29 and listed nearly all the artifacts as coming from the Lost Mission site.

Most of the Squire material at the Ameliasburgh Museum can be divided into four groupings: Late Iroquoian ceramic vessel rims and pipe sherds, bone tools, chert bifaces, and polished red and green slate objects. Many of the polished stones are pendants, either drilled or grooved at one end to form a nubbin for attachment. There are also other stones, polished into winged triangular forms similar to a brachiopod fossil. Fifteen of these stone objects are illustrated in Squire's 1958a article in the same plate as two chert drills, three barbed bone points, and two stone pipe fragments. Most of these artifacts could be matched between the collection and the drawings. It should be noted that there are a considerable number of pendants, which, if authentic, would represent a significant collection. There are several bone tools, mainly awls, barbed points, and needles, as well as a few chert points and drills. What was absent from the collection when Gromoff examined it were the two bannerstones Squire was photographed with and the catlinite bird effigy that he illustrated in his 1958a article.

There were also artifacts that had clearly been manufactured by Squire, including several stone clubs made from beach cobbles bound to the ends of whittled wooden handles. There was a plaster pot marked "made by Bowen Squire" on the base and a strange piece termed the "owl stone," which appeared in the 1956 *Globe and Mail* article and was made from cement. Although most of the pipes were clearly Iroquoian, at least two were very crude, with an atypically coarse paste, and the addition of a wash or stain. A small bird carving with "pop eyes" that also appeared in his 1958a article was made from plaster or chalk and then covered with a wash to antique it (Figure 3.5).

There are a few metal artifacts, although curiously none of these were listed as coming from the Lost Mission site in the museum's catalogue, although they had the same accession number prefix as the rest of the Squire Collection. These metal objects consist of three crude crosses cut from thin mesh strapping, three triangular ferrous points, a ferrous knife blade, two scraps of ferrous sheet, and an unidentified fragment cut from thin sheet brass. There are no apparent attachments on the crosses, and although the sides are smooth, the ends are rough-cut. Crosses found on French-period sites are typically cast or stamped pendants. The only decoration is hammered bossing on one surface of the thin metal. These appear to be expedient crosses possibly manufactured by Squire in an attempt to legitimize his site as Kenté (see Figure 3.6).

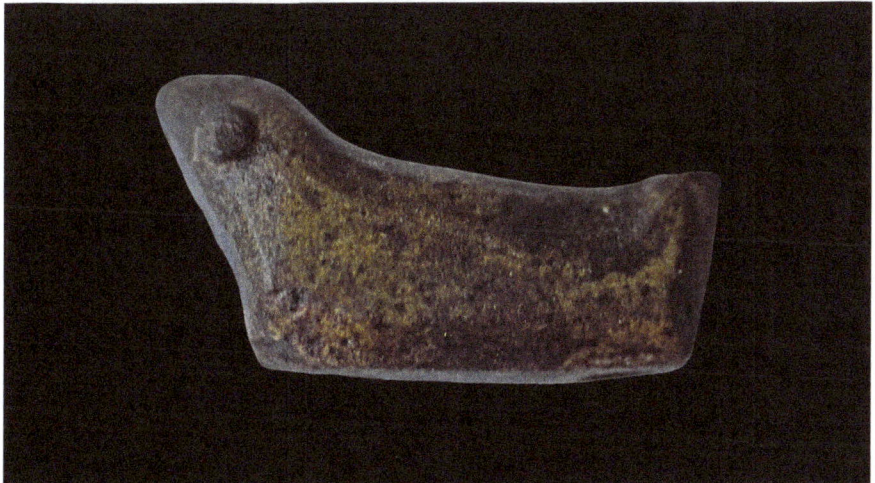

Figure 3.5. Fake birdstone from the Squire Collection.
Source: Photograph by Nick Gromoff; digital enhancement by John Howarth.

The ferrous points are rough-cut with ragged edges. Each of the ferrous points is of a different shape, one resembling a Jack's Reef Pentagonal point, another a Levanna point, and the last an isosceles triangle with one corner broken (see Figure 3.7). Although trade points are generally better made (see Cooper, this volume), with even edges, crude versions like these are known. The knife blade is thin, like cutlery rather than a clasp knife, and would not be out of place on a nineteenth-century homestead site.

Figure 3.6. Example of metal cross possibly manufactured by Squire.
Source: Photograph by Nick Gromoff; digital enhancement by John Howarth.

Figure 3.7. Metal projectile points.
Source: Photograph by Nick Gromoff; digital enhancement by John Howarth.

The two artifacts held by the Ameliasburgh Museum that could be contemporary with the Kenté mission are a brass kettle and an iron trade axe. The kettle, however, is tagged Jack Hazard, indicating that it is most likely from BaGj-1, the Kettle Burial site, recorded by Hakas in 1967 as having been found on Jack Hazard's property (Swayze 1976). The trade axe is not listed as coming from the Lost Mission site but, rather, from a lot and concession east of Lake Consecon.

The twenty-seven artifacts from Squire's collection held by Glanmore House are similar to those curated by the Ameliasburgh Museum. Three historic artifacts were present: a copper alloy triangular point, a leaf-shaped point, and a bone handle from a piece of cutlery. The copper alloy triangular point has a verdigris patina and clean-cut edges and does resemble some points recovered from contact-period Wendat villages.

The leaf-shaped point is cut from thin sheet copper and is not patinated, meaning it is unlikely to have come from an archaeological context. It is also too flimsy to have functioned as a point. The cutlery bone handle is decorated with a grooved herringbone pattern commonly found on late eighteenth- and early nineteenth-century sites.

In summary, there is little evidence that the Squire site is either the mission or the Cayuga village of Kenté. This connection is solely based on Squire's assertion that it is. The Iroquoian pottery and pipes in Squire's Collection are, for the most, from the Middle Iroquoian period and suspiciously similar to those recovered from the nearby Payne site. There are no formal trade goods, such as glass beads, musket flints, or kettle lugs.

The metal points are possibly from the seventeenth century, but it would require metallographic analysis to determine this. Even if they were contemporary with Kenté, there is no documentation for them, and they cannot be associated with any site, whether Kenté, the Kettle Burial site, or any other site from which Squire collected. Given the small size of Squire's collection and the broad temporal range of the artifacts, it is quite possible that there was no site on his property. He may simply have taken the artifacts he collected elsewhere and manufactured a site, just as he manufactured some of the artifacts in his collection.

Swayze, who registered Squire's Consecon (BaGi-8) site with a secondary name of "Kenté Mission," did acknowledge that he had strong reservations about relying on Bowen Squire as a credible source of information, writing "It has not been determined if the Squire site really is the Kenté site" (Swayze 1976:54). Data provided in this chapter have precluded Squire's notion of Kenté being located at Consecon, and hence the "Kenté Mission" alternative name has now been removed from the database record for BaGi-8.

2. Spatial Analysis

A spatial analysis of artifacts from the G. J. Chadd Collection, now in the care of the Royal Ontario Museum, was undertaken with a focus on those that were thought to date to the mid- to late seventeenth century to provide additional evidence of the location of Kenté at Wellers Bay. Analyses of most of these artifacts, as well as some discovered more recently, can be found in Cooper (this volume); Williamson and von Bitter (this volume); Fox et al. (this volume); and Engelbrecht and Williamson (this volume).

The collection consists of artifacts collected in the late nineteenth century, primarily in and around Prince Edward County by G. J. Chadd of Trenton (see Harris 2020). He recorded at least general provenance for most of his artifacts, and from those data, the locations of artifacts were plotted. Chadd documented at a minimum the geographic township in which an item was found, although most of the provenances are even more detailed, providing lot and concession. Some have merely a name, such as Smokes Point, Trenton Mountain, or Gardenville. The initial process was to digitize Chadd's notes into a searchable form, in this case Microsoft Excel. One field recorded the type of artifact, another the artifact count, and four others held the location details. To conduct an analysis on the spatial component of the data, a geographic information system was employed (ESRI's ArcMap). The data model used consisted of a base polygon, either a geographic lot from the Ministry of Natural Resources' lot and concession data or a hexagon centred on a place name. The model assigned the artifacts to one of twenty-eight fields for each polygon (such as iron tomahawk, glass bead, chert specimen), and each field requires a yes/no answer indicating presence/absence of that artifact in that polygon. In this way, the data could be queried for specific artifacts. Finally, a count field was added that summarizes all artifacts found in that polygon.

The resulting polygons were then categorized into general time periods. The "pre-contact" polygons were categorized by containing only lithic artifacts that Chadd mainly classified as "chert tools"; the "Woodland," by including ceramics; the "contact period," by including iron/brass objects and/or glass beads; and the "Iroquois du Nord," by having diagnostic Haudenosaunee artifacts, such as certain ceramic types and antler combs. The "Iroquois du Nord possible" category has ceramics that could date to the latter half of the seventeenth century, likely Iroquois du Nord period ceramics that were accompanied by an incomplete entry and so was inferred to a geographic locale, and brass rings that cannot be definitively dated to only the Iroquois du Nord time period.

There is, however, uncertainty regarding artifacts found in Concession 1, Murray Township. The concessions on either side of the portage route, modern County Road 64 and the boundary between Prince Edward and Northumberland Counties, are "Concession East/West of the Carrying Place." On the Ameliasburgh Township side, Chadd collected a large amount from "Lots 1–12, Concession 1, Ameliasburgh." Yet those lots do not technically exist, as Concession 1 only contains Lots 60–106, with the numbers starting in the east and increasing westward. It was assumed, therefore, that "Lot 12, Concession 1, Ameliasburgh" was in fact "Lot 12, Concession East of the Carrying Place,

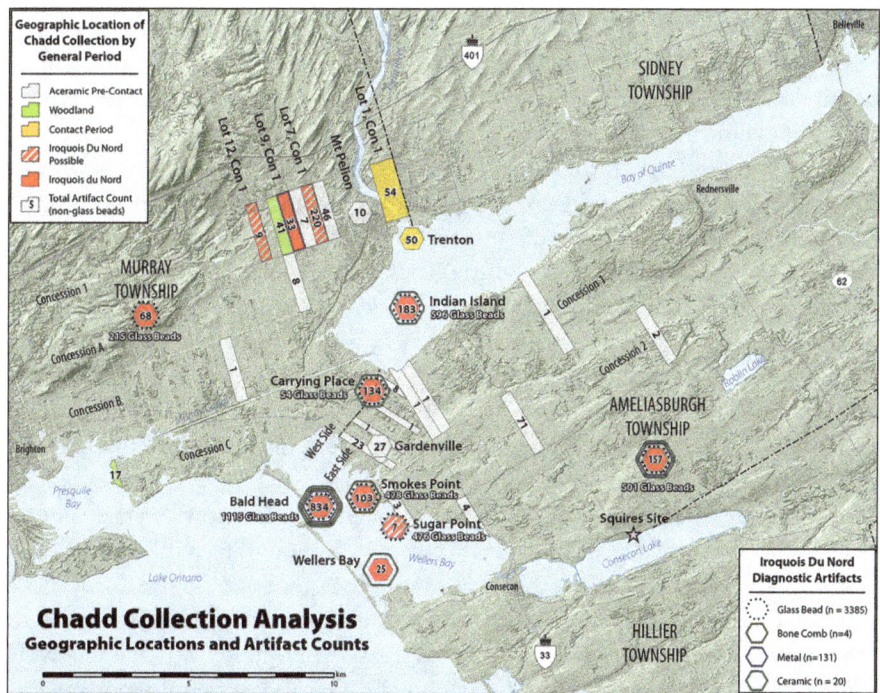

Figure 3.8. First option for spatial analysis of the Chadd Collection.
Source: Map by Chris Menary.

Ameliasburgh." There are four lots in total that had this issue and that were adjusted in this manner (Figure 3.8).

On the Murray Township side, Chadd recorded lots in a similar manner. For instance, he recorded "Lot 12, Concession 1, Murray." But this lot does exist, unlike those in Ameliasburgh Township, and is three concessions north of the Carrying Place (Figure 3.8). The concession immediately north of West of the Carrying Place is Concession B. The artifacts have been placed into the lots where Chadd recorded they were from, but there is a chance they could be from Concession West of The Carrying Place instead. To attempt to confirm their location, the online census was searched for the names of the people from whom Chadd collected in the 1880s. One individual was traceable from the 1891 census through to the 1921 census. The 1921 census, unlike censuses of previous years, includes a geographic location, and this individual lived on the First Concession, Murray Township. Based on this, and on the fact that Chadd recorded artifacts from Concessions A and B and lived in Trenton (which is in Concession 1, Murray Township), the locations in Figure 3.8 represent one possibility.

It is unlikely, however, that Chadd recovered material on the east side of the Old Portage Road (Ameliasburgh Township) but none on the west side (Murray Township), for two reasons. First, Chadd collected primarily in the Carrying Place, where he lived, and his original museum was at Young's Point, where he was a customs officer, so it is improbable that artifacts were recovered only on the one side of the road. Second, Figure 3.8 creates a twelve-lot artifact density 5 km away, resulting in a corresponding void west of the road, exactly where it would not be expected. Chadd was likely assuming that, since lots were counted off east of the Old Portage Road in Ameliasburgh, lots west of the road, in Murray Township, were counted off in the direction. Mapping the finds as shown in Figure 3.9 also accords with discoveries made by others since Chadd, such as the Kettle Burial (BaGj-1). Figure 3.9, therefore, likely represents the correct location of Chadd's Lot 1–12 Murray Township finds.

The general clustering of IDN artifacts is along the Carrying Place to Smokes Point, including offshore islands. The symbols showing counts for artifacts labelled "Ameliasburgh" and "Murray" are centred on each township in Figures 3.8 and 3.9; however, those, too, were likely found closer to the main concentration.

Together, these data, plus analysis of seventeenth-century maps, suggest that Kenté was situated at Smokes Point, on Wellers Bay, with use around Carrying Place, rather than at the location of the Squire site, on the north shore of Lake Consecon. Smokes Point is situated where a river extends 1 km into the interior, which shortens the portage to the Bay of Quinte. This is a relatively similar place to the locations of Teiaiagon and Ganatsekwyagon—both occupying strategic positions at the foot of a portage. Although the location of two western sites allowed a new watershed to be accessed, Kenté's position, in

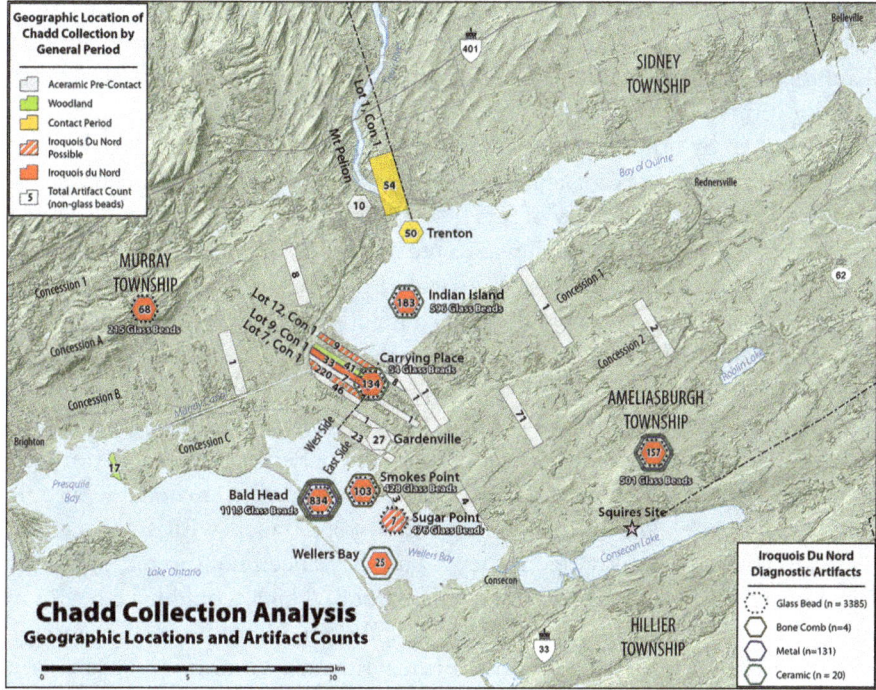

Figure 3.9. Second option for spatial analysis of the Chadd Collection.
Source: Map by Chris Menary.

contrast, simply allowed a safe and quicker passage in comparison with travelling around the southern tip of Prince Edward County, where treacherous shoals and open water were present. It also differed from Teiaiagon and Ganatsekwyagon in that the isthmus represented a very short portage, which could be used to traverse a natural choke point on the landscape.

In the past, the focus has been on IDN settlements and their propensity for "occupying isolated positions on Lake Ontario, locations that commanded the major thoroughfares of the region" (Konrad 1974:2). Although this may be true, Kenté appears to represent a potentially more complex north-shore IDN settlement system. Claude Trouvé in 1672, for example, noted "We have three villages (Kenté, Ganetsygon and Ganaraské) within the bounds of our mission, not counting scattered huts" (de Casson 1928:369). This observation reveals that north-shore occupations, at least in some cases, were more than just isolated villages. Artifacts from the Chadd Collection also point to a second portage between Picton and Wellington, such that a network of interception points covering the landscape may have been present. The density of IDN material shown in Figure 3.9 points to the occupation having spread to cover all strategic locations. Tannouate, an IDN settlement that is shown on a few seventeenth-century maps, speaks to a strategy of diffused settlement designed to control all strategic nodes. The fact that this village was not mentioned by Trouvé by 1672 shows that north-shore settlement was constantly evolving, possibly with Tannouate no longer extant by 1672. It could also represent differences in identification in that what was viewed by some Europeans as a few isolated huts was identified by others as a village with a name. Although Konrad (1981:136) stated "that at no other points and with no fewer villages could the Haudenosaunee as effectively control the flow of furs ...," it was likely a combination of villages and associated special purpose sites at Kenté that represent the settlement pattern. A discussion of similar findings is provided by Menary and von Bitter (this volume) for Quintio, Ganaraské, and Ganneious.

Although much has been written about the reasons for the decline of Kenté, including the Sulpicians' falling from the governor's favour, lack of funding, and lack of success (Pritchard 1973a:141), we wonder if what had given Kenté its initial advantage was also a factor in its demise, namely, its location at a shortcut on the landscape that maximized safe passage when material was being moved by canoe. With time, as more furs were traded with Europeans at Teiaiagon and Ganatsekwyagon, they would have been transported down the lake by a type of water vessel known as a barque, which would have been too big to have been portaged easily at Kenté and would have been large enough to sail safely around what is now Prince Edward County (Figure 3.10). Teiaiagon, which does not even receive mention in Trouvé's 1672 correspondence and fails to show up on maps made prior to 1673, later, by the 1680s, becomes the most significant north-shore Haudenosaunee village (Konrad 1981:140) and "gained importance, in part, because of its superior anchorage for French trade barques" (Konrad 1981:134). This suggests that once the movement of furs shifted to larger boats that could not be easily portaged, they did not need the safe passage of what is now referred to as the Bay of Quinte. *The Griffon* has received a great deal of attention and was indeed dismantled and portaged at one point, but it should be remembered that three ten-ton ships sailed Lake Ontario, which "fully expressed La Salle's principles—the employment of shipping rather than of canoes and the establishment of widely separated posts, contact being maintained by the ships" (Cooper 1978:77). It is difficult to verify this hypothesis because only records of aggregations of furs received for the entire lake are available (Lamontagne 1958), not records of who delivered them or by what means. Certainly, prior to and during the early years of the IDN period, there are accounts of large canoe brigades carrying furs to Quebec (e.g., Pritchard 1973:134; Trigger 1976:754). What gave Toronto its advantage for trading with Europeans who had barques could have deprived the Kenté village of its strategic advantage. This, along with the fact that the Seneca shifted the flow of furs around the west end of Lake Ontario and south through their homeland (Konrad 1981:134, 143), led to its abandonment. The fact that there were only eight inhabitants at Kenté village in 1679 has been

Figure 3.10. Detail from the 1688 Raffeix map showing a barque; map published in 1688 by Jesuit Father Pierre Raffeix, titled "Le lac Ontario avec les lieux circonvoisins & particulièrement les cinq nations Iroquoises." The map shows Lake Ontario, also known as the Lake of Saint Louis, with the surrounding area marked as including territory belonging to the "five Iroquois nations." Current-day Lake Simcoe is marked as "Lac Taronthe." The villages of "theyagon" (Teiaiagon) and "Ganestikiagon" (Ganatsekwyagon) are also marked. *Source:* Map and Data Library, University of Toronto.

linked with the later European preference to visit other villages and the abandonment of the Kenté mission (Konrad 1981:139). If Kenté was located at Wellers Bay, it becomes easier to make sense of the evolution of the north-shore settlement system and the decline of the mission.

Returning to the Reverend Squire briefly, it is worth noting that he failed to include any mention of Chadd's collection in his articles and seemed eager to discount earlier research in order to forward his own agenda. In the first section of his 1959 article, he records his tour of Wellers Bay, where he attempts to cast doubt on Bald Head as being of much importance. Elsewhere in the article (1959), he mentions Canniff's publication but describes the reference to earlier finds at "Bald Head" as "rumours," even though by that time, Squire had seen Chadd's amazing artifact collection from Bald Head. Swayze (1976:82) notes the following information about conversations with Squire:

> Squire says he first got interested in archaeology when he was 19; he is now 75. He can remember seeing Mr. Chadd, who may have inspired him somewhat. He says the Chadd Collection was mislabelled "Prince Edward Island" by the Royal Ontario Museum and thus the collection is mixed up. [Swayze 1976:82]

Squire may also have provided some information that is consistent with the spatial analysis and helps to confirm the Wellers Bay location. In his 1959 article, Squire also notes, "A later reconnaissance of the bay area disclosed other apparently undisturbed mounds close to the shoreline. Whether these are of natural or artificial raising will require careful investigation to determine." Even though the "bay area" Squire is referring to is most likely the bay area of Bald Bluff and not the rest of Wellers Bay, it raises the prospect of surviving undisturbed mounded features of potential cultural origin in the vicinity. Forty-four years later, construction activities related to the building of a house on a small rise on Smokes Point at Wellers Bay resulted in the discovery of human remains and artifacts, which led to the analysis by Northeastern Archaeological Associates

(2010) and its designation as the Hilton site (BaGj-24). The investigation yielded two antler combs (see Williamson and von Bitter, this volume), one conical ring pipe (see Engelbrecht and Williamson, this volume), fifty red round beads (see Fox et al., this volume), and two trade axes (see Cooper, this volume).

3. Conclusion

The French mission of Kenté, established at a Haudenosaunee village of the same name, was initially on the edge of New France's frontier. This change mirrored the major shifts in power, reliance and goodwill that took place between the French and Haudenosaunee over the twelve years the mission operated. The rapidly shifting geographical, religious and political landscape added to the significance of Kenté, as did it being a hub for the religious conversion of Indigenous Peoples—initially to three north-shore villages (Trouvé 1871) and then later to five (Pritchard 1973a:140). This chapter has shown that Kenté was not located at Consecon, as Squire claimed, but at Wellers Bay.

Trouvé (1871:369) wrote, "I have never set myself to keep any record, knowing very well that God is a great enlightener, and that when He wills that the things which concern His glory should be known, He would rather make the trees and stones proclaim it." Menary has used LiDAR to locate a number of potential targets within the 2 km^2 Wellers Bay search area, although landowner permissions to investigate have not yet been obtained. Use of LiDAR and other new technologies might allow for "the trees and stones [to] proclaim it," although research undertaken as far back as 1870s and some carried out more recently has already clarified the site's location.

Acknowledgements

The authors would like to Brianna Logan and François Paré from the University of Waterloo for initiating the study on Kenté and making valuable contributions to the research. Mima Kapches and Ken Swayze both generously shared information about Rev. Squire. We are appreciative of the assistance provided by other Iroquois du Nord researchers with a special word of thanks to Ron Williamson.

4

CLUES IN THE LANDSCAPE

The Search for Ganaraské, Quintio, and Ganneious

CHRIS MENARY AND ROBERT VON BITTER

Ganneious, Quintio, and Ganaraské, along with Kenté, represent the eastern Iroquois du Nord (IDN) villages that are traditionally linked with Cayuga and Oneida settlement (Figures 1.1 and 1.3). While the location of Kenté has been linked with Smokes Point and Bald Head Island on Wellers Bay (see von Bitter et al., this volume), none of the remaining three villages have been definitively found, and the primary sources of evidence for their location consist of several inconsistent seventeenth-century maps and documents from French missionaries. Unlike at Kenté, no archaeological evidence or nineteenth-century artifact collections exist that can be examined to aid in the search. This chapter uses the documentary record in concert with modern landscape analysis and remote sensing to discern a general location for each settlement. Although historical maps proved useful, missionary letters and accounts, being focused on spiritual matters, include limited geographic information. The letters do tell us that one of the Kenté Sulpician missionaries, François-Saturnin Lascaris d'Urfé, visited Ganaraské and may have visited Quintio.

The suspected locations of the eastern villages differ from those of the western village sites of Teiaiagon (see Robertson, this volume) and Ganatsekwyagon (see Poulton, this volume), which are located defensively atop of high bluffs at bends in rivers. The eastern sites instead are mostly low-lying and seem to favour exposed locales, as if the occupants were less concerned with defence. The villages were settled during a period of peace, after the treaty of 1666 and during the renewed peace of 1673 between the French and Haudenosaunee (Williamson, this volume). This was also a time of cooperation between the Haudenosaunee and various Anishinaabeg (Williamson, this volume). The locations of Quintio and Ganneious suggest that in that particular region, the proximity of agricultural fields for food production may have been an important criterion for their settings. There is also documentary evidence to suggest that Quintio began as a satellite settlement of Ganaraské and only became large enough to assume its own identity sometime after 1673 (de Casson 1871). This east-west dichotomy in geographical location is also reflected in the recovered material culture from the Kenté area, especially in the trade beads, and may be indicative of intra-Haudenosaunee differences (Fox et al., this volume).

1. Documentary Record: Accounts

1.1. Ganaraské and Quintio

For the purposes of this study, Ganaraské and Quintio were treated as one community, as they represent the ends of a portage from Rice Lake to Lake Ontario, with both points possibly functioning as tollgates for Anishinaabe fur brigades (Adams 1986). Like Kenté, both settlements are thought to have been established by Cayuga populations in the late 1660s (Konrad 1981; Jordan, this volume). Ganaraské is mentioned as one of three villages within the bounds of the Kenté mission, along with Kenté and Ganatsekwyagon. D'Urfé visited Ganaraské in 1671, as indicated in a letter by François Dollier de Casson. While little was written about his visit to this village (all that de Casson notes is that he visited and stayed awhile), a detailed episode is recorded of d'Urfé's visit to a group of people living five leagues away (de Casson 1871:363).

The story de Casson recounts is that d'Urfé departed from Ganaraské and visited a nearby group to conduct missionary work. At this settlement he encountered a pregnant Haudenosaunee woman, who was staying in the same hut. The woman left the hut for modesty and, with help from other women in the settlement, gave birth to an infant in the snow. As d'Urfé felt he was the cause of her distress, he returned to Ganaraské. Three days later he went back to the settlement because he had forgotten his alter service in the hut. On his return, he discovered that the woman had given birth to another infant but unfortunately both the woman and one of her infants had died. As there were no other nursing women for the surviving infant, d'Urfé went to Kenté to search for one but on his return, found the second infant had died as well. All three had been baptized by d'Urfé and were buried in the settlement.

Three interesting lines of evidence regarding the relative locations of Ganaraské and this other settlement, which may be Quintio, arise from this story. The first is the ease with which d'Urfé comes and goes between them and the fact that no canoe is mentioned. (In contrast, de Casson goes into great detail about the arduous initial journey of the Kenté missionaries from Montréal to Kenté.) It was also winter, with snow on the ground, so in order for d'Urfé to have found his way, the route between Ganaraské and the settlement must have been well travelled and well marked. The fact that it was cold enough for there to be snow on the ground is a further indication that travel would not have been by canoe. The second is that there is a burial of a woman and two infants at the site, the discovery of which archaeologically could tie this story directly to the settlement. The third is that this settlement had no other nursing women present in 1671 but did have other women present who assisted the mother to give birth. It may have functioned at that time as a hunting/fishing camp and had yet to become a large settlement with family units, and this would explain why de Casson does not mention a name.

The distance between Ganaraské and the settlement noted by de Casson is five leagues: "il prit la résolution d'aller visiter quelques sauvages établis à cinq lieues de là" (de Casson 1928:363). There are numerous pre-revolutionary French measurements referred to as *lieue,* or league, which vary in length from 3–5 km. Which *lieue* de Casson was using is not known.

Heidenreich (1978:104) has suggested that, using Samuel de Champlain's 1632 map as an example, one can determine that Champlain used three different measures of distance: the Spanish league in the Gulf of St. Lawrence, the French *lieue commune* on the St. Lawrence, and what is probably the short *lieue de poste* or possibly the *petite lieue* for his inland explorations. Heidenreich later concluded that for overland routes, Champlain most likely used the *lieue d'une heure de chemin,* or one-hour league, at 4.9 km (Heidenreich 2014). De Casson does not indicate that travel was by canoe. Therefore, using Heidenreich's information, we can calculate that the settlement d'Urfé visited must be within 15–24.5 km of Ganaraské. From the mouth of the Ganaraska River to the most southerly point of Rice Lake is 16 km; the next closest IDN villages are at least 40 km away.

François Vachon de Belmont's 1680 "Carte du cours du fleuve Saint Laurent depuis son embouchure jusques et y compris le Lac supérieur," (Figure 4.1) depicts the portage route between Quintio and Ganaraské and gives a length of four leagues (12–20 km). Belmont's map does not contain a legend, so it is impossible to know which league he used. It is unlikely that he would have used the longer *lieue commune,* which was primarily for maritime cartography. Following Heidenreich's (2014) logic, we suggest that d'Urfé may have used the shorter *lieue de poste* or *petite lieue,* which range from 3.5–4.5 km. This would give a portage length of 14–18 km.

While it is not certain that the settlement that d'Urfé visited was Quintio, we know that it was a satellite community of Ganaraské much like those found at Kenté (see von Bitter et al., this volume) and possibly Ganneious. If it was Quintio, it is strange, however, that no name was provided in the account. Jean-Baptiste-Louis Franquelin's map of 1678 (Figure 4.2) only shows Ganaraské and does not include Quintio or even Rice Lake. Quintio was not among the villages invited to send representatives by La Salle in 1673 to meet Governor Frontenac at Kenté. Included were Ganatsekwyagon, Ganaraské, Tannaouate (a possible satellite of Kenté), and Ganneious (Pritchard 1973b:25). It may be that Quintio began as a small farming and fishing settlement and only acquired a name when it grew into a larger village. It gave its name to Rice Lake, as later maps omit the village but retain the name Lake Kentsio.

Figure 4.1. Detail of François Vachon de Belmont's "Carte du cours du fleuve Saint-Laurent depuis son embouchure jusques et y compris le Lac supérieur," 1680.
Source: Bibliothèque nationale de France, département Cartes et plans, CPL GE DD-2987 (8662 B).

Figure 4.2. Detail of Jean-Baptiste-Louis Franquelin's "Carte pour servir a l'éclaircissement du papier terrier de la Nouvelle-France," 1678.
Source: Bibliothèque nationale de France, département Cartes et plans, Service hydrographique, pf. 125, div. 1, p.1.

1.2. Ganneious
In the winter of 1675, Father Louis Hennepin and René-Robert Cavelier La Salle journeyed to the village of Ganneious from Fort Frontenac in order to entice the inhabitants to relocate to the fort. Father Hennepin wrote:

> While the brink of the lake was frozen, I walk'd upon the ice to an Iroquois village called Ganneious, near to Kente (Quinte), about nine leagues from the fort—in the company of Sieur de La Salle above mentioned. These savages presented us with the flesh of elks and porcupine, which we fed upon. After having discours'd them some time, we returned bringing with us a considerable number of the natives, in order to form a little village of about forty cottages to be inhabited by them lying betwixt the fort and our House of Mission. [Thwaites 1903:47–48]

A distance of nine leagues is roughly 44 km, and following the north shore of Lake Ontario, Hay Bay is 40 km from Fort Frontenac. The mention of them having to cross ice suggests the village was on the north side of the bay, as walking overland from the lake to the bay would not necessitate this. The size of Ganneious may be approximated by the mention of "forty cottages" moving to Fort Frontenac. Nick Adams cautions that this number may have been inflated to increase the prestige of Father Hennepin; a map of the fort from 1682 includes only six Indigenous houses (Adams 1986). Father Hennepin also writes that Ganneious and Kenté supplied Fort Frontenac with provisions, as the soils around the fort were of poor quality (Thwaites 1905:122). Deer may have been part of those provisions since they have been identified in the faunal remains from the French occupation of the fort (Needs-Howarth 2008:48).

The occupation of Ganneious continued until 1687, when it was destroyed (along with Kenté) during the Marquis de Denonville's raids against the Haudenosaunee (see Jordan, this volume):

> Among the number ensnared by this disgraceful artifice of Denonville were the leading representatives of the villages of Kenté and Ganneious; in fact, some eighteen men and sixty women and children were made prisoners at the latter village while pursuing their peaceful occupations. During these years of strife, they had remained neutral, living on friendly terms with the garrison at Cataraqui, for whom they hunted and fished, receiving in return such merchandise as the French were able to supply them. [Herrington 1913:14]

2. Documentary Record: Historical Maps
The primary source for the village's locations is a series of maps dating to between 1670 and 1700. While these can provide a general area for each village,

the quality of seventeenth-century cartography varies considerably based on the source(s), the cartographer, and the scale. The earliest maps of the Great Lakes region were created by Champlain based on first-hand accounts, yet in the decades following the French withdrawal from Wendake, Jesuit missionaries created maps based on second-hand accounts of Indigenous groups and fur traders. Conrad Heidenreich described how these maps were drawn and how they should be viewed:

> Some maps [...] portray native knowledge of lands beyond European exploration. The precision with which such information was incorporated was highly dependent on the rapport established between an explorer and his native informants. In some cases, native sketch maps were employed, while elsewhere verbal accounts were rendered graphically. These maps provide interesting information on the space perception as well as the extent of knowledge about an area by native groups. [Heidenreich 1978:111]

The most detailed maps are small-scale and focus on the Great Lakes region or Lake Ontario; other maps depict New France and Louisiana and are of less use due to their level of detail. The quality of French cartography improved with the peace treaty of 1666 and the ability of surveyors and cartographers to return to the Great Lakes region. This is also the beginning of the French expansion into the interior of North America and the expeditions of La Salle, Jolliet, and Marquette. Their notes and sketches were then returned to Quebec and the Hydrographe du Roi; in Quebec, a centralized office maintained maps of the colony (Heidenreich 1978).

The first map to show precise details of the Lake Ontario shoreline is René Bréhant de Galinée's "Cart du Lac Ontario" of 1670, which survives only as late eighteenth-century copies, because the original was lost. Previous maps, including Champlain's, show some of the Trent River system, but Bréhant de Galinée's includes accurate details of the Bay of Quinte and the Thousand Islands region (Figure 4.3). While no Iroquois du Nord villages are included, this map was later copied and became the basis of the Sulpician François Vachon de Belmont's 1680 map (Figure 4.1). Here, Ganaraské is placed on the east bank of the river and Quintio (here called Kenitſſio) is situated on the north shore of Rice Lake, between two rivers. The eastern river, which has its confluence with Rice Lake opposite several islands, could be either the Otonabee River or the Indian River. The western river is at the end of the lake and flows to the west, where a portage connects it to another river that joins the body of water labelled Lac du Tronteau (now known as Lake Simcoe). It is most likely that this western river is the Otonabee, which would place Quintio between it and the Indian River.

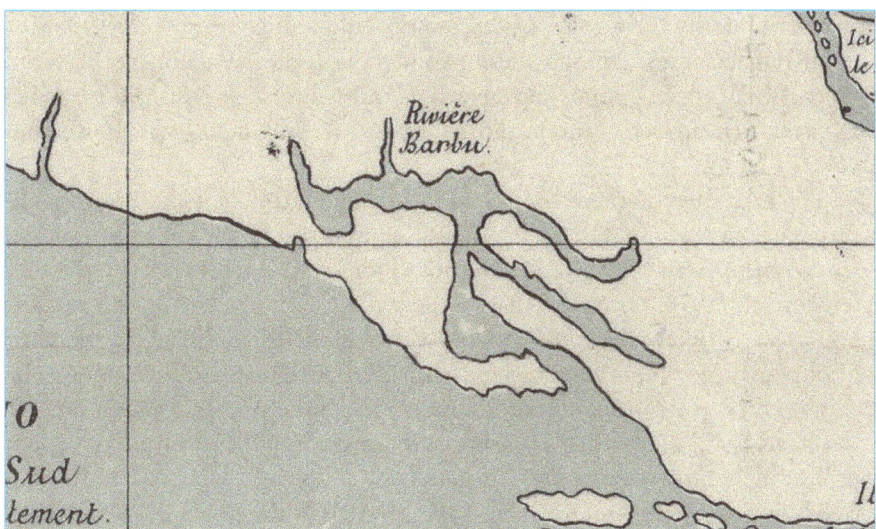

Figure 4.3. Detail of René Bréhant de Galinée's "Carte du lac Ontario et des habitations qui l'environnent. Ensemble le pays que M.M. Dollier et Galinée, missionnaires du Séminaire de St-Sulpice ont parcouru. 1670: Vraie copie (fac-similé) de l'original déposé aux Archives des cartes et plans de la marine impériale faite à Paris en May 1854." Extrait de Carte des grands lacs de l'Amérique du Nord dressée en 1670 par Bréhant de Galinée.
Source: Bibliothèque nationale de France, département Cartes et plans, GE C-3829.

Interestingly, the village symbol used for Quintio (a longhouse icon) is marked over the label "Lac de Kentsio" using a darker ink also used for the village label. Heidenreich remarks: "The importance of the map lies in Belmont's marginal notes and additions, especially the route from the Bay of Quinte through the Kawartha Lakes to Georgian Bay" (Heidenreich 1978:94). In this instance, the label for Quintio seems to be a later addition, because the symbol overlays another label, the spelling is different than the one that was overwritten for the lake (Kenitſſio versus Kentsio), and the ink is darker than that used for Ganaraské and the Rice Lake portage. The location of Quintio on this map seems to be expedient rather than accurate (Vachon de Belmont essentially ran out of space) and perhaps supports the idea that Quintio was originally a small satellite settlement of Ganaraské and that it later grew in importance, and hence was a later addition to the map.

Vachon de Belmont's map also adds detail to de Galinée's map of the Bay of Quinte/Hay Bay area. Vachon de Belmont correctly depicts Adolphus Reach and the confluence of Hay Bay and the Napanee River and the general shape of the Bay of Quinte, with the mouths of the Moira and Trent Rivers. Vachon de Belmont places Ganneious on the north side of Hay Bay, between a watercourse and the portage route to the Napanee River. Most importantly, this map includes portage routes, some with distances listed. These include the Lake Ontario-Rice Lake, Lake Ontario-Lake Simcoe, and Lake Ontario-Grand River routes. Among these major trade routes, Vachon de Belmont noted a small route connecting Hay Bay and Ganneious with the Napanee River, which attracted the authors' attention. This detail will be further explored below.

The next map of interest was initially attributed to Jolliet and was thought to have been created in the earlier 1670s (Figure 1.4) but has since been shown to have been drawn by Claude Bernou after 1680 (Heidenreich 1978:94). Heidenreich (1978:92) argued that "the excellence of the cartography of these maps makes it likely that the originals were supplied by either Franquelin or La Salle, both of whom had contacts with Bernou, since Jolliet was not sufficiently skilled as a cartographer to have produced the originals which Bernou must have used." In this map, Ganaraské is depicted on the east bank of a river, but instead turning west, as the Ganaraska does, this river turns east. Quintio is placed on the north shore of Rice Lake, near the outlet of the Trent River. Ganneious is placed on the south shore of a large inlet of the Bay of Quinte. There is only one inlet depicted, and it is unclear if this is Hay Bay or the Napanee River. The geographic errors of this map are puzzling, as this map contained an incredible level of detail for the Wellers Bay/Kenté area (see von Bitter et al., this volume). The problem of interpretation is compounded by the contemporary Belmont map, which is based on an earlier 1670 map that correctly shows a separate Hay Bay and Napanee River.

Several maps created by Jean-Baptiste-Louis Franquelin (a trained cartographer appointed *hydrographe du roi* in 1686) between 1675 and 1702 clearly mark village locations. Franquelin was provided with information from Louis Jolliet on his and Jacques Marquette's journey down the Mississippi. Marquette had initially created a simple map of the journey in 1674; Franquelin subsequently used this as a base to create a map that was "much more elegant than Marquette's bare-bones effort" (Kupfer 2019:64). The 1675 map depicts only Ganneious, Kenté, and Tannaouate in the east. Kenté and Ganneious are depicted with a longhouse-like symbol, whereas Tannaouate is not. Indeed, the label may refer to the Trent River instead of the village. Ganneious has the longhouse symbol on the north shore of a dead-end waterbody off the Bay of Quinte, while the label is placed above another dead-end waterbody farther north, to avoid overlap with the placement of another label on the map. This has led to confusion over Ganneious' position, as the label places the village on the north side of the Napanee River, whereas the symbol (which is harder to see) places it on the north side of Hay Bay.

Franquelin's subsequent maps, however, "are good works of art rather than accurate renditions of the known geography of North America; geographic features are depicted so crudely that the maps can only be described as free-hand drawings. The second-last Franquelin map of this period, tentatively dated 1679 and apparently an adaptation of a Jolliet map, is also a dreadful piece of cartography" (Heidenreich 1978:94). The 1679 map places Ganaraské on the east side of a river at its mouth, does not include Quintio, and places Ganneious at the end of a square-shaped inlet off the Bay of Quinte. The symbols for the villages on this map vary; Ganaraské is depicted with the longhouse symbol used for other Haudenosaunee villages, Kenté is depicted with a European church, and Ganneious has no symbol at all.

Franquelin's 1688 "Carte de l'Amérique Septentrionnale" (Figure 4.4) also omits Quintio but does include Rice Lake, as "Lac Kentsio." Ganneious is placed on the north side of a water body connected to the Bay of Quinte by a river; this is most likely Hay Bay, but this is difficult to determine because the Napanee River is missing. Ganaraské is on the east bank of a river with a distinctive westward bend, which is the correct configuration of the Ganaraska. Subsequent maps by Franquelin up to 1700 all copy this same configuration.

The final map of interest is the Jesuit Pierre Raffeix's 1688 map, titled "Le Lac Ontario avec les lieux circonvoisins et particulièrement les cinq nations Iroquoises" (Figure 1.1). It shows two village icons, on either side of a river; only the western one is named (Ganaraské), while the eastern one is connected to Quintio, on the south shores of Rice Lake, via a portage. Ganneious is located

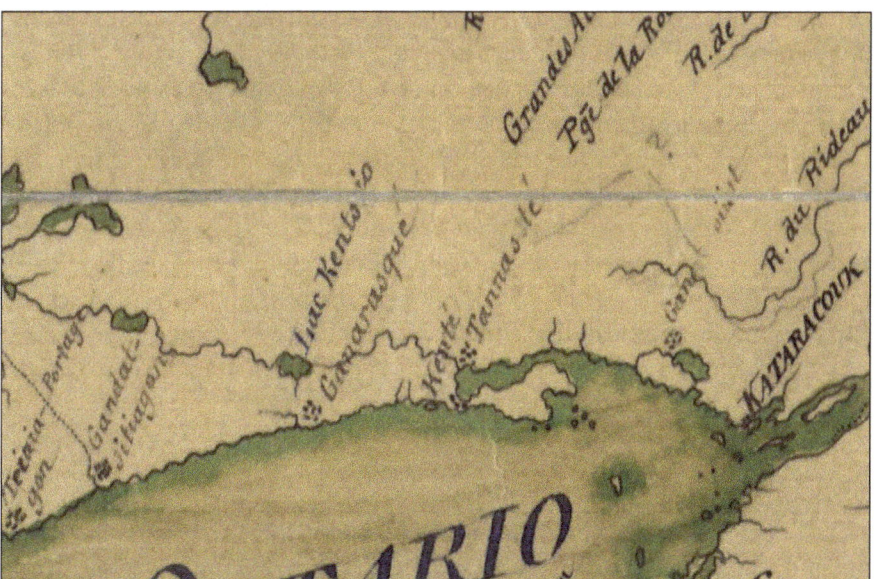

Figure 4.4. Detail of Jean-Baptiste-Louis Franquelin's "Carte de la Louisiane en l'Amérique septentrionale, depuis la Nouvelle France jusqu'au golfe du Mexique, où sont décris les pays que le sieur de La Salle a découverts dans un grand continent compris depuis 50 degr. de l'elevation du Pole jusques à 25', les années 1679, 80, 81, 82."
Source: Bibliothèque nationale de France, département Cartes et plans, Ge. D. 2987.

on the north side of an inlet, most likely Hay Bay, although this is difficult to determine because on this map, too, the Napanee River is not depicted.

The Iroquois du Nord villages continue to appear on maps until shortly before the conquest of New France, in the late 1750s. Cartographers unfamiliar with the area, including those from other European nations, would copy earlier map symbols even though the villages were long abandoned or destroyed. This erroneously gives the impression that the IDN settlements survived later than they did. Some later maps also show the villages with additional details not found in earlier maps. The 1726 "Carte du Lac Ontario et de la Rivière jusques au dela de L'Isle de Montréal celle de Niagara et partie du Lac Erie," by Chaussegros de Léry, for instance, is a copy of Franquelin's 1688 map but contains additional details, such as the portage between the Ganaraska River and Rice Lake and a small watercourse flowing out of the east end of Hay Bay. The latest map with IDN villages found by the authors is a British map of the American Colonies published in 1755 (Lewis 1755). It only shows Kenté and Ganneious, which were both destroyed in 1687 (Denonville 1687).

3. Relocating the Villages: Landscape Analysis

Using the seventeenth-century maps as a rough guide to the village's locations, we examined their geography, topography, and aerial photographs to determine why exactly that location might have been selected. What advantages, such as defence, trade, and resource extraction, were available at each? Some maps placed the same village in contradictory positions to others; therefore, an examination of each was necessary to determine the mostly likely position. There is a remote possibility that some of the villages may have relocated, as was Ontario Iroquoian practice (Warrick 1988). This relocation was due mainly to soil infertility over time that led to abandonment and resettlement every ten to forty years, depending on the size of their population. The IDN settlements were based on trade and linked with portage routes necessitating a fixed geographic location and were in existence for no longer than twenty years. This section expands on our examination of the landscape of each location on the historic maps and attempt to glean additional information in an effort at relocation.

3.1. Quintio

As noted above, seventeenth-century maps place Quintio on both the north shore and the south shore of Rice Lake. At first glance, only a village location on the north shore, near where the Trent River flows out of Rice Lake, would seem like a place where the flow of furs down the Trent River Valley could be controlled. Bernou's map of 1680 places Quintio in this location (see "Kentsio" on Figure 1.4).

Looking at a modern map of the Trent River watershed (Figure 4.5), one may get the impression that it represented a fast and efficient transportation corridor, eventually leading from Rice Lake to Lake Ontario. It should be remembered, however, that the later Ojibwa name for the Trent River was Sagetewedgewam, which means "difficult to navigate river," presumably because of the rapids from Meyersburg to the village of Hastings. A trail referred to as the Percy Portage allowed these rapids to be avoided.

Those attempting to travel the Trent River would be subjected to a further set of obstacles downstream. The section of the river south of Frankford to the mouth on the Bay of Quinte was called Nine Mile Rapids. In "Forgotten Pathways of the Trent," Frost refers to this as a further portage one would have to traverse after taking the Percy Portage if descending the river from Wendake (Frost 1973:79–80). It possibly was not identified as a portage by Frost because, unlike the other cross-country routes he shows, it was simply a footpath along the river. The Trent-Severn Waterway, built in the nineteenth century to make the Trent navigable, has eighteen locks between Lake Ontario and Rice Lake, rising roughly 110 m in elevation over 85 km of river. Due to the lengthy portages involved, the Trent River is not the optimal route south to Lake Ontario from the west end of Rice Lake.

An 11–12 km portage running south from Rice Lake would allow the Trent and its portages to be avoided entirely, effectively cutting the length of the required portages in half. A village location on Rice Lake at the terminus

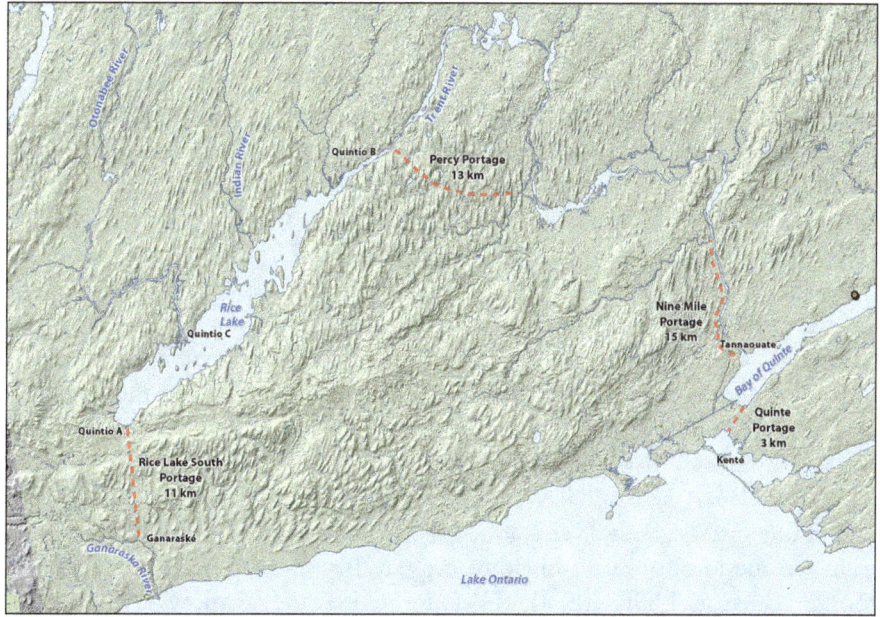

Figure 4.5. The portage routes from Rice Lake to Lake Ontario and the probable locations of IDN villages and possible location options for Quintio on the Trent Waterway.
Source: Map by Chris Menary.

of the portage route north from Lake Ontario would also be superior to a location at the Trent River outlet, as it would control the flow of furs down both the Otonabee River and the Indian River, not just the former ("Quintio A" on Figure 4.5). Raffeix's map of 1688 places Quintio in this location.

The stream of trade goods coming down the Rice Lake portage to Ganaraské is also more consistent with the documentary record. If material had been transported down the Trent River, Kenté would have been bypassed entirely, yet we know that the missionaries there participated in the fur trade (see von Bitter et al., this volume). Some maps, such as Franquelin's 1688 map of North America (Figure 4.4), show "Tannaouate" at the mouth of the Trent River, a settlement that, while considered a possible subsidiary of Kenté, was significant enough to be included in La Salle's invitation to send representatives to meet with Frontenac in 1673 (Adams 1986). If the main flow of trade were down the Trent River, this settlement would have risen in importance and Kenté would have been bypassed.

Another possibility for the location of Quintio is at the mouth of the Otonabee River ("Quintio C" on Figure 4.5), as Vachon de Belmont's map of 1680 (Figure 4.1) places the village in this location. There is a record of an "Indian trading post" there in 1790 (Guillet 1933:61), which is in a good strategic location to act as a tollgate to control the flow of furs coming from Georgian Bay. Using light detection and ranging (LiDAR) data, we identified a rectangular enclosure measuring 50 × 70 m on Hatrick Point. This is in the same location as a hand-drawn rectangle on the 1819 patent map of Otonabee Township (Ontario 1819) and is not located near any settlement or farms. It is likely that this enclosure, with ninety-degree corners, is European influenced in construction design, because pre-contact Indigenous enclosures in Ontario usually follow a circular or oval shape. Further research on this feature is required for identification. While this enclosure does not appear to be pre-contact Indigenous, the general location at the mouth of the Otonabee could have been occupied repeatedly because of its strategic position. Hatrick Point also contains several Middle Woodland earthworks known as the Miller Mounds (Kenyon 1986). These earlier structures could have functioned in later periods as navigational landmarks; this, too, is seen near Ganneious, on the Napanee River, as will be discussed below.

One question that remains is: Why would Quintio have been required as a tollgate? Ganaraské could have easily controlled the flow of goods at the south end of the portage, as did Teiaiagon and Ganatsekwyagon. The answer may be found in the location of Ganneious, on Hay Bay, perhaps for the purpose of food production. Unlike the IDN sites located on the fast-flowing Ganaraska, Humber, and Rouge Rivers, both Quintio and Ganneious are located near rich sources of wild rice, on large bodies of water. They could have functioned as rice and fishing outposts supplying the larger villages. Ganneious and Kenté were provisioning Fort Frontenac after 1673 (Thwaites 1903), so these larger settlements must have been producing surplus resources. This idea of satellite settlements as resource producers arises in the documentary record with d'Urfé's visit to a group living five leagues from Ganaraské; in the dispersed spatial patterning of artifacts found in the vicinity of Kenté (see von Bitter et al., this volume); and in the geographic analyses of the village locations.

There are no registered sites in the area of the northern terminus of the portage route around the village of Bewdley.

3.2. Ganaraské

Ganaraské is located on the eponymous Ganaraska River and is placed on both its east and west banks in seventeenth-century maps. Most of the maps, such as Franquelin's from 1688 (Figure 4.4) and Belmont's from 1680 (Figure 4.1), show the village on the east bank, near a distinctive westward bend in the river. This location represents the end point of the portage north of Lake Ontario to Rice Lake, as the river continues west for many kilometres before turning north again. While some maps show an icon for a village near the mouth of the Ganaraska River, this may simply be a cartographic device.

Unlike at Kenté, there are no nineteenth-century artifact collections from the local township, Hope Township, and while there are registered sites in the vicinity of the Ganaraska River, none are clearly of the contact period. An isolated triangular Late Woodland chert projectile point was found on a farm 1,500 m east of the westward bend of the river; it could date to the IDN period or to pre-contact times (see Jordan, this volume and Cooper, this volume). A survey of a pipeline conducted immediately south of this location in 2017 produced only a Hi-Lo (late Paleo) projectile point on the west bank (Golder 2017:87).

3.3. Ganneious

While it has been postulated by Adams that IDN villages "acted as tollgates where the Iroquois could control and regulate the flow of furs from the north and west to the markets at Albany" (Adams 1986), Victor Konrad has suggested that to do this, north-shore villages had to have occupied "positions that command the major thoroughfares of the region." He argued further that "[a]t no other points and with no fewer villages could the Iroquois as effectively facilitate and control the flow of furs" (Konrad 1981:136).

As was the case with Kenté (see von Bitter et al., this volume), there was one map that contained the most detail and therefore seems the most useful in terms of the search for Ganneious. Belmont's map of 1680 shows not only the distinctive Z shape of the Bay of Quinte, but also accurately and most clearly Hay Bay midway between the Napanee River and Adolphus Reach. There are four islands drawn at the end of the bay, and while there are several islands in Hay Bay, they are in a different configuration and so appear to be cartographic approximations that cannot be used to locate the village (Figure 4.6). These islands were mentioned in the 1869 *History of Settlement of Upper Canada*:

> Upon an old plan of Fredericksburg, dated 1784, is to be seen in Hay Bay, three islands; one near the north shore, at its eastern extremity, is called *Hare Island*. To the south, at the eastern shore, are the other two; the north one is called *Nut Island*; the more southern one is *Wappoose Island*. This island, from its name, must have been the place of a residence of the principal chief of some Indian tribe, probably the Kente Indians. Here, "must have been a place of considerable importance to the Indian rendezvous, whereat they met, and whereat the chief held his simple, but dignified court." [Canniff 1869:405]

Wappoose or Waupoos is an Ojibwe word meaning "rabbit" (Nichols 1995), which does not connect to the Oneida inhabitants at Ganneious; it may, instead, relate to later Mississauga settlement of the area (see Warrick and Williamson, this volume). The name Waupoos is also found in neighbouring Prince Edward County.

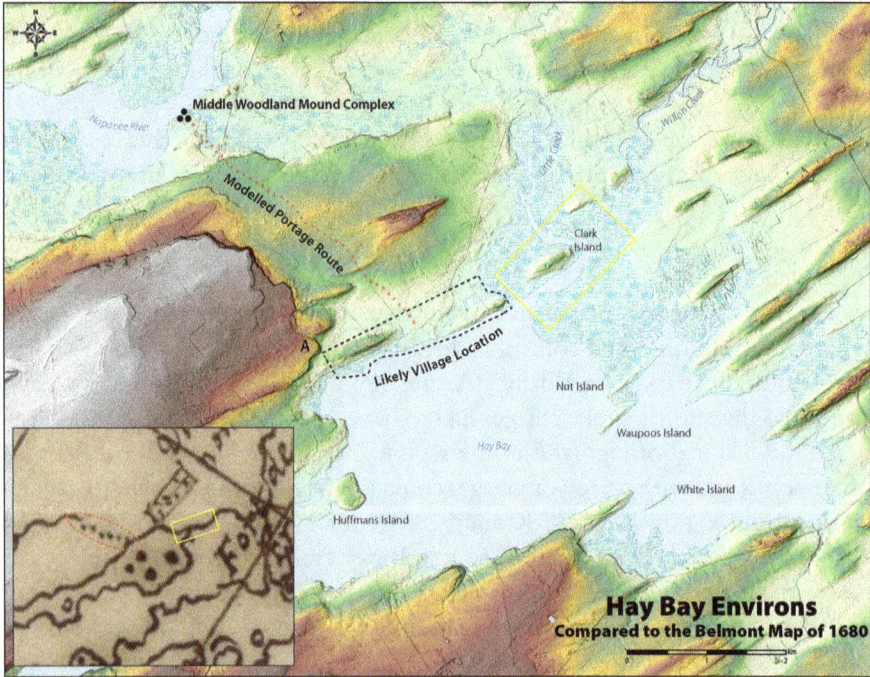

Figure 4.6. Topographical map of Hay Bay and comparison with Belmont 1680. *Source:* Map by Chris Menary.

In some ways, Ganneious represents the biggest riddle, because Hay Bay has no outlet and is well away from any rivers bringing furs downstream from the north. If Ganneious was in Hay Bay, how could it have functioned as a tollgate? The authors noticed a short portage on the Belmont map shown extending north-northwest from Hay Bay to the Napanee River. If the main village had been located on the north shore of Hay Bay and a smaller cabin had been located at the opposite end of the portage, the flow of furs coming down the Napanee River could have been controlled. If the village had been in this location, it would also have been situated adjacent to a rich biotic zone.

There are several woodland sites along the south shore of the Napanee River 5 km from Hay Bay (Roberts 1978) including two Middle Woodland mounds. Two stone pipes recovered by Douglas Alkenbrak by the Napanee River may be IDN. Although they do not match any common Haudenosaunee styles, they do match the small size of seventeenth-century pipes found at Fort Frontenac (Adams 1986:17).

4. Relocating the Villages: LiDAR and Remote Sensing

Locating the eastern villages through early maps and topographic analysis provided a rough geographic area of where each village may have been located. To further refine the search, modern remote sensing and geographic information systems were used. Employing airborne-derived LiDAR data, we examined each village location and compared it with the two known IDN village locations to see if trends in the western Seneca sites are repeated in the eastern Cayuga and Oneida sites. We also used LiDAR data in conducting a search for the portage routes themselves, since if we could identify those, we would be able to locate the villages in the vicinity of either end.

4.1. Ganaraské and Quintio

We know that Ganaraské and Quintio were linked via a portage and that the total distance between Lake Ontario and Rice Lake is 16 km. If Ganaraské was located where the Ganaraska River makes its westward bend (roughly 4 km upstream from Lake Ontario) and Quintio was near the south shore of Rice Lake, the total portage route needed would be 10–11 km. As the general location of each village is known, the research goal then became to find the portage itself. If a remote sensing exercise could identify the route, the location of the portage's terminuses could refine the search area.

Airborne LiDAR data from 2017 was acquired from Ontario's Ministry of Natural Resources and Forestry (MNR) for Northumberland County in the form of a classified point cloud. As light pulses can penetrate vegetation cover, LiDAR allows one to view the ground surface beneath forest cover. From the raw data, we developed a 50 cm digital elevation model (DEM) for an area stretching from Lake Ontario to Rice Lake (Figure 4.7). We also created a

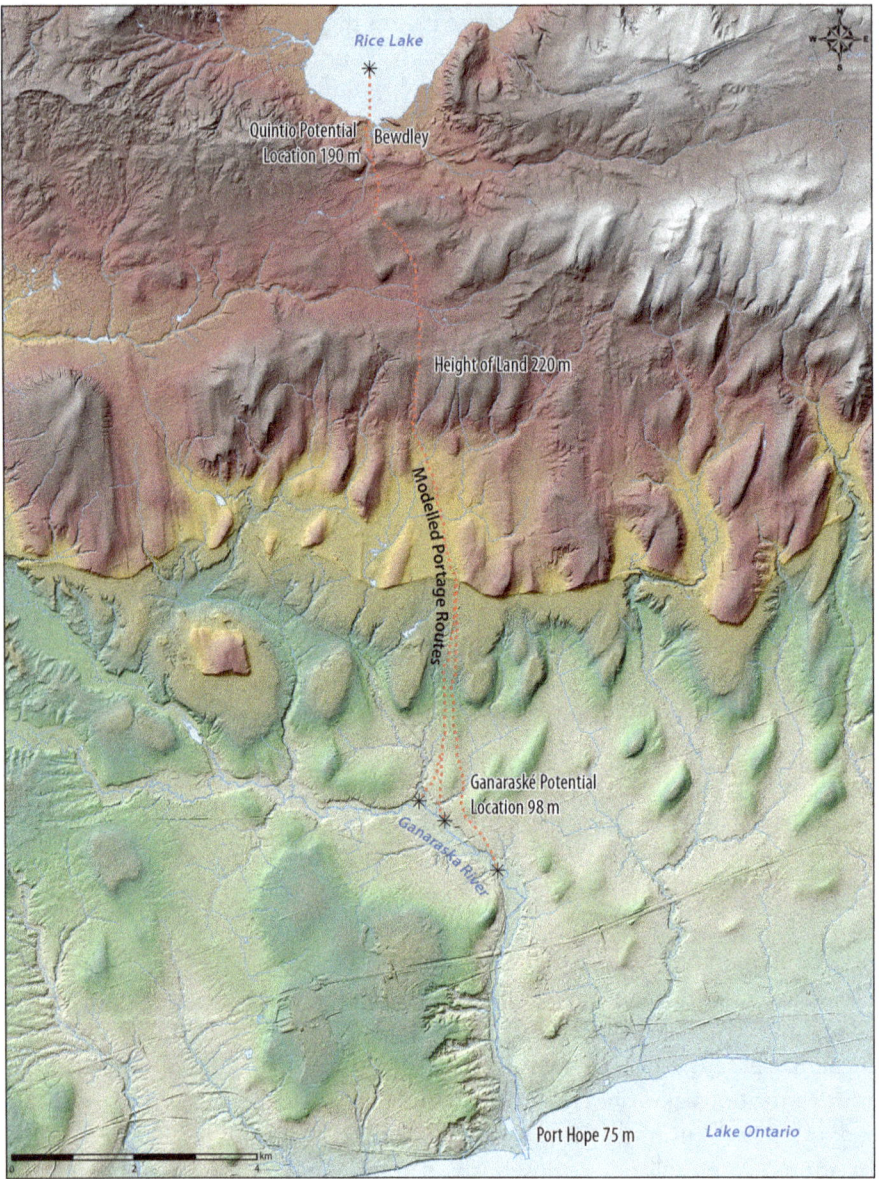

Figure 4.7. The topography of the Rice Lake–Lake Ontario portage.
Source: Map by Chris Menary.

hillshade (a greyscale image of shadows produced from the DEM), slope model, and contours from the DEM.

The initial exercise consisted of using a hillshade to conduct a visual search for any anthropomorphic ground disturbances (e.g., earthworks, mounds) in the general area where each village was suspected of being from the documentary record, including early maps. As there were small burial mounds recorded at both Teiaiagon and Ganatsekwyagon (Archaeological Services Inc. 2016), we thought it possible that similar mounds would exist at Ganaraské or Quintio if Cayuga burial practices were like those of the Seneca. While nothing definitive was identified in the search, two mound-like anomalies in the Ganaraské area were observed measuring 4 m in diameter and 60 cm in height. Both were located on the crest of slope on the tableland above the Ganaraska River and were far enough from agricultural areas to preclude them being field clearance piles, which could also be seen. From Kenyon's "Mounds of Sacred Earth" and from examining the LiDAR of the Serpent Mounds area, we know that undisturbed Middle Woodland mounds are typically 5–6 m in diameter and 1.5 m in height (Kenyon 1986). Permission to enter the property was not granted, so no further examination could occur.

A comparison between the western Seneca village locations and the possible sites for Quintio and Ganaraské was also undertaken. According to Konrad, IDN villages were located at strategic, defensible positions. This is true of Teiaiagon and Ganatsekwyagon, both situated on promontories with 30 m high bluffs overlooking a river. There is no similar location around the westward bend of the Ganaraska River, yet there are landforms that could offer some

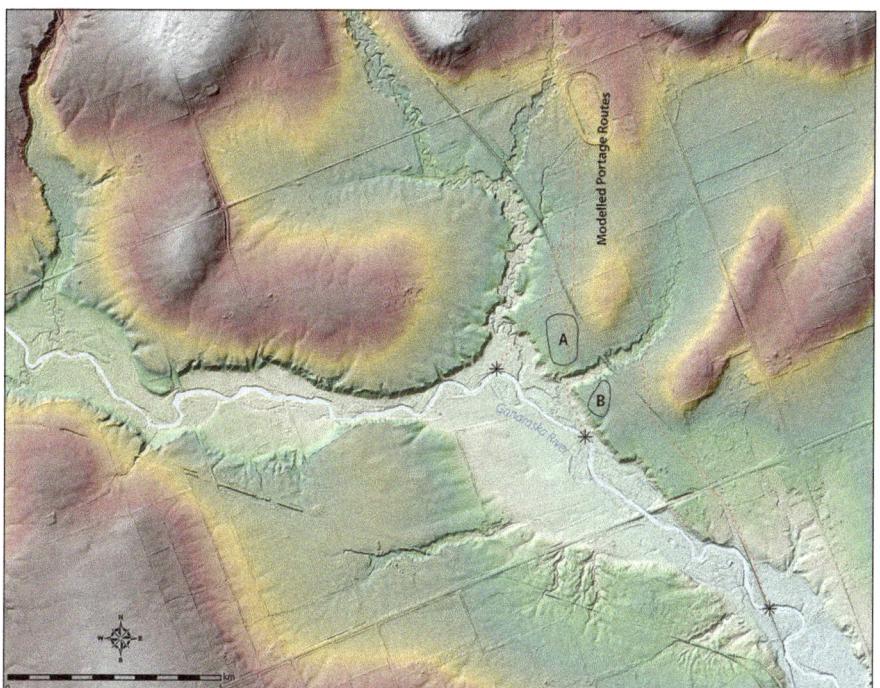

Figure 4.8. Potential locations of Ganaraské and least cost path analysis of portage routes.
Source: Map by Chris Menary.

protection in order to situate defensibly a village. On Figure 4.8, they are marked as "A" and "B"; for comparison, two sixteenth-century ancestral Wendat village outlines are added for scale. Location A is the Jean-Baptiste Lainé (Mantle) site, at 2.9 ha, and Location B is the Seed-Barker site, at 1.2 ha. The tableland is 10 m above the river in both places, and both could be easily enclosed by a palisade. Most importantly, the modelled portage routes from Rice Lake pass less than 300 m from each.

At the possible site of Quintio, there are no steep bluffs, river valleys, or major defensive locations whatsoever. The most promising area, an agricultural field marked as "A" on Figure 4.9, was surveyed by Laurie Jackson and yielded only an Early Woodland projectile point and several other stone artifacts (Jackson 1976). If the hypothesis of Quintio being focused on food production is correct, then there would be no need for a defensive setting. It would be likely, then, that the village was closer to the lake edge, now either covered by the Town of Bewdley or drowned when the Hastings dam raised the level of Rice Lake during the construction of the Trent-Severn Waterway (Figure 4.7). Aerial photography from 1954 shows agricultural fields above the settlement, which are now mostly reforested, and a small gravel pit to the west of Rice Lake Drive North, which is present on topographic maps dating back to 1932. The area to the west of the modelled portage route offers the most likely lakeside location for the village.

An interesting possibility is that the modern Rice Lake Drive South, from Rosemount to Bewdley, represents the route of the portage (Figure 4.9). It was first mentioned as a gravel road in 1817, "when Charles Fothergill went on horseback to Rice Lake. He could follow the road to concession five, but after that there was only an Indian trail. He was lost for an hour" (Reeve 1967). The route was improved to a plank road in the 1840s and eventually realigned as modern Highway 28, with Rice Lake Drive South becoming a local road. It is seen on Ridout's 1826 map of Upper Canada (as is the Percy Portage) and on the 1870 Hamilton Township map, with the northern section shown deviating from the other surveyed roads. In other areas of the province, old portage routes became "given," or non-surveyed roads, such as Davenport Road in Toronto and Highway 48 through Goodwood (McIlwraith 1998). A similar situation may have occurred in Bewdley, as our modelled portage route closely follows sections of Rice Lake Drive South.

In an attempt to further refine the route of the historic portage from Rice Lake to the Ganaraska River, a GIS modelling exercise, called a least cost path analysis, was conducted. The initial step was to produce a new 2 m DEM, as courser data was adequate to analyze roughly 80 km^2 of terrain between the two points. As a raster dataset, a DEM is comprised of squares called cells (much like pixels in a digital photograph) that contain information, in this case elevation. The analysis involves creating a new, combined raster that assigns a "cost"

Figure 4.9. Potential location of Quintio and portage, least cost path analysis.
Source: Map by Chris Menary.

to each cell and then calculates the "cheapest" path, moving along each cell from the start to the end points. The cost was a combination of several datasets: the distance from the finish point, the slope, and the presence of wetlands. The slope was broken down into five classes, with a flat surface having the value of 1 and a steep slope a value of 5. Combined with distance and wetlands, there were eight potential costs for each cell; a level, non-wetland cell on a direct path was assigned a value of 1, while a very steep cell not on a direct path was assigned a value of 8. The software then analyzes thousands of potential routes and may, for example, identify a path that is longer and steeper but that avoids a swamp. Three start points were included in the model, all clustered around the westward bend in the Ganaraska River, both in the valley and on the tableland. The end point was placed in the middle of Rice Lake in order to not prejudge the evaluation by having it on the shore edge. The analysis was performed in ArcGIS Pro, and the results are presented in Figure 4.9. The modelled route was 11.5 km in length.

An issue encountered was the over-accuracy of the LiDAR. The analysis was run with the DEM, slope, and wetlands, and the resulting route basically followed Highway 28, as it was the flattest, shortest route and avoided all wetlands. To overcome this, it was necessary to purge the DEM of all traces of settlement, such as roads, drainage ditches, driveways, and railways. LiDAR data can be cut and selected like any other GIS data, so we created a mask, based on the township's lot and concession plan, that excluded everything within the sixty-six-foot road allowance. We then removed other traces of settlement, such as houses and railway beds, manually and subsequently used the mask to select LiDAR points and create a new DEM. The software automatically bridges any gaps or holes with the surrounding elevation, so this process created a new, "pre-contact" DEM. This was then used in the model, with satisfactory results.

Upon completion, we examined the modelled portage route visibly with the hillshade to look for earthworks, mounds, and other potential traces of the villages. A cluster of features was identified on the ridgeline of a drumlin 1 km west of the route. Upon closer examination, we saw that they consisted of four mounds, varying in height from 1–1.2 m and in diameter from 6–7 m. Three of these were in a row, and the fourth was offset, forming a "T" formation. The dimensions were similar to those at the Serpent Mounds and were within the range of the size of other Middle Woodland mounds (Kenyon 1986). They are unlikely to be glacial kames, given that they are located on the top of a drumlin (which was smoothed by glacial action), and they are too large for field clearance piles. Further examination of these features is warranted. If they are confirmed to be Middle Woodland mounds, they could have functioned as a waypoint along the portage route. Using GIS software, a viewshed analysis was conducted to see if they would have been visible from the portage. The portage runs along a small ridge of high land, and the land slopes downward into a small valley between the ridge and the drumlin. The analysis concluded that the top of the drumlin would have been visible from the portage and that the line of three mounds would have been silhouetted against the sky.

4.2. Ganneious

For Ganneious, LiDAR was acquired from the MNR in the form of a 1 m DEM flown in 2009. A similar search for earthworks was conducted and a least cost path analysis undertaken. The results of the modelling can be seen in Figure 4.6. The portage route is most likely in the narrowest point of land between Hay Bay and the Napanee River, and the modelled results follow this narrow point for more than 3.8 km. Multiple start points were created along a 2.3 km stretch of waterfront on Hay Bay where the most likely location for the village would be; the end point was located at the narrowest section of the Napanee River, in a bend that provided unobstructed views both upstream and downstream. This is the likely location of a subsidiary cabin that would have functioned as a tollgate on the Napanee River. The secondary reason for this end point is the presence of a Middle Woodland mound complex at this location. There are two registered mounds at this spot. Using LiDAR, we detected two more potential mounds in the vicinity. The mounds could have served as a navigational aid on the Napanee indicating the location of the portage as well as a sacred site near the settlement.

The village location is most likely along the waterfront, between the portage route and the mouth of Little Creek; there are no defensible locations save for a small bluff 500 m from the water's edge ("A" on Figure 4.6). This area and an area farther inland on the ridge were investigated by the authors in the summer of 2019 for evidence of the village and to examine several potential small mounds. No evidence of a village was found, and the mounds were a false positive created when the LiDAR mistook large, dense juniper bushes for the ground surface. The soil conditions on the ridge were extremely poor, with large nodules of limestone present only 10 cm below the ground surface. It was difficult to excavate more than 30 cm down, so one cannot imagine building longhouses or other structures in those conditions. The lack of agricultural fields upon the ridge also testifies to the quality of the soil, and this was confirmed by examining the Canada Land Inventory soils data. The best soils are located on the waterfront (CLI 1 and 2) closer to the wild rice beds, while those on the ridge are very poor (CLI 6). As this village was supplying Fort Frontenac, it would have been located on the best soils available. Aerial photography from 1954 shows that the waterfront is largely unaltered and represents a site for further investigation. The village location then is most likely on the north shore of Hay Bay, east of the mouth of Little Creek below the limestone ridge.

5. Conclusion

Ganaraské, Quintio, and Ganneious represent villages established at strategic locations across the landscape, with connected subsidiary sites. This is the same pattern as observed at Kenté (von Bitter et al., this volume), where IDN material found some distance from the village indicates the presence of subsidiary sites. Ganneious appears to represent the main settlement. It is connected to a secondary outpost located on the Napanee River. The portage between Ganaraské and Quintio reflects another example of a village and paired subsidiary site, although Quintio may have begun as a subsidiary location that later solidified into a named settlement.

Maps made starting in 1668 show the villages generally separated by vast spaces. There are two possible reasons why not all locations are shown. The map scales used may simply have been too large for important locations to be shown, and many cartographers copied earlier maps, compounding errors in geography (Heidenreich 1978). Archaeological evidence in addition to the documentary record suggests that IDN villages may not have been as isolated as previously thought; d'Urfé's visit to the smaller settlement associated with Ganaraské (possibly Quintio) and his subsequent return three days later show the ease of travel between two village sites. The notion that IDN villages were defensive outposts primarily focused on trade (Konrad 1981) may lead researchers to miss other functions. The locations of Quintio and Ganneious, for example, no doubt offered rich sources of food, but the sites were in areas impossible to fortify to the degree of Teiaiagon and Ganatsekwyagon. The production of crops or harvesting of natural resources may have become very important with the founding of Fort Frontenac in 1673, as it was easier to acquire supplies from Ganneious, less than 40 km away, rather than from Montréal, 300 km upstream (Adams 1986).

Mounds are found at all three village locations. This is to be expected, as the three villages are located in the area where mounds are found in Ontario: Peterborough and Northumberland Counties along Rice Lake and along the south shore of the Bay of Quinte (Kenyon 1986). Middle Woodland mounds are found on the Napanee River at the presumptive end of the portage from Ganneious; at the mouth of the Otonabee River, where a 1790 trading post may hint at the location of Quintio; and possibly along the Rice Lake-Lake Ontario portage route in Hamilton Township. These mounds would have served both as navigational aids and as sacred sites that the newly arrived Haudenosaunee would have recognized. The western IDN Seneca villages contain burial mounds (ASI 2016), so it is possible that burial mounds may be found at the eastern Cayuga and Oneida villages. This is reinforced by human remains recovered from a mound on Smokes Point in 2003, which the authors believe relates to the location of Kenté (see von Bitter et al., this volume). Two small mounds were also observed at the southern end of the modelled Rice Lake-Lake Ontario portage route, near where the village of Ganaraské may lie.

Further fieldwork will hopefully allow the important IDN settlements of Quintio, Ganaraské, and Ganneious to be discovered and protected. This chapter should serve as a new basis for research and stimulate the search for these sites of national importance.

5

THE BEAD HILL SITE

A Late Seventeenth-Century Seneca Village on the Lower Rouge River

Dana R. Poulton

Bead Hill is a multi-component archaeological site. It is situated on the lower Rouge River Valley, on the eastern edge of Toronto, within Rouge National Urban Park (Figures 5.1 and 5.2). The main component is a late seventeenth-century Seneca village; it has yielded the largest artifact sample of any Iroquois du Nord (IDN) settlement. The site also includes a Mississauga occupation. In 1991, Bead Hill was designated a National Historic Site and was added to the Canadian Register of Historic Places.

This chapter details the archaeological discoveries and investigations at the site between the mid-nineteenth and late twentieth centuries. It places the Seneca occupation and the Mississauga reoccupation in an historical context. Contemporary sources document two IDN villages in the Toronto area: Teiaiagon, at Baby Point on the lower Humber River in Toronto (Robertson, this volume) and Ganatsekwyagon, somewhere on or near the lower Rouge River. Based on the evidence, Bead Hill is the best candidate for the historically documented village of Ganatsekwyagon.

As detailed in the description of the material culture, with few exceptions, the available sample of Seneca artifacts from the Bead Hill site dates to the 1670s and 1680s. Six contemporary Seneca settlements beyond the lower Rouge Valley provide historical and, in some cases, archaeological context for Bead Hill. Two of the settlements were among the IDN villages considered in this volume: the aforementioned Teiaiagon; and Outinaouatoua, a two-day journey westward from the head of Lake Ontario; although Neal Ferris (this volume) does not believe that the latter should be regarded as a strictly Seneca settlement. The other four were in the Seneca homeland south of Lake Ontario. They were the western principal town of Tiotohatton (likely the Rochester Junction site) and its satellite village, Keinte-he (likely Kirkwood), and the eastern principal Seneca town of Ganondagan, (also Gannagaro or Boughton Hill) and its satellite village, with the addition of a small Wendat village (Jordan 2018a, 2018b). All these settlements in western New York State are believed to have

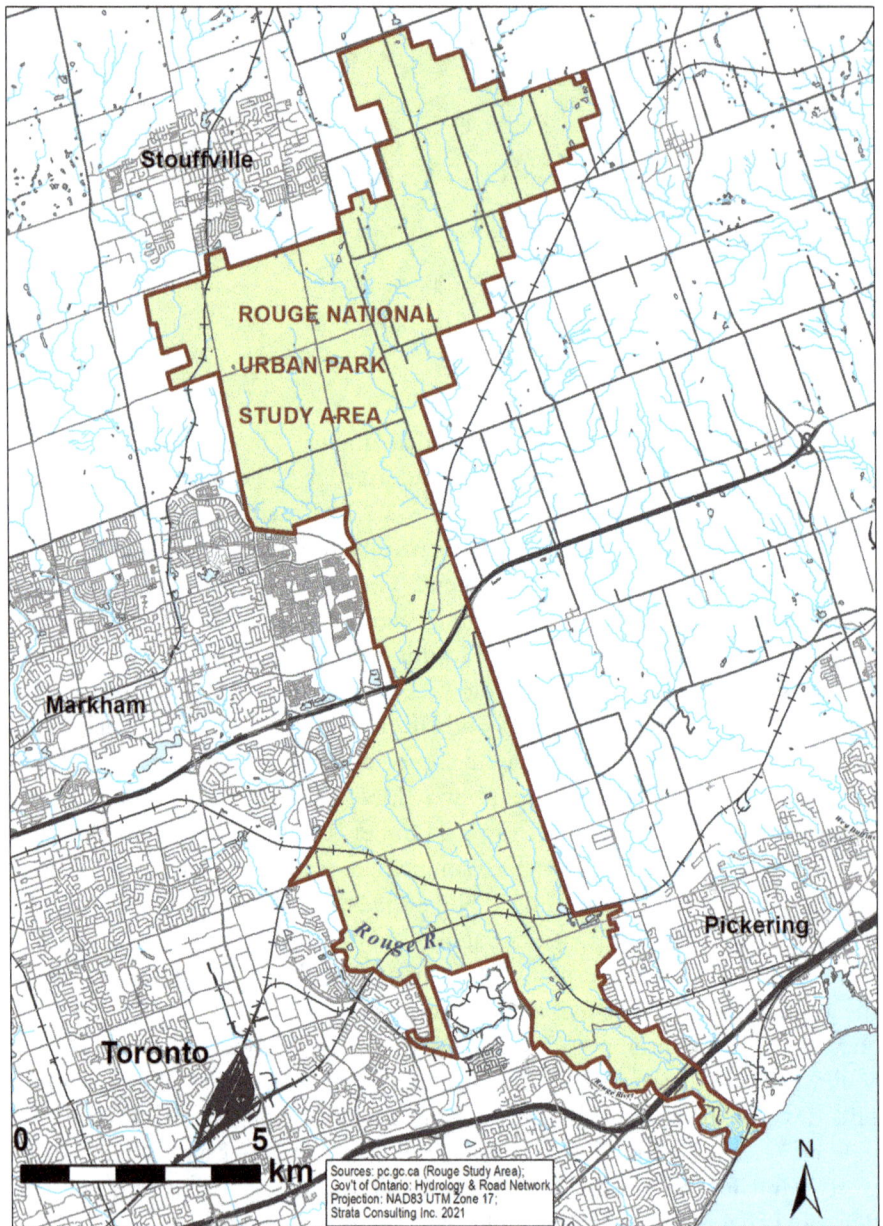

Figure 5.1. Location of the Rouge National Urban Park.
Source: Map by Dana Poulton.

been established in the early to mid-1670s, with Tiotohatton perhaps the last to be founded, circa 1675 (Jordan 2018a:179). New York agent Wentworth Greenhalgh described these settlements after he visited them in 1677 (see Jordan, this volume).

Figure 5.2. The lower Rouge River, Joseph Adamson Blakely, 1908. *Source:* Toronto Public Library.

As with other IDN settlements (Adams 1986:8; Konrad 1981:136–138), Ganatsekwyagon occupied a strategic location that enabled it to fulfill its wider frontier functions in the fur trade, and it had an advantageous setting that allowed it to be self-sustaining. The vicinity of the lower Rouge Valley, with its proximity to the Rouge marsh and the first rapids on the river, would have provided abundant resources of deer, smaller game, fish, and wildfowl, as well as both edible and medicinal plants. In addition, early maps depict historic salmon fisheries off the mouths of the Rouge River and nearby Duffins Creek (e.g., Bouchette and Faden 1815), the French name for which was "Rivière au Saumon;" the same applies to the mouth of the Humber River off Teiaiagon. Further, the loam and sandy loam soils on the tablelands that flank the lower Rouge Valley were the same as those that had been farmed by the ancestral Wendat villagers upstream on the Rouge River drainage and adjacent West Duffins Creek. Finally, again as with the other IDN settlements (Adams 1986:9), it is likely that the Haudenosaunee had frequented the lower Rouge River in the past, initially through their conflicts with the Wendat and the Tionontaté up until 1651 (see Williamson, this volume), then subsequently as part of their extended hunting territory in south-central Ontario.

1. The Lower Rouge River Valley, ca. 1665–1687

Ganatsekwyagon is depicted on dozens of maps spanning a full century, from René de Bréhant de Galinée's two 1670 maps to the Pehr Kalm map of 1771, first as a Seneca village and later as what was presumably a succession of Mississauga settlements. On the many maps that show it in relation to the Rouge trail and the Rouge River, the village is always depicted at the base of the trail (although on both the east and west sides of the river), and the trail is always depicted on the east side of the Rouge (e.g., Figures 1.1 and 1.4). The names of some seventeenth-century Seneca villages were hereditary (Hamell 1980:94), and it is clear from the documentation that this name continued in use for several decades after the Seneca abandoned the north shore.

The seventeenth-century Seneca place names were descriptive (e.g., Hamell 1980:93). In discussing the etymology of Ganatsekwyagon, Percy Robinson (1933:243) cites J. N. B. Hewitt of the US Bureau of Indian Affairs when stating that it signifies "Among the Birches or the birch trees." Elsewhere, however, he cites a conflicting translation by Professor Lewis Allen, "who suggests that Ganatschekiagon, as it is sometimes spelled, may mean sand cut, i.e., opening in sand cliffs, from gandechia, 'sand,' and giagon, 'cut'" (Robinson 1933:17, Footnote 2). Neither translation serves to suggest a specific location on or near the lower Rouge River.

Key information on the early history of the lower Rouge River is provided by a French document of about 1730 (Robinson 1939:18–19). In a description that corresponds almost exactly with several landmarks depicted in Pierre Raffeix's 1688 map (Figure 1.1), this document states the following:

> It is 15 leagues from Quinté [Kenté] (the Bay of Quinté) to the river Ganestiagon [Rouge]; at the mouth of said river there used to be an Iroquois village [Ganatsekwyagon]; after them (came) the Mississauga; the said river is navigable for 2 leagues; at the end of the 2 leagues there is a portage of 12 leagues (30 miles) through a good country of low hills [the Oak Ridges Moraine]. The route is northerly and at the end is the River Escayondy [East Holland River]. [Robinson 1939:18–19]

This quote contains the earliest recorded name for the Rouge River, and the same name is identified on an unsigned French map (Delisle 1703) as "R. ganstiagon." This indicates that the river and the village shared the same Haudenosaunee name.

It has been surmised that almost all the IDN villages were established circa 1665 and that Ganatsekwyagon was among them (Konrad 1981:135; Preston and Lamontagne 1958:85; see Robertson, this volume, regarding the later establishment date for Teiaiagon; see Fox et al., this volume, in regard to the relative dating of eastern and western IDN settlements).

Ganatsekwyagon was one of several villages that were included in the Sulpician mission beginning in the fall of 1668 (von Bitter et al., this volume). In May or June of 1669, Jean Peré and Adrien Jolliet (brother of Louis Jolliet) left Montréal in search of a fabled copper mine on the north shore of Lake Superior. En route, their party, which included René-Robert Cavelier de La Salle and François Dollier de Casson, visited Ganatsekwyagon before continuing north on the Rouge trail (Robinson 1933:18, 20). Casson was a priest and missionary and was François de Salignac de La Mothe-Fénelon's superior in the Sulpician mission to the IDN.

From this sequence of events, we know Ganatsekwyagon existed at least as early as the summer of 1669. It must have been established sometime late in the occupations of the two principal Seneca settlements of western New York State that preceded the Rochester Junction and Boughton Hill sites: the Marsh site (1650–1670); and the Dann site (1655–1675) (Wray 1983:44; also, Jordan, this volume).

Some time after Peré's visit, a delegation of north shore Seneca visited Kenté and asked that a Sulpician school and mission be established at Ganatsekwyagon. In response, Fénelon established one there beginning in the fall of 1669. That winter was unusually harsh, with deep snow, and the winter hunt failed. In consequence, some villagers starved to death, and others, Fénelon among them, were forced to disperse through the forest to forage, where he reportedly subsisted on porcupine and fungi. When the spring came, he abandoned the mission there (Preston and Lamontagne 1958:8), and thereafter the Seneca village on the lower Rouge was once again administered from Kenté (de Casson 1928:359; von Bitter et al., this volume). His presence at Ganatsekwyagon in 1669–1670 has been described as "the first recorded residence of white men in the neighbourhood of Toronto" (Robinson 1933:17) and as "the first school in Pickering Township and Ontario County" (Johnson 1973:14).

The strategic importance of Ganatsekwyagon during this time was that it commanded the base of the Rouge trail. Until Teiaiagon was established, the Haudenosaunee who travelled west along the north shore of Lake Ontario all used this route to reach the upper Great Lakes (Robinson 1933:133–134), and it was a transit point for explorers. Most importantly, every spring Ottawa fur brigades brought their pelts down the Rouge trail to barter at Ganatsekwyagon with English, Dutch, and French traders. Finally, one of the 1670 maps by Galinée states of the Rouge trail that "The French are beginning to take this route to the Ottawas; the peace with the Iroquois will keep it open" (Robinson 1939:18).

The construction of Fort Frontenac, in July 1673, was the culmination of years of strategic planning by the French (see also Robinson 1933:22–23). Its purpose is clear from a letter Louis de Buade, Comte de Frontenac et de Palluau wrote to Jean-Baptiste Colbert on November 12, 1674: to establish control over the fur trade on Lake Ontario, by checking the Haudenosaunee middlemen in the commerce between the Ottawa fur brigades and the Dutch and English traders at Ganatsekwyagon (Preston and Lamontagne 1958:109, 115). In fact, the perceived success of this military post is alluded to in a notation beside this village and the Rouge trail on an early map attributed to Claude Bernou (Figure 1.4); it states, "Road by which the Iroquois go to the Ottawa that they would have taken to trade in New Holland had fort Frontenac not been built on their route."

The Seneca response was to begin trading 37 km to the west, at Teiaiagon, whereafter many of the furs now passed around the western end of the lake and on to their partners on the Hudson River (Adams 1986:9; Konrad 1981:134; Preston and Lamontagne 1958:158; Robinson 1933:23–24). Putting these events in context, Victor Konrad (1981:133–134) states of Teiaiagon that there is no documentary evidence that it existed by 1673 and that if it had, it may only have been as an offshoot of Ganatsekwyagon. Regardless of the specifics, the result was that the importance of Ganatsekwyagon and the Rouge trail declined over time and that by the 1680s, Teiaiagon was the most important village on the north shore (Konrad 1981:140).

2. Archaeological Investigations

The first overview of the Bead Hill site was undertaken between 1986 and 1989 as part of an archaeological masterplan of the lower Rouge River Valley (Mayer, Pihl, Poulton [MPP] 1988). It determined that a systemic lack of knowledge and understanding of previous and related discoveries had long been an issue for a fuller appreciation of this site. In researching the matter, the author correlated it with the discovery in the 1840s of a large historic First Nations cemetery on a slope of the lower Rouge River Valley (MPP 1988: I:116–117). This cemetery was described by William Brown (1849:79–80). He concluded that "as among the relics dug up there were some gun barrels, it must have been used since the settlement of the French in Canada; and I was informed that the gun barrels found were the manufacture of that nation."

The site first entered the literature by name in the centennial history of Scarborough Township by David Boyle (1896). He states, "At the place known as Bead Hill, specimens connected with the Mississaugas have been unearthed, consisting of Queen Anne gun barrels with copper sights, hunting knives, copper kettles and other articles of European manufacture" (1896:24). Boyle knew of Brown's cemetery but did not connect it with Bead Hill.

Crucial information was recorded twenty years after Boyle, by the noted avocational archaeologist A. J. Clark (1916). His brief fieldnote entry states, "Visited Bead Hill. [...] Many relics found there (including great number of beads—hence the name) during life of elder [stating the surname of the current owner] but not much of late years." Clark was somehow aware of Boyle's Bead Hill (how is not known) but not of Brown's cemetery.

In 1944, some children digging an underground fort on the east slope of Bead Hill discovered the skeletal remains of a subadult, an adult male, and an adult female with grave goods (Bathurst 2008; Cooper 2007). The Ontario Provincial Police (OPP), who investigated this discovery, treated it as an isolated occurrence.

In 1964, the OPP responded to the discovery of a burial in a shallow grave at the opposite end of the village. It was excavated by Walter Kenyon of the Royal Ontario Museum (ROM) and proved to be a single flexed interment of an adult female with grave goods. In 1973, the burial was registered by Victor Konrad and Bill Ross during the North Pickering survey; it was identified as historic Haudenosaunee burial, possibly Seneca (AkGs-5 site record form). Konrad and Ross were not aware of any previous discoveries at the site and did not investigate the surrounding area. Finally, in April 1985, the author rediscovered the Bead Hill site using Clark's 1916 fieldnote data.

Limited fieldwork was carried out at the site by MPP in 1987. Conditions permitted controlled surface collections at the western end of the site; the remainder of the site, in secondary-growth forest, was partially assessed by shovel test pitting (MPP 1988). Another surface collection at the western end of the village, together with test excavations in three sequentially numbered trenches, followed in 1991, undertaken by Mayer, Poulton and Associates (MPA) under contract to Parks Canada (MPA 1991) (Figure 5.3). The assessment was conducted in consultation with the Elected Council of Six Nations of the Grand River and with Seneca officials from Ganondagan State Historic Site in western New York State. The fieldwork included the manual excavation of 108 one-metre test squares; this represents less than 0.5 percent of the surface area of the village. In an attempt to recover embroidery seed beads, lead shot, and other small but useful artifacts for dating purposes, all the matrix from the test units was screened through 1/8" (3.2 mm) mesh.

3. Site Description

Bead Hill is on a point of land that is flanked by slopes on three sides. Excluding the burials on its eastern and western sides and one known hillside midden, the village has a length of about 220 m, a width that varies from 50 to 120 m, and a surface area of 1.65 ha. This site and Teiaiagon occupy similar locations, with strong natural defences, and both are examples of the larger defended Haudenosaunee villages the Dutch and English termed "castles." In addition, each commanded a nexus of important east-west and north-south communication routes, the latter being the Humber trail for Teiaiagon and the Rouge trail for this site. The entire habitable portion of the Bead Hill village was plowed by horse until 1943, then by tractor for another dozen years, until all cultivation ceased in 1955. The hillside deposits are largely disturbed. In consequence, Bead Hill is much better preserved than the site of Teiaiagon, and the archaeology of this former site may help inform that of the latter.

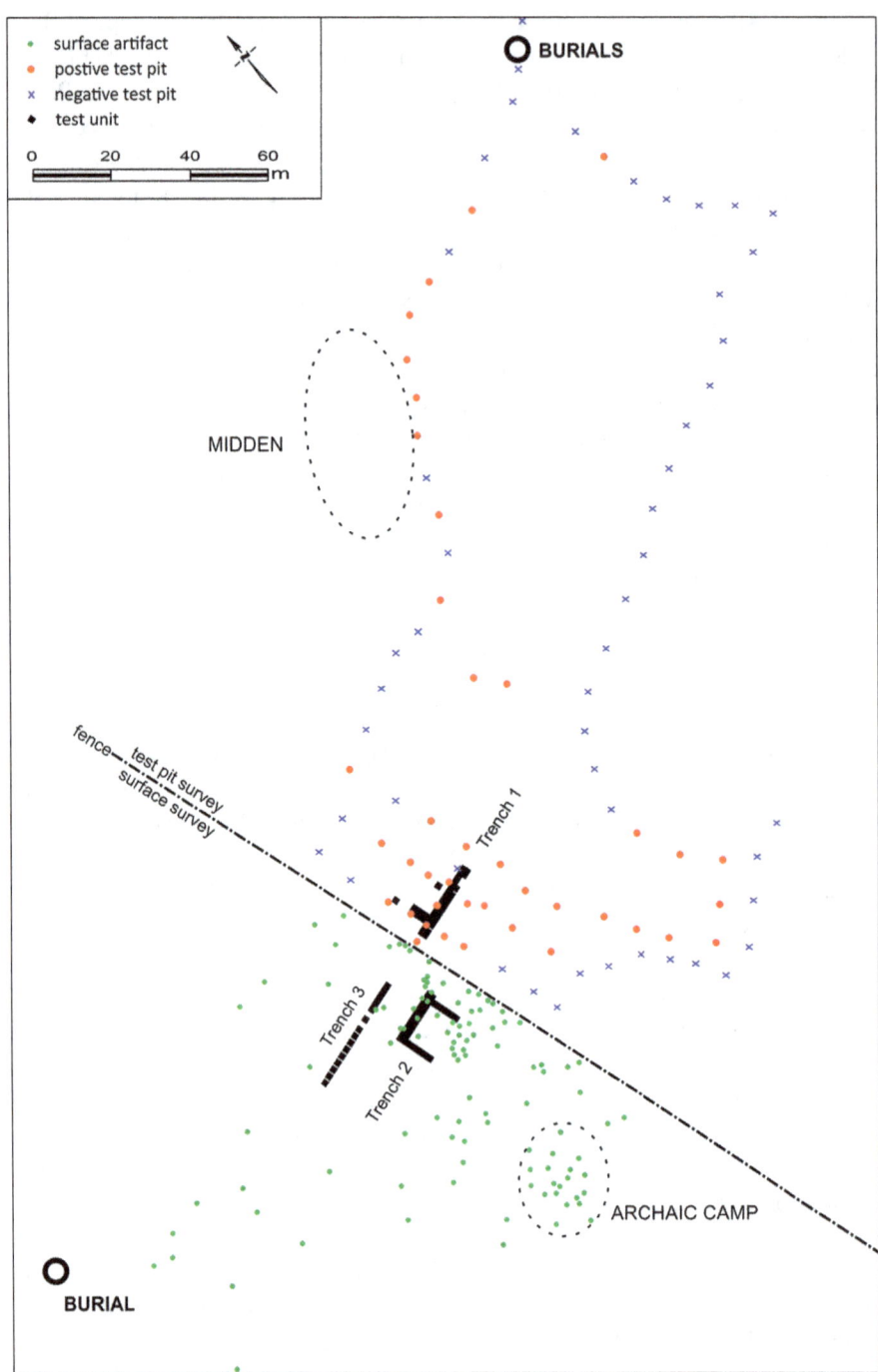

Figure 5.3. Bead Hill site plan showing 1987 and 1991 archaeological investigations.
Source: Plan by Dana Poulton.

Two springs would have provided the villagers with ready sources of potable water, as would the nearby Rouge River. Investigations have identified one large hillside midden. The single burial found in 1964 was just west of the village, and the 1840s and 1944 burials were at the eastern end. This pattern of cemeteries around the edges matches that of other late seventeenth-century Seneca settlements.

The test excavations recorded 133 post moulds, 7 pits, and 1 hearth, almost all of which were concentrated in Trench 1 (Figure 5.4); they were mapped but not excavated, as the site was not threatened. The settlement patterns suggest the presence of one or two longhouses in this area. Of note is a linear stain that was 3 m from the hearth; it is inferred to be an example of the linear end features that define the storage cubicles at the ends of many historic Neutral longhouses (MPA 1991:18). This stain suggests that the construction of this house involved one or more Seneca inhabitants of Bead Hill who had been Neutral prior to the conflicts of 1647–1651, and it has been described by Jordan (2018b:18) as the "best example of atypical Haudenosaunee architectural practices." This is but one expression of cultural identity by the occupants of the village. In fact, every tribe of this region practised the coercive adoption of its enemies in endemic warfare, and for the Seneca, the consequence was that, by the mid-seventeenth century, they had become "biologically, linguistically, and culturally diverse" (Hamell and John 1987:1). The same must have been true for Ganatsekwyagon.

4. Material Culture Remains

There was a clear concentration of artifacts in the plow zone in Trench 1, in association with most of the post moulds and features (Figure 5.5). The artifact frequencies and distributions fell off rapidly to the west (compare Figure 5.4

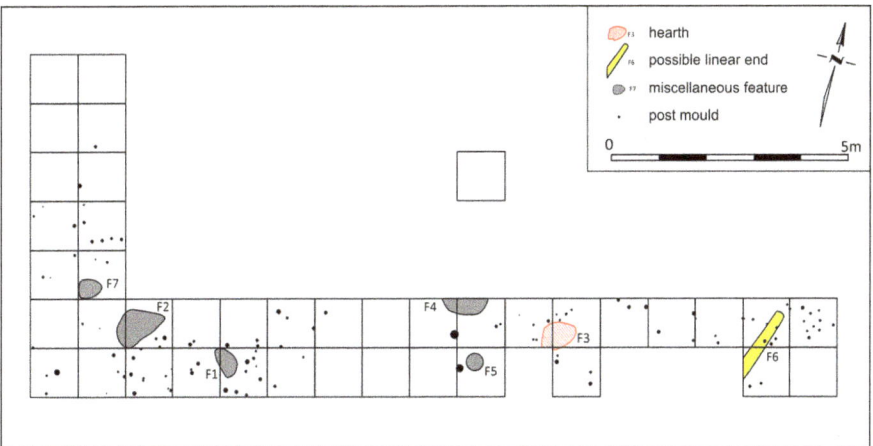

Figure 5.4. Bead Hill site, Trench 1 plan showing settlement patterns.
Source: Plan by Dana Poulton.

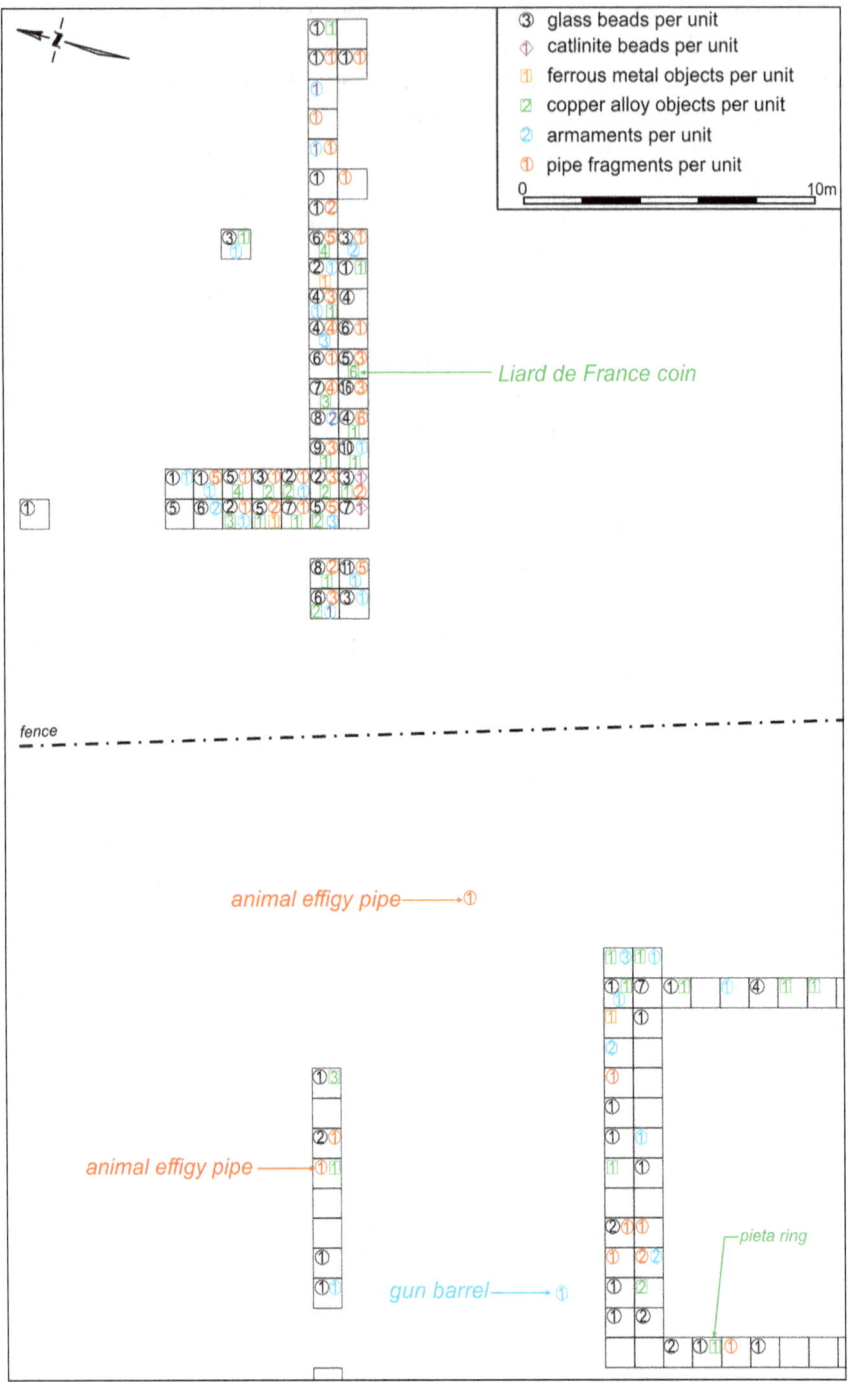

Figure 5.5. Bead Hill site, distribution of selected artifacts in the 1991 investigations sample.
Source: Plan by Dana Poulton.

and Figure 5.5), suggesting that Trench 2 straddled the maximum western edge of the village.

The extant collections total 3,938 artifacts, of which 78 percent are from the 1991 test excavations and much smaller but roughly equal amounts are from the burials, each of which had a concentration of diagnostics (Table 5.1). The combined sample is dominated by flaked lithics (72 percent), followed by European trade goods (18 percent), worked marine shell (5 percent), and ceramics (4 percent). The absence of ground stone celts and the virtual absence of ceramic vessels reflect the changes in Haudenosaunee material culture that followed the widespread adoption of European-made analogues (Wray 1973:9, 12, 22–23, 29–30) (see also chapters by Jordan, Cooper, and Engelbrecht and Williamson, this volume).

As for flaked stone, debitage forms 70 percent of the Bead Hill sample. This may seem anomalous for a site of the 1670s and 1680s, as the production of flaked stone tools declined greatly in the latter half of the seventeenth century. By the 1670s, traditional flaked stone tools were largely confined to triangular arrowheads, then those that were willow-leaf-shaped (Wray 1973:9, 29). The comparative data, however, show that flaked lithics are present in some quantity on Haudenosaunee sites that were contemporary with Bead Hill, including the Seneca Ganondagan site (1670–1687) and the Mohawk Jackson-Everson site (1660–1680), and are well represented on the next generation of Seneca sites, as indicated by White Springs and Townley-Read (1688–1715) (Krohn 2010). What changed over time was that far fewer types of formal flaked lithic tools were being made, and most of those that were made were gunflints and expedient tools such as spokeshaves and utilized flakes (Krohn 2010:1–2, 13–15; Dean 1984:31–33; Cushman 1986:27). This resulted in quantities of debitage but with few tools. In summary, the comparative data, added to the fact that the soils on the Bead Hill site screen well and they were screened through 3 mm mesh, explain the high frequency of debitage recovered from the site, and the lack of formal Seneca flaked stone diagnostics other than gunflints. As a final consideration, it is possible some proportion of the flaked stone in the Bead Hill sample may relate to the pre-contact components although the distributions do not tend to substantiate that hypothesis.[1]

---

1. The undiagnostic flaked stone frequencies in association with Seneca diagnostics in the Trench 1 house area average forty-four pieces per one-metre unit compared to nine and seven pieces per one-metre unit in Trenches 2 and 3, respectively. The Trench 1 lithics include a Late Archaic Perkiomen Broad Point type (Ritchie 1961), ca. 3650–3550 BP (Ellis et al. 1990:101), which pertains to the Broad Point Archaic (ibid.: 99–105), and two points of the Terminal Archaic Hind type, ca. 3000–2800 BP (ibid.: 115), which pertain to the Glacial Kame Complex. These bifaces may represent curios, a behaviour that has been documented elsewhere for the historic Seneca (Wray 1973:9; Ritchie 1965:Plate 112). In addition,

Table 5.1. Artifact samples from the Bead Hill site

Artifact Class and Category		Sample by Year of Investigation					Total	%
		1944	1964	1985–1988	1991	2009		
Worked Marine Shells	columella			1			1	0.03
	wampum beads	14	162				176	4.47
	tubular shell beads	16	10				26	0.66
	Subtotal – Marine Shell	**30**	**172**	**1**			**203**	**5.15**
European Trade Goods	glass trade beads	349	53	9	216		627	15.92
	metals		2	3	61		66	1.68
	lithics	European gunflint			2	5		7	0.18
		European gunflint flakes				19		19	0.48
	Subtotal – European Trade Goods	**349**	**55**	**14**	**301**		**719**	**18.26**
Ceramics	partially reconstructed pottery vessel		1				1	0.03
	juvenile sherd				1		1	0.03
	fragmentary sherds			5	5		10	0.25
	pipe fragment			11	86		97	2.46
	lump of clay			1	51		52	1.32
	miscellaneous				1		1	0.03
	Subtotal - Ceramics		**1**	**17**	**144**		**162**	**4.11**

Bead Hill had periodic occupations during the Archaic period, between ca. 2500 and 1000 BC. Those components are mostly centred around a knoll southwest of the village, but the Trench 2 excavations recovered single projectile points of the Middle and Late Archaic Brewerton Corner-Notched and Genesee types in the plow zone above and beside a large pre-Iroquoian subsoil feature (MPP 1991:5–6, Figure 10).

Artifact Class and Category		1944	1964	1985–1988	1991	2009	Total	%
Flaked Lithics	native gunflint			2	3		5	0.13
	native gunflint flake				3		3	0.08
	projectile point			9	7	1	17	0.43
	biface			8	13		21	0.53
	drill				2		2	0.05
	scraper			2	4		6	0.15
	utilized flake			6	26		32	0.81
	bipolar wedge				1		1	0.03
	core			1	2		3	0.08
	chipping detritus			164	2552	43	2759	70.06
	Subtotal – Native Chipped Lithics			**192**	**2613**	**44**	**2849**	**72.35**
Ground Stone	catlinite bead				2		2	0.05
	Subtotal – Ground Stone				**2**		**2**	**0.05**
Rough Stone	hammerstone				1		1	0.03
	Subtotal – Rough Stone				**1**		**1**	**0.03**
Other	effigy antler comb		1				1	0.03
	leather pouch		1				1	0.03
	Subtotal – Other		**2**				**2**	**0.05**
	Total	379	230	224	3061	44	3938	100.00
	%	9.62	5.84	5.69	77.73	1.12	100.00	
Other	fire-cracked rock			p	p		p	
	floral remains				p		p	
	carbonized plant remains				p		p	
	charcoal			p	p		p	
	faunal remains			155	11631		11786	

p = present but not enumerated in percentages column and in some totals. The samples only include a few pieces of fire-cracked rock. The 2009 sample derived from the assessment of a proposed fence replacement.
Source: Dana Poulton.

The trade goods are dominated by 627 glass beads, 66 pieces of metal, and 29 gunflints and flakes of European flint. Other classes and categories in the sample are limited to a single effigy antler comb, two stone beads, one hammerstone, and a leather pouch that was preserved by copper salts.

The glass trade bead samples from the 1991 test excavations and the two burials are quite consistent with each other, with high representations of the major drawn varieties of the 1670–1687 era in each (Table 5.2; see also Fox et al., this volume). Further, Karlis Karklins (1992), who compared the 1991 sample with the samples from the Mohawk, Oneida, and Seneca sequences, noted close similarities between Bead Hill and sites dating between 1677 and 1693. He concluded that the mean date for all of them is a uniform 1680–1681. In addition, he suggested a "juncture date" of 1682 for what he termed the "red-black-bead" period, which is what is represented here. Finally, he described the resemblance between the beads from Bead Hill and those from Boughton Hill and Rochester Junction as "striking."

Table 5.2. Glass trade beads from the Bead Hill site

Beads		Sample by Year of Investigation*				Total	%
Type	Description	1944	1964	1985–1988	1991		
IIa1	round opaque red		36	6	71	113	18.0
IIa2	doughnut opaque red				8	8	1.3
IIa1, IIa2 & IIa3	lumped sample – round red oval and seed beads	344				344	54.9
IIa6	round opaque black			2	71	73	11.6
IIa7	doughnut opaque black				12	12	1.9
IIa8	oval opaque black	1			10	11	1.8
IIa13	round opaque white				1	1	0.2
IIa14	doughnut opaque white				1	1	0.2
IIa15	oval opaque white				2	2	0.3
IIa24	red opaque apple green				5	5	0.8
IIa34	doughnut translucent light aqua blue				1	1	0.2
IIa35	round opaque light aqua blue			1		1	0.2
IIa37	doughnut opaque aqua blue				8	8	1.3
IIa40	round opaque robin's egg blue				3	3	0.5
IIb'3 variant	oval opaque black with 4 white stripes				1	1	0.2
IIIa3	tubular opaque red with clear apple green core				1	1	0.2
IVa1	round red with black core	4				4	0.6

Beads		Sample by Year of Investigation*				Total	%
Type	Description	1944	1964	1985–1988	1991		
IVa5	round opaque red with clear apple green core		11		3	14	2.2
IVa6	doughnut opaque red with clear apple green core		1		18	19	3.0
IVa7	oval opaque red with clear apple green core		5			5	0.8
Total		349	53	9	216	627	100.0
%		55.7	8.5	1.4	34.4		

*Kidd and Kidd 1970 types. The fifty-three beads in the 1964 burial sample were analyzed by Ian Kenyon (6 December 1990 letter to Dana Poulton). The analysis of the 1944 burial sample by Cooper (n.d.) identifies specific frequencies for two types and a lumped frequency for three others. See also Fox et al., this volume.
Source: Dana Poulton.

Several other artifact traits at Bead Hill have date ranges that encompass the time span 1670–1680 (but cannot be narrowed down to that specific decade) and that are replicated at contemporary Seneca sites in western New York State. Examples include the armaments, the effigy clay pipes, the serrated catlinite bead, the octagonal gun barrel, and the antler effigy comb. The latter is the most remarkable of these artifacts (Williamson and von Bitter, this volume: Figure 10.10); it shares several elements with an effigy of a Seneca hunter with his musket and dog on an antler comb from Boughton Hill (Hamell 2012).

The sample includes only a few earlier Seneca traits. Of the sixteen key drawn-glass trade bead types and three wound bead types of the period of the Marsh and Dann sites (1650/55 to 1670/75), the only one present is a single drawn bead of the IIIa3 type; it is the only tubular bead from Bead Hill. Other early traits are two brass omega kettle lugs and a 1655 Liard de France (a copper coin) (see Cooper, this volume). Finally, the paucity of ceramic vessels supports a later date for the sample, as they were scarce by 1675 (Wray 1973:27) and had disappeared by 1700 (Hayes 1980:89; see Engelbrecht and Williamson, this volume). Fragments of a ceramic vessel that has now been partially reconstructed (Figure 5.6) were found with the 1964 burial. It has a plain lower body with short, possibly rocker dentate-stamped lines on the upper body and neck; the rim is missing. As this vessel clearly dates to the Middle Woodland period, it is likely material that was in the back dirt from the initial disturbance to the burial by machine and was subsequently collected and included with the otherwise IDN-period grave goods.

Figure 5.6. Partially reconstructed Middle Woodland ceramic vessel.
Source: Photograph by Ian Kenyon.

As a cautionary note, any consideration of the Bead Hill artifact samples must begin with the recognition that they undoubtedly reflect sample bias, a consequence of the limited extent of the excavations. That is the simplest explanation for the absence of such artifacts as iron trade axes and triangular projectile points of brass and chert. As for possible sample bias resulting from the unauthorized use of investigations using metal detectors, while it cannot be discounted, there is no evidence for it at Bead Hill.

Bead Hill has the only appreciable sample of faunal remains from an IDN site. The 11,786 specimens represent 75 percent of all the finds recovered. Mammal remains account for 99.9 percent of the large 1991 sample, but the species identification rate is only 0.27 percent; this is because most of the remains consist of burned and calcined fragments (Rick 1992). Including both calcined and uncalcined remains but excluding smaller rodents, the minimum numbers of individuals of native taxa are as follows: white-tailed deer (3); black bear (2); rabbit/hare (2); muskrat and carnivore (1 each); porcupine and beaver/porcupine (2 and 3, respectively); duck (1); marsh or pond turtle (1); whitefish/cisco (1); perching bird (1); and unidentified bird (3). Of the above, the mammals represented by uncalcined bone alone are carnivore, rabbit/hare, porcupine, and beaver/porcupine. Because sampling of the hillside midden was not one of the stated objectives of the 1991 test excavations, no resources were available to sample for faunal remains from this area. The excavators were able to observe, however, that the most obvious aspect of the hillside midden (Figure 5.3) is that its surface was littered with faunal remains, most of which were small, calcined fragments.

The Bead Hill faunal sample can be compared with those from two other historic Seneca sites, both of which are also dominated by fragmented calcined remains. Bead Hill is the earliest of the three sites that help fill a previous gap for historic Seneca faunal studies between the early seventeenth century and the post-1790 reservation era (Watson and Thomas 2013:82). The second is the White Springs site, the eastern capital town (ca. 1688–1715) (Jordan 2018a:181; see also Jordan, this volume), the analysis of the latest sample from which is currently in progress. The third is the Townley-Read site, a dispersed Seneca settlement (ca. 1715–1754). Adam Watson and Stephen Cox Thomas (2013:81, 114–115) determined that the subsistence strategies represented in the Townley-Read faunal remains parallel earlier Mohawk practices, and that they are evidence of the standard practice of marrow extraction and bone grease production as an integral part in meeting the community's yearly dietary needs, rather than as a response to times of nutritional stress. These observations also apply to the White Springs site (Kurt Jordan, personal communication 2020 to William Engelbrecht and Ron Williamson), and the sample from Bead Hill is but a slightly earlier expression of the same subsistence strategy. Further, it is a strategy that may only have been made possible, or at least more efficient, by the use of trade metal kettles.

As detailed by Gary Warrick and Ron Williamson (this volume), the prevalence of highly fragmented burned faunal remains that is evident at Bead Hill is also characteristic of eighteenth- and nineteenth-century Anishinaabe archaeological sites in Ontario. As Warrick and Williamson note, artifact frequencies on Anishinaabe camp sites are low outside of midden deposits, and the sites themselves can be difficult to discover by a standard 5 m interval shovel test pit survey, even when using 1/8" (3 mm) mesh, as the most characteristic diagnostics are quite small (glass embroidery seed beads and lead shot). These considerations suggest the possibility that some or all the faunal remains recovered from Bead Hill may relate to the subsequent Mississauga occupation of the site. It is more than likely that some proportion of the faunal remains from Bead Hill do indeed relate to that later component, especially those recovered to the east of the 1991 test excavations, notably those from the surface of the hillside midden. On the other hand, most, if not all, of the faunal remains recovered by the 1991 excavations that were in direct association with typical Seneca diagnostics of this period likely relate to the earlier and presumably much more populous occupation. Certainly, the Seneca villagers of this site were eating other than vegetable matter.

It should also be noted that the Bead Hill faunal remains do not provide any conclusive evidence of the fur trade, even though it was arguably the raison d'être for the village. As Konrad (1981:137) explains, the north shore settlements acted as bases for extensive winter hunting at some distance, as far as two hundred leagues to the north and west. The lack of evidence for large-scale primary processing of animals is likely because the remains of beaver that the Haudenosaunee and northern Algonquians brought down the trail had already been readied for the European market, having been processed into pelts before transport.

5. Discussion

At the very least, the glass trade beads and other artifacts recovered from the Bead Hill site demonstrate that the village was largely contemporary with the other Seneca settlements identified at the beginning of this chapter. However, because of the inescapable issue of sample bias at this site, it is possible the village was established as early as the mid-1660s. If there is proof of that, it lies in the 99.5 percent of the site that has not been excavated.

As points of land with strong natural defences that were occupied by the historic Seneca, the settings of the two frontier "castles" at Bead Hill and Teiaiagon are virtually identical. Teiaiagon had a palisade, and it is inconceivable that the Bead Hill village, as a fellow Seneca village of equivalent importance, was also not palisaded.[2] In fact, defence was paramount for the Seneca villages

---

2. A. F. Hunter observed the remnants of the palisade at Teiaiagon when he visited Baby Point on May 24, 1889 (Hunter n.d., notebook on file, ROM, "Village Site

on the lower Humber and Rouge Rivers, as in the event of an imminent attack by an enemy, they could only look to each other for mutual support. In the case of the Bead Hill site, it is safe to assume the palisade awaits discovery in the 99.5 percent of the site that has not been tested, and that a few test trenches at right angles to the south, east and/or north edges of the point would confirm that in short order.

Bead Hill and other IDN villages are all examples of Haudenosaunee "extraterritorial settlements" (Jordan 2018b:30; see also Jordan, this volume). In terms of size and function, the best comparison for this site is the aforementioned Kirkwood site (Keinte-he), which was the satellite village of Tiotohatton (Jordan 2018a:178). It is reportedly 1.0 ha in size (Vandrei 1987:Table 1). In 1677, Wentworth Greenhalgh observed that Kirkwood had "about 24 longhouses" (O'Callaghan 1849–1851:3:252). Applying this information to the 1.65 ha Bead Hill site, the numbers indicate it was about half again as large as Kirkwood and may have had forty longhouses, with a population of perhaps 825 individuals. These calculations assume that both sites had similar residential densities; they also assume a site density of about five hundred people per hectare of residential space for nucleated Haudenosaunee villages (Jordan 2018a:176).

The larger relative size of the Bead Hill village is inferred to be a reflection of its importance to the Seneca as a frontier settlement, as the entire Seneca population in 1670–1690 has been estimated at only four thousand (Snow 1996:Table 7.1), including (as of 1677) an estimated one thousand warriors (O'Callaghan 1849–1851:3:252). Further, in 1687, Jacques-René Brisay de Denonville stated of the north-shore Haudenosaunee villages that they included "some fine and large (towns)" (Konrad 1981:140). Because the contemporary documents describe most of these villages as being small (Konrad 1981:138), it is suggested here that Denonville's comment likely only applied to Ganatsekwyagon and Teiaiagon.

The trail from the lower Rouge around the western end of Lake Ontario to the Seneca homeland was about 320 km long. Unlike Kirkwood and the other satellites of the two Seneca capitals, the IDN villages all had to be fully autonomous. But there is an additional reason why Bead Hill was larger than

#7" of York County.); it is one of three documentary accounts from the 1880s of the ruins of palisaded village sites in southern Ontario. The second site, which was near the mouth of the Rouge River (C. B. Robinson 1885), is discussed elsewhere in this chapter. The third is the historic Neutral McDonald (Mount) village (AiHa-9) in what is now the rural part of the city of Hamilton. When David Boyle (1888:11) visited that site on May 20, 1887, the landowner, who was the first-generation pioneer on the property, informed him that he had observed the palisade when he had broken up the land *upwards of 40 years ago* (i.e., about 1847). The glass trade beads from the McDonald site date to GBP 2 and 3 (Fitzgerald 1990:287), indicating an occupation in the second quarter of the seventeenth century.

Kirkwood. It is that the lower Rouge controlled one of two key choke points in the fur trade that was vital to Seneca interests. Simply put, whatever major settlement there was on this valley in the 1670s and 1680s, it had a wider strategic function than did the two small Seneca satellite villages of this time.

6. Historical Identity

As Ganatsekwyagon is the only village the French documented on or in the immediate vicinity of the Rouge River between the 1660s and the 1680s, the inference is that only one Seneca village population was ever resident here. This suggests two possibilities for Bead Hill. The first is that it is the one and only village of Ganatsekwyagon. The second is that at some point in time the villagers moved. If that were the case, the current artifact sample would suggest Bead Hill was the second Ganatsekwyagon.

Since the 1880s, numerous locations have been suggested for this historically documented village, but only four have received serious consideration. One is on Frenchman's Bay, 4 km east of the mouth of the Rouge River. The other three are on the lower Rouge River; they are Bead Hill and the Rouge River I and II sites (Mohr 1988; MPP 1988:III). One source that researchers have cited in this regard is an 1885 history (C. B. Robinson 1885:I:107). It records "a considerable Indian village [...] near the mouth of the River Rouge" that was surrounded by "the remains of the logs that formed a wooden palisade," with glass beads and "implements" of copper and iron, and "a few yards [away] a number of graves..." It is difficult to conceive that this is anything other than a description of what remained of the Seneca village of Ganatsekwyagon.

Based on multiple lines of evidence, in 1972, Konrad (1973:127) registered a location on Frenchman's Bay as Ganatsekwyagon (AkGs-2 site record form). At the same time, he registered the Rouge River I and II sites, considering them to be smaller Seneca villages, and citing as evidence for them the 1885 account (AkGs-3 and AkGs-34 site record forms). However, Frenchman's Bay can be discounted, and the evidence for Rouge River I and II is problematic.[3] This leaves Bead Hill to be considered.

---

3. As authorities for the Frenchman's Bay location, Konrad cited the Reverend William Wood (1911), the ROM (see Mohr 1998:25), the 1688 Raffeix map, and a 1682 map by Abbé Claude Bernou. His inference followed several generations of historians who had placed Ganatsekwyagon there (e.g., Hunter 1882:621; McKay 1961:205; Pritchard 1973a:138). However, there has never been a report of archaeological discoveries of any kind at Frenchman's Bay, nor is there any documentation of a site there at the ROM (April Hawkins, personal communication 2019). As for Rouge River I and II, both have suffered past impacts (MPP 1988:III:103–106, 107–108): the former by construction, by grading to a depth of 6 m, and by erosion, and the latter by the construction of a residential subdivision.

The author has identified this site as the best candidate for Ganatsekwyagon and has correlated it with the 1885 account of the palisaded village (MPA 1991:40, 41–43, Table 10; MPP 1988:I:136–137). Further, in a detailed assessment of the Rouge trail, Archaeological Services Inc. (ASI 2009:18, 25) concurs with both correlations. For his part, Mohr (1998:35) considers that Ganatsekwyagon was located elsewhere on the lower Rouge, specifically identifying it as the Rouge River I site (Tom Mohr, personal communication 2020). His only caveat is that if there were two sequential Seneca villages, the final occupation was at Bead Hill (1998:31, 35).

6.1. Abandonment

Contemporary sources identified several reasons for the abandonment and relocation of Iroquoian villages, a common one being the depletion of soil fertility and firewood (Engelbrecht 2003:101–107; Heidenreich 1971:213; Jordan 2018a:175). At most, the Seneca occupation of the lower Rouge spanned some twenty-two years. This raises the question whether Bead Hill, a village of fewer than one thousand people living in such an environmentally rich area, would have been compelled to relocate for environmental reasons within that time frame.

Another cause cited for Wendat village abandonment, and one that was especially true of frontier villages, was the threat of enemy attack, the response to which was to withdraw to a tribal stronghold (Heidenreich 1971:133–134, 215). This was the reality the Seneca and other Haudenosaunee of the north shore faced in mid-1687. Between June 20 and July 3, the French, based at Fort Cataraqui, had seized 201 Cayuga, Oneida, and other Haudenosaunee; they included "forty of the principal chiefs of all the Iroquois villages" (Preston and Lamontagne 1958:47–48). Then, on July 4, Denonville's army set out from Cataraqui on its campaign to crush the Seneca in their homeland in western New York State.

The French plan for the scorched earth campaign was succinct: "All their corn plantations will be destroyed, their villages burned, their women, children and old men captured, and their warriors driven into the woods where they will be pursued and annihilated by the other Indians" (Preston and Lamontagne 1958:47). The French and their northern and western Native allies numbered some three thousand; they outnumbered the Seneca warriors by almost four to one. As executed in the thirteen days from July 12 to 23 (O'Callaghan 1849–1851:9:369), the campaign was extremely destructive, but it failed in its main objective: to eliminate the Seneca once and for all time as a threat to New France. Afterwards, one of the western Native allies stated disparagingly of the

---

Finally, there are no extant artifact collections from Rouge River II, and those from the multi-component Rouge River I site lack any Seneca diagnostics.

French that "they were good for nothing but to make war on hogs and corn" (Parkman 1905:162).

The IDN response to these hostilities was to abandon their villages (Konrad 1981:140–141), and the French accounts by those returning from the campaign after leaving Fort Denonville almost literally only mention them in passing. On August 2, Denonville sent his militia and the northern native allies from Niagara on foot around the west end of Lake Ontario, and the next day he followed by *batteau*. On August 5, he rendezvoused with them, making landfall at Ganatsekwyagon; there, he found "the Indian allies were clearly in control" (Konrad 1981:140).[4] All Denonville states of this day is that "we [...] arrived at the place [...] to which I had sent forward our Christian Indians from below. We found them with two hundred deer they had killed, a good share of which they gave to our army, that thus profited by this fortunate chase" (O'Callaghan 1855:9:369; Robinson 1933:56).[5]

On August 25, Denonville wrote a letter to Colbert from Ville Marie describing the campaign (Preston and Lamontagne 1958:163). In it, he stated that the Haudenosaunee of the south shore were compelling the north-shore villagers to rejoin them and that the latter's villages were being abandoned, adding, "Our interest would be to repeople these villages because they would be better allies and more under our control." If Denonville's plan was to repopulate them with reliable Algonquian allies and trading partners, that is exactly what came to pass (Konrad 1981:141; see also Warrick and Williamson, this volume).

For the lower Rouge River, there is historical documentation for an early Mississauga reoccupation of Ganatsekwyagon; I consider it to be the first of what was a succession of Anishinaabe village occupations along the lower Rouge. On June 30, 1700, a Five Nations delegation in Albany reported that by the winter of that year one group of the Dowaganhaes (Ottawa) had chosen to "desert their habitations and come to settle upon Ye Lake of Cadarackgui [...] at a place called Kanatiochtiage [Ganatsekwyagon]" (O'Callaghan 1854:4:694). The same passage adds of the Dowaganhaes that they "have sent five of their people to Onondaga to treat being sent from three nations who are very strong, having sixteen castles." The subject of this passage was a peace treaty between the Algonquins and the Haudenosaunee; it was a precursor to the following year's Great Peace of Montréal (Havard 2001). As noted by

---

4. In the publication of Denonville's expedition against the Seneca, O'Callaghan (ibid.) erroneously identifies "5th July" as the date of his rendezvous with the militia on the north shore.
5. This quantity of game for a victory feast implies the use of deer drives; it also attests to the abundance of game in the area, even after a lengthy and sizeable Seneca occupation.

Robinson (1933:59), the June 1700 account is the first documentary proof of the reappearance of Algonquians on Lake Ontario since Champlain's time, with Ganatsekwyagon being one of the "sixteen castles." It is also the first contemporary documentation of an Algonquian reoccupation of a specific abandoned Iroquois du Nord village.

As described previously, the artifacts from Bead Hill that were described by Boyle (1896:24) included Queen Anne guns with "copper sights." Opinions may differ on Boyle's 1896 identification of these gun barrels, but I accept it at face value.[6] I also consider that the muskets Boyle describes were almost certainly Mississauga grave goods, and that they were most likely found in the east cemetery. Based on the Seneca burial(s) that was found there in 1944 and on Brown's description of the extensive graves and his mention of guns of French manufacture from that cemetery, it was probably the main Seneca burial ground for the Seneca village. Further, if the above inferences are correct, this cemetery was also used by the subsequent Mississauga occupants of the site. Apart from the many practical benefits Bead Hill had to offer, including the close proximity of extensive bottomlands of the kind on which the historic Anishinaabeg are known to have planted their corn, this component of the site also represented a symbolic re-occupation of one of their historic enemy's key strongholds. The same applied to Teiaiagon following its abandonment by the Seneca, and it seems likely that other of the former IDN settlements were also among the "sixteen castles" the Algonquians established following the desertion of the north shore by the IDN.

Two aspects of this village abandonment and reoccupation are not known. One is their individual timings. The other is what state the Iroquois du Nord villages were in by the time they were reoccupied. The French records of Denonville's campaign are silent on what condition his forces found Ganatsekwyagon in when they reached it on or about August 4, and on what condition they left it in, but the recent events in the campaign against the Seneca indicate two possibilities. Faced with the impending invasion by an overwhelming enemy force, the main response by the Seneca had been to set fire to most of their own settlements upon abandoning them, then flee southeast to seek

---

6. Boyle's identification of the material of the gunsights is probably incorrect; they were almost certainly of brass, and there are Queen Anne British Land Pattern flintlock muskets with rounded brass blade sights (Queen Anne British Land Pattern Flintlock Musket and Plug Bayonet | Rock Island Auction). As Queen Anne reigned from 1702 to 1714, any firearms produced during her reign that are found in an archaeological context could date to any time within that thirteen-year period or later. The peace negotiations between the Algonquians and the Haudenosaunee in 1700 and the Great Peace of Montréal in 1701 explains why early English trade goods may be expected on the Algonquian re-occupation of Ganatsekwyagon, and why early eighteenth-century British trade guns could be present at Bead Hill.

refuge among the Cayuga. Upon their arrival, Denonville's forces then torched whatever remained, before withdrawing. This suggests the likelihood that Ganatsekwyagon was burned by the Seneca as they abandoned it, or by their enemies soon afterward. An alternative possibility, which is suggested by Denonville's statement to Colbert, is that he had directed that the village be spared so that it could be re-occupied by his loyal Algonquian allies, and that it may have survived intact.

Leaving aside the historical identity of the Seneca village on Bead Hill, the above possibilities apply to its fate, but as with so many other unanswered questions, this issue cannot be addressed, as almost nothing of this site has been excavated. What can be said is that it is entirely plausible Denonville's forces looted the Seneca cemetery or cemeteries at this village, just as archaeology demonstrates they had done only weeks before to multiple current and abandoned Seneca cemeteries (Wray 1973:27–28; 1983:45).

7. Conclusion

For three centuries following its abandonment by the Seneca, the Bead Hill site survived by a combination of happenstance and benign neglect; due to wise planning and public land acquisition, the entire site is now preserved. The record of accidental discoveries prior to the mid-twentieth century and the limited fieldwork that followed provide a groundwork for a better understanding of the Seneca occupation of this village and the lower Rouge. Despite that, many questions remain about Bead Hill. Limiting the discussion to the Seneca component, we have no idea of the number, density, or orientation of the longhouses at this site or how the settlement evolved over time, or whether it encompassed non-residential areas. We also do not know the extent of the eastern cemetery. Nor do we know the presence, location, and extent of other as-yet undiscovered middens and cemeteries. Finally, even if we accept that Bead Hill was the Ganatsekwyagon the Seneca abandoned upon leaving the lower Rouge, we still do not know when it was first settled, or if it does indeed contain the 1669–1670 Sulpician mission and residence of Fénelon.

Many and perhaps most of these questions could be answered through a judicious combination of archaeogeophysical survey and archaeological test excavations, always provided that whatever was to be undertaken abided by Parks Canada's overriding mandate to preserve and protect this nationally significant historic site.

Acknowledgements

First, I would like to acknowledge the governments of Canada and Ontario and the City of Scarborough for funding the 1986–1989 and 1991 investigations, and I extend my gratitude to the City of Toronto and the federal and provincial governments for the public acquisition of the site in the 1950s and

1990s and to Save the Rouge for its advocacy in its successful efforts to live up to its name. Second, I would like to thank Barbara Leskovec, Jenneth Curtis, Bill Ross, Sheryl Smith, and Lisa Buchanan of Parks Canada for the different roles they have played in the site. Finally, I appreciate the many insights my colleagues have shared on matters relating to Bead Hill: Nick Adams, Martin Cooper, Neal Ferris, William Fox, Nick Gromoff, George Hamell, David Harris, April Hawkins, Kurt Jordan, Karlis Karklins, Ian Kenyon, Victor Konrad, Chris Menary, Tom Mohr, David Robertson, Robert von Bitter, and Ron Williamson.

6

TEIAIAGON
A Village on the West Branch of the Toronto Carrying Place

DAVID ROBERTSON

The settlement of Teiaiagon, located on the Humber River near the limit of upstream travel by canoe, existed for less than a generation, between the early 1670s and late 1680s. During this brief period, however, it may have become the most important of the Haudenosaunee villages established on the north shore of Lake Ontario, as the western branch of the Toronto Carrying Place overtook the eastern arm along the Rouge River as the more heavily used route to the interior. The site now lies within the Toronto neighbourhood known as Baby Point, an early twentieth-century residential enclave designed following the principles of the English garden suburb. While undoubtedly highly destructivee, the development of Baby Point has not entirely eradicated the archaeological remains of the seventeenth-century settlement. This chapter reviews the history and archaeology of Teiaiagon, as well as the planning and management measures intended to address the potential survival of remnants of the site beneath the pavements and lawns of Baby Point.

1. The Toronto Carrying Place

Throughout much of time, the linear fabric of the major rivers draining the north shore of Lake Ontario provided a permanent system of landmarks to orient travellers. Canoe travel was limited to the lower portions of these waterways, but also tended to orient foot travel to a parallel path, as trails would have been directed parallel to the watercourse orientation by virtue of the difficulty of negotiating steep ravines, swampy lowlands, and troublesome water crossings.

In the late seventeenth century, the Haudenosaunee established a series of settlements on the north shore to control each of the major routes to the interior. These consisted of villages oriented toward the routes that followed various parts of the Trent River system, such as the Rice Lake Portage and the Scugog Carrying Place, and of two villages on the Toronto Carrying Place and one at the Head-of-the-Lake.

Perhaps the best documented of the routes was the Toronto Carrying Place trail, the west branch of which followed the Humber River Valley northward across the drainage divide created by the Oak Ridges Moraine, to the headwaters of the west branch of the Holland River. The east branch of the Toronto Carrying Place ran from the mouth of the Rouge River northward to the headwaters of the Little Rouge and over the moraine to the east branch of the Holland River at Holland Landing. A third route, between these two, along the Don River, may have been used on occasion as well. Both branches of the Toronto Carrying Place, like the Rice Lake and Scugog Carrying Place to the east, took advantage of the only stretches where the moraine narrows to just 1 km or 2 km.

The site of Teiaiagon, in the modern Toronto neighbourhood of Baby Point, served as a natural stopping place for traffic along the Humber (west) branch of the Toronto Carrying Place (Figure 6.1). It occupied a broad promontory on the east side of the river, approximately 4 km upstream from the Lake Ontario shore. It is likely that, prior to European clearance of the local forest cover, the water levels of the river were lower and Teiaiagon represented the upstream limit of canoe travel (Fisher 1985:29). It may not even have been navigable this far inland. It has been suggested that the actual landing point for northbound canoe traffic upstream from Lake Ontario was at the narrow end of a "hog's back" ridge on the east bank of the river, about 400 m north of the river mouth. This location corresponds roughly to the intersection of Riverside Drive and the South Kingsway (Austin 1995:5; Robinson 1933:33). The trail extended north along the crest of the "hog's back," more or less along the present course of Riverside Drive, veering slightly to the east, away from the river, and then northward to the approximate location of the intersection of present-day Bloor Street and Armadale Avenue. At this point, it turned sharply northwest, across Jane Street and along the line of Humberview Road and Humbercrest Boulevard, to put travellers directly in line with Teiaiagon to the immediate west (Austin 1995:6).

2. The Historical Context of the Site of Teiaiagon

Although there is evidence for the use of the Baby Point promontory from the Archaic period through to the Late Woodland period, the most intensive occupation of the site evidently occurred over a span of little more than a decade during the later seventeenth century, with the emergence of the community of Teiaiagon. The occupants of the settlement were predominantly Seneca, although like most communities after the upheavals of the 1640s and 1650s, the population likely consisted of people of diverse origins including, in all probability, Wendat adoptees returning to territory with which they were familiar (Konrad 1981:136; Richter 1992:121; Thwaites 1896–1901:53:19, 54:79, 81).

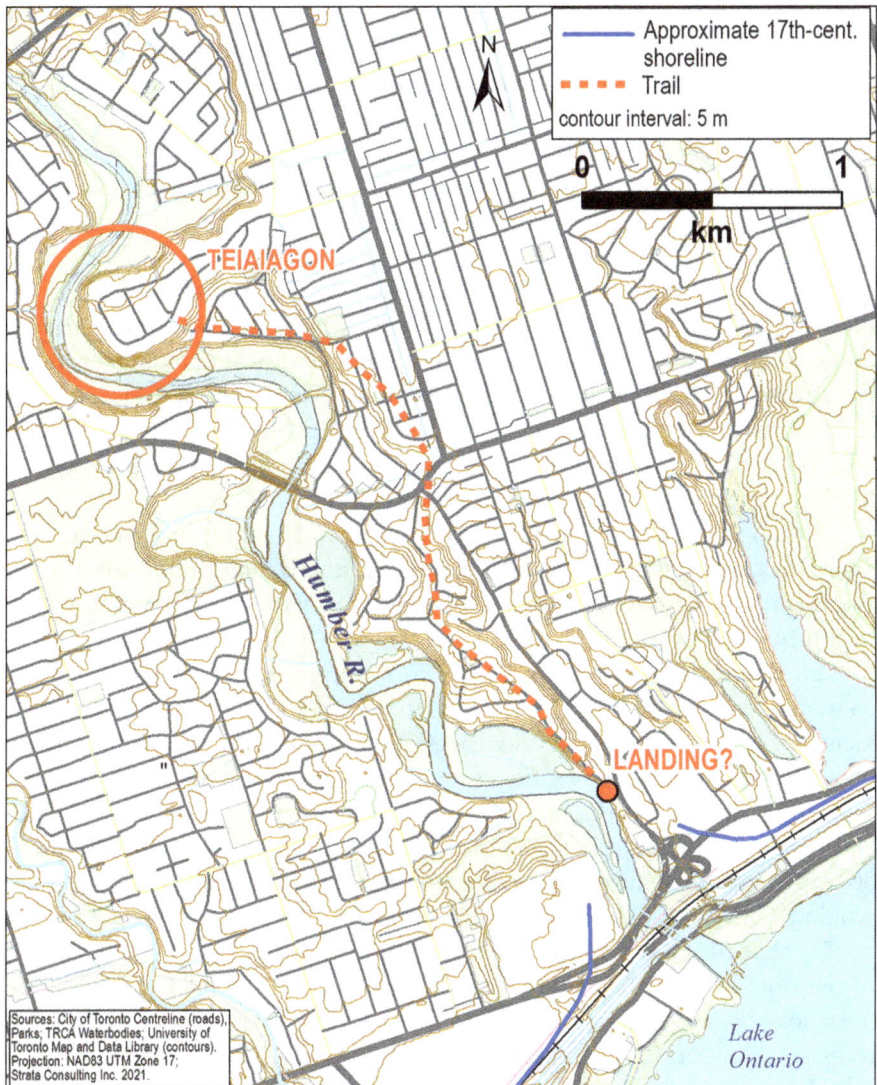

Figure 6.1. Map showing the location of the village of Teiaiagon on the lower Humber River and the southern terminus of the west branch of the Toronto Carrying Place.
Source: Map by David Robertson.

There are limited references to Teiaiagon in the historical sources, which have been summarized by Percy Robinson in his 1933 *Toronto During the French Régime* and by Victor Konrad, in 1981, in his article "An Iroquois Frontier: The North Shore of Lake Ontario During the Late Seventeenth Century." Although Robinson (1933:20, 24) assumes that the village of Teiaiagon had been established prior to 1673, Konrad (1981:133) does not wholly accept this assumption, given the failure of any deputations from Teiaiagon to attend the

1673 negotiations between the Haudenosaunee and the French, held at Cataraqui. Konrad (1981:133) suggests that either the settlement had not yet been established or, if it had been, it was only a satellite of Ganatsekwyagon, on the Rouge, rather than an autonomous village.

The main accounts of French traders, missionaries, and explorers visiting the site date to the later part of the 1670s and the early 1680s. Sometime in the 1670s, possibly in 1676, a party of traders from Cataraqui who were employed by René-Robert Cavelier La Salle apparently visited Teiaiagon and may have sparked an outbreak of considerable disorder (de Belmont 1840:15–16, 19; Robinson 1933:31). The Recollect missionary and explorer Father Louis Hennepin is known to have spent three weeks at the settlement in the late autumn of 1678, while La Salle spent time there in the summer of 1680 and perhaps on two occasions in 1681 (Lizars 1913:24–26; Robinson 1933:37–39). In 1682, three Frenchmen at the site were robbed of their goods (Robinson 1933:31–32).

Although the major importance of Teiaiagon derived from its position as a terminal for fur trade traffic between the northern interior and the French and English outposts to the east and south, it is likely that the settlement exhibited many attributes common to the Iroquoian village settlement pattern, though it and the other Iroquois du Nord villages were smaller than their contemporaries in the Haudenosaunee homelands. The north-shore sites are identified on some maps as small villages of the Iroquois, as opposed to towns, which is the term used to identify some of the New York sites (see Jordan, this volume). This has led Konrad to suggest a population of perhaps 500 to 800 people for the largest of the north-shore sites, occupying between 20 and 30 longhouses. Any further population estimate for the Humber community would be purely speculative.

By about 1680, Teiaiagon appears to have emerged as the most important of the north-shore sites, as the west branch of the Toronto Carrying Place overtook the east branch, along the Rouge River, as the more heavily used route to the interior. The Sulpician missionary Abbé Joseph Mariet set up a subsidiary mission at Teiaiagon around this time. This was the only one the order established among the Iroquois du Nord other than the one at their main base at Kenté.

Due, in part, to increased military pressure from the French upon their homelands south of Lake Ontario, the Haudenosaunee abandoned their north-shore frontier settlements by the late 1680s, although they did not relinquish their interest in the resources of the area, as they continued to claim the north shore as part of their traditional hunting territory (e.g., Lytwyn 1997). Some of the former Iroquois du Nord sites, Teiaiagon among them, were reoccupied by Mississauga groups. There is explicit mention of a Mississauga presence near Teiaiagon in the records of a June 30, 1700, council meeting held between the

Haudenosaunee and the English at Albany (O'Callaghan 1853–1887:4:693–695). A 1736 French report on the disposition of people on the north shore of Lake Ontario includes a reference to Mississauga at the River Toronto, or the Humber River (O'Callaghan 1853–1887:9:1054–1058).

The French, at various times, established fortified posts for trade with the Mississauga on the Humber River. The first of these was the *magasin royal* of 1720, which was one of several installations constructed around Lake Ontario that year at key trading sites. Whether it was at the former site of Teiaiagon or closer to the mouth of the Humber is not known (Robinson 1933:77). In 1750, René Robinau de Bécancour, the Chevalier de Portneuf, constructed a storehouse enclosed by a palisade, known as Fort Toronto, on the east bank of the Humber. However, the structure was deemed too small for an adequate garrison, and a new establishment, variously called Fort Toronto, Fort Rouillé, or Fort Saint-Victor, was built farther to the east, on the shore of Lake Ontario, just outside the narrow entrance to Toronto Bay, on what are now the grounds of Exhibition Place (Brown 1983; Robinson 1933:100). All these installations were essentially outposts to the larger French presence established at Fort Niagara. The relationships between the military, mercantile, and civilian occupants of these posts and the local Mississaugas were, at times, unstable (Benn 2018:10–11; Brown 1983:9).

The French abandoned Fort Toronto in 1759, during the Seven Years' War, which ended with the British takeover of French possessions in Canada. When British troops arrived at Fort Toronto, they found a "Chippewa" man and took him to Niagara, where the British commander Sir William Johnson released him and gave him gifts to try to open communications with the Ojibwa and other nations who had been allies of the French. The British then held council with the "Missassagas and other Indians" from the north and west side of Lake Ontario (Sullivan 1921:3:131). For further discussion of the Mississauga at Teiaiagon and the other former Iroquois du Nord sites, see Warrick and Williamson (this volume).

Following the Toronto Purchase of 1787, the territory that would become York Township was surveyed in 1791, and the first patents were granted in 1796. The former site of Teiaiagon fell within Lots 2 and 3 of Concession 5, west of Yonge Street. These lands, and others, were initially granted to John Lawrence, who was a friend of Lieutenant Governor John Graves Simcoe and had the intention of establishing milling operations on the Humber River (Fisher 1985:25, 38–39).

The site was later acquired by the Honourable James (Jacques) Baby, who moved from Sandwich (modern-day Windsor) to York Township after being appointed the Inspector General of Upper Canada in 1815 (Clark 2003). Baby's primary residence was in the Town of York; his Humber property was a "recreational" estate. He did, however, have a house built on the southwestern part of the point, surrounding it with orchard trees. Upon James's death in 1833, the property passed to his sons Raymond and Francis.

Approximately half of the promontory on which Teiaiagon had stood had been cleared by the mid-nineteenth century (Browne 1851). This work, which may have been accomplished in large part by tenants or hired labour, undoubtedly brought to light many artifacts. Although Raymond and Francis Baby were farmers, they do not appear to have occupied the Lot 2–3 lands full time, as records tend to place them elsewhere throughout much of the nineteenth century.

By 1910, the Baby estate had been purchased by entrepreneur Robert Home Smith. The property was just one of many that Home Smith accumulated along the Humber, with an eye to their long-term development for residential purposes. Between 1908 and 1911, his company had quietly assembled some 1,200 ha on either side of the river, which he called "The Humber Valley Surveys." Home Smith was a member of the Toronto Guild of Civic Art, an advocacy group concerned with the quality and comprehensiveness of development planning and design that was strongly influenced by the City Beautiful Movement (Roberts and Roberts 2017).

The Baby Point subdivision, in particular, was planned and marketed as an exclusive residential subdivision modelled on the English and American principles of the "garden suburb," with large houses referencing Tudor- and Colonial-period architecture set back from the streets on large lots. The design of such neighbourhoods relied on maintaining and working with the natural landscape and preserving features such as tree canopy to the degree possible. Indeed, each property sale to a prospective resident was accompanied by a restrictive covenant (Home Smith and Co. 1914) that contained two clauses intended to minimize landscape alterations:

> 5. No excavations shall be made on any of the said lots except for the purpose of building on said lot, and at the time when the person holding said lot is commencing such operations and no sand or earth shall be removed from any of the said lots except as part of such excavations….
> 6. On any of the bank lots as shown on said plan no trees situate between the summit and bottom of said bank shall be cut down or removed without obtaining the consent of the Vendor thereto in writing. [Home Smith and Co. 1914]

The restrictive covenant remained in effect until 1941, at which time it was replaced by a new bylaw that maintained some of the conditions of the original, although these were limited largely to control over built-form character of new houses.

Another integral feature of any garden suburb was the provision of ample public green space, and Home Smith entered into a number of arrangements with the City of York related to the Humber valley lands and other areas that remain public parks today. Some servicing work for the Baby Point subdivision appears to have occurred shortly after Home Smith had acquired the Baby land, and a few houses had been built by 1913, although these were located well to the east of the site of Teiaiagon. Around three quarters of the residential lots on Baby Point had been developed by the mid-1930s. Most of the remaining properties were developed after the Second World War, by which time the original restrictive covenant had expired.

3. The Archaeology of Teiaiagon

The first public accounts of archaeological discoveries on the Baby farm date to the 1880s, two centuries after the Seneca had abandoned the site.

Antiquarian Charles Hirschfelder acquired a complete pipe and a number of fragments from the site in the early 1880s (see Engelbrecht and Williamson, this volume) and became embroiled in a debate played out in the *Toronto Mail* newspaper in late 1885 to early 1886 over the authenticity of his claims of the discovery of an inscribed stone grave marker on the site. Although some supported his claims concerning the find, comparing it to petroglyphs found elsewhere in southern Ontario, the consensus is that it was fraudulent. One newspaper correspondent even claimed that he knew the boys who had created the piece to trick one of their companions (Hamilton 2010:49; Kapches 1983:2013).

In 1888, David Boyle published a general description of the site in the 1886–1887 annual report of the Canadian Institute:

> Within easy distance of Toronto is the Village of Lambton Mills, on the River Humber. This locality has long been noted as one rich in Indian relics. An old trail to Lake Simcoe and the Georgian Bay followed the valley of this river for a good many miles, and here and there throughout its course are found indications of the old encampments and potteries.
>
> A little south of Lambton Mills, on the Baby Estate, there must have been at one time a considerable Indian population of as stationary character as it was possible for the nature and habits of the aborigines to permit.
>
> On the summit of a club-shaped plateau, having an area of about ten acres, and being fully one hundred feet above the bed of the Humber, a number of native burial pits have been opened at various times, and much valuable material taken from them. It is quite certain that when this portion of the farm is freed from underbrush further interesting discoveries will be made.

On the flats to the south of this elevation, and facing the Baby residence, Mr. Raymond Baby pointed out a camping ground, or village site, as indicated by remains still turned up by the plough, and I am quite sure that inspection of the corresponding flats to the north would reveal even more numerous proofs of old time habitation [...].

Mr. and Mrs. R. Baby did everything possible to further the views of the Institute, and expressed their intention to give our Society due notice of any local archaeological developments. [Boyle 1888:12]

Boyle's 1886–1887 report reproduces illustrations of two Middle Archaic (Laurentian) ground stone gouges found on the Baby farm that had been donated to the Institute by Mr. Kirkwood, "an enthusiastic collector" (Boyle 1888:40, Figures 65 and 66). He also provides a description of a Late Archaic birdstone that "has been ingeniously shaped from a piece of richly grained slate as to make an oval mark containing a dark spot, take the place of the eye" (Boyle 1888:37).

In the Canadian Institute report for 1887–1888, Boyle included an illustration of a finely made conical ring-type ceramic smoking pipe "from the Baby farm at Lambton" (Boyle 1889:Figure 15). This item was attributed to James Kirkwood. The annual report for 1888–1889 makes it clear that a substantial number of other artifacts from the site had made their way into the Institute's collections. The listings of seventeenth-century items from the Baby farm in the various display or storage cabinets that are provided in the 1888–1889 report include glass and shell beads, finger rings, a ring brooch, kettle fragments, various pieces of reworked copper or brass, gun parts, a white ball clay pipe with a fleur-de-lys motif, a stone pipe roughout or preform, clay pipes, and different other items (Boyle 1889:48–50, 52, 62–64) (see Fox et al., this volume and Cooper, this volume). James Kirkwood was the donor of some of this material, which was attributed either to the Baby farm or, more generally, to York Township. Other artifacts were donated by a Miss Kirkwood and a W. Kirkwood. Clearly, the Kirkwoods were active explorers of the site; one of the correspondents in the debate of the previous year over the authenticity of Hirschfelder's grave marker from the site in the *Toronto Mail* was Robert Kirkwood.

James, Robert, and probably Miss Kirkwood were the children of Alexander Kirkwood, a career civil servant who held positions in the Bureau of Agriculture, the Crown Lands Department, and later in a Royal Commission that led to the establishment of Algonquin Park (Killan 2003). Boyle was probably well acquainted with the Kirkwood family through his connections with the provincial government, and the Canadian Institute actively supported the creation of Algonquin Park (Killan 1993:11–13). Toronto city directories indicate that the Kirkwoods lived on the east side of Jane Street in Lambton Mills, or the West Toronto Junction, between 1881 and 1890, conveniently close to the Baby estate. James was around eighteen years old when the family moved to the area, while Robert was about thirteen. Miss Kirkwood may have been either Marie Anna, Margaret, or Eve Kirkwood, who, in 1881, were twenty-four, fifteen, and eleven years old, respectively (Census of Canada 1881). W. Kirkwood may have been another of Alexander Kirkwood's thirteen children or perhaps a nephew; the records are not clear.

Other individuals who donated artifacts to the Institute that were likely collected from the Baby farm before it was developed include Wardie and Ottie White (Boyle 1889:97), a Mr. Wallace (Boyle 1908:7), and H. Smith (Orr 1913:96). Details about these individuals are scant. Wardie and Ottie White's artifact collecting activities may have rivalled the Kirkwoods' and may even have been carried out with them, as they were possibly relatives of Aubrey White, a close colleague of Alexander Kirkwood's at the Crown Lands Department (Cottam 2003). Smith may have been Hugh Smith, an engineer who lived on St. John's Road; Herbert Smith, a carpenter who lived on Jane Street; or Henry Smith, another carpenter, who lived on St. Clair Avenue West, all at addresses a short distance northeast of Baby Point.

In 1889, Andrew F. Hunter visited the site and was shown various features of the landscape by Raymond Baby, including a "burial ground" on the promontory and settlement areas on the lower plateau, and possibly traces of a palisade. Robinson, commenting on Hunter's visit, noted that "these relics of a fortification might be ascribed to Teiaiagon, the Mississauga village, or the Toronto Post of 1720" (Robinson 1933:30, 33). Arthur J. Clark made a copy of Hunter's sketch map many years later, and the accompanying key identifies four areas variously described as camps or burial grounds, as well as the course of the Humber trail (Figure 6.2).

Clark first visited Baby Point on November 11, 1916. His records note that he found an adapted metal tool—a gouge or scraper—while digging in a refuse heap on the north side of the point. He returned to Baby Point every November 11 until his death, in 1934. These visits do not appear to have involved active investigations, or at least there are no records for any resultant discoveries.

Construction work resulted in the discovery of human remains on more than one occasion during the development of the residential neighbourhood. A short Toronto *Globe* newspaper article, of August 7, 1920, reported that a "human skeleton in a fair state of preservation was unearthed yesterday morning by workmen employed in the pavement work for York Township in the Baby Point district on the Humber River […]. 'I was told today that skeletons were also found while excavations were being made for some of the dwellings in the district' said Foreman James Orr" (*The Globe* 7 August 1920:9). The Canadian Institute's accessions for 1928 include a skull and skeleton from the site, donated

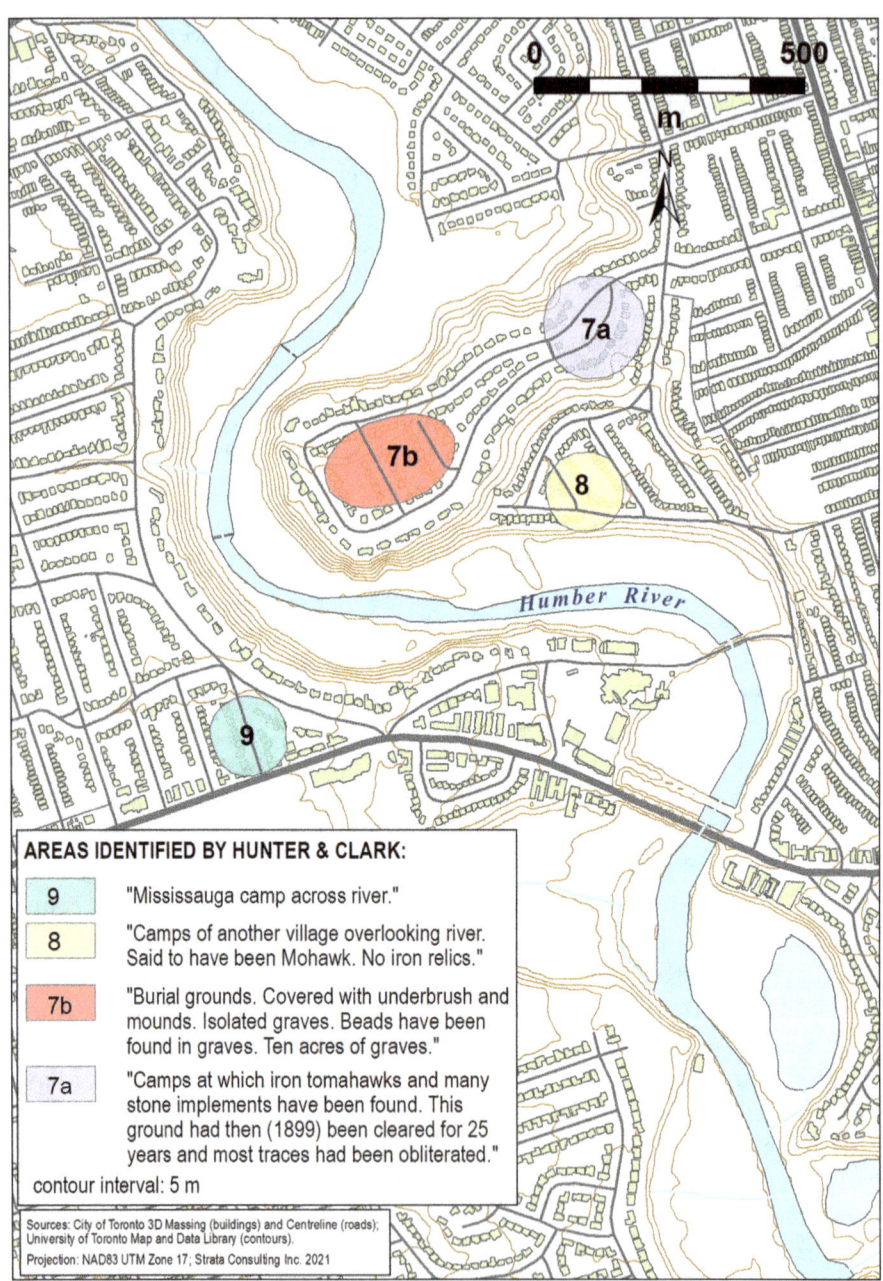

Figure 6.2. Andrew Hunter's and A. J. Clark's sketches of the principal areas of archaeological finds at Baby Point, Toronto, overlaid on a map of the modern neighbourhood.
Source: Courtesy Archaeological Services Inc., based on unpublished field notes of A. J. Clark, Canadian Museum of History.

by Etobicoke physician Emerson Bull (Orr 1928:78). Perhaps he was called to attend one of these discoveries during the initial development of the neighbourhood.

Residents of the new neighbourhood continued to unearth items on their properties as well. Robinson, writing in the 1920s and 1930s, noted that "relics have been discovered by Mr. R. J. Dilworth" (Robinson 1933:33). Robert Dilworth was a prominent financier who lived on Baby Point Crescent, according to the City of Toronto directories of the period.

Robinson also reported that Mr. William Mansell made discoveries on the brow of the hill behind his residence on Baby Point in 1924 (Robinson 1933:34). City directories place Mansell on the north side of Baby Point Road, with his house backing onto the north slope of the promontory. Robinson described Mansell's finds as consisting of

> a large number of iron trade axes bearing the usual markings, some nondescript fragments of metal and two broken clay pipes of European manufacture [...]. The tomahawks were found on the crest of the hill where it overlooks the Humber sweeping down from Lambton Mills. At the foot of the hill there is a stretch of swampy land; the slope is still well-wooded and intersected with numerous paths. Quantities of bone of every description, found on the slope of the hill, jawbones of deer, ribs of bears, and fragments of partridge bones, indicate that the inhabitants of the village found the slope of the hill a convenient place for the disposal of refuse. Eight of the iron tomahawks discovered in 1924 were found in a cluster or circle, and suggest the gloomy thought that this lovely spot was at some time desecrated by one of the atrocities described so minutely by the early missionaries and explorers. In burning a prisoner, it was customary for the Indians to add to the torment of the victim by suspending from his neck a collar of axe-heads heated in the flames and held together by a withe. [Robinson 1933:34–35]

Mansell donated at least two of these axes and a "worked stone" to the Canadian Institute shortly after he discovered them (Orr 1925:118).

Following the publication of Robinson's *Toronto During the French Régime*, the archaeology of Teiaiagon/Baby Point seemed to fade from view. Only in the early 1970s did the site receive renewed attention from an archaeological perspective. Victor Konrad reviewed the available documentation concerning Baby Point as part of his effort to develop a comprehensive inventory of archaeological sites in the Toronto region (Konrad 1973). He also spoke to some residents about their memories of discoveries or their knowledge of accounts of such discoveries. On this basis, he registered four separate sites within the provincial site database, two of which were assigned specific municipal addresses, while the other two were more vaguely defined.

The first professional investigation of the site only occurred in 1999, when Heather Henderson of Historic Horizon Inc. (HHI) carried out a Stage 1–2 archaeological assessment in advance of the construction of an addition to a house on Baby Point Crescent, across the street from the former home of Robert Dilworth. Test pitting in the area to be affected by the construction project did not result in any discoveries, as these portions of the property proved to be heavily disturbed (HHI 1999). However, Henderson noted that the front lawn of the house appeared to be largely intact and exhibited potential for the presence of archaeological deposits. Because this portion of the property was not to be impacted by the construction, it was not investigated. Her conclusions were confirmed when, a few months later, backhoe excavation of a trench for a new gas line through the front yard of the property disturbed a human burial. Henderson returned to the site to carry out the burial investigation (HHI 2001). The remains were those of a woman in her twenties, who was laid in an extended position, with her head to the west and her left arm placed across her chest. The right arm and portions of the right half of the torso had been removed by the backhoe. The interment lay approximately 1.25 m below modern grade. The grave had been excavated to a depth of approximately 1 m below the original grade, which was capped by a thin soil horizon associated with the 1930s construction of the house and subsequent importation of topsoil.

The interment was accompanied by five artifacts: a brass finger ring was recovered from soil disturbed by the backhoe and was assumed to have been worn on her right hand; two additional brass rings were found in situ on the fingers of her left hand; a small, fragmentary brass kettle containing a piece of a fur pelt was found on the right side of the body; and, finally, a finely made antler comb was recovered from the soils disturbed by the backhoe. The grave goods are all consistent with a date of the middle to the third quarter of the seventeenth century. The antler comb, which bears a carved openwork motif of two human figures wearing European-style clothes, suggests a Seneca affiliation (for further discussion of the artifacts, see Cooper, this volume; Williamson and von Bitter, this volume).

This burial discovery was one of a number of events at the turn of the millennium that, in 2005, sparked the City of Toronto to initiate an archaeological management plan in order to ensure that development projects were more consistently subject to archaeological evaluation and mitigation as part of the municipal approvals process (Williamson et al. 2017). One element of this plan was the definition of a number of archaeologically sensitive areas (ASAs) within the city. ASAs are archaeological sites or combinations of sites and other landscape features or historical land uses with known boundaries that require greater planning scrutiny. For obvious reasons, Baby Point was an early candidate for consideration as an ASA, not just because of the historical significance of Teiaiagon, but because of the 1999 burial discovery and the possibility that other substantial areas of the site remained somewhat intact, thanks to the restrictions Home Smith had placed on the types of development permitted at Baby Point (Ganatsekwyagon-Bead Hill was also established as an ASA; see Poulton, this volume). Although the basement excavations were massively destructive, it seemed that wholesale grading of properties was not likely to have been the norm, at least in the older parts of the neighbourhood.

In 2006, while the archaeological management plan was still in its embryonic phases, and before the Teiaiagon/Baby Point ASA, or indeed any ASA, had been formalized, a substantial program of natural gas service upgrades began in the neighbourhood. This project had not been communicated to City Heritage staff, but once they became aware of it, they moved quickly to ensure that archaeological concerns would be addressed. Given the schedule, it was determined that the archaeological measures would take the form of monitoring all the excavations required for the replacement of the gas mains and laterals. This work led to the discovery of another burial on Baby Point Crescent, approximately 300 m northeast of the burial found in 1999 (Archaeological Services Inc. 2007).

The remains, which had been partially disturbed at some point in the past, most probably by an original utility installation, were those of a woman, laid in an extended position at a depth of approximately 0.75 m below existing grade. She was aged between thirty-five and sixty or older and had suffered from several pathologies: caries and tooth loss; arthritis; a non-specific infection; and possibly tuberculosis (Archaeological Services Inc. 2007:11–18). She was accompanied by a suite of grave goods corresponding to a date in the middle to the third quarter of the seventeenth century. The offerings consisted of a brass pot containing an ash wood bowl that, in turn, contained squash, acorn, and grapes; a moose antler hair comb; two iron awls; an iron knife; and an iron axe (for more on the metal artifacts, see Cooper, this volume). The basic form of the antler comb is openwork carving of an elaborated combination of panther, bear, human, and possibly rattlesnake. Secondary decoration in the form of fine incised motifs includes linear, spherical, and geometric designs on the bodies of the animal figures (Archaeological Services Inc. 2007:19–23). Taken together, these various symbols represent a complex amalgam of concepts related to spiritual power, shapeshifting, and medicine (see Williamson and Veilleux 2005; Williamson and von Bitter, this volume; Hill, this volume).

The Baby Point ASA came into effect as a planning tool in 2007. It basically flagged every single residential property within the neighbourhood as having archaeological potential, regardless of surface appearances. Since that time, most intrusive works have been subject to archaeological review, regardless of their status in terms of planning legislation or permitting. This proved timely because the area was starting to undergo changes, as many individual properties were being altered by substantial additions to the existing century houses or their wholesale replacement with new buildings. These redevelopments have generally all been subject to Stage 1–2 archaeological assessments and often subsequent monitoring of the construction excavations.

More than twenty such investigations have taken place between 2007 and 2021. None have resulted in new finds of archaeological remains, and it has become clear that some of the assumptions about the degree of landscape preservation in the area were overly optimistic. Home Smith's designers, architects, and construction contractors had significant impacts when the neighbourhood was first developed. Much of the existing topography of the area represents an evocation of the original landscape rather than its preservation. Throughout most of the site area, only those archaeological features that were deeply excavated in the first place, such as burials, are likely to survive under some of the residential lawns and gardens. There is also the possibility for the survival of slope middens at the rears of the properties ranged along the edge of the promontory.

Despite the largely negative results of testing on individual properties, the continued management of the site remains a concern. In 2016, the City commissioned a Heritage Conservation District (HCD) Study of Baby Point, providing an opportunity to refine the blanket characterization of archaeological potential within the neighbourhood. This was undertaken on the basis of a detailed review of early aerial photography and of a field review on a property-by-property basis.

There were some limiting factors to the effectiveness of this work. Aerial photographic coverage of the area post-dates the main period of subdivision development, although it does make it possible to get a sense of construction impacts on the lower terrace, on the south side of the promontory, as this area was only built up in the 1940s. A field review was conducted, but only from the streets, so for the most part, only the front yards could be evaluated. Modern aerial photography revealed relatively little about the backyards because the properties are heavily treed. It also proved challenging to differentiate natural or essentially unaltered topography from areas of heavy modification to create building envelopes in some locations. Overall, therefore, the removal of an archaeological potential rating for an individual property was undertaken conservatively. In cases where yards had complex landscape treatments, for instance, there was a presumption that these have had only superficial impacts and were achieved through filling rather than cutting of the original grade.

The HCD Study reinforced the ASA requirements and specifically identified those situations in which archaeological assessments must be carried out in advance of any proposed works. These will be implemented as part of the development controls that will form part of the HCD Plan for the neighbourhood. There may also be an opportunity to more proactively investigate the archaeology of the site through testing within selected city-owned lands to further inform planning measures for the area, but this is only an idea at this time. Nonetheless, the ASA and HCD measures will ensure that the surviving archaeological remains of Teiaiagon are managed as well as they can be given the context of the site. This is only fitting given the importance of Teiaiagon during a critical period of history and the clearly sensitive nature of its limited physical remains.

Acknowledgements

Thanks are due to Martin Cooper, William Fox, Dana Poulton, and Peter Carruthers for sharing information and their thoughts on the archaeology of Teiaiagon over the years and to Ron Williamson for his comments on an earlier version of this chapter.

7

CHANGING CONTINUITIES OF HOME

Outinaouatoua in the Context of Seventeenth-Century Indigenous Heritage Landscapes

NEAL FERRIS

Of all the Iroquois du Nord settlements described in European accounts from the second half of the seventeenth century, the most westerly settlement remains a historical enigma. Generally understood to be somewhere inland west from the western end of Lake Ontario and east of the Grand River within that region of Ontario that broadly falls within the inter-lakes area between Lakes Ontario and Erie, the location of this place remains unknown. Nonetheless, local histories have readily proclaimed where the settlement was located, and scholarship over the past century has explained the logic of that location within conventional historical constructs, framing this place as specifically situated to control the movement of people and trade during a period of Seneca expansionism. In other words, the Indigenous community at this place is framed by scholars with European-centric economic and political priorities interpreted from European written accounts. The particulars of this narrative arose specifically from the connections of this place to the European wanderers René-Robert Cavelier de La Salle and Adrien Jolliet (brother of Louis Jolliet), and to the Sulpician priests René de Bréhant de Galinée and François Dollier de Casson, who all briefly found themselves in the community in the early fall of 1669.

The singular historical source about this settlement is Galinée's recollection of the expedition he was a part of in 1669–1670, which was translated into English by James Coyne and published in 1903. In Coyne's translation of Galinée's account, the settlement they visited in September of 1669 is first referred to as Ganastogué Sonontoua Outinaouatoua and later as Tinaòùtòûa (Coyne 1903:40, 44). Various iterations of this name, including the variant

Quinaouatoua, have appeared on maps between the 1670s and the late eighteenth century, though, as Heidenreich has noted, later maps simply mimic the general location derived from Galinée's cartographic accounting (e.g., Gentilcore and Head 1984; Heidenreich 1978, 1980). Coyne (1903:45) translated the iteration Tinaòùtòûa into English as Tinawatawa. This label has been favoured in local histories (e.g., Henderson 2005; Lajeunesse 1960; Robinson 1965; Woodhouse 1969), while Tinawatawa/Quinaouatoua tends to be the preferred designation used in historical scholarship (e.g., Adams 1986; Konrad 1981; Laprairie 2018). In deference to Galinée, the designation Outinaouatoua is used here and throughout this volume.[1]

According to Galinée, Outinaouatoua was located near the head of Lake Ontario (Coyne 1903:39), or, more specifically, after two days' travel overland from what is known today as Cootes Paradise (Coyne 1903:43) (see Figures 1.1 and 1.3). Galinée also reports that the settlement was a further three days' overland travel away from the banks of the Grand River (Coyne 1903:49). In modern geographic parlance, then, the site would appear to have been somewhere within a vast geography between the modern-day Ontario cities of Hamilton, Cambridge, and Brantford. Despite this lack of precision, we can still "follow" the footsteps of these Europeans today with certainty along established trails and parks, complete with historical plaques marking Galinée's and La Salle's voyage (e.g., Henderson 2005). Laden in this certainty are assumptions about the location of Outinaouatoua and the routes connecting it to Lake Ontario and the Grand River, with scholars and local historians relying heavily on a kind of speculative mapping: transposing seventeenth-century cartographic depictions onto modern topography, and then using Galinée's estimation of the duration of the journey undertaken from that place to "pinpoint" the route (e.g., Brouwer 2018; White 1972:68).

A number of known seventeenth-century archaeological sites in the region, including Lake Medad, Freelton, Christianson, and Walker, have all been cited as candidates for Outinaouatoua (Fox 2013a; Henderson and Bandow 2009). So, an association of this historic place to a known seventeenth-century archaeological site from the region has long been assumed. That association was reinforced by the extensive amount of European "trade goods" recovered from these sites, which were a particular focus of amateur digs dating back well into the nineteenth century (e.g., Breithaupt 1920; Fox 2013b; Hamilton 2010; Ionico 2018). Before refined seriations (e.g., Fitzgerald 1990; Kenyon and Kenyon 1983) confirmed that the objects from these places all date to the first half of the seventeenth century, the presence of glass beads or axe heads from

---

1. Other terminology in this chapter has also been revised to ensure consistency with the remainder of the volume.

a site that also happened to align with a possible location for Outinaouatoua was assumed to be proof of its location.

Ernest Lajeunesse (1960:xxxii) went further and argued that Outinaouatoua was intentionally built onto the ruins of one of these earlier seventeenth-century villages. The residents of these earlier settlements were people whom Europeans described as part of a range of nations and village communities extending across the inter-lakes region east of the Grand River. These people, collectively and generically referred to by the Wendat as the Attawandaron[2] and by others as "Neutral peoples," by 1652 had dispersed from the inter-lakes region due to conflicts with Haudenosaunee nations (e.g., Ridley 1961; Wright 1963). Over the years, archaeologists have further ascribed this generic appellation to a wide range of archaeological sites documented across southwestern Ontario, from the Niagara Escarpment west to Chatham, and dating back to the fifteenth century and earlier; lumping this Late Woodland archaeology within a generalized "Neutral" archaeological record (e.g., Finlayson 1998; Foster 1990; Lennox and Fitzgerald 1990; Noble 1978). Lajeunesse's suggestion helps frame the popular understanding of the settlement of Outinaouatoua as overlying a deeper Indigenous archaeology and heritage. Notably, Outinaouatoua was laid over and thus erased the palimpsest of the deeper past of the "Neutral Nation," often identified as "destruite" (destroyed), as it was thought of and depicted on maps from the later seventeenth and eighteenth centuries (e.g., Vincenzo Coronelli's 1688 map and Guillaume de l'Isle's 1730 map; see Gentilcore and Head 1984:20–22).

Speculating on where Outinaouatoua was (and archaeologically is) remains a puzzle, and other "new" candidates come to light regularly. My brief encounter with a material suggestion of where the site may be took place in 2001, when I happened to be in the Department of Anthropology at McMaster University. An individual had dropped by to see if someone would look at a sizeable collection he had, including a range of undiagnostic material: a fragment of a high-collared smoking pipe bowl, some copper or brass scraps, and a substantial number of glass beads. In the limited notes I made at the time, I wrote that this bead assemblage included a large number of short, polychrome tubular beads, notably Ib16 beads, as well as monochrome red and black rounds, and a few red beads with an apple green core (following Kenyon and Kenyon 1983). These are generally consistent with other north-shore of Lake Ontario and Seneca sites post-dating 1650 (e.g., Wray and Graham 1966; see also Fox et al., this volume). Charles Wray's (1973, 1983) suggestion that the decline in tubular

---

2. The term Attawandaron is reported to mean "Peoples of a slightly different language" (Thwaites 1896–1901:21:191), and this name distinguished the peoples of this region from an even more generic application of Akwanake, or "strangers," which was applied to people whose language the Wendat "in no wise understand [...]" (Thwaites 1896–1901:21:191).

beads and rise in round beads occurred somewhere around 1670 was in my mind as I looked over the beads in this collection. At least to me, the beads supposed the collector had recovered a post-1650 assemblage from a site along the upper Spencer Creek drainage, just west of the Beverly Swamp, and within the archaeological landscape of earlier seventeenth-century settlements so well known to archaeologists and artifact collectors in this area. Unfortunately, the collector was reticent to discuss details of the site, what he had done there, and whether he would be willing to take me to the location. He would only say that it was on farmland owned by an individual who let him, and only him, onto it to collect. I did try to follow up with him, but he stopped being communicative after that first meeting.

That we cannot here consider whether this collection originated from Outinaouatoua is the result of my failure to properly type glass beads in that moment I found myself standing in the department's hallway. But as that material is now beyond my ability to investigate further, I do not want to speculate on X-marks-the-spot hypotheses for where Outinaouatoua—the archaeological site—might be.

But I do want to consider here why the historical fact of the recorded, momentary encounter with this place by a handful of Frenchmen in 1669 has come to be framed in a historical certainty within conventional scholarly constructs. After all, Galinée's account is not unambiguous, and represents the recalled, single perspective of a poorly-understood landscape and the peoples of the region at the time of his journey. And yet that account is cited as explaining the reasons why Outinaouatoua was where it was, albeit from within a Eurocentric economic and political understanding of the time. That conventional construct suggests Outinaouatoua was a stratagem of Seneca political and economic expansionism, placed where it was to control the east-west flow of furs and trade goods, and to control the region from encroaching French (e.g., Adams 1984; Konrad 1981, 1987; Robinson 1933). Moreover, the fact of Galinée and La Salle coming across this community in 1669 "makes sense" within that logic if we accept the assumption that, at that time, the broader inter-lakes region was a blank slate after the erasure of the earlier ancestral Indigenous heritage of this region.

But I would argue that the archaeological history of the region—a deep time narrative of material continuity within and through change (Ferris 2006, 2009)—invites us to see this encounter as connected to that deeper heritage, rather than an act of erasing it. Indeed, as I will suggest below, Galinée's account can be better understood as a reflection of how, in the early autumn of 1669, the inter-lakes region was a liminal and fluid place that directly connected to that deeper Indigenous heritage. I will first examine what Galinée actually does and does not say in the context of that moment. I then consider that historical moment within the context of the archaeological history of this region. I believe this perspective offers a more nuanced reading of Outinaouatoua, one that helps explain the "why" of the site, as well as the "where" and "when" of it, beyond the conventional Eurocentric logic that scholarship has assumed for this place.

The embedded Eurocentric biases which shape conventional historical narratives tend to advance what Jordan (2008) refers to as the "Negative Master Narrative" of Indigenous ruin and lack of agency (see also Ferris 2014; Rubertone 2000; Silliman 2005; C. Williamson 2004, among others). The assumptions that underlay this narrative are read in historic accounts, piecing together partial historic facts and observer biases into a certainty of historical knowing, at least until further documents or other ways of reading the record undermine the certainty. Much like some scholars were certain that the location of Outinaouatoua had to be associated with early seventeenth-century archaeological sites until it was clear those sites were too early for that association. I argue (Ferris 2009) that reading historical accounts such as Galinée's from within a deeper archaeological history of this region can offer a different understanding of Outinaouatoua, one more consistent with the Indigenous-centric logic and heritage that undoubtedly shaped the inter-lakes region at least as much, and likely more, than European ones did in 1669.

1. The Galinée and Dollier Expedition in the Context of 1669

The year 1669 was a fluid time in the lower Great Lakes, as people and communities negotiated the consequences of significant changes in the recent past, unstable presents, and uncertain futures (e.g., Brandão 1997; Parmenter 2010). Military confrontation and conflict between the French colonial presence along the St. Lawrence River and the Nations of the Haudenosaunee gave way to an uneasy tolerance, if not truce, following French incursions that ended in 1666. This allowed French expeditions to travel more openly through the lower Great Lakes in the following years, creating an opportunity for a more sustained and formal French return to a region the French had vacated during the pan-regional conflicts that had played out across the lower Great Lakes less than twenty years earlier (Heidenreich 1987, 1990; Williamson, this volume). This period of "tolerance" also invited the possibility for the French to travel farther afield, linking up with Indigenous nations to the north, and to push exploration to the west and south. These were the immediate motivations that brought together Galinée, Dollier, and La Salle in the summer of 1669, accompanied by a crew of around a dozen individuals, with the intent of travelling beyond Lake Ontario toward their respective routes to upper Lake Huron (Galinée and Dollier) and south beyond Lake Erie (La Salle) (Coyne 1903) (Figure 7.1).

From Galinée's account, it is clear that Outinaouatoua and an overland route from Burlington Bay to Lake Erie were unknown to his group when their expedition, sponsored by Daniel de Rémy de Courcelle, the governor of New France, set out from Montréal in early July of 1669 (Coyne 1903:5–7).

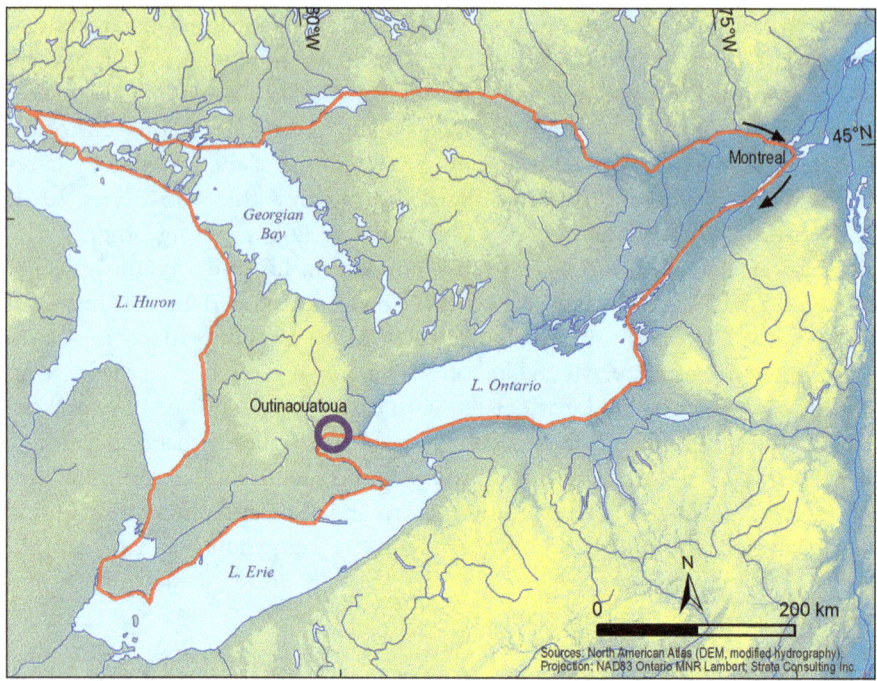

Figure 7.1. Speculative route of Galinée's 1669–1670 journey based on Coyne (1903) and the area in which Outinaouatoua is likely located.
Source: Map by Neal Ferris.

Their initial plan focused on travelling to Irondequoit Bay (near present-day Rochester), on the southwest shore of Lake Ontario, in the heart of Seneca Territory. There they hoped to speak to the Seneca about the best way to travel west, with the vague thought that they could then head overland down to Lake Erie. Once they reached the bay in early August, they travelled by land to a principal town and met with the Seneca Nation council on August 13, to whom they explained their aim to travel west along the Lake Erie shore to the Ohio River (Coyne 1903:25). They were told they would have to wait for appropriate guides to take them to the Ohio River, so La Salle, Galinée, and several other members of their expedition spent the next couple of weeks in the Seneca village. During that time, they did manage to learn that they would need to take a six-day overland portage to get to Lake Erie, and they doubted the viability of undertaking such a long portage so soon into their journey given all their baggage (Coyne 1903:37).

Moreover, as they lingered in the town, their Dutch interpreter reported that he was being told by people that they did not want to accompany the French on this route, as the region along the eastern shore of Lake Erie was unsafe due to the presence of the Andaste-Susquehannock of that region, who were currently in open conflict with the Seneca (Coyne 1903:37). At the same time, Galinée notes an increasing sense of unease settling into his group as their expedition stalled. In part, this unease arose from stretching their welcome among their Seneca hosts and from the tensions they felt as individuals representing a nation that had so recently been in conflict with the Haudenosaunee. But mostly their unease came from not knowing how they would proceed west, as they lost precious weeks while summer slowly approached the fall.

2. The Context of Outinaouatoua in 1669

As August of 1669 dragged on, Galinée's expedition floundered. By late August, the members of the expedition waiting in the Seneca town had returned to their landing and camp on Irondequoit Bay. And by luck, as Galinée suggests, there they met an Indigenous person who was passing through and chose to rest at the French camp for the night. According to Galinée, this individual was travelling "from the Dutch"—presumably, Albany—on his way back to his community of Outinaouatoua, at the end of Lake Ontario (Coyne 1903:39). Upon hearing of the expedition's aim to travel to Lake Erie and westward, and their lack of guides, he told Galinée that the overland portion of the journey to his settlement was only three days long. He also mentioned that his community included individuals who had previously been part of Indigenous nations living to the west, and who could therefore serve as guides. Given that following this person would also mean that the French expedition could immediately put some distance between themselves and the tension of staying near the Seneca town, they decided to take up the offer.

They set out the next day and travelled west along the south shore of Lake Ontario, passing the mouth of the Niagara River, and then travelled for five days along the western end of the lake, to what is known today as Burlington Bay. They paddled through the bay to a "little lake" (Cootes Paradise), which they crossed in "half a league" (just shy of 3 km) and unloaded their canoes. Galinée indicated this location was "nearest the village, which is, however, five or six good leagues away" (roughly 28–33 km). Here they waited, while their companion travelled to Outinaouatoua to bring back the "principal men" and other people who could help carry their baggage (Coyne 1903:41).

Three days later, their companion returned with "almost everyone from the village" (Coyne 1903:41). According to Galinée, the principal members of the community welcomed the expedition and invited them to their settlement, but also asked that this French expedition "do them no harm, and not to burn them as the French had burned the Mohawks" (Coyne 1903:43). These comments are a reference to the earlier French military attacks of 1666, underscoring an uncertain present in 1669, and an anxiety that encompassed both European aliens and Indigenous residents of the region.

The group that came from Outinaouatoua to greet the French expedition numbered more than fifty people (Coyne 1903:43). Among them were two individuals referred to as formerly belonging to western Indigenous nations. Galinée identified them as coming from the "Shawanon," or people from the south [Shawnee], and wrote that they were to serve as La Salle's guides. An individual Galinée suspected was "from a nation near the Pottowattamies" was to guide him and Dollier (Coyne 1903:42). These individuals were referred to as "slaves" by Galinée. However, Galinée's account also suggests that the individual who was to be his guide was not indentured or otherwise obligated to do the bidding of others. Indeed, a dispute between the individual and Galinée led the individual to refuse to accompany Galinée's group. Another figure, who was also referred to as Shawanon, subsequently volunteered himself to serve as Galinée's guide (Coyne 1903:47). These observations suggest that the term "slave," at least as understood by a European in 1669 or scholars conventionally reading this account in the present, may not have been an entirely adequate description of these individuals' identities and the roles they held as residents of Outinaouatoua (see Fox 2009 for further discussion).[3] However, these comments do suggest that individuals' identities could be both shaped by being part of that community in the present, and by the heritage of who they were commonly understood to have been previously.

The group from Outinaouatoua led their French guests from Cootes Paradise in an overland trip that Galinée claims took two days, including wading through mid-thigh-deep waters close to the settlement (Coyne 1903:43). During the journey, Galinée learned that two Frenchmen (Adrien Jolliet and likely Jean Peré) had also just arrived at the village. They were travelling east on their way back from the upper Great Lakes, with a young "Iroquois" man previously held prisoner by the Ottawa. Jolliet had agreed to return the man home to further the peace between the Ottawa and the Haudenosaunee (Coyne 1903).

This coincidence has been interpreted as proof that Outinaouatoua was a vital gateway, strategically placed along the principal east-west travel corridor into Haudenosaunee country (e.g., Konrad 1981, 1987; Robinson 1965). But this is certainly not how the situation was described in Galinée's account. Notably, Jolliet is said to have arrived at Outinaouatoua as the result of having to take a very inconvenient detour. Specifically, Jolliet mentioned he had not known of the route he was travelling prior to his Haudenosaunee companion telling him of it, and that the journey down the Detroit River and along Lake

---

3. I recognize that there was a wide spectrum to the experiences individuals had as a "slave," and that these could differ from those had by individuals as "captives." Nonetheless, it is also certainly the case that individuals incorporated into community settlements as captives or slaves also persisted and would become incorporated as members of those communities. So clearly the identity of these individuals was more nuanced than the more specific European notion of the term, at least as it became understood through the colonial era.

Erie was "heretofore unknown to the French for returning from the Ottawa to the country of the Iroquois" (Coyne 1903:45). Also, Jolliet noted that the route should have included travelling farther east along Lake Erie, then up the Niagara River, and would have required only a half-league overland portage around Niagara Falls. However, Jolliet's Haudenosaunee companion refused to go that way, for fear of running into an Andaste-Susquehannock group, and what they would do to him if that happened. Instead, he persuaded Jolliet to abandon their canoes on the Lake Erie shore not far from the mouth of the Grand River, and then travel by land to Lake Ontario. Outinaouatoua, at least as reportedly described by Jolliet to Galinée, was simply serving as a momentary lay-by along this fifty-league (241 km) detour (Coyne 1903:45).

Jolliet's complaint and his Haudenosaunee companion's fear of travelling along eastern Lake Erie in the fall of 1669 undermines the notion that Outinaouatoua was situated strategically along a major east-west travel corridor controlled by the Seneca. Instead, it suggests that knowledge of the settlement and the region offered a temporary means of avoiding the extra-regional and contested space of eastern Lake Erie, at least as it existed in the moment of 1669.

The company of hosts and guests arrived at Outinaouatoua on September 24. Coyne translated Galinée's description of the community as a "little village" (Coyne 1903:43), which had 18–20 "cabins" or longhouses (Coyne 1903:39), and a population of more than fifty men and women (Coyne 1903:43). In contrast, Galinée described the Seneca principal towns, including the one they visited, as containing 100–150 cabins and described smaller towns in Seneca country as containing 30 cabins (Coyne 1903:25). From Galinée's descriptions, then, Outinaouatoua, on the outer edge of the country "of the Iroquois" (Coyne 1903:45), was neither a substantial settlement nor a vital gateway along a major travel corridor.

Prior to Galinée and company moving on, La Salle decided to return to Montréal to overwinter (Coyne 1903:49). Galinée and Dollier chose to continue, heading west with a dozen men on October 1. Three days' overland travel, covering nine to ten leagues (50–56 km), brought the party to the Grand River, along a stretch of shallow rapids. At that point, the party separated into two groups, with Galinée, Dollier, and a few others travelling downriver by canoe. Galinée describes the subsequent forty-league (160 km) journey downriver as being "marvellous [for] how much difficulty we had in descending the river, for we had to be in the river almost all the time dragging the canoe..." because the water was so shallow. They arrived at Lake Erie by mid-October. They then travelled another three days west along the north shore, another twenty leagues or so, to a location—reputedly near present-day Port Dover (Canada 1934)—where they decided to spend the winter (Coyne 1903:49–51).

Galinée's descriptions of the expedition's travels are a singular account of happenstance encounters with individuals and communities across a liminal space and time. What he offers is an "I-witness" (Denning 1994, 1997) experience of the unfamiliar and mostly unknown once the party moved on from the southwest shore of Lake Ontario. His observations of time and distance can only be accepted as general and imprecise, but so too are his observations of geopolitical realities and the logic of the peoples and nations he encountered. There is little in his account that invites an understanding of the "why" and where of Outinaouatoua in 1669, and much that, from a close read, would suggest that daily life at this place was not as preoccupied with the geopolitical and economic interests of the French as assumed in later conventional scholarship. If we think of his account from within the deeper Indigenous heritage and archaeological history of this region that, at the time, would have been well understood by the Indigenous residents of Outinaouatoua, perhaps we can discern another, more Indigenous-centric logic to this place.

3. Outinaouatoua Within the Context of an Indigenous Heritage Landscape

The solution Galinée's company stumbled across to get to Lake Erie in the fall of 1669 took them along a path they had not known would be an option for them before they left Montréal. That path took them through a region and community they did not previously know about firsthand—a place they mostly thought of as being on the edge and beyond the Seneca and Haudenosaunee heartland. But everyone in the expedition would also have been aware that the region had recently been a landscape of cosmopolitan Indigenous towns, villages, and nations of people known to the French as the Neutral. And the expedition would have entirely expected the absence of settlements they found in the region in 1669, understood as the consequence of conflicts the French had heard about between these groups and the Seneca and other Haudenosaunee nations, and that had concluded less than twenty years earlier. These accounts had come to Montréal third hand since no French observers were in the region at the time. The absence of communities would have been reinforced by visible markers of abandoned villages across this landscape "that was formerly Neutral" (Coyne 1903:Map Insert) and would have been read as confirmation of the wholesale devastation and loss that had occurred here.

This narrative of annihilation and loss is a trope that dominates conventional historical narratives of the seventeenth- to eighteenth-century period in the lower Great Lakes generally, and southwestern Ontario archaeology specifically (see, for example, Jackes 2008; Lennox and Fitzgerald 1990; Noble 1978; Trigger 1985; White 1978; see Ferris 2006, 2009; Jordan 2008 for a review). It is also a visible marker in the local archaeological record, since an immediate consequence of the 1647–1651 conflict is a lack of post-1650 archaeological deposits across the inter-lakes region, a stark difference from pre-1650 (e.g., Lennox and Fitzgerald 1990). Moreover, the region's subsequent historical narrative during the eighteenth and nineteenth centuries tends to focus on new beginnings unconnected to those deeper pasts.

I do not want to rehash the problematics of those narrative constructions here, or the distinction between material record and the heritage of place. But transformation is not the same as destruction. As many scholars have pointed out (e.g., Brandão 1997; Engelbrecht 2003; Ferris 2006; Fitzgerald 1990; Fox 2009; Garrad et al. 2003; Heidenreich 1990; Jordan 2013), there are extensive archaeological, historical, and oral histories that note the sophisticated and nuanced social adoptive and coalescent processes practised within and beyond the palisade, and across the Indigenous nations of the lower Great Lakes, in the 1600s and the centuries prior. These processes collectively allowed for the incorporation of individuals, families, and village and multiple village-level populations, formerly distinct, into other communities and nations. These processes, sometimes coercive, led to individuals, families, or larger social units becoming something else: members of the community they had been adopted into, while retaining their former identity. This social becoming often included relocation, which is readily evident across the archaeological history of the region as reflected in the patterns of village growth and expansion, and of formerly distinct archaeological settlements and households merging with other settlements to become something new (e.g., Birch 2015, 2018). Indeed, this fluid and constant social transformation is a hallmark of the Late Woodland archaeological record from southern Ontario, reflecting a millennium of becoming and of being connected to a deep heritage through the changing continuities of place and community (Ferris 2014). In short, people and places changed, and by changing, they continued.

As elsewhere in the lower Great Lakes, the archaeology of the "country of the Neutral" illustrates how significant this coalescence and adoptive becoming was in shaping Indigenous heritage landscapes and intra-nation and inter-nation connections across the generations of people the French, and subsequent historians and archaeologists, assumed were one. The material record in the 250-year period before 1650 certainly reflects a continual tendency of village or multi-village regional relocations across what is now southwestern Ontario, including relocations that subsequently left parts of that region archaeologically "lacking" formal settlements (e.g., Lennox and Fitzgerald 1990). Other areas reflected inter-regional coalescence (e.g., Fox et al. 2018; Garrad 2014), reflecting a continuation of even deeper time patterns of material innovation and group identity transformation (e.g., St. John and Ferris 2019). This process culminates, archaeologically, in the second half of the sixteenth century, with the entire north shore of Lake Erie peninsula west of the Grand River being characterized as largely "abandoned," with very few large settlements and only limited evidence of seasonal use (Ferris 1986; Ferris et al. 1990; Lennox and

Fitzgerald 1990; Murphy and Ferris 1990). In contrast, the inter-lakes region east of the Grand River is marked by extensive and numerous village and town settlement clusters (Ferris and Spence 1995; Finlayson 1998; Lennox and Fitzgerald 1990; Noble 1984, 1985). In addition, there is a suggestion that the increase in the number of these village clusters was, in part, aided by community relocations, including from the Chatham area of southwestern Ontario (Fitzgerald 1982, 1990; Fox et al. 2018; Ionico 2018). Notably, the archaeological record from this period, then, is read as the coalescence of previously distinct peoples and communities, despite archaeological absences over the broader region.

Earlier in the seventeenth century there is further evidence of this kind of relocation and adoption occurring in the inter-lakes region east of the Grand River. Notably, people of the Atsistaehronon (part of the Fire Nation), living west of Lake Erie, were reported by the Jesuit Gabriel Lalemant to have been brought back to the "country of the Neutrals" as prisoners due to warfare: "last year a hundred prisoners; and this year [...] more than a hundred and seventy" (Thwaites 1896–1901:21:195; see also Heidenreich 1988; Lennox 1981). These "captives" were thought to have augmented local populations following a period of loss due to epidemics, through a process of coercive adoption. They are also assumed to have ended up within the cluster of sites associated with that earlier, late sixteenth-century community relocation from southwestern Ontario (Lennox and Fitzgerald 1990). These actions also created an "abandonment" of Indigenous settlements in northwestern Ohio and a break in the local archaeological record (Stothers 1981). The westerly connection between people "of the Neutral" and people "of the Fire Nation" speaks to a continuation of ancient and complex east-west social inter-regional interactions that played out among peoples across the north shore of the Lake Erie peninsula through many generations of revised self and group identity (Ferris 2006, 2014).

Such relocations, archaeologically, are all manifested at the same scale, regardless of motivations attributed to any given instance. Coalescence is interpreted as the rationale for "abandonment" of formal settlements west of the Grand River by the late sixteenth century. And in the seventeenth century, thanks to a limited third-hand historical report, the rationale for "abandonment" in northwestern Ohio is assumed to be warfare and coercion, though leaving the same archaeological material traces and absences are seen over and over again through the Late Woodland. These are the material traces of continuities that archaeology clearly accounts for as social and community transformation through time.

So, the notion that the transformations of the inter-lakes region during the mid-seventeenth-century can only be due to the "destruction" of societies as reported by Europeans from third-hand accounts, might not fully embody the deeper social complexities occurring through this region at the end of the 1640s, despite the region appearing to be "abandoned" by the time it was visited in 1669. For example, references to the incorporation in Haudenosaunee societies of hundreds of people who formerly resided in the inter-lakes region are readily accessible in the historical record if we read past the European assumptions of destruction. This incorporation of peoples into Haudenosaunee societies was readily acknowledged as the motivation for the capture and adoption of "different" peoples by the Haudenosaunee (see Brandão 1997; Heidenreich 1990 for a detailed review). Indeed, the notion that these various nations could come together, be adopted, or separate over time is reflected in Lalemant's observation (Thwaites 1896–1901:21:191–193) of all Iroquoian peoples that "not long ago they all made but one People, —both Hurons and Iroquois, and those of the Neutral Nation; and that they came from one and the same family." Such observations offer insight into the trans-generational social transformation of always becoming within and across communities, similar to that reflected in the archaeological history of southwestern Ontario (Ferris 2006, 2014).

In the late 1660s, the Jesuits Julien Garnier and Jacques Fremin, in their travels through Seneca country, noted large numbers of "formerly" Neutral people, including a village almost entirely populated by Neutral, Erie, Wendat, and other non-Seneca individuals "formerly overthrown by the Iroquois" (Thwaites 1896–1901:54:81). Similar accounts are noted in Onondaga country (Thwaites 1896–1901:43:365), of the Mohawk (Thwaites 1896–1901:43:187, 45:205–209) and of the Oneida (Thwaites 1896–1901:51:123; see also Engelbrecht 2003; Wright 1963). It is also worth noting that Morgan (1962 [1851]:76) reports two centuries later that Haudenosaunee oral tradition recalls that Erie and Neutral peoples were offered the choice to either join the Confederacy or face death. These references all suggest, at least for the inter-lakes region, that the depopulation of the mid-seventeenth century was due primarily to coercive relocation of communities than to annihilation.

Considering this complex movement of people and communities, and the implications these processes have for revising notions of identity and heritage, it is worth thinking about just who the residents of Outinaouatoua were and were not in 1669. Significantly, although some scholarship has suggested they were Seneca (e.g., Adams 1986; Konrad 1981), Galinée does not refer to the community as Seneca, though he does when referring to towns and settlements when he is in Seneca country. Instead, he describes the individual who first told them of Outinaouatoua, and the settlement itself, as being from "a village of *Iroquois of the Five Nations* at the end of Lake Ontario" (Coyne 1903:39; emphasis added). This distinct appellation suggests that Galinée did not recognize the community, although they were of the Haudenosaunee, as formally aligned with a particular Haudenosaunee nation, at least as he understood them to be in the fall of 1669. This distinction suggests that the community was more a place where people were becoming Iroquois (Ferris 2014). Thinking of the people of Outinaouatoua this way makes sense given the immediate, disruptive pasts and uncertain presents playing out in the region at the time, and the living memory of individuals' polyphonic identities. At the very least, if we can draw meaning from Galinée's distinction in designation in his writing, it is that the residents of Outinaouatoua were something other than Seneca in this transitory moment. Also noteworthy is the fact that some of the residents of Outinaouatoua are referred to as formerly belonging to western Indigenous nations. Given slightly earlier forced relocations of large numbers of people from west of Lake Erie, these individuals could well have been connected to or descended from the people who had been brought back and incorporated into these inter-lakes communities around 1640, before another relocation and coercive adoption around 1650.

Considering the strong presence of people formerly "of the Neutral" noted by Europeans residing within Haudenosaunee settlements at the time, I would suggest that many of the residents of Outinaouatoua likely had previously been part of those communities, returning some eighteen years later to a place they knew well, because they had, in effect, returned to their homescape, albeit now negotiating revised identities. This connection also makes sense, given the extensive earlier seventeenth-century archaeological record known for the region the French expedition traversed in 1669. The landscape around the settlement would have been well-known and understood within the needs of daily living for the residents. This begins to point at an Indigenous-centric logic and heritage as to why Outinaouatoua was where it was in 1669.

According to Galinée's account, the stated reason inhabitants of the site were there was "for the convenience of hunting roebuck [deer] and bear, which are plentiful at that place" (Coyne 1903:39). Also worth noting is that the upper Spencer Creek drainage, which is known to contain a dense cluster of earlier seventeenth-century archaeological sites, is fed by the marsh and edge environments of the Beverly Swamp. Such a landscape would have been a vital region for successful summer and fall deer and bear hunting. Also, that Galinée complained of having to trek through water mid-leg deep further suggests that their trail to Outinaouatoua led their party through, if not to, the upper Spencer Creek drainage. In other words, Galinée's party presumably entered into a landscape known for successful hunts and livelihood, perhaps fondly remembered by some if not most of the inhabitants of Outinaouatoua, and thus an important reason why they were back there by the late 1660s.

If Outinaouatoua does represent the return to a recently lived landscape to pursue a range of subsistence practices, which the residents' prior knowledge of the place indicated could be successfully carried out there, then the heritage of this knowledge is readily reflected in the archaeological record of the earlier seventeenth century. In particular, Fitzgerald (1990) has documented a remarkably extensive concentration of Glass Bead Period III village sites (ca.

1630s–1640s) in the area of the upper Spencer Creek drainage. These sites comprise some of a cluster of mostly seventeenth-century sites he refers to as part of the Spencer-Bronte Creek cluster (Fitzgerald 1990; Ionico 2018; Lennox and Fitzgerald 1990). This cluster is also where he noted evidence of an influx of material traits suggestive of westerly relocations into the region. Both Fitzgerald (1990) and Ionico (2018) have suggested that these earlier towns and villages encompassed cosmopolitan assemblages of people and communities becoming—changing and in the process continuing their identity after relocating, coercively or otherwise, from places and peoples well to the west. And the archaeological record speaks to the rich livelihood and material innovation sustained through the first half of the seventeenth century in those communities, and especially in the period immediately before the events of the late 1640s (Fitzgerald 1982, 1990; Lennox 1981, 1984a, 1984b; MacDonald 1991). This recent history in 1669, rich connection to and knowledge of the region, and Indigenous heritage of the place where Outinaouatoua was located should simply be understood, then, as the connection of people to place and beyond transitory historical moments of "abandonment" and "loss." The Indigenous families of this settlement who greeted Galinée's company in the fall of 1669 were the next generation's becoming within their ancestral/recent homeland and heritage.

4. Conclusion

I suggest that the events referred to in the historical record for the inter-lakes region during the seventeenth century conveys a deep certainty within conventional historical understandings of change through this time; one resistant to alternative explanatory narratives or the ability to contextualize those events as representing something beyond Eurocentric logic and explanation. As well, I acknowledge that those events greatly affected the Indigenous communities and nations in the region, however they played out and at whatever scale. The transformation of the inter-lakes region before and after 1650, especially the end of extensive settlements afterward, is readily visible archaeologically. But what I wanted to offer here is to think about Outinaouatoua as a result of continuing the Indigenous heritage of this region, rather than as an erasure of it. This perspective allows us to see the residents of this community as connected to and preoccupied with dynamics of their lives and their place in the world as understood in 1669, and as connected to the deeper heritage of the region, and not as furthering European preoccupations, or subsequent conventional historical assumptions.

The place and idea of Outinaouatoua remains elusive to identify or know today beyond the brief observations Galinée offered in the account of his travels of 1669–1670. Scholarship has interpreted the historical fact and happenstance of the expedition encountering this community within a conventional narrative that frames Galinée's encounter within European-centric explanations of geopolitical, military, and economic expansionism. But this interpretative approach to Indigenous pasts is about the tyranny of transitory moments preserved in written European accounts imposing a permanency on the past that masks the more complex and nuanced realities underlying those transitory moments, erasing a richer and deeper context informed by the archaeological history and Indigenous heritage of this region as it existed in 1669.

In the case of Outinaouatoua, its significance and importance in understanding the community in 1669 and in understanding the complexities of seventeenth-century Indigenous social identities and histories comes not from detailed material assemblages or written records, but from the fact of where and when it existed. This fact speaks to deep connections and social continuities within change experienced by the residents in their lifetimes, connecting them to the same changing continuities of their ancestors, and to be shared by their descendants. Indeed, beyond the tyranny of recorded moments, the fortuitous happenstance of Galinée's travel means that his group's passing acquaintance with a community and place has situated Outinaouatoua within our collective consciousness today; it might well have been "lost" to knowing without this happenstance.

Buried in Galinée's observations, then, is the proof of the "why" of Outinaouatoua: it was situated within a homescape of daily living and familiarity to some if not most of the residents of the settlement—a place where game was known to be abundant, and a place to continue on, even if individuals there were, in 1669, thought of as "of the Iroquois of the Five Nations" and no longer as "of the Neutral." And through that continuity, it continued an Indigenous heritage tied to the deep traditions and innovations of people and communities becoming across the inter-lakes region and the north shore of Lake Erie peninsula in the centuries prior.

To sum up this discussion of a site we do not know and can only access through a cacophony of historical speculation, we do know that, in the fall of 1669, Galinée and his party found themselves travelling across a region of deep traditions in transition, embodied both in the people of Outinaouatoua they met, dined with, and were guests of, and in the landscapes, environment, and animals that continued to influence and shape the heritage and practices of this ancestral homeland. This was a borderland of becoming between pasts, presents, and futures that scholarship still seeks to know beyond distant French preoccupations of the time, and beyond the transitory contexts of the moment Galinée's group found themselves connecting with the time-immemorial heritage of a place that we, too, strive to understand in our transitory moment today.

SECTION 3
THE MATERIAL CULTURE
OF THE IROQUOIS
DU NORD SITES

8
DRAWING A BEAD ON THE IROQUOIS DU NORD NARRATIVE

WILLIAM A. FOX, APRIL HAWKINS, AND DAVID HARRIS

This chapter presents information concerning the evolution of Indigenous and European ornament-production industries and distribution networks during the seventeenth century. It characterizes the beads manufactured from stone, shell, bone, and glass recovered from Iroquois du Nord sites in southern Ontario and situates them within the rapidly evolving technical trajectories of this dynamic century. It then compares these assemblages with those recovered from late seventeenth-century villages in the upstate New York homeland of the Haudenosaunee, in particular the well-documented Seneca bead assemblages. The varying character of the Iroquois du Nord bead assemblages is also interpreted utilizing extant historic documentation.

Over the past thirty years, the study of seventeenth-century glass trade bead assemblages in the Northeast has been dominated by the chemical analyses undertaken by Ron Hancock and collaborators (1994, 1995, 2000, 2013), such as Ian Kenyon (1995) and Martha Sempowski (2001), and most recently Heather Walder (2013; 2018). The identification of bead production sites in Europe has been pursued by Karlis Karklins (1974, 2015, 2019). Together, these two research initiatives have generated a more nuanced understanding of European trader commodity acquisition and marketing to the Indigenous communities of the Northeast and of the identification of temporally significant chemical markers in the evolving technology of glass bead production. At the same time, there have been important advances in our understanding of the dramatic seventeenth-century changes in shell bead production, an industry whose Indigenous history stretches back many millennia in the Atlantic coastal region (Ceci 1988). This is followed by a brief description of the European lathe turned bone bead industry represented on the eastern Iroquois du Nord sites collected by Chadd, particularly in the Wellers Bay area. Finally, this chapter considers the fluorescence of Indigenous stone bead production during the seventeenth century, as has been documented in southern Ontario and northern Michigan for more than a century (Boyle 1888:12; Cleland 1971:41–52; Fox 1980).

To place the Iroquois du Nord sites in archaeological context, it is important to review the character of the preceding Ontario Iroquoian glass trade bead sequence. Ian and Tim Kenyon initiated an extensive program of research and documentation during the 1960s of Huron-Wendat, Tionontaté (also known as Petun), and Neutral glass bead assemblages dating from circa 1580–1650 (Kenyon and Kenyon 1983). Not only did they study and describe Ontario collections, they also, in 1968, visited Charles Wray to study his Seneca collections of western New York. Their proposed chronology of glass bead styles, using the Kidd typology (Kidd and Kidd 1970), has stood the test of time with minor revision. Period 1 dates from circa 1580–1600, period 2 from circa 1600–1620, and period 3 from circa 1620–1650. There has been some dispute about the start date of period 3 as Fitzgerald (1983:21) has proposed 1632. It has also been suggested that this period be divided into periods 3a and 3b (Kenyon and Kenyon 1983:74, Table 4). Glass bead period (GBP) 3 is, of course, the most relevant in differentiating terminal Ontario Iroquoian glass bead assemblages from those present on late seventeenth-century Iroquois du Nord sites. On circa 1632–1651 terminal Ontario Iroquoian sites, drawn red tubes (Kidd Type Ia1) constitute roughly a quarter of the assemblages (Figure 8.1).

Figure 8.1. Glass Bead Period 3 beads from the Lake Medad site.
Source: Courtesy of the Canadian Museum of History, photograph by William A. Fox; digital enhancement by John Howarth.

1. Evidence from the Haudenosaunee Homeland

Assuming that Bishop François de Laval's information was correct, the "place situated close to the nearest part of the lake called Ontario," or the present-day Prince Edward County region, seems to have been occupied by Haudenosaunee at around 1665 (Preston and Lamontagne 1958:85). The population of this region is identified as Cayuga for the most part. There were Oneida farther east, at Ganneious (Konrad 1981:136; see Menary and von Bitter, this volume), and Seneca farther west, at Teiaiagon and Ganatsekwyagon (see Robertson, this volume; Poulton, this volume). Comparative bead data for the Oneida (Bennett 1983; Pratt 1961) and Cayuga (Mandzy 1990, 1994) homeland settlements are limited. Those for the Seneca are more robust, thanks to Charles Wray, who has identified the Dann and Marsh villages as contemporary with the initial Iroquois du Nord occupation (Wray et al. 1987:3) (Figure 8.2). The Marsh village appears to be the predecessor to the Boughton Hill village, which has been identified as the village of Ganondagan (also Gannagaro), attacked and

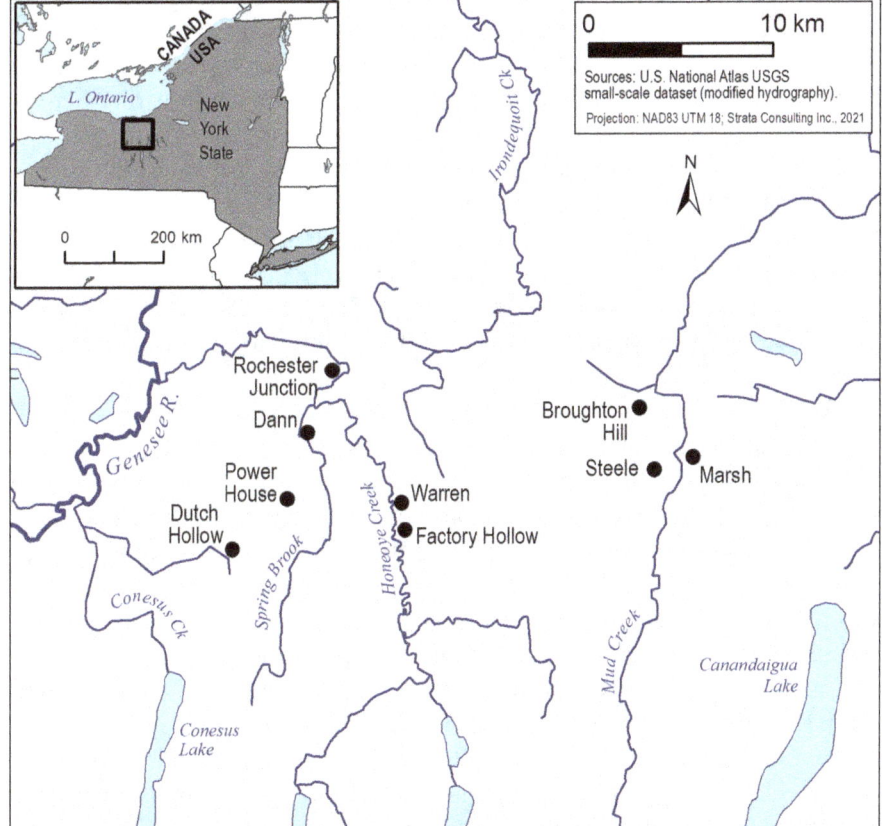

Figure 8.2. Map showing locations of Haudenosaunee sites mentioned in the text.
Source: Map by William A. Fox.

sacked by French forces led by Jacques-René de Brisay de Denonville in 1687 (Wray et al. 1987:2). The Dann village is proposed by Charles Wray to be the predecessor of the Rochester Junction site, which has been identified as the village of Totiakton, the second major Seneca village attacked by Denonville.

Unfortunately, none of the aforementioned Seneca sites have been subject to the comprehensive and excellent material culture description and analysis of the *Charles F. Wray Series in Seneca Archaeology*—the final villages studied being the Dutch Hollow and Factory Hollow sites, which were argued by Wray et al. (1987) to date from circa 1590–1620. A subsequent revision by Martha Sempowski and Lorraine Saunders (2001:19) puts them at circa 1605–1625, and in our opinion a more realistic occupation date may be 1615–1630 (see also Birch et al. 2021: 68, 74, 78–80), which is still prior to the dispersal of the Ontario Iroquoians and their Algonquian allies. Since we are not in a position to undertake a detailed analysis of the more than 95,000 glass beads from the four aforementioned late seventeenth-century Seneca villages (Wray 1983:44–45), we must rely on Wray's summary of the key bead types for the time period. The Kidd glass bead types characteristic of collections from the Marsh and Dann villages include drawn tubes, which continue to dominate over round bead forms, but there is a slightly greater range of colours than in earlier Seneca assemblages (Ryan and Dewbury 2010:22) (Figure 8.3).

Beginning in the 1670s and throughout the 1680s, there is an abrupt change to predominately round beads in a limited range of colours. To quote Wray (1983:45): "the numerous tubular varieties of the Marsh-Dann period are nearly gone and are replaced by monotonous round red, black, green and white drawn beads" (Figure 8.4). Support for this summary observation is presented in Wray and Graham's 1966 inventory of beads from the Boughton Hill site (Wray and Graham 1985:23–24).

We have combined Wray's (1983) overview of Seneca glass bead trends through the late seventeenth century with personal observation by one of us (WF) of the Rock Foundation collections at the Rochester Museum & Science Center to generate directly comparable data for the western Iroquois du Nord communities, identified as Seneca despite their strongly multi-ethnic composition (Thwaites 1896–1901:45:207). Intensive looting of seventeenth-century Cayuga sites, particularly during the 1870s (Skinner 1921:37–38), has resulted in limited subsequent archaeological excavation and reporting on these sites, as well as little studied legacy collections held by various New York State museums (Mandzy 1994:136) and even the Royal Ontario Museum (Boyle 1898:15). Extant Oneida information includes Pratt's 1961 colour guide to Oneida glass beads, which precedes the Kidds' seminal publication, and an update using the Kidd typology by Monte Bennett (1983).

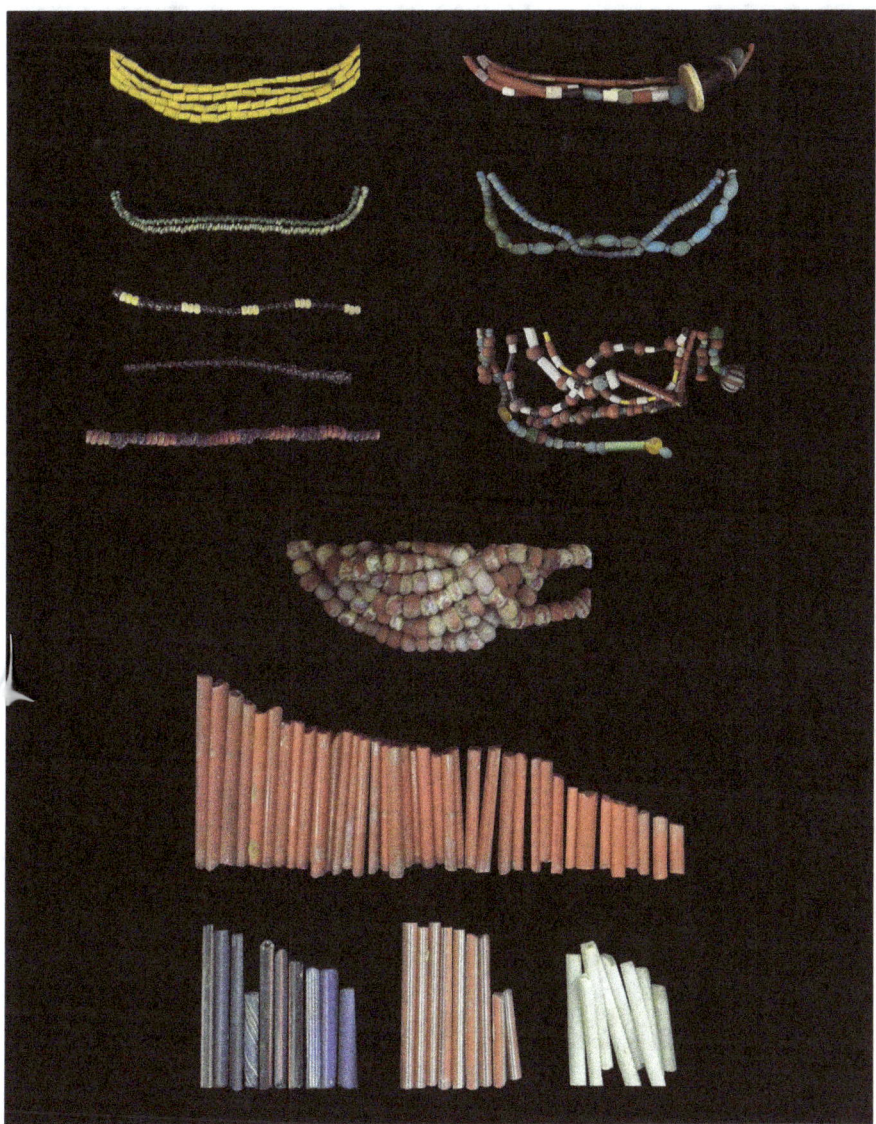

Figure 8.3. Glass beads from the Dann site.
Source: Rochester Museum & Science Center, photograph by William A. Fox; digital enhancement by John Howarth.

2. Glass Beads

Before we consider the glass bead data from Teiaiagon and Ganatsekwyagon, the two historically identified IDN sites in the Toronto area, and from ten collection localities in Prince Edward and Hastings counties (see Tables 8.1–8.12), we need to present a number of caveats. As described by Ron Williamson (this volume), there are serious constraints to the archaeological interpretation

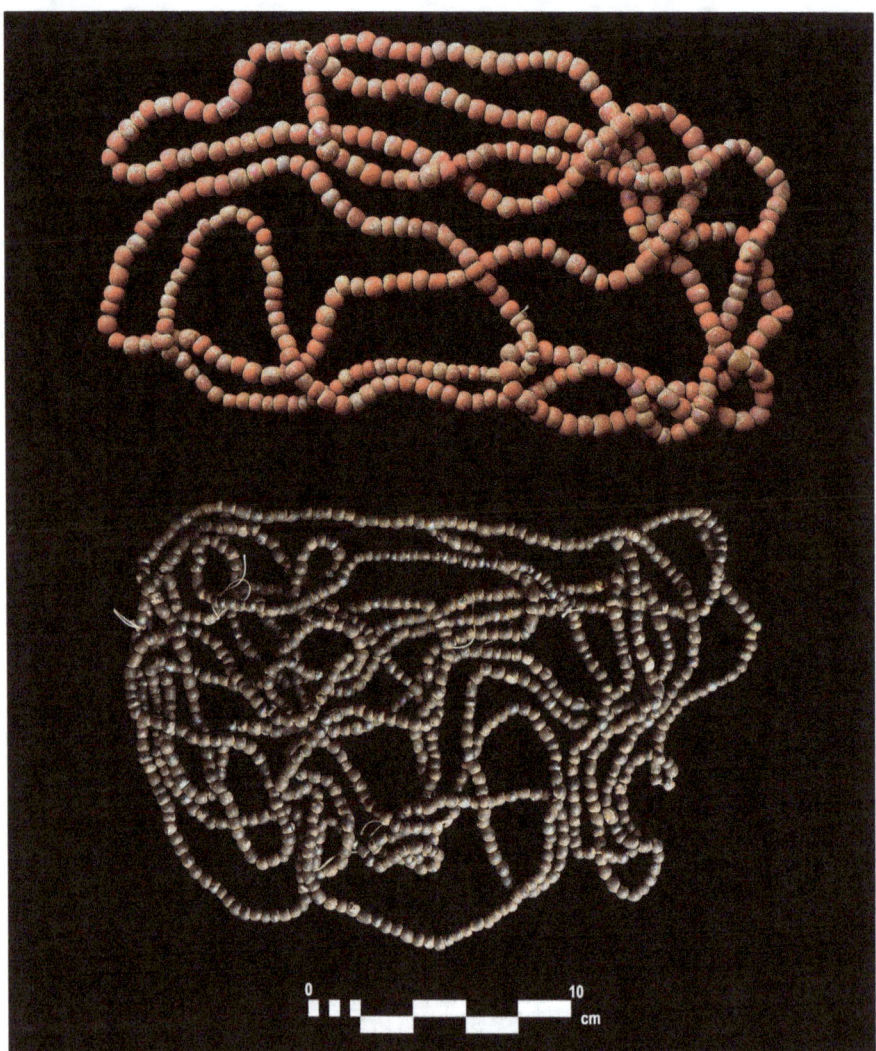

Figure 8.4. Glass beads from the Boughton Hill and Rochester Junction sites.
Source: Rochester Museum & Science Center, photograph by William A. Fox; digital enhancement by John Howarth.

of the subject legacy collections, resulting from a dearth of information concerning the exact context and the methods used to recover the bead assemblages (Boyle 1897:48). Also, due to recent, pandemic-related constraints on access to the Royal Ontario Museum collections, where most of the bead assemblages discussed here are curated, our typological analysis is based to a considerable extent on a series of digital images taken by WF in 2011, supplemented by limited "truthing" of these identifications during a February 2020 visit. Despite the relatively high resolution of the digital images, application of the Kidd typology has proved challenging due to varying degrees of patination, which has all but completely obscured colouration in some cases. This is particularly true for blue-coloured beads, which appear to patinate more rapidly than other colours, perhaps due to inadequate amounts of calcium in their production recipe (Hancock et al. 1994:263). Because of the limitation of working with digital images and following consultation with Karklins (personal communication 2019) concerning glass bead production variables, we have decided to roll together all the "cored" (Type IV) varieties of round beads with their Type II solid colour forms. The resulting analysis, although not exact regarding core colour for round beads, still provides some clear conclusions concerning comparisons with bead assemblages from Haudenosaunee villages in the homeland.

Glass beads from the Dann village, illustrated in Figure 8.3, reflect an unprecedented diversity of colour and form in the decades immediately following the mid-century, similar to collections from the Wellers Bay localities, the Indian Island locality on the Bay of Quinte, and from the Sandbanks locality (Figure 1.2; Figure 8.5). These assemblages from the eastern part of the north shore of Lake Ontario are dominated by tubular red (Ia1) and black (Ia2); round red (IIa1); and, to a lesser extent, round black (IIa6) beads (see Tables 8.1–8.10). The tubular red forms range in size from small to very large (as defined by Kidd and Kidd 1970:66), with the majority in the medium to lower-large range (5–8 mm long, 2 mm thick), similar in size to wampum, and considerably smaller than the Type Ia1 red tubes characteristic of the preceding GBP 3 assemblages from Ontario. Other minority bead types of temporal significance include the twisted red tubes (Ic′1, 0.2%–10%) that are characteristic of GBP 3 assemblages, as well as black tubes with three red stripes (Ib3, 0.8%–4.8%), which are never found on Ontario GBP 3 sites. One eastern site stands out as anomalous in not containing the aforementioned range of bead forms, at least based on a 2003–2004 salvage excavation of a mortuary site at Smokes Point (Northeastern Archaeological Associates 2010). The 397 complete and 27 half pea-sized round red beads are clearly Kidd type IIa1 beads, while the four red tubes are a thinner Ia1 type (Northeastern Archaeological Associates 2010:43–44, Plate 17), consistent with the following western site assemblages.

Table 8.1. Glass beads from the Sandbanks locality

Kidd Code	Shape	Size	Description	Qty.
IIa1	round	VS–L	opaque redwood	34
Ia2	tubular	S–M	opaque black	33
Ia1	tubular	M–VL	opaque redwood	21
IIa6	round	MS–M	opaque black	21
Ia7	tubular	S–M	opaque light gold	8

Kidd Code	Shape	Size	Description	Qty.
Ib3	tubular	M	opaque black; 3 redwood stripes	7
IIg1	round	M	opaque black; 3 white dots	7
IIa13	round	VS–L	opaque white	5
IIa18	round	S	opaque amber	5
IIa24	round	VS	opaque apple green	2
Ic'1	tubular	VL	opaque redwood	1
IIa40	round	S	opaque robin's egg blue	1
IIa46	round	L	opaque shadow blue	1

Notes: VL = very large; L = large; M = medium; S = small; V = very small
Source: William A. Fox.

Table 8.2. Glass beads from Indian Island locality

Kidd Code	Shape	Size	Description	Qty.
Ia1	tubular	M	opaque redwood	194
IIa1	round	S–L	opaque redwood	38
Ia7	tubular	S–M	opaque light gold	28
Ia2	tubular	S–M	opaque black	13
IIa6	round	S	opaque black	10
IIa13	round	S	opaque white	7
IIg1	round	M–L	opaque black; 3 white dots	4
Ib3	tubular	M	opaque black; 3 redwood stripes	3
IIa2	circular	S	opaque redwood	2
IIa35	round	M–L	opaque light aqua blue	2
Ic'1	tubular	VL	opaque redwood	1
IIa3	oval	M	opaque redwood	1
IIa7	circular	S	opaque black	1
IIIb1	tubular	M	opaque redwood; black core; opaque white stripes	1

Source: William A. Fox.

Table 8.3. Glass beads from the Ameliasburgh Township

Kidd Code	Shape	Size	Description	Qty.
IIa1	round	M–L	opaque redwood	92
IIa2	circular	S	opaque redwood	90
Ia1	tubular	M–L	opaque redwood	38
Ia2	tubular	L	opaque black	36
IIa35	round	S–M	opaque light aqua blue	24
IIa6	round	S	opaque black	16

Kidd Code	Shape	Size	Description	Qty.
Ia7	tubular	S–M	opaque light gold	15
IIa7	circular	S	opaque black	14
Ic'1	tubular	M–VL	opaque redwood	12
IIa14	circular	S	opaque white	6
IIa13	round	M	opaque white	5
IIa48	round	S	opaque shadow blue	5
IIa3	oval	M–L	opaque redwood	4
IIa12	circular	S	opaque oyster white	4
Ib3	tubular	L	opaque black; 3 redwood stripes	3
IIa26	round	S	clear emerald green	3
IIa34	circular	S	opaque light aqua blue	3
IIg1	round	L	opaque black; 3 white dots	3
Ia21	tubular	S	clear rose wine	1
IIa15	oval	L	opaque white	1
IIa16	round	L	opaque pale blue	1
IIa18	round	M–L	opaque amber	1
IIa40	round	M	opaque robin's egg blue	1
IIa61	round	M	clear dark rose brown	1

Source: William A. Fox.

Table 8.4. Glass beads from Bloomfield locality

Kidd Code	Shape	Size	Description	Qty.
IIa1	round	M–L	opaque redwood	19
Ia1	tubular	M–VL	opaque redwood	12
IIa35	round	M–L	opaque light aqua blue	5
IIa36	round	M	opaque aqua blue	5
Ia2	tubular	M–L	opaque black	4
Ia7	tubular	S–M	opaque light gold	3
IIa2	circular	S–M	opaque redwood	3
IIa3	oval	M–L	opaque redwood	2
Ib3	tubular	M	opaque black; 3 redwood stripes	1
Ic'1	tubular	VL	opaque redwood	1
IIa6	round	S	opaque black	1
IIa17	round	S	opaque light gold	1
IIa18	round	M	opaque amber	1
IIa34	circular	M	opaque light aqua blue	1
IIa44	round	S	clear cerulean blue	1

Source: William A. Fox.

Table 8.5. Glass beads from the Carrying Place area

Kidd Code	Shape	Size	Description	Qty.
Ia1	tubular	M–VL	opaque redwood	15
IIa37	circular	M	opaque aqua blue	7
IIa36	round	M–L	opaque aqua blue	5
Ic'1	tubular	VL	opaque redwood	4
Ia2	tubular	L	opaque black	3
Ia7	tubular	S–M	opaque light gold	3
IIa6	round	S	opaque black	2
Ia19	tubular	VL	opaque bright navy	1
IIa1	round	M	opaque redwood	1
IIg1	round	L	opaque black; 3 white dots	1
IIIk1	tubular	VL	opaque redwood; white; bright blue; white; bright blue	1

Source: William A. Fox.

Table 8.6. Glass beads from the Coe Hill area

Kidd Code	Shape	Size	Description	Qty.
Ia1	tubular	M–L	opaque redwood	162
Ia2	tubular	M–L	opaque black	57
IIa2	circular	S	opaque redwood	55
IIa7	circular	VS–S	opaque black	41
IIa1	round	M–L	opaque redwood	33
IIa6	round	S–M	opaque black	25
Ia8	tubular	S–M	translucent citron	21
IIa14	circular	S	opaque white	18
IIg1	round	L	opaque black; 3 white dots	14
Ia7	tubular	S–M	opaque light gold	8
Ib3	tubular	M–L	opaque black; 3 redwood stripes	7
IIa27	circular	S	clear emerald green	7
IIa35	round	M	opaque light aqua blue	6
IIa3	oval	L	opaque redwood	2
Ic'1	tubular	L	opaque redwood	1
IIa55	round	M	clear bright navy	1
IIa61	round	M	clear dark rose brown	1

Source: William A. Fox.

Table 8.7. Glass beads from the Picton area

Kidd Code	Shape	Size	Description	Qty.
IIa1	round	S–L	opaque redwood	141
IIa2	circular	S–M	opaque redwood	88
Ia1	tubular	M–L	opaque redwood	60
IIa35	round	M–L	opaque light aqua blue	38
Ia2	tubular	S–M	opaque black	30
IIa6	round	S–M	opaque black	27
Ib3	tubular	M–L	opaque black; 3 redwood stripes	10
IIa14	circular	S	opaque white	8
IIa17	round	S–L	opaque light gold	8
Ic'1	tubular	L–VL	opaque redwood	7
IIa44	round	S	clear cerulean blue	7
Ia7	tubular	S–M	opaque light gold	5
IIa18	round	L	opaque amber	4
IIg1	round	M	opaque black; 3 white dots	2
Ia14	round	VL	opaque robin's egg blue	1
IIa9	round	L	opaque light grey	1
IIa34	circular	M	opaque light aqua blue	1
IIa41	circular	S	opaque robin's egg blue	1
IIa49	oval	M	opaque dark shadow blue	1

Source: William A. Fox.

Table 8.8. Glass beads from Sugar Point

Kidd Code	Shape	Size	Description	Qty.
Ia1	tubular	S–L	opaque redwood	116
IIa1	round	S–L	opaque redwood	61
Ia7	tubular	S–M	opaque light gold	41
IIa2	circular	S–M	opaque redwood	25
IIa7	circular	S	opaque black	21
Ia2	tubular	M–L	opaque redwood	15
IIa35	round	M	opaque light aqua blue	12
Ib3	tubular	L	opaque black; 3 redwood stripes	7
IIa6	round	S–M	opaque black	7
Ic'1	tubular	VL	opaque redwood	5
IIa14	circular	S	opaque white	4
IIa61	round	M	clear dark rose brown	4
IIa22	round	M	opaque mustard tan	2
IIa44	round	S	opaque robin's egg blue	2

Kidd Code	Shape	Size	Description	Qty.
Ia8	tubular	S	translucent citron	1
Ia15	tubular	M	translucent bright blue (facetted)	1
IIa3	oval	L	opaque redwood	1
IIa9	round	L	opaque light grey	1
IIa11	round	M	opaque oyster white	1
IIa15	oval	M	opaque white	1
IIa19	circular	S	opaque amber	1
IIa24	round	S	opaque apple green	1

Source: William A. Fox.

Table 8.9. Glass beads from the Trent River mouth (Murray Township)

Kidd Code	Shape	Size	Description	Qty.
IIa1	round	M–VL	opaque redwood	29
Ia1	tubular	M–VL	opaque redwood	24
IIa2	circular	S–M	opaque redwood	15
IIa6	round	S–L	opaque black	15
Ia2	tubular	M–VL	opaque black	14
Ia8	tubular	S–M	translucent citron	9
IIa12	circular	S	opaque oyster white	9
IIa36	round	M	opaque aqua blue	9
IIg1	circular/round	M–L	opaque black; 3 white dots	7
Ib3	tubular	L	opaque black; 3 redwood stripes	5
IIa13	round	S–L	opaque white	3
IIa17	round	S–L	opaque light gold	3
IIa27	circular	S	clear emerald green	3
IIa37	circular	M	opaque aqua blue	3
Ia21	tubular	VL	opaque rose wine	2
Ic'1	tubular	VL	opaque redwood	2
Ia7	tubular	S	opaque light gold	1
IIa14	circular	M	opaque white	1
IIa20	round	M	opaque cinnamon	1
IIa28	round	M	opaque dark palm green	1

Source: William A. Fox.

Table 8.10. Glass beads from the Wellers Bay locality

Kidd Code	Shape	Size	Description	Qty.
IIa1	round	M–L	opaque redwood	218
Ia1	tubular	M–VL	opaque redwood	88
Ia2	tubular	S–L	opaque black	82
IIa2	circular	S	opaque redwood	75
Ia7	tubular	S–M	opaque light gold	42
IIa6	round	S	opaque black	32
IIa13	round	VS–S	opaque white	20
Ib3	tubular	M	opaque black; 3 redwood stripes	19
Ic'1	tubular	VL	opaque redwood	13
IIa24	round	S	opaque apple green	12
IIg1	round	L	opaque black; 3 white dots	12
IIa19	circular	S	opaque amber	9
IIa7	circular	S	opaque black	6
IIa35	round	M	opaque light aqua blue	6
IIa46	round	M	opaque shadow blue	6
IIa3	oval	M	opaque redwood	4
IIa36	round	M	opaque aqua blue	4
IIa40	round	M	opaque robin's egg blue	3
Ia5	tubular	S–L	opaque white	2
IIa8	oval	M	opaque black	2
IIa14	circular	S–M	opaque white	2
IIa49	oval	M	opaque dark shadow blue	2
IIa55	round	S	clear bright navy	2
IVa1	round	L	opaque redwood; black core	2
Ib4	tubular	M	opaque black; 3 white stripes	1
IIIf2	tubular	L	tr. ultramarine; light aqua blue core	1

Source: William A. Fox.

Table 8.11. Glass beads from Ganatsekwyagon

Kidd Code	Shape	Size	Description	Qty.
IIa1	round	M–L	opaque redwood	113
IIa6	round	S–L	opaque black	73
IVa6	circular	S	opaque redwood; clear apple green core	19
IVa5	round	L	opaque redwood; clear apple green core	14
IIa7	circular	S–L	opaque black	12
IIa8	oval	S–L	opaque black	10

Kidd Code	Shape	Size	Description	Qty.
IIa2	circular	S–L	opaque redwood	8
IIa37	circular	S	opaque aqua blue	8
IIa24	round	M	opaque apple green	5
IVa7	oval	M	opaque redwood; clear apple green core	5
IIa40	round	L	opaque robin's egg blue	3
IIa15	oval	S–M	opaque white	2
IIa13	round	L	opaque white	1
IIa14	circular	S	opaque white	1
IIa34	circular	M	opaque light aqua blue	1
IIa35	round	M	opaque light aqua blue	1
IIb'3	oval	M	opaque black; white stripes	1
IIIa3	tubular	M	opaque redwood; clear apple green core	1

Source: William A. Fox.

Table 8.12. Glass beads from Teiaiagon

Kidd Code	Shape	Size	Description	Qty.
IIa1	round	VS–L	opaque redwood	743
IIa6	round	VS–L	opaque black	131
IIa40	round	VS–M	opaque robin's egg blue	50
Ia1	tubular	M–VL	opaque redwood	35
IIa2	circular	S–L	opaque redwood	19
IIa13	round	M	opaque white	16
Ia2	tubular	M	opaque black	7
IIa24	round	M	opaque apple green	6
Ib3	tubular	M–L	opaque black; 3 redwood stripes	3
IIa55	round	M	clear bright navy	2
Ia19	tubular	M	clear bright navy	1
IIa7	circular	M	opaque black	1
IIa8	oval	M	opaque black	1
IIa15	oval	L	opaque white	1
IIb12	round	M	opaque black; 4 opaque white stripes	1
IIbb6	oval	L	opaque black; 3 thin redwood on white stripes	1
WIb2	round	L	opaque white	1
WIc1	oval	M	opaque white	1

Source: William A. Fox.

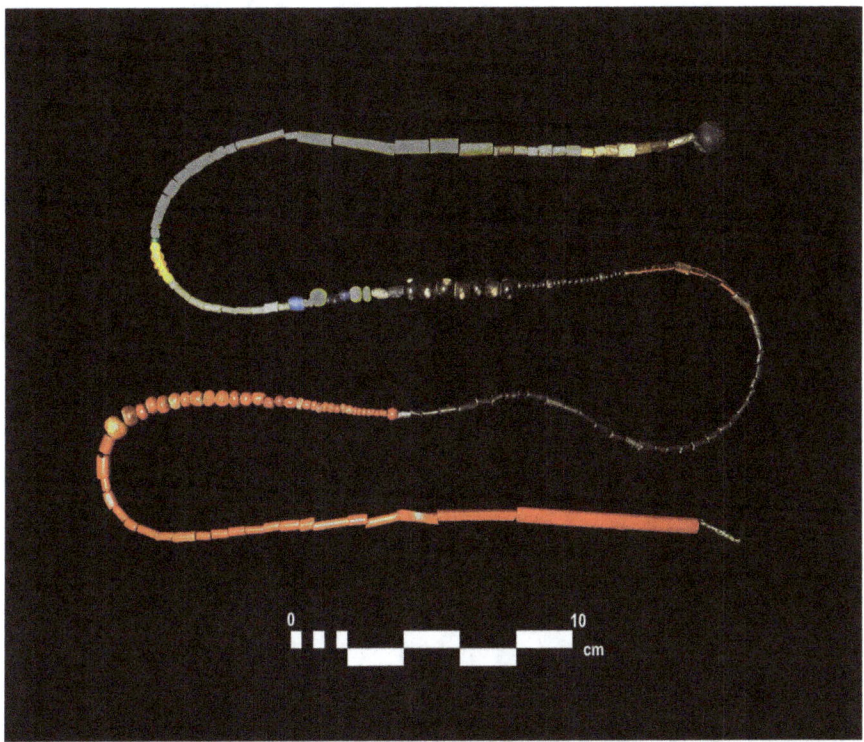

Figure 8.5. Glass beads from the Wellers Bay localities.
Source: Courtesy of the Royal Ontario Museum, photograph by William A. Fox; digital enhancement by John Howarth.

Excavations at Ganatsekwyagon (Poulton, this volume) have produced hundreds of pea-sized, round red and round black beads (Cooper 2007; Figure 8.6), as have the collections from Teiaiagon (Robertson, this volume). A handful of the earlier, tubular forms have also been recovered at Teiaiagon (see Tables 8.11 to 8.12). The round red (IIa1) and round black (IIa6) beads range in size from very small to large, but they are larger on average than those from the eastern sites. These two bead types constitute 72% and 85.6%, respectively, of the total glass bead recoveries from Ganatsekwyagon and Teiaiagon. With the exception of the Hilton site on Smokes Point (Northeastern Archaeological Associates 2010), none of the assemblages from the eastern sites produced more than 40% of these two bead types. Neither western site has produced twisted red tubes (Ic′1), and only three black tube beads with three red stripes (Ib3, 0.003%) were identified in a total assemblage of 1,021 beads from Teiaiagon (Figure 8.7).

174 The History and Archaeology of the Iroquois du Nord

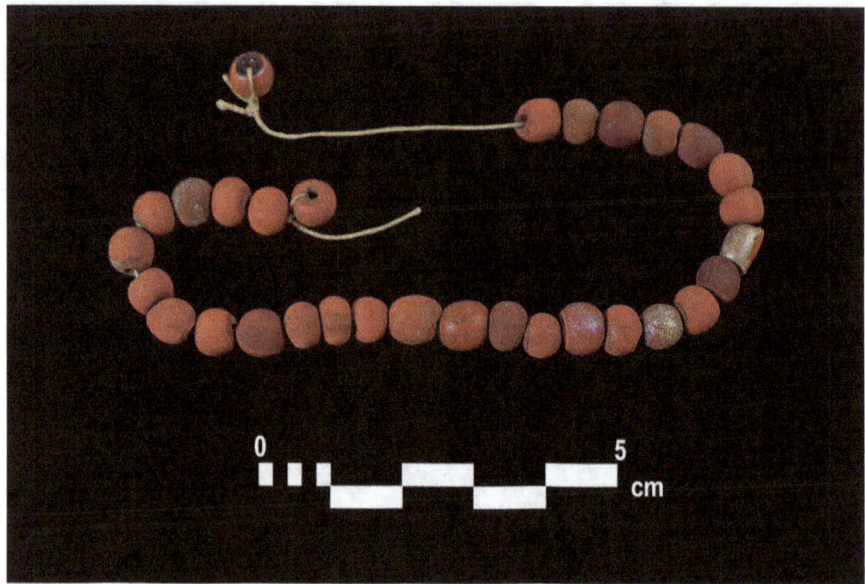

Figure 8.6. Glass beads from Ganatsekwyagon.
Source: Courtesy of the Royal Ontario Museum, photograph by William A. Fox; digital enhancement by John Howarth.

Figure 8.7. Glass beads from Teiaiagon.
Source: Courtesy of the Royal Ontario Museum, photograph by William A. Fox; digital enhancement by John Howarth.

3. Marine Shell Beads

Martha Sempowski (1988:87) has noted the substantial and increasing abundance of marine shell beads and pendants on Seneca sites dating to the second half of the seventeenth century. Ontario Iroquoian populations, in contrast, were acquiring large quantities of marine shells and ornaments from the mid-Atlantic coastal region from the late sixteenth century onward. There is evidence of marine shell ornament manufacturing during the 1630s based on this imported whelk shell on the Blue Mountain-area Hamilton-Lougheed village (Ehwae; Garrad 2014:357) at the same time as the red siltstone bead industry was flourishing (Boyle 1888:12; Fox 1980). From the mid-seventeenth century on, by far the most common shell bead is the "true or belt wampum" (Bradley 2011:42) form, which is present on lower Great Lakes Indigenous sites starting in the 1630s (Fox 2020: Figure 1; Kenyon 1982:31, Plates 30, 211, and 185; Kenyon and Fox 1982:13; Warrick 1983:49–50). A complete wampum belt was recovered from the site of Ganatsekwyagon (Figure 8.8).

Archaeological evidence from coastal New England, where seventeenth-century Indigenous wampum production was centred, indicates that the purple quahog clam shell beads first appear during the 1630s, later than the white whelk shell "Early Wampum" form (Ceci 1989:72) and at about the same time that Europeans began to participate in the industry (Esarey 2013:58). Although purple wampum is abundant on 1640s Ontario Iroquoian sites (Fox 2020; Warrick 1983), whelk shell disk runtee-style beads are rare (Wintemberg 1908:49, Plate IX, l, m, 69), and they appear cruder than the later seventeenth-century specimens associated with the Iroquois du Nord occupation (Boyle 1903:87, Figure 54; Wintemberg 1908:50, Plate X.e.69). These and a range of other bead and pendant ornament forms have been defined by Duane Esarey as the standardized marine shell (SMS) industry (Esarey 2013:4–7, Figures 1.1–1.3, Table 1.1), which subsumes almost all marine shell goods on Iroquois du

Figure 8.8. Marine shell wampum belt from Ganatsekwyagon.
Source: Courtesy of the Royal Ontario Museum, photograph by William A. Fox; digital enhancement by John Howarth.

Nord sites. There are some holdovers of traditional pre-contact Indigenous bead forms, such as perforated *Marginella* shells and the ubiquitous whelk shell discoidal beads, but the vast majority of marine shell ornaments relate to the SMS industry. These include pipe beads and classic disk runtee-style beads or pendants, as well as crescent, bear claw, and loon effigy pendants (Cowin 2000:4–5, Figure 3; Esarey 2013:5, Figures 1.2 and 1.3; Hayes 1988:40, Figures 5 and 6; Wintemberg 1908:59, Plate 19, j). Loon pendants (Beauchamp 1901:362–363, Plates 5, 65, 68, 70, Plates 17, 218; Bradley 2011:40; Wintemberg 1908:59, Plate XIX, j, 77) certainly post-date the Ontario Iroquoian diaspora. Therefore, these ornaments and the classic disk runtee-style beads (Beauchamp 1901:372–376, Plate 10; Esarey 2013:6, Figure 1.3) are excellent late seventeenth-century time markers. Loon effigy pendants are present in the material collected by G. J. Chadd (Harris 2020; Williamson, this volume) from the Picton and Bloomfield localities (Orr 1922:122, Figure "Small Shell Pendants") (Figure 8.9), as are wampum and pipe beads.

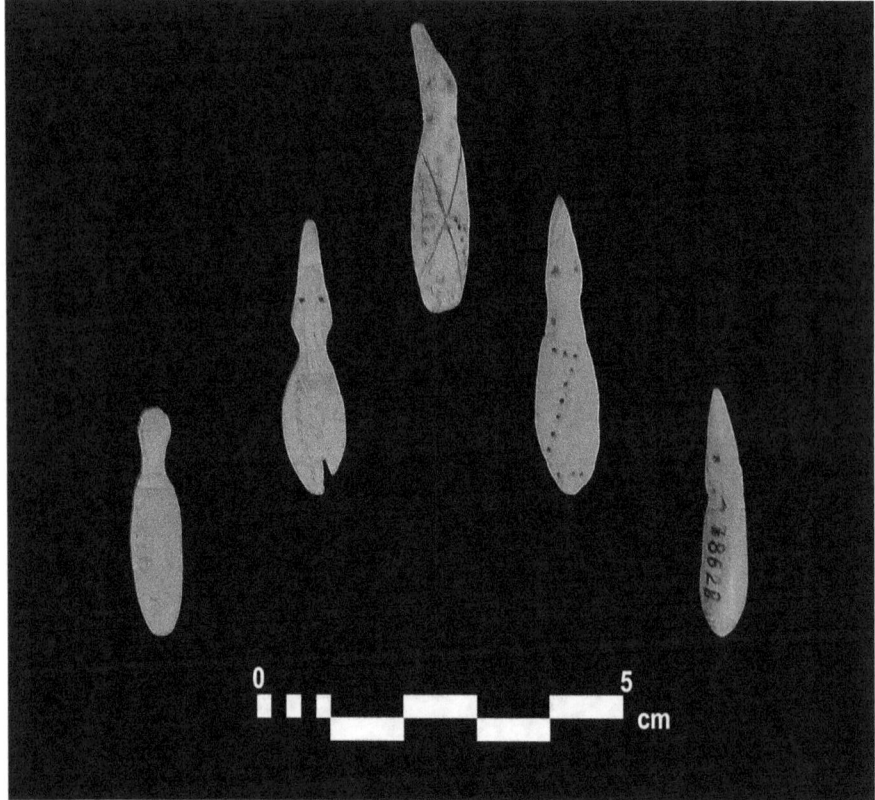

Figure 8.9. Marine shell loon effigy pendants from the Picton and Bloomfield localities.
Source: Courtesy of the Royal Ontario Museum, photograph by William A. Fox; digital enhancement by John Howarth.

Classic decorated runtee beads or pendants have been recovered from three Ontario sites (Boyle 1904:87, Figure 54; Wintemberg 1908:50, Plate X.e.69; Laura Peers, personal communication 2019) (Figure 8.10).

Pipe beads (Figure 8.11) and wampum are also included in Chadd's collection from the mouth of the Trent River, and the latter have been recovered in abundance from all Iroquois du Nord sites, except the Hilton site (Northeastern Archaeological Associates 2010:40).

Two additional SMS ornament forms have been recovered from Teiaiagon: a loon effigy pendant and a crescent. Although many marine shell artifacts have been eroded over time by acidic soils (Davis 1988:14), some of the Teiaiagon white and purple wampum beads remain in remarkable condition, providing a glimpse of their former beauty (Figure 8.12).

Figure 8.10. Classic late seventeenth-century marine shell runtee beads and catlinite tubes, assumed to be from King Township, York County, in the John R. Mortimer Collection at the Hull and East Riding Museum, England.
Source: Photograph courtesy of A. Rose.

Figure 8.11. Marine shell pipe beads from Ganatsekwyagon.
Source: Courtesy of the Royal Ontario Museum, photograph by William A. Fox; digital enhancement by John Howarth.

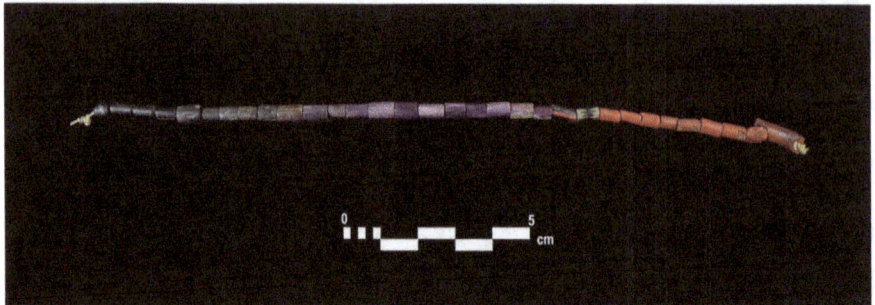

Figure 8.12. Marine shell wampum beads from Teiaiagon.
Source: Courtesy of the Royal Ontario Museum, photograph by William A. Fox; digital enhancement by John Howarth.

4. Bone Beads

A preliminary review by WF in 2011 of the Chadd Collection focused on strings of glass beads, and no observations were made regarding bone beads. All bone specimens are of European manufacture and lathe turned (Léouffre et al.

2019). There are thirty-one round, three oval, and two tubular (Figure 8.13) in the Chadd Collection. The latter form is described by Stone (1971:75) as "single jointed," forming "a part of the rosary crucifix" (Figure 8.14) as seen in a complete rosary from Ste. Marie I illustrated by Kenneth Kidd (1949:129; Figure 23B). They measure 7.7 mm, 4.1 mm, and 1.9 mm, and 6.3 mm, 4.0 mm, and 1.6 mm in maximum length, diameter and bore diameter, respectively, consistent with the late seventeenth-century Lasanen site metrics (Stone 1971:75, Table 18). Similar beads from the eighteenth-century site of Fort

Figure 8.13. A string of glass and bone beads from the Wellers Bay locality with close-ups of round and oval bone rosary beads.
Source: Courtesy of the Royal Ontario Museum; photograph by William A. Fox; digital enhancement by John Howarth.

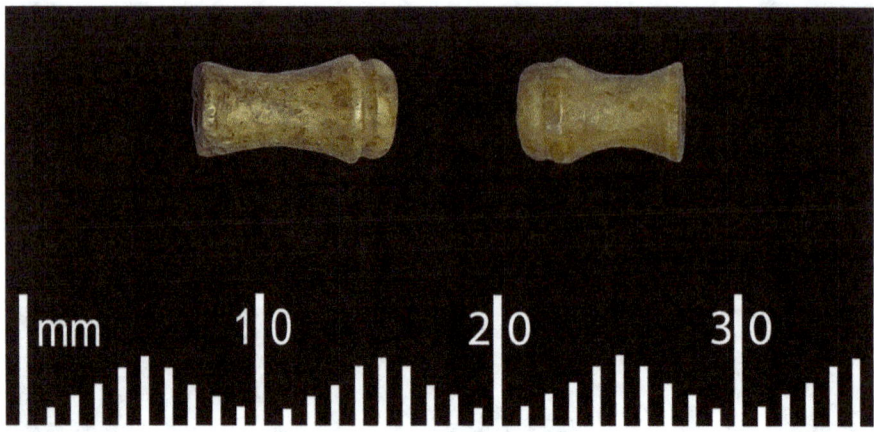

Figure 8.14. Tubular bone crucifix beads from the Wellers Bay locality.
Source: Courtesy of the Royal Ontario Museum; photograph by William A. Fox; digital enhancement by John Howarth.

Michilimackinac are described as tubular—SA T4c (Stone 1974:115–116M, 117; Figure 52). The three grooved oval specimens may be gaudes or decade separators on a rosary (d'Allemtejo 2003:1), and range from 7.7 to 8.7 mm, 5.3 to 6.0 mm, and 2.2 to 2.7 mm in maximum length, diameter, and bore diameter. These dimensions are consistent with the Lasanen site "ovate shaped" rosary beads (Stone 1971:74) and slightly smaller than the Fort Michilimackinac oval form—SA T1a (Stone 1974:114, 116A, 117, Figure 52). The remaining thirty-one round beads range from 4.3 to 11.0 mm and 2.0 to 2.8 mm in maximum diameter and bore diameter. They would be classified as small to large at the Lasanen site (Stone 1971:74), and as round—SA T2 in the Fort Michilimackinac assemblage (Stone 1974:115–116 E–G, 117, Figure 52).

The two tubular rosary beads derive from "Ameliasburgh Township" according to Chadd's catalogue, along with fourteen of the round specimens. The only other site producing anything like this number of rosary beads, including the three oval gaudes, is Wellers Bay, with nine round specimens, suggesting that the general township collection derives from one or more of the Wellers Bay localities. The only other locality on Wellers Bay that produced rosary beads is Sugar Point, with three round specimens. Outside of Wellers Bay, the Trent River mouth produced four round beads and the distant Coe Hill site, one round specimen. There is a possibility that round amber-coloured glass beads categorized as Kidd type IIa18 also functioned as rosary beads (Loewen 2019), although the majority so-classified were subsequently identified as bone.

5. Stone Beads

Stone beads continued to be manufactured and exchanged during the late seventeenth century. A red stone bead production industry sprang up circa

1615–1620 on southern Ontario Wendat and Tionontaté sites that also evidence Odawa/Anishinaabe residents (Fox and Garrad 2004:129), during what Ian Kenyon has referred to as the "red shift" in glass beads anticipating GBP 3 assemblages (Kenyon and Kenyon 1983:69). A discoidal stone bead production industry existed on the circa-1600 Wendat (and Anishinaabe) Ball village, where the application of heat to create pink to red colouration in a naturally grey-coloured steatite seems to anticipate the initiation of the Indigenous red siltstone bead industry (Fox 2014). As the source of the red siltstone raw material for the later tubular beads is situated along the north shore of Georgian Bay and the most intensive bead production occurred on Blue Mountain-region village sites, such as Ehwae (Boyle 1888:12; Garrad 2014:208, Figure 5.1), that were shared by the Odawa and the Tionontaté (Fox 1980:94), we strongly suspect that it was a primarily Odawa industry (Fox 1992). By the 1630s and into the 1640s, red catlinite beads began arriving from the west and became increasingly popular among Ontario Iroquoian groups (Kenyon and Fox 1982:12–13). These tubular beads are usually square or triangular in cross-section, can display notching along one or more edges, and occasionally display incised zigzag serpentine motifs. One of the earliest Ontario examples of this catlinite bead type is a 29 mm long tube of triangular cross-section, with a 3 mm bore and eleven lateral edge notches, recovered from the GBP IIIa Grave 11 in the Grimsby Neutral cemetery (Kenyon 1982:63–64, 76, Plate 77, S; Kenyon and Fox 1982:9, 12). The collection from the later 1640s Lake Medad Neutral site, examined by WF, includes fifty-four catlinite beads, six of which display edge notching. Of these six, three display serpentine motifs.

No evidence of this catlinite bead production industry has been identified in the Midwest catlinite heartland (Dale Henning, personal communication 2019); however, there is evidence for catlinite working from the late seventeenth-century Lasanen site, at St. Ignace, Michigan (Shu-wu How 1971:41), which Cleland (1971:95) suggests is Odawa-Wyandot. With the departure of the Tionontaté and the Odawa from the Georgian Bay region in 1650, the Blue Mountain siltstone bead production system would have collapsed; however, a catlinite-based industry appears to have continued in the northern Lake Michigan region to which this population retreated. The Odawa may have acquired catlinite through their connections with the Ioway (Fox 2002:146).

Early seventeenth-century stone bead evidence from the Seneca homeland parallels that from Ontario Iroquoian sites (Kenyon and Fox 1982:12), with tubular red siltstone forms replacing earlier discoidal-style stone beads during the 1620s on the Dutch Hollow (Sempowski et al. 2001:1:271–272, Figure 3–217) and Factory Hollow (Sempowski et al. 2001:2:544–545, Figure 7–224) sites. The twenty-four tubular red siltstone specimens from these two Seneca sites were likely acquired through the Neutral, who imported large numbers of these beads from the Blue Mountain producers. Catlinite beads are not reported from the contemporary Seneca sites of Dutch Hollow and Factory Hollow; however, WF has recorded four tubular specimens from its successor site, the Warren site (circa 1635–1650), along with a single red siltstone tubular bead. The latter bead form disappeared, as we would have expected, on the post-1649 Steele and Power House sites. The four Warren site catlinite beads are quite variable in length (10–76 mm) but are consistently narrower than the Ontario siltstone forms (5–9 mm, as opposed to 6–13 mm), with a narrower bore of 2 mm. One of these specimens displays notching along two opposing edges. Twelve catlinite tubular beads from the Steele site are shorter and narrower on average than those from the Warren site, with slightly narrower bores. The ten beads from the circa 1645–1660 Power House site display similar metrics to those from the Warren site. One bead from the circa 1650–1665 Steele site displays a zigzag serpentine motif on two opposing faces. Nine catlinite tubes from the circa 1680–1687 Boughton Hill village all display notching on two to all four edges.

Although stone beads of any form are rare on Iroquois du Nord sites, a bead string from the Trent River mouth, and another from Teiaiagon, include red siltstone specimens. No catlinite beads have been identified on the eastern Cayuga sites, and no stone beads of any kind are included in the accession list for Chadd's Collection (Orr 1922:123–132). A review by WF of the bead string containing one red siltstone bead from Chadd's site(s) at the mouth of the Trent River revealed that it also includes a very large faceted star bead (Type IVk4), plus forty discoidal marine shell beads, both bead types characteristic of the early

Figure 8.15. Glass beads from Trent River Mouth, including a red siltstone tubular bead.
Source: Courtesy of the Royal Ontario Museum, photograph by William A. Fox; digital enhancement by John Howarth.

seventeenth century (Figure 8.15). This anomalous string may well reflect an early seventeenth-century presence at this high-traffic location.

The only siltstone specimens ($n = 3$) found on the western sites are on a string from Teiaiagon that includes both catlinite and thin red tubular glass beads. Three of the six catlinite beads display edge notching. A second string from this site includes three catlinite beads, one of which displays an incised serpentine motif (Figure 8.16). We argue that the presence of red siltstone at Teiaiagon could mean that the Teiaiagon vicinity was occupied from immediately post-1650 or even shortly before, a date that the tubular glass (Type Ia1) bead forms would support. The recovery of a limestone elbow pipe, which had broken in production, supports the possibility of an earlier occupation (Boyle 1891:57–58, Figure 138). Two catlinite beads were recovered from Ganatsekwyagon (Poulton, this volume). One was reworked. The other, which was complete, displayed notching along two opposing edges (Poulton 1991:26, 100, Plate 25). In total, Teiaiagon and Ganatsekwyagon have produced nine tubular catlinite beads, four of which are decorated.

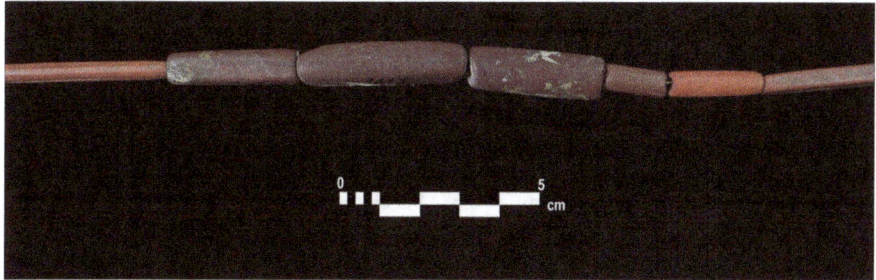

Figure 8.16. Red siltstone beads from Teiaiagon.
Source: Courtesy of the Royal Ontario Museum; photograph by William A. Fox; digital enhancement by John Howarth.

6. Discussion

Considering the rich biotic character of the Prince Edward County region, it is not surprising that some Wellers Bay localities present a palimpsest of occupations spanning thousands of years, as evidenced by the Chadd Collection (Orr 1922). Many are strategic locations for wildfowl hunting and fishing, which may well have been particularly productive following decades of conflict between the Haudenosaunee, on the one hand, and the Wendat and the Tionontaté and their Algonquian allies, on the other hand, which would have rendered the region dangerous for people looking to settle there or even exploit its natural resources. The initial Haudenosaunee movement into this region may have been associated with subsistence activities similar to those already occurring on Lake Ontario south-shore fishing camps (Konrad 1981:135). Certainly, no substantial late seventeenth-century settlements identifiable as "villages" have been located in this region to date, unlike the settlements to the west on the Rouge and Humber Rivers though, Ganaraské, 60 km to the west, has yet to be located (Menary and von Bitter, this volume). In our opinion, the bead assemblages from the Prince Edward County region, which, with few exceptions, such as a single-faceted nineteenth-century bead from the Sandbanks locality, are remarkably similar, argue for a series of contemporary and, for the most part, relatively early and transient occupations following initial settlement circa 1665.

Between 5 percent and 19 percent of the glass beads in collections from the eleven eastern region localities are Kidd types identified by Wray in his analysis of Seneca beads (1983:44–45) as characteristic of the Marsh and Dann sites assemblages, with the same four types present (Ia7, Ib3, Ic'1, IIg1) (see Tables 8.1–8.10). Only the Wellers Bay locality produced two additional types (Ia5 and Ib4), while the Hilton site at Smokes Point on Wellers Bay produced an assemblage apparently dominated by 411 Kidd type IIa1 beads and 4 thin Ia1 specimens (NEAA 2010:43–44, Plate 17). The two western villages, Teiaiagon and Ganatsekwyagon, produced a mere 3 beads characteristic of the Marsh and Dann sites, out of a combined total of 1,299 beads (see Tables 8.11–8.12): Teiaiagon yielded 948 (92.8%) Boughton Hill/Rochester Junction bead types, and Ganatsekwyagon yielded 209 (75.2%). With the exception of the anomalous Hilton site assemblage, the eastern sites contained only 15% to 45% of the bead types characteristic of the Boughton Hill and Rochester Junction village assemblages as defined by Wray (1983:45).

Turning to the limited Cayuga data, we note that Mandzy (1990) has convincingly correlated the Rogers Farm site with the Jesuit mission site of St. René (see Niemczycki 1984: 95, Figure 28), dating to circa 1668–1684. The glass bead assemblage of 2,457 specimens is dominated by red and black tubes and red and black round beads (total 79%), and it also includes black tubes with red stripes (Ib3; 6%) (Mandzy 1990:21–22). The site has also produced "purple and white wampum" and "duck billed shell pendants, shell crescent pendants, shell runtees" (Mandzy 1990:24), consistent with the majority of eastern IDN sites (Mandzy 1990:22).

An intriguing geographic outlier during this early period are the six strings of glass and shell beads obtained by Chadd from a location 90 km north of Kenté and northeast of Quintio, at Coe Hill. Whether this discovery reflects the former location of one of the Iroquois du Nord interior hunting camps (Konrad 1981:136) is impossible to determine at present.

The above percentages of bead types describe an apparent dichotomy in glass trade bead assemblages between eastern sites, with the exception of the Hilton site, in the Prince Edward County region, and western sites, in the Toronto region—the former relating more closely to the circa 1660–1675 Dann and Marsh villages of the homeland Seneca and the latter relating more closely to the succeeding, circa 1675–1687 Rochester Junction and Boughton Hill villages. These differences are particularly evident given the "monotonous round red, black, green and white drawn beads" (Wray 1983:45) that constitute the vast majority of the beads recovered from Teiaiagon and Ganatsekayagon. As Victor Konrad (1981:133) notes, up until the establishment of Fort Frontenac, in 1673, the eastern end of Lake Ontario was the preferred route to the north shore by the Haudenosaunee. That same year, representatives from the villages of Ganatsekwyagon, Ganaraské, Kenté, and Ganneious met with Louis de Buade, Comte de Frontenac et de Palluau. Immediately thereafter, the Haudenosaunee began to frequent the western route around Lake Ontario (Konrad 1981:134), utilizing the alternate route north along the Humber River, as opposed to the Rouge River, and enhancing the importance of the nascent settlement of Teiaiagon.

Although we have yet to pinpoint exactly the location of Ganaraské (see Menary and von Bitter, this volume), it is interesting to note that the topographic settings of Teiaiagon and Ganatsekwyagon are similar to those of the classic steep-sided Haudenosaunee "castle" locations, to use contemporary seventeenth-century terminology (Gehring and Starna 1988:3), whereas those of the eastern sites, so far as we can see, do not resemble this pattern. In fact, most of the Chadd collecting sites appear to represent fishing camps around Wellers Bay and transient portage camps—the "scattered huts" described by Claude Trouvé in 1672 (de Casson 1928:369)—and this may be an accurate reflection of all the Cayuga and Oneida sites located on the eastern route around the lake, other than Ganaraské, Ganneious, and the Kenté mission community. The Haudenosaunee had dedicated fishing settlements along the south shore of the lake (Konrad 1981:133), and, following 1650, there was nothing and no one to stop them from establishing hunting and fishing camps in the rich lacustrine environment of the Prince Edward County region. The bead assemblages suggest that this is exactly what some coalescent Haudenosaunee populations did between 1650 and 1680. And it is just such a diffuse settlement pattern, including Quintio, that may have encouraged the Sulpicians to establish a central mission to satisfy the spiritual needs of their scattered "flock" in 1668.

The "castles" to the west appear to have been established—at least in a more substantial form—circa 1670–1675, due to increasing tensions with the French and the growing strategic importance of the Rouge and Humber routes between the fur trapping regions to the north and the Albany traders to the south (see von Bitter et al., this volume). This evolving political situation and increasing importance of the winter beaver hunt may even explain in part the apparently circuitous Outinaouatoua portage route or trail, which heads to the northwest from Burlington Bay (see Ferris, this volume). In fact, the importance of the "castles" to the fur trade brought the English and French traders with their rum directly to these settlements by the 1670s (Konrad 1981:137–138), the period in which the distinctive Rochester Junction/Boughton Hill bead assemblages were established. All these events reduced the attraction of the eastern region to the Haudenosaunee, leading to the abandonment of the Kenté mission in 1680, following a substantial decline in Haudenosaunee population and the arrival of the Recollect priests at Fort Frontenac (see also von Bitter et al., this volume).

7. Conclusion

The entire bead and pendant assemblage for the Iroquois du Nord sites scattered along the north shore of Lake Ontario is consistent with contemporary assemblages from Haudenosaunee communities south of the lake. Although the east-west dichotomy in glass trade bead assemblages on the north shore of Lake Ontario may be explained by more intensive artifact recovery evidently practised on eastern sites, there are also small tubular and round "seed" beads among the western assemblages that are dominated by the larger round red and black bead types. The regionally anomalous late 1670s glass bead assemblage from the Hilton site, combined with the variety of bone bead rosary components and religious medallion from the adjacent Wellers Bay site (Cooper, this volume) suggest that the Kenté mission site may have been situated nearby, perhaps on Smokes Point. Considering the political realities of the late seventeenth century (Adams 1986), it seems likely that the east-west glass bead type dichotomy and the temporal occupation pattern that it reflects is explained by the Haudenosaunee strategic response to French encroachment into the Lake Ontario basin—a response that consisted of shifting their economic and settlement activities westward.

Acknowledgements

The authors wish to thank the following individuals and institutions, without whose support this research would not have been possible: Craig Cipolla, of the Department of New World Archaeology at the Royal Ontario Museum; Martin Cooper, of Archaeological Services Inc.; Stacey Girling-Christie, of the Canadian Museum of History; George Hamell, of the Rock Foundation Trust at the Rochester Museum & Science Center; Ron Hancock; Kurt Jordan, of the Department of Anthropology and American Indian and Indigenous Studies Program, Cornell University; Karlis Karklins; and Dana Poulton, of D.R. Poulton and Associates Inc. We also thank Suzanne Needs and Kurt Jordan for their reviews of an earlier draft of this chapter and volume editors Robert von Bitter and Ron Williamson as well as the incisive commentary provided by Jennifer Birch and Carl Benn.

9

COME FROM THE SHADOWS
Metals on the Iroquois Frontier

Martin S. Cooper

By the latter half of the seventeenth century, European trade goods had become readily available to Indigenous groups in the Great Lakes area through trade with the French, the Dutch, and the English, and with Indigenous intermediaries. Indeed, by this period metal tools were rapidly replacing Indigenous-manufactured goods, such as ceramic cooking vessels, which were being superseded by brass kettles (see Engelbrecht and Williamson, this volume). By the mid-century, stone axes had already been replaced by iron trade axes, and flaked stone artifacts, such as chert knives and projectile points, were being supplanted by their iron and copper alloy counterparts.

This chapter examines the metal assemblages from archaeological sites that have been identified with the Haudenosaunee settlement of the north shore of Lake Ontario during the second half of the seventeenth century, more specifically between circa 1660 and 1680. These include the Baby Point site, associated with the Seneca village of Teiaiagon (Robertson, this volume), located at the mouth of the Humber River; the Bead Hill site, associated with Ganatsekwyagon, located at the mouth of the Rouge (Poulton, this volume); and the Smokes Point and Bald Head Island sites, associated with the Cayuga village and Sulpician mission of Kenté, situated on Wellers Bay, near Carrying Place, in what is now Prince Edward County (von Bitter et al., this volume). In addition to these Iroquois du Nord (IDN) villages, I also discuss the material culture from an additional archaeological site that I believe represents a similar period Haudenosaunee occupation, the Van Son cemetery, which is situated on Grand Island, in the Niagara River, above the falls. I argue that it is primarily on the basis of the metal artifacts that the identification of the site long considered by Frederick Houghton (1909) and Marian White (1968) to be associated with a pre-1650 Neutral community should be considered a post-1670 IDN Seneca cemetery.

I examine the temporal and spatial distribution of IDN metal tools, and contrasting IDN assemblages from Teiaiagon, Ganatsekwyagon, and the vicinity of Kenté with pre-dispersal Huron-Wendat and Neutral assemblages, as well as contemporary Haudenosaunee assemblages on the south shore of Lake Ontario. The frequencies of metal items from IDN sites are listed in Tables 9.1 and 9.2 and the locations found in Figures 1.2, 1.3, and 4.9.

Table 9.1. Metal artifacts from Iroquois du Nord sites

Artifact Type	Teiaiagon		Ganatsekwyagon		Chadd Collection		Van Son	
	n	%	n	%	n	%	n	%
Kettle	4	13.7	0		1	1.1	3	15
Lug	0		2	2.8	0		0	
Scrap	1	3.4	42	60	0		0	
Copper clip	0	6.9	2	2.8	0		0	
Copper bead	0		3	4.2	0		0	
Tinkling cone	0		2	2.8	0		0	
Bell	0		1 (hawk bell)	1.4	0		1 (hawk bell)	5
Projectile point	3	10.3	0		59	66.2	10	50
Awl	1 (brass)	3.4	0		0		3 (iron)	15
Iron axe	4	13.7	0		6	6.7	2	10
Iron hoe	1	3.4	0		0		0	
Iron knife	2	6.9	2	2.8	0		0	
Firearm	1	3.4	1	1.4	0		0	
Lead bar	1	3.4	2	2.8	0		0	
Lead ball	0		4	5.7	0		0	
Gunflint	7	24	8	11.4	0		0	
Medallion	1	3.4	0		1	1.1	0	
Iconographic ring	3	10.3	1 (Pieta type)	1.4	21	23.5	1 (AM type)	5
Other ring	0		0		1	1.1	0	
Coin	0		1	1.4	0		0	
Total	29	70		89			20	

Source: Martin Cooper.

Table 9.2. Iconographic finger rings from Iroquois du Nord sites

Ring Motif	Tionontaté	Huron-Wendat	Neutral	Teiaiagon	Chadd Collection	Ganatsekwyagon
IHS	3	5	5		10	
L-heart		6	2		13	
Pieta						1
AM						
Portrait					1	
Indeterminate			3			
Total	3	11	7	3	24	1

Source: Martin Cooper.

1. Kettles

Copper alloy or brass kettles were highly desired trade items among the Huron-Wendat and the Neutral, as attested to by European observers and by their prominent placement in cemeteries and ossuaries. By the latter part of the seventeenth century, they begin to replace Indigenous-manufactured ceramic vessels (see Engelbrecht and Williamson, this volume). Fitzgerald (1990) noted that the earliest kettles found in Ontario contain the highest proportions of copper and that, through time, as more tin and other elements were added to the alloy, the kettles became cheaper to manufacture, as well as thinner, lighter, and more brittle. These later kettles can be distinguished from the earlier ones by their brassy colour (Fitzgerald and Ramsden 1988). Damaged kettles were repaired with copper patches that were riveted or, in some cases, laced or stapled into place. Kettles that were damaged beyond repair were recycled into an array of tools, such as awls, knives, and projectile points, and items of personal adornment, such as bracelets, rings, tinkling cones, pendants, earrings, and nose ornaments. The iron bail was repurposed for the manufacture of iron awls, drills, and gravers. Kettles were available in a wide range of sizes and were often transported for Indigenous trade nested together to preserve cargo space (Wheeler et al. 1975).

1.1. Teiaiagon

A total of four brass kettles have been recovered from Teiaiagon: two that are now curated at the Royal Ontario Museum (ROM), a third excavated by Historic Horizon Inc. in 1999, and a fourth recovered by Archaeological Services Inc. (ASI) in 2006. The latter two were reinterred with the ancestors, as were all the grave goods from the two burials discussed in this chapter. The first ROM kettle (33732) has been conserved, revealing its brass colour. It is 10 cm in height and approximately 20 cm in diameter, and it weighs 550 g.

There are several cracks and perforations near the base. It is flat-bottomed and has a near-vertical exterior profile.

The second ROM kettle (33731) has not been conserved and has a preserved beaver pelt in the bottom (Figure 9.1). The pelt was probably overlying the kettle, and only the portion that came into contact with copper oxide was preserved, causing the preserved remains of the pelt to fall into the pot. The maximum width of the pot is 19 cm, the height is 10 cm, and the weight is 555 g. There are several cracks and perforations near the base. It is flat-bottomed and has slightly out-sloping sides, probably to facilitate nesting. The iron bail is complete and is still attached to both lugs. The lugs are typical of those found on most seventeenth-century kettles. They consist primarily of square pieces of sheet brass that have been riveted to the kettle and folded over at the rim. The rim of the kettle has been rolled over an iron rod, as can be determined from the iron oxide staining just below the rim.

A third kettle was recovered by Historic Horizon Inc. during an archaeological investigation in 1999 (Historic Horizon Inc. 2001). This kettle, which was inadvertently damaged by a backhoe, was approximately 19 cm in diameter and had rolled-brass, omega-style lugs. It was also associated with a fragment of a preserved animal pelt.

A fourth kettle was found during an ASI investigation in 2006 (Archaeological Services Inc. 2006) (Figure 9.2). It is slightly larger than the two ROM

Figure 9.1. Brass kettle from Teiaiagon.
Source: Courtesy of the Royal Ontario Museum, photograph by Martin Cooper; digital enhancement by John Howarth.

Figure 9.2. Brass kettle from Teiaiagon.
Source: Archaeological Services Inc. with digital enhancement by John Howarth.

examples, being 24 cm in diameter at the rim and 13.5 cm in height. Approximately half of the bail is intact, and it is still fastened to one lug. The opposite lug is missing. The bail is made of iron and is rectangular in cross-section. It tapers toward the lug, where it has been fastened by bending.

The lug is unlike those found on kettles on archaeological sites in Ontario dating to the first half of the seventeenth century, which consist primarily of square pieces of sheet copper that have been folded and riveted to the side of the pot. The lug on this kettle has an inverted-U shape. It has flattened ends to accommodate a rivet for attachment to the pot. The lug was made of rolled brass. James Bradley refers to these as omega lugs and described them as uncommon on Onondaga sites prior to 1655 (Bradley 1987:197). Omega-lugged kettles were also found at the Mohawk Allen site, which dates to 1646–1666 (Snow 1995a:396), and at the Mohawk Rumrill-Naylor and Freeman sites, which date to the 1640s and 1660s, respectively (Snow 1995a:4, 1995b:171). The rim of the kettle excavated by ASI has been rolled over an iron rod, as can be determined by iron oxide staining just below the rim. There are several cracks and perforations near the base. It is relatively flat-bottomed, with slightly out-sloping sides to facilitate nesting.

Also found at Teiaiagon (Baby Farm) was a single wire spiral (Boyle 1890–91:63). Wire forms of this size have been found on IDN period sites such as Indian Castle, Indian Hill, Power House, and Marsh and the slightly earlier Steele site (Bradley 2020:229–231). According to Engelbrecht (2003:136), single brass or copper spirals perhaps made of altered kettle scrap are common on late sixteenth-century Haudenosaunee locations and may represent the tail of the powerful underwater panther.

1.2. Ganatsekwyagon

Although no complete kettles were recovered from Ganatsekwyagon, two kettles are represented by their omega lugs, one of rolled brass, the other of cast brass (MPA 1991). The rolled copper specimen is similar to the omega lug on the Teiaiagon kettle described above (Figure 9.3).

Figure 9.3. Omega lug from brass kettle from Ganatsekwyagon.
Source: Parks Canada and D. R. Poulton and Associates; digital enhancement by John Howarth.

1.3. Chadd Collection

A complete brass kettle in the Chadd Collection was likely derived from the Kenté village. It has been conserved, revealing its brassy colour. It is missing the iron bail, and the lugs are square sheet brass with the top corners of the lugs removed. This type of lug with the corners removed has been associated with French-sourced trade kettles (Bradley 1987:198). All twenty-two brass kettles from the Grimsby cemetery, which according to Kenyon and Fox (1982) was in use between circa 1615 and 1650, have this style of lug.

The omega-lugged kettles present at both Teiaiagon and Ganatsekwyagon are exceedingly rare on pre-dispersal Neutral and Huron-Wendat sites, a single example occurring on the terminal, circa 1640–1650 Neutral Walker site. Omega lugs are also found on kettles at the contemporaneous Seneca Dutch Hollow and Factory Hollow sites, which were occupied during the first quarter of the seventeenth century (Sempowski and Sanders 2001:124). Omega brass lugs also frequently occur on seventeenth-century Hudson's Bay Company sites (Kenyon 1986:149); this suggests that those occurring on Seneca, Onondaga, and Iroquois du Nord sites may be of English origin.

2. Projectile Points

On pre-1650 Huron-Wendat and Neutral sites, chert projectile points far outnumber those made of brass. For example, the Neutral Grimsby cemetery contained no metal projectile points but did produce forty-four triangular chert points. Triangular brass projectiles points do occur, however, in limited numbers on pre-dispersal Neutral and Huron-Wendat sites. By the third quarter of the seventeenth century, on Seneca and Onondaga sites, chert projectile points are being replaced by ones made of sheet brass, typically derived from kettles (Bradley 1987; Wray 1973; Wray and Graham 1985).

Brass points are usually isosceles triangle-shaped and sometimes have a single, centrally placed perforation to facilitate hafting. Some brass points have bevelled edges. Broken points were reused as drills, gravers, and awls. The manufacturing process is relatively straightforward. It began with scoring, bending, and cutting a sheet of brass. Iron knives would have simplified the process, and scissors, which in Ontario occur in the 1640s, may also have been used to cut the thin sheets of brass.

2.1. Teiaiagon

There are three triangular brass projectile points from Teiaiagon in the ROM collections (Figure 9.4). These range in length from 27 mm to 33 mm and in width from 17 mm to 22 mm. Two of the three have a centrally placed perforation to facilitate hafting.

Figure 9.4. Three triangular brass projectile points from Teiaiagon.
Source: Courtesy of the Royal Ontario Museum, photograph by Martin Cooper; digital enhancement by John Howarth.

2.2. Ganatsekwyagon

No sheet brass projectiles points were recovered from Ganatsekwyagon. There were twelve pre-Iroquoian chert projectile points that probably represent earlier occupations at the site (see Poulton, this volume). It is interesting to note that pre-Iroquoian chert projectile points are found in features on seventeenth-century Haudenosaunee sites on the south shore of Lake Ontario, which appear to represent the curation of earlier projectile points (Wray and Graham 1975). This may also be the case for three of the pre-Iroquoian projectile points recovered from Ganatsekwyagon.

2.3. Chadd Collection

There are fifty-nine brass projectile points in the Chadd Collection at the ROM, five of which are conical points similar in form to earlier conical projectile points manufactured from deer antler tines. Of the brass points, fifty-four are triangular, a small majority of which ($n = 29$; 53.7 percent) have centrally placed perforations to facilitate hafting. Two triangular points are unfinished, and two have been reworked, one as a graver/awl, the other as an awl.

3. Axes

Iron axes rapidly replaced their ground stone counterparts. By the middle of the seventeenth century, stone axes are almost absent from Huron-Wendat and Neutral assemblages. Indeed, the Jesuit Joseph-Marie Chaumonot remarked that the Neutral had formerly used stone axes (Revel 1982:6), suggesting that they were no longer using them when he visited them in 1641.

The major difference in iron axes between pre- and post-1650 Haudenosaunee sites is their variability in size. Almost all pre-1650 iron axes are large felling-type axes. After 1650, smaller axes appear (Bradley 1987; Wray 1973), which functioned as belt axes or tomahawks. They could be easily transported and then wielded for clearing trails and portages or as a very effective weapon.

No iron axes were recovered from Ganatsekwyagon during the 1991 excavations.

3.1. Teiaiagon

Four iron axes have been examined from Teiaiagon: three in the ROM collection and one excavated by ASI in 2006, which was in a burial. Three of the axes are small hatchet or belt axe types, one of which has a symmetrical shape, unique for the period. One is a large felling axe (Figure 9.5).

The iron axe recovered by ASI in 2006 was a belt axe (Kenyon 1984) (Figure 9.6). This style has most of the weight on the blade below the handle; this specimen has a rounded poll and a square ear. The leading edge is flat, and

Figure 9.5. Conserved iron axe from Teiaiagon.
Source: Courtesy of the Royal Ontario Museum, photograph by Martin Cooper; digital enhancement by John Howarth.

Figure 9.6. Iron axe from Teiaiagon.
Source: Archaeological Services In., photograph by John Howarth.

the heel is very pronounced. Wood was still present in the eye, indicating that a whole axe, and not just the head, had been placed with the individual. The bit (blade) is still sharp and there are no observable armourers' marks, although extensive iron oxide corrosion on the blade may have obscured or destroyed them.

3.2. Chadd Collection

Four iron axes are in the Chadd Collection from Wellers Bay. Three are small belt axes and the fourth is a large felling axe. Two of the belt axes have battered polls, suggesting a secondary use, possibly as a wedge for splitting wood.

4. Hoes

Hoes are absent on pre-dispersal Huron-Wendat, Tionontaté, and Neutral sites in Ontario, although there was a single, crude example from Sainte-Marie I (Kidd 1949:115). Iron hoes appear on Haudenosaunee sites on the south shore of Lake Ontario around 1670 (Wray 1973:22).

4.1. Teiaiagon

There is a single conserved hoe in the ROM collections from Teiaiagon (Figure 9.7). It is a socketed hoe with a circular maker's mark on the underside. The blade is somewhat corroded; it appears to have measured approximately 100 mm in width.

Figure 9.7. Conserved hoe from Teiaiagon.
Source: Courtesy of the Royal Ontario Museum, photograph by Martin Cooper; digital enhancement by John Howarth.

5. Knives

Iron knives are found throughout Iroquoia during the seventeenth century and were important trade items along with iron axes. Iron knives quickly replaced Indigenous-made chert cutting tools. No knives were identified in the Chadd Collection.

5.1. Teiaiagon

A bone-handled knife is in the ROM collection from Teiaiagon (Figure 9.8). Four iron rivets hold the handle to the haft. The metal blade has a bolster at the handle, which has a spur at the heel and a rounded, expanding edge. It appears that after the blade of the knife had broken, it was used as a scraper.

ASI recovered a second, very similar bone-handled knife from the burial in 2006. The knife has a flat tang and the bone scales that form the handle area are fastened with four rivets. The bone scales widen at the butt and are undecorated. The blade has a heel at the bolster, and the back and edge of the blade are parallel to each other. This relatively large iron knife is unlike other iron knives recovered on pre-1650 archaeological sites in Ontario.

The recovery of intact, four-rivet bone handles is rare.

Figure 9.8. Bone-handled knife from Teiaiagon.
Source: Courtesy of the Royal Ontario Museum, photograph by Martin Cooper; digital enhancement by John Howarth.

5.2. Ganatsekwyagon

A highly corroded knife blade and the blade of a clasp knife were recovered from Ganatsekwyagon. The clasp knife, which is a form of folding knife, appears to occur primarily after the mid-century, with a few examples occurring on late glass bead period (GBP) 3 Tionontaté, Huron-Wendat, and Neutral sites in Ontario (Fitzgerald 1990:467; Garrad 2014:369). Their ubiquity during the late seventeenth century is attested to by the presence of twenty-four clasp knives at Ganondagan.

6. Firearms

With the exception of a few items from the terminal GBP 3 Neutral Hood site (Lennox 1984); the Huron-Wendat/French Sainte-Marie II site on Christian Island (Carruthers 2014); the GPB 3 Le Caron site (Johnston and Jackson 1980); and some early, unsubstantiated references to the recovery of firearms from several Tionontaté ossuaries (Garrad 2014), there is very little evidence of firearms on Indigenous archaeological sites in Ontario prior to 1650. The presence of arms in Wendake is, however, evident from historic documentation and the large amount of archaeological evidence at Sainte-Marie I, which was a French colonial settlement (Hunter 1985; Kidd 1949). There appears to have been a policy of the French not trading guns to the Huron-Wendat until after 1643 and then only to Christian converts (Trigger 1985:255).

Iroquois du Nord sites do have ample evidence of firearms and related materials, reflecting their greater availability in the second half of the seventeenth century, due to the fact that the Dutch and the English had been trading firearms to the Haudenosaunee, particularly the Mohawk, since the first quarter of the seventeenth century (Snow 1995b).

Except for a lead cruciform or bird effigy, which was probably made from lead musket balls or sprue, no firearms-related artifacts were identified in the Chadd Collection. Lead turtle effigies were recovered from the 1655–1663 Onondaga Indian Castle site (Bradley 1987:155) and cut lead human figures have been recovered from the 1655–1675 Seneca Dann site.

6.1. Teiaiagon

Evidence of firearms at Teiaiagon consists of a lead bar in the ROM collection (Figure 9.9). The lead bar is 250 mm in length and has a maximum width of 33 mm, tapering to 25 mm at the opposite end. It weighs approximately 920 g.

These items were used to produce lead musket balls. Due to lead's low melting temperature (327.5°C), musket balls could be produced by melting the lead bar over an open fire and pouring the molten lead into a mould. Such moulds have been found at the contemporaneous Seneca Ganondagan site in New York State. Lead was also used in the eighteenth century by Indigenous craftspeople in the Great Lakes area to produce inlay decoration on stone smoking pipes. The ROM accession records also listed a gun lock donated by Miss Kirkwood, which I was not able to find in the collections (see Robertson, this volume, for a discussion of Miss Kirkwood and her family).

Figure 9.9. Lead bar from Teiaiagon.
Source: Courtesy of the Royal Ontario Museum, photograph by Martin Cooper; digital enhancement by John Howarth.

6.2. Ganatsekwyagon

At Ganatsekwyagon, two small lead bars, lead scrap, and four lead balls were recovered in 1991; two of the lead balls were finished and smooth, while two retained the sprue, or waste metal, left over from the mould. Dana Poulton has suggested that this constitutes indirect evidence that the site inhabitants were manufacturing lead balls in a mould on-site (MPA 1991:35).

In addition, a portion of a reworked iron musket barrel was recovered (Figure 9.10). The 96 mm octagonal barrel with a rear sight has a 15 mm bore. A similar octagonal specimen with rear sight was among the nineteen gun barrel portions recovered from the Ganondagan site (MPA 1991:35).

Figure 9.10. Portion of a reworked iron musket barrel from Ganatsekwyagon.
Source: Parks Canada and D. R. Poulton and Associates; digital enhancement by John Howarth.

7. Gunflints

Gunflints, although not metallic, are discussed here because they may indicate the presence of firearms. Their presence in pre-dispersal times should not necessarily be interpreted as the presence of arms since gunflints are often reworked into scrapers and may have been used as strike-a-lights for starting fires. It should be noted that gunflints should only occur after 1630, since that is when the flintlock was introduced. Indeed, the sites that produce gunflints and other gun-related materials appear to date to the 1640s, the decade prior to the Ontario Iroquoian diaspora.

According to Roets et al. (2014), bifacial gunflints, which appear to be Indigenous-made, first occur during the first half of the seventeenth century and continue in use until the last quarter of that century. A bifacially worked gunflint made from Kettle Point chert was identified at the GPB 3 Neutral Hood site. This location also produced three pieces of lead shot (Lennox 1984). Poulton has recently identified gunflints made of Onondaga and Kettle Point chert at the Neutral Rattlesnake Point (three gunflints and one possible gunflint) and Pipeline (one gunflint and two possible gunflints) sites (Dana Poulton, personal communication 2020). A single French spall gunflint, which had a secondary use as a strike-a-light, was identified at the GBP 3 Tionontaté Plater-Martin site (Fox 1971; Garrad 2014).

As for IDN sites, seven gunflints are in the ROM accession records for Teiaiagon; however, I was able to locate only a single Onondaga chert gunflint in the collection. A total of eight gunflints were recovered from Ganatsekwyagon, including five European-made and three Indigenous-made (Figure 9.11) (MPA 1991:36). At the Hilton site (BaGj-24) on Smokes Point, Northeastern

Figure 9.11. Three European gunflints from Ganatsekwyagon.
Source: Parks Canada and D. R. Poulton and Associates; digital enhancement by John Howarth.

Archaeological Associates (2010:24) documented four French gunflints which ranged in colour from blond to light brown.

8. Iconographic Rings

In terms of metal trade goods, religious items, such as so-called Jesuit rings and medallions, are among the most temporally sensitive artifacts on IDN sites and therefore can be used for dating assemblages. There is, however, some doubt as to whether iconographic rings can be directly related to missionaries, Jesuit or otherwise. Toward the middle of the seventeenth century, they become popular trade items, and it is clear from both traders' manifests and the recently discovered wreck of La Salle's ship *La Belle* that they were being imported from France in large quantities for trade to Indigenous intermediaries (Birmingham and Mason 2017). The fact that the motifs have religious themes is not at all surprising given the pervasive nature of the Catholic Church in French culture at the time. The popular L-heart motif has been interpreted by some researchers as signifying love for Ignacio Loyola, a co-founder of the Jesuit order, and by others as love for King Louis XIV (Wood 1974). The equally popular IHS motif, known as the Christogram, signifies the name of Jesus. Carol Mason (2003) has pointed out that the L-heart motif was a common symbol of love and that IHS can be considered both a religious and a secular motif. In other words, there is likely no direct association between so-called Jesuit rings and missionary activity. Similarly, there may or may not have been a direct relationship between Jesuit and Sulpician missionaries and medallions with religious themes.

Based on interments from the late seventeenth-century Seneca Ganondagan site, we can surmise that rings were worn not only on the fingers, but also in multiples on necklaces. They may also have been sewn onto clothing.

In terms of temporal range, rings with engraved and embossed bezels increase in frequency after the middle of the seventeenth century. Pre-dispersal Huron-Wendat, Tionontaté, and Neutral sites have yielded very few iconographic rings. For example, with a single exception, these items occur in Ontario only on GBP 3 sites, the majority on sites dating to the final decade or year before the diaspora. Of the twenty-five or so Jesuit rings identified from pre-dispersal sites, the greatest number occur on terminal occupations, such as Sainte-Marie II, on Christian Island, which accounts for eight rings, and the Neutral Hood site, which is believed to be a terminal Neutral village and which accounts for six rings. These two sites comprise 56 percent of all the so-called devotional items from the pre-dispersal period in Ontario. The Ossossané ossuary, which is thought to date from 1636, contained four rings. Three rings have been found on Tionontaté sites: two on Plater-Martin and one on Kelly-Campbell (Garrad 1994).

In contrast, Ganondagan and the other post-1650 Seneca villages have a total of ninety-one rings, the majority of which were found in graves. There is a clear difference not only in the frequency of rings and other religious items, but also in the variety of decorative motifs on the rings before and after the mid-century in both Ontario and New York State. All twenty-five of the pre-1650 rings in Ontario have either IHS or L-heart motifs. During the second half of the seventeenth century, IHS and L-heart rings continue in popularity, but a wide variety of other designs become available.

8.1. Teiaiagon

Three brass rings were recovered from a single burial during Historic Horizon Inc.'s investigation in 1999 (Historic Horizon Inc. 2001). Unfortunately, the three rings were too corroded to determine the motif on the ring's bezel. One of the rings had a distinctive and unique bowtie-shaped bezel.

8.2. Ganatsekwyagon

The single ring from this site, which was recovered in 1991, is of the Pieta type, which occurs on Seneca sites in New York State exclusively after 1650 (Figure 9.12). At the Seneca Ganondagan location, there are seven Pieta-type rings, representing just under 20 percent of all the rings with decorated bezels from the site.

Figure 9.12. Pieta-type iconographic ring from Ganatsekwyagon.
Source: Parks Canada and D. R. Poulton and Associates; digital enhancement by John Howarth.

8.3. Chadd Collection

A total of twenty-four brass bezel rings have been identified in the Chadd Collection from Bald Head Island, relating to the Kenté village, many of which likely derive from burials. A total of thirteen Bald Head Island rings are L-heart, while ten are IHS (Figures 9.13 and 9.14). There is a single example of a unique portrait ring. It appears to be a woman wearing a cassock or dress and grasping her breasts (Figure 9.15). There appear to be angel wings on her back and long, flowing hair on her head. This ring may depict a saint, possibly either Teresa or Mary. I have seen no iconographic ring or religious image that compares to this unique ring.

Figure 9.13. L-heart-type iconographic ring from Bald Head Island/Kenté.
Source: Courtesy of the Royal Ontario Museum, photograph by Martin Cooper; digital enhancement by John Howarth.

Figure 9.14. IHS-type iconographic ring from Bald Head Island/Kenté.
Source: Courtesy of the Royal Ontario Museum, photograph by Martin Cooper; digital enhancement by John Howarth.

Figure 9.15. Unique portrait ring from Bald Head Island/Kenté.
Source: Courtesy of the Royal Ontario Museum, photograph by Martin Cooper; digital enhancement by John Howarth.

9. Religious Medallions

Religious medallions have been found on IDN sites, including single examples from Teiaiagon and Kenté.

9.1. Teiaiagon

The Teiaiagon medallion has been described elsewhere by Bill Fitzgerald and colleagues (1994) (Figure 9.16). One face contains the inscription ".S.MARI. POPVLO.ROMA," which refers to the Augustinian Church of Santa Maria del Popolo in Rome, whose reconstruction was completed in 1477, and a portrait of Mary with the child Jesus. The obverse is a portrait of St. Augustine of Hippo and his mother, St. Monica of Ostia.

Figure 9.16. Unique religious medallion from Teiaiagon.
Source: Courtesy of the Royal Ontario Museum, photograph by Martin Cooper; digital enhancement.

9.2. Chadd Collection

A unique religious medallion is included in the ROM's Chadd Collection from Bald Head Island (Figure 9.17). It is heart-shaped and bears a portrait of Mary and the baby Jesus, with two angels suspending a crown or halo over Mary's head. On the obverse are the five saints who were canonized by Pope Gregory XV in 1622: the co-founders of the Jesuits, Ignacio Loyola and Francis Xavier; Teresa of Ávila; Francesco Saverio; Felipe Neri; and Isidore the Farmer. Below this group portrait is inscribed "Roma," the place of their canonization.

Both medallions would have been widely distributed as commemorative pieces, and although medallions do increase in frequency in archaeological assemblages after 1650, we can only say for certain that the five-saints medallion from the Chadd Collection post-dates 1622.

Figure 9.17. Unique religious medallion from Bald Head Island/Kenté.
Source: Courtesy of the Royal Ontario Museum, photograph by Martin Cooper; digital enhancement by John Howarth.

It should be noted that other religious objects such as crosses and crucifixes, which do occur in very limited frequencies on contemporary Seneca sites such as Ganondagan (Wray and Graham 1985), are absent on IDN sites. A silver cross reported by Coyne (1904:15) from Bald Head Point certainly relates to a later, possibly Mississauga cemetery. Silver crosses and brooches do not appear on Haudenosaunee sites until the mid-eighteenth century (Wray 1973:20).

10. Coins

European coins are found in limited quantities on Northern Iroquoian sites during the seventeenth century and are not necessarily indicative of European presence. Coins were used primarily for adornment, as evidenced by the fact that they were often perforated so they could be worn suspended around the neck, ears, or nose. Because coins were in circulation for many decades or even centuries, they provide only a *terminus post quem* date for the site.

Coins have been found on pre-dispersal sites in Ontario, including two copper 1640 double *tournois* Louis XIII coins, one each at Sainte-Marie I (Kidd 1949:130) and Sainte-Marie II (Carruthers 2014:134). A perforated 1591 French silver coin was found about 1 km from the Neutral Freelton site (Fitzgerald 1990:514); its specific archaeological context is unknown.

Several coins have also been recovered from late seventeenth-century Seneca sites. Ganondagan produced a 1640 copper double *tournois* coin perforated in three places (Dean 1984:41), while the later Indian Hill village produced another 1640 double *tournois* coin, as well as two 1656 French *liard* coins (Beauchamp 1903; Tuck 1971:186).

10.1. Ganatsekwyagon

Of the IDN sites, only Ganatsekwyagon produced a coin (Figure 9.18). This item is a centrally perforated copper French 1655 *liard* coin with a bust of the seventeen-year-old Louis XIV. Figure 9.18 includes a photograph of the reverse of the coin and an X-ray of the same side; *FR..CE*, for France, as well as fleurs-de-lis at the bottom and *LIARD* across the top, are visible. The letters faintly visible around the edge of the coin are likely "bleeding" through from the other side of the coin.

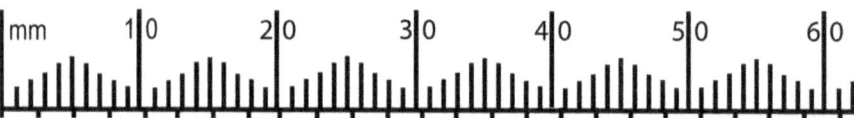

Figure 9.18. French 1655 *liard* coin from Ganatsekwyagon.
Source: Parks Canada and D. R. Poulton and Associates; X-ray taken by the Canadian Mint, both with digital enhancement.

11. Is the Van Son Cemetery an Iroquois du Nord Site?

More than a century ago, the archaeologist Frederick Houghton salvage excavated an Iroquoian cemetery, known as the Van Son site, on Grand Island, in the Niagara River. It was situated approximately 6 km upriver from the Niagara Falls and within view of the rising mist of the falls. The burials, located on a gravel knoll, were being threatened by a quarry operation. He noted a nearby village but provided no details (Houghton 1909).

One of Houghton's goals was to identify the specific ethnicity of Iroquoian groups in the Niagara Frontier. During the first half of the seventeenth century, four or more Iroquoian groups resided in the region, including the Neutral, the Erie, the Wenro, the Seneca, and possibly one or more unnamed groups. Houghton believed that if he could determine the sites that the Neutral were known to have inhabited on the east side of the Niagara River, he would be able to define the identity of the village occupants on the west side. The ethnic identification of the Van Son cemetery was critical to his hypothesis that those on the west side were Neutral.

Half a century later, Marian White, of the University of Buffalo, took on the task of sorting out these affiliations on both sides of the border, in New York State and Ontario, including a re-examination of the Van Son cemetery (White 1968, 1969, 1972).

Despite burial patterns indicative of the Seneca, consisting exclusively of single primary interments, both Houghton and White concluded that the Van Son site was Neutral. They based their assessment primarily on the presence of bone sucking tubes, which Houghton identified as a Neutral trait, and on several complete ceramic vessels and a limestone human-effigy pipe, which appeared to be distinctively Neutral.

The site also produced a single so-called devotional ring with "AM" inscribed on the bezel. Fitzgerald (1990), who identified the ring as what is known as an Ave Maria ring, indicated that, based on the presence of this type of ring at the late seventeenth-century Seneca Ganondagan site, the Van Son site was likely a post-dispersal Seneca site. The post-1650 date of the ring has since been confirmed by Carol Mason in her extensive research on iconographic rings in northeastern North America (Birmingham and Mason 2017; Mason 2009). It is probable that the AM inscription stands not for *Ave Maria* but for *Auspices Maria*, which is the motto of the Sulpicians. Sulpician missionaries, such as François Salignac de La Mothe-Fénelon, who were known to have visited several IDN villages, including Kenté, did not arrive in North America until the late 1660s. Therefore, it is likely that the AM rings do not appear in the lower Great Lakes until the late 1660s and Van Son thus post-dates the dispersal of the Neutral by almost twenty years.

As part of my doctoral research on the seventeenth-century Neutral occupation of the eastern Niagara Peninsula, I examined the Van Son artifacts, which are now housed at the Buffalo History Museum (Cooper 2020). Unfortunately, the bulk of the collection analyzed by White in the 1960s could not be relocated, including the ring and all the glass trade beads. However, her description of the beads indicates the presence of bead types that would not be out of place on late seventeenth-century Seneca sites, including IDN settlements. These include black round and tubular; red cored; and blue with white stripes, which further supports the theory that Van Son is a post-1650 Seneca site. Other supporting evidence includes the presence of ten finely made brass projectile points (Figure 9.19).

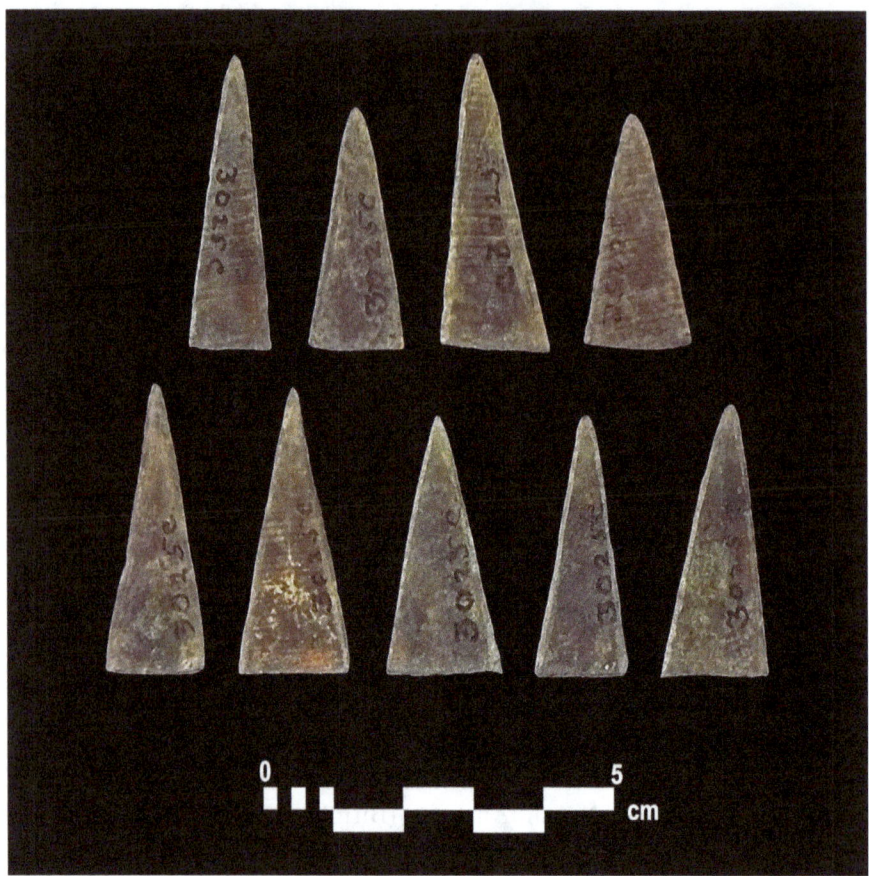

Figure 9.19. Brass projectile points from the Van Son cemetery site.
Source: Buffalo Museum of Science, photograph by Martin Cooper; digital enhancement by John Howarth.

The location of Van Son at the north end of Grand Island, in view of Niagara Falls, would provide a commanding vista of anyone travelling between Lake Ontario and Lake Erie. In 1678, the Recollect Louis Hennepin was escorted to and around Niagara Falls by Seneca who were living on the east shore near the mouth of the Niagara River. Hennepin also mentioned that René-Robert Cavelier de La Salle had asked permission from the Seneca to build Fort Conti at the mouth of the lower Niagara River at Lake Ontario (Thwaites 1903). This confirms that by the mid-1670s, the Seneca were in possession of what was formerly Neutral territory along the Niagara River, which is about the time that they had defeated the Andastogues (Thwaites 1896–1901:59:251), who had, as late as 1669, threatened Haudenosaunee in the vicinity of the Niagara River (Coyne 1903:45).

One might ask if there was a late-1670s Seneca cemetery on Grand Island, why was it not mentioned by European visitors to the area? First, a Seneca cemetery on Grand Island in the Niagara River would not have been noted if it was unassociated with a nearby village. Second, if there had been an associated village, it is possible the village was occupied after the La Salle journey.

I would posit, therefore, that Van Son is a post-Sulpician IDN Seneca cemetery in which the remains of post-dispersal Neutral adoptees were placed, since it yielded material culture attributed to the Seneca, as well as Neutral ceramic vessels and a distinctive Neutral-style limestone pipe. The location of it and a likely associated village is consistent with the post-dispersal expansion of Haudenosaunee, in particular the Seneca, in the Niagara region, into what was formerly Neutral territory, beginning around AD 1670. It is in a strategic location along a major transportation and communication corridor with which the Neutral and Huron-Wendat were intimately familiar, and which would have allowed the inhabitants to take advantage of trade and monitor the movement of others. It is also consistent with Kurt Jordan's (2013) description of extra-regional satellites (see also Jordan, this volume), which are Haudenosaunee colonies, and which often contained incorporated populations.

12. Conclusion

Based on the data presented, it is apparent there are significant temporal and spatial trends in both the quantity and the types of metal goods available to IDN communities during the second half of the seventeenth century. The differences in these goods among communities are certainly due to the function of the archaeological sites, whether village or cemetery, and the amount of archaeological investigation, as well as the degree of nineteenth- and early twentieth-century collecting activities. However, despite these differences, general trends in metal artifact type and frequency can be discerned. Brass kettles with omega-type lugs appear in the second half of the century, likely related to the availability of English-sourced trade goods. Brass projectile points made from kettle scrap or sheet brass increase in number, and chert projectile points suddenly decrease in number. Iron axes decrease in size and weight and appear to be available in a wider range of sizes, reflecting the growing popularity of belt axes and hatchets for clearing trails and for use in warfare. Iron tools increase in number and variety, including knives and task-specific items, such as hoes. Arms-related materials, such as European gunflints, significantly increase in frequency after mid-century, reflecting the widespread availability of and increased dependence on guns, for both hunting and warfare. It would appear that European gunflints precede actual firearms and were used for secondary purposes, such as hide scrapers and strike-a-lights. High-quality European flint would have been desired for its purity and relative rarity, although in the latter part of the seventeenth century, Haudenosaunee on both sides of Lake Ontario were manufacturing gunflints from local materials, such as Onondaga chert.

There is also a considerable increase in the frequency and variety of iconographic finger rings on IDN sites and on Haudenosaunee sites on the south side of Lake Ontario. Prior to the middle of the seventeenth century, so-called Jesuit rings are limited in number and consist almost exclusively of the IHS and L-heart types. These ring types and their variations persist post-dispersal, but assemblages of the IDN period also include additional portrait-type rings, such as the Pieta type found at Ganatsekwyagon and the anomalous portrait ring from Bald Head Island. Other varieties of note that occur after the mid-century include the AM type, argued here to refer to *Auspices Maria*, the motto of the Sulpicians, which occurs in comparative abundance on post-1670 sites in the Haudenosaunee homeland and was found at the Van Son site on Grand Island. Religious-themed medallions occur in limited numbers on IDN sites as well as on pre-dispersal Neutral, Tionontaté, and Huron-Wendat sites.

Finally, a re-examination of the evidence from the Van Son cemetery on Grand Island in the Niagara River shows that it post-dates the dispersal of the Neutral and that the cemetery and its enigmatic associated village are likely part of a Seneca-Neutral settlement that represents an early attempt of the Seneca at colonization in newly acquired territory. Van Son may thus be regarded as an additional Iroquois du Nord site.

Acknowledgements

I would like to thank Ken Lister and April Hawkins, Royal Ontario Museum; Kathy Leacock, Buffalo Museum of Science; Carol Mason, University of Kansas (Lawrence); and Walter Mayer, Buffalo History Museum, for their assistance. I am also grateful to Suzanne Needs-Howarth and Ron Williamson for their comments on an early draft of this chapter.

10

IROQUOIS DU NORD DECORATED ANTLER COMBS
Reflections of Ideology

RONALD F. WILLIAMSON AND ROBERT VON BITTER

This chapter examines the antler combs found on the Iroquois du Nord sites with reference to the ideological contexts of their production and use and compares them to those discovered on homeland sites. There have been few comprehensive studies of Northern Iroquoian bone and antler combs. The best known is a review of ornamental Seneca combs published in 1963 in *Pennsylvania Archaeologist* by Charles Wray. He documented 251 Seneca combs known to be in private and institutional collections, although he assumed the actual total number of extant objects to be closer to 275 or 300 (Wray 1963:38).

It was not until 1991 that another major study emerged, a master's thesis by April Vasey, entitled "Seneca Hair Combs as Material Culture." Vasey examined thirty-seven Seneca hair combs in the decorative hair comb collection at the Rochester Museum & Science Center featuring human figure motifs. The combs are associated with fourteen sites, which were occupied between circa 1550 and 1700. She recognized that all the decorative hair combs, regardless of form or subject matter, seemed to depict the origin and nature of the Haudenosaunee Confederacy (or League) and thus identity, historical events, or myths. More generally, she argued that they were indicative of how the Haudenosaunee viewed and valued the world around them and that they represent stability during a time of change. She noted that the variation in the combs reflects the variation in the myths which they sought to portray—a specific myth offered by different individuals (or even the same individual at different times) is prone to variation. Whatever the subject, she argued, they reflect Haudenosaunee ideology.

A second master's thesis on combs was prepared in 2004, by Karine Weisshuhn, entitled "Native American Combs in the Northeastern United States." In her analysis, based largely on decorative hair combs in the collections at the Rochester Museum & Science Center and New York State Museum, she stressed that animal figures represent both the world as seen and the spiritual world, and that these two worlds are reinforced by the symmetry on most of these combs. She also argued that the human characters on combs reflect both everyday activities and mythological beings, such as the Trickster, who was used to integrate the European and Indigenous worlds.

In 2005, Williamson and Annie Veilleux prepared a compendium of bone and antler combs as part of a study of Northern Iroquoian decorated bone tools, but they did not include all the unpublished examples recovered during the nineteenth and early twentieth centuries from documented or suspected Iroquois du Nord (IDN) sites.

A thoughtful undergraduate thesis, written in 2008 by Amy Dianne Bergseth, entitled "'Reversing the Gaze' with Early Native American Visual Imagery," examines Indigenous visual art in the form of Seneca combs, rock art, and wampum belts from the seventeenth to the mid-nineteenth century that depicted Euro-Americans. Her analysis, while exploring Indigenous perceptions of the "other," at the same time focused on how art reflected evolving Indigenous identities.

Seneca combs have also been analyzed by Haudenosaunee scholar Rick Hill (2012) at the Indigenous Knowledge Centre and published online as "Hodinohso: ni Art Lesson 1," in which he describes combs as media for recording cultural change, especially encounters with colonialists and their strange clothing and their horses, as well as performance involving mythical animals and ancient beliefs. He describes the use of positive and negative spaces and symmetry to depict power relationships. In an earlier analysis of the art from the Seneca town of Ganondagan, Hill (1986a) explained that combs "remind us that art in the Seneca community has a long history of manifesting personal identity and providing a Seneca perspective to their changing world." Although non-Indigenous scholars employ analyses of Haudenosaunee combs as signifiers of identity and tools to understand the past, these combs hold a special place in the Haudenosaunee worldview. According to the Haudenosaunee creation story, the man and woman who lived in the Sky World only interacted when the woman attended to the man to comb his hair, yet she mysteriously became pregnant. The daughter who was born became known as Sky Woman. Haudenosaunee people would create carved combs and give them to loved ones, an act that Hill describes as symbolizing the combing of Sky Woman's father's hair. In this way, combs "connected them to the spirit world" and were "prized possessions in life and in death" (Bergseth 2008:15; Richter 1992:9, 28).

Finally, George Hamell has also commented extensively on the meaning of designs on these combs and other material culture as reflections of Indigenous ideology. In a general way, Hamell (1979:15) has suggested that the symbolic content of combs reflects the connection between human hair and sympathetic and contagious magic and power. This would explain in part the links between the taking of scalps and scalp locks with the capture of souls and the painting of scalps red (Hall 1997; Williamson 2007:216–217).

Few combs have been found that predate the Middle Woodland period—a notable exception is from the four-thousand- to five-thousand-year-old Frontenac Island site, featuring two opposing but symmetrical bird's heads with a common beak (Figure 10.1). Combs are found more frequently on Middle Woodland sites and are characterized by elaborate incised and filled triangular, v-shaped, and box designs (Figure 10.2). Later Transitional Woodland and pre-contact Late Woodland forms, such as the one from the Lawson site in London, Ontario (Figure 10.3), while still relatively rare, tend to be larger and consist of three to five thick and sturdy teeth. The tops were occasionally carved to represent animal or bird figures (Wray 1963:36). Early sixteenth-century Seneca combs have also been found that feature symmetrical bears or panthers joined at their snouts and that feature four or five sturdy teeth.

With the arrival of Europeans and the introduction of metal trade tools, combs became more finely made, with smaller, fine teeth and intricate, etched designs. Williamson and Veilleux, in their 2005 review of decorated Iroquoian bone objects, documented a near absence of these combs on contact-period St. Lawrence Iroquoian and Huron-Wendat sites but noted they are present in numbers on historic Neutral sites. There are five specimens, for example, from the historic Neutral Grimsby cemetery, one of which is near complete (Figure 10.4), and more than a dozen from various other Neutral cemeteries or village burials.

The Seneca seem to have produced more combs than any other Iroquoian-speaking group, an increase in their production being coincident with the introduction of iron tools and the growth of Seneca political and military strength in the post-1650 period (Wray 1963:40). Their geographical proximity to, and at times peaceful relationship with, the Neutral is probably responsible for the number of antler combs on Neutral sites, perhaps even manufactured by Seneca. It is not known who made the combs on the eastern IDN sites; it is assumed the Oneida and the Cayuga made their own.

Most combs have been found in the graves of women, but some have been uncovered in the graves of men and children, often behind or beside the head, as one might expect. They have also been found frequently within caches of artifacts accompanying the individual, either as a burial offering or as part of his or her personal belongings. In flexed burials, these artifact caches were usually placed between the knees and the face. In extended burials, they were usually placed beside the chest or the hips (Wray 1963:41–42). According to Wray (1963:42–43), both men and women wore combs, but men's combs were smaller and simpler, and had shorter teeth, than those of women and children, which generally featured more complex decoration. Children's combs would obviously have been made by their adult relatives.

Figure 10.1. Comb from the Late Archaic Frontenac Island site, New York, collection of Rochester Museum & Science Center.
Source: Reproduced from 1993 New York State Archaeology Week poster with digital enhancement, originally illustrated in Ritchie 1965:116, Plate 39, and cover.

The great majority of combs are made from the flat section of moose or elk antler, although wood and bone were sometimes used. Their primary function was likely for cleaning and fashioning hair, although they should also be

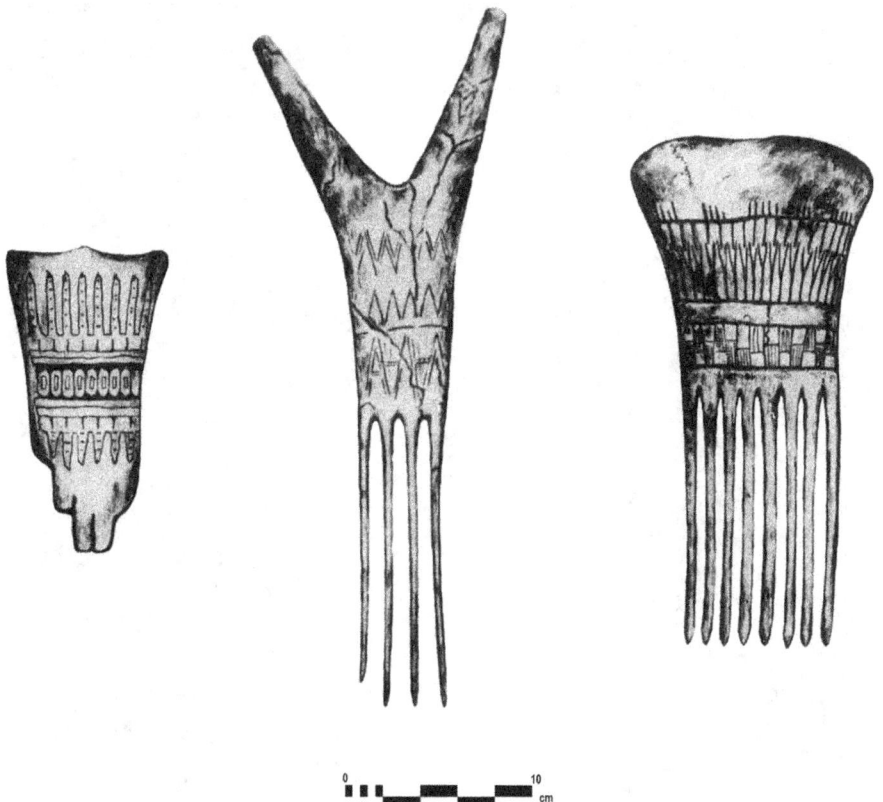

Figure 10.2. Combs from the Middle Woodland period: *left*, Bay of Quinte; *middle*, Kipp Island site, New York; *right*, Port Maitland, Ontario
Source: Reproduced with digital enhancement by John Howarth from illustrations in Ritchie 1944:185.

considered ornamental (Gates St-Pierre 2018). According to Christian Gates St-Pierre, preforms and manufacturing debris indicate that they were manufactured by first obtaining a rectangular or trapezoidal shape, which was then divided into two sections by means of an engraved horizontal line. The bottom portion was engraved with guiding lines indicating where to carve to form the teeth. The handle was carved after the teeth. A rough draft was first marked out, and one or a series of holes served as decoration or as starting points for more elaborate carvings. The guiding lines may also have been important for an even layout of the teeth and for effecting bilateral symmetry.

In William Engelbrecht's *Iroquoia: Development of a Native World* (2003:153–154), he suggests that combs may be objects of transformation and that bilateral symmetry was employed to create a reflection of the other. He suggests that since many of these bilaterally symmetrical combs have been found in burials, perhaps the reflected one represents the spirit world. In some accounts, it seems as if the afterlife is viewed as a reflection of this life. Engelbrecht argues that a

Figure 10.3. Comb from the Late Woodland Lawson site, collection of Museum of Ontario Archaeology. *Source:* Photograph courtesy of Museum of Ontario Archaeology; digital enhancement by John Howarth.

comb with bilateral symmetry in a burial could have been seen by the Haudenosaunee as assisting the transformation of the individual's spirit to the spirit world. The presence of bilateral symmetry on the comb that is thousands of years old from the Frontenac Island site may, therefore, signify the antiquity of Haudenosaunee ideology in their linguistic homeland in central New York State (Schillaci et al. 2017).

Figure 10.4. Comb from the Neutral Grimsby site.
Source: Collection of Royal Ontario Museum, illustration by Savannah Parent.

Vasey (1991:180) argues that the combs' function was as a fundamentally efficient vehicle for conveying symbolic information, in miniature form, about significant events and details of Haudenosaunee culture. Although they were used in life, their placement in graves meant neither they nor their symbolic information were intended to be destroyed. In Haudenosaunee ideology, the soul of the comb transcends the boundary between life and death, accompanying one of the souls of the deceased ancestor.

Combs are often adorned with carvings of human, mammal, or bird effigies, or with less complex geometrical shapes. Approximately 90 percent of Northern Iroquoian human and animal effigies that are not stand-alone figurines or maskettes (face effigies) appear on combs (Williamson and Veilleux 2005:5). Identified mammal effigies on Seneca combs include bear, panther, otter, beaver, wolf, dog, horse, lynx, and deer, while commonly identified birds include heron, snipe, and woodcock. Many of the animals, such as bear, wolf, beaver, and heron, are Seneca clan animals and possibly are used as designs that signify the special relationships between those animals and the people who share their name. In the case of mammals, beings with a large head with ears, powerful abdomen, and long tail may be panthers; those with a tiny head, curved abdomen, and long tail may be otters; and those with a head curving down to the ground, rounded back, flat stomach, and long tail may represent beavers. Although it is not always clear what animal is being depicted, it should be remembered that otter, beaver, and water panther are all sacred beings—in Hamell's words, long-tailed and long-bodied animal man-beings (Hamell 1998).

Reptiles and amphibians, such as the snake, lizard, and frog, have also been identified (Wray 1963:45). When human figures are represented, Europeans can be differentiated from Indigenous individuals, usually based on the depicted hairstyle or details of dress, especially cloaks and hats. Combinations of representations are common (see Hill 2012).

Combs also feature intricate and fine engravings (Wray 1963:Figure 2), including hourglass figures, stars, filled triangles, crosses, and X forms, as well as zigzags. Wray (1963:45) believed that the hourglass, star, and X forms represent humans, while the zigzag lines are reflective of snakes, all symbols that are present in some of the images presented in this chapter.

Hourglass motifs are among the most prevalent form included on combs. Rick Hill (2012) noted that the manipulation of positive and negative space has been used to create hourglass motifs in addition to etching. In the examples in Figure 10.5, this space can be seen to have been created by the sometimes-unnatural positioning of the legs of the various panther beings.

The modified hourglass/star motifs are described by Wray as possible human figures (1963:45–46), but they have also been described by others as thunderbird representations (Hamell 1998:278–279). The motif is characteristic of panther effigy combs, and, according to Hamell, "a bi-association of panther man-being

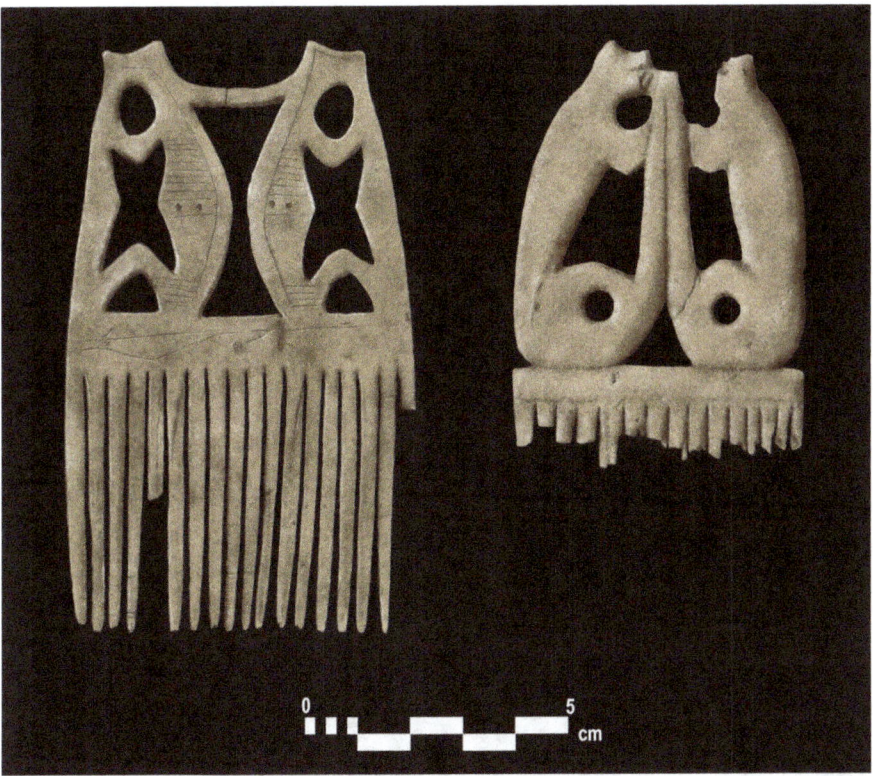

Figure 10.5. Two combs illustrating hourglasses, from Ganondagan (*left*) and the Grimsby site (*right*). *Source:* Collections of Rochester Museum & Science Center and Royal Ontario Museum, respectively; illustrations by Savannah Parent.

and hourglass shape suggests a Northern Iroquoian universe in microcosm, specifically the conceptual symmetry and complementary synergism between powers below, exemplified by the panther/fire-dragon/great serpent man-beings, and the powers above, typified by the thunder (bird) man-beings" (1998:279).

Figure 10.6 is a Seneca "doorkeeper" comb (Hamell 1979) from Rochester Junction, likely the Seneca town of Tiotohatton, which was destroyed during de Denonville's 1687 punitive expedition. Although they perhaps represent the Confederacy function of the Seneca as the "keepers of the western door," Hamell and Dean (1987:10–12) further argue that combs such as this one represent the specific functions of the cross-moiety paired doorkeeper chiefs— numbers 49 and 50 in the Roll Call of the Haudenosaunee chiefs, with the conceptual image of wolves representing the Wolf clan doorkeeper, number 50, named "It-keeps-the-doorway-open." That particular comb, however, also features long-beaked birds, possibly snipe, engraved on the comb's base, perhaps representing a clan. The arbour-like motif may represent the sky dome or the symbolic Haudenosaunee Confederacy longhouse. A hocker (squatting figure)

Figure 10.6. "Doorkeeper" comb from the Seneca Rochester Junction site, New York.
Source: Collection of the Rochester Museum & Science Center, illustration by Savannah Parent.

placed within such a framework and grasping its sides has been interpreted by Hamell (1979) as supporting the longhouse and, by extension, the sky dome.

Combs of this doorkeeper type are, to this date, unknown from IDN sites, although a ceramic pipe bowl recovered near Wellington, Prince Edward County, has a similar image (see Engelbrecht and Williamson, this volume: Figure 11.3). George Hamell has described an early twelfth-century ceramic pipe from central New York that featured "continuous bas relief hockers—a frog alternating with a headless human" (Hill 2012:9). A small, separate wolf effigy, perhaps from a similar comb, was found at Teiaiagon (see below).

Anthony Wonderley (2005) has also demonstrated that, with certain types of Mohawk and Onondaga effigy pipes, there exist matching combs. He argued that those pipes were focused on origin stories and themes related to the confederation of the League (see also Wonderley and Sempowski 2019). Those same Dougherty pipe-style confederacy motifs do not seem to be present on the sample of combs recovered from the IDN sites.

1. Iroquois du Nord Antler Combs

Seven complete or partial combs have been documented from Iroquois du Nord sites: six from Teiaiagon (Robertson, this volume) and one from Bead Hill, the site identified with the IDN village of Ganatsekwyagon (Poulton, this volume). There are also seven combs known from the suspected location of Kenté and environs (von Bitter et al., this volume).

1.1. Teiaiagon

One of the antler combs from Teiaiagon was found by Archaeological Services Inc. (2007) with the burial of an adult woman, who had been placed in an extended position. During the removal of soil approximately 25 cm above the burial, the rim of a brass pot was discovered. The comb was recovered teeth upwards, to the west of the pot, with the body of the comb underneath the pot. Both the pot and the comb were above the torso and over the left arm. Several other artifacts were found, including a bone-handled iron knife at the right knee, along with two iron awls. An iron axe had been placed at the left foot.

The design of the comb is elaborate and consists of a combination of human and multiple animal figures (Figure 10.7). It also has fine, detailed engravings on both faces of the comb. The animal figures are illustrated in profile, and the human figure is situated on the back of one of them. The human form is represented from the waist up, with two definite arms and a portion of a squared arbour. The human form's incomplete arm—bent at the elbow—likely involved the lower arm extending to grasp the now missing side of the arbour to the left. This is a common motif, which also provides structural strength for the figure(s) free carved within the arbour. As noted above, comb designs are usually symmetrical, and this was almost certainly originally the case with this comb. The attachment areas for the missing figures had, however, been carefully smoothed and polished.

A detailed description of the engraved designs can be found in the Williamson and Veilleux article (2005:14–16); suffice it to say that the animal figures on this comb fit Hamell's (1998) description of a Seneca panther effigy, although we wondered if it is a panther morphing into a bear, as the shape of the second animal head is quite bearlike. The distal end of the panther's long tail has a series of engraved bands, which likely represent the rattle of a rattlesnake. According to Hamell, "panther, dragon, and serpent tails and tales are

Figure 10.7. Comb from the Teiaiagon site, found by Archaeological Services Inc. *Source:* Photo of resin replica by John Howarth with digital enhancement.

closely entwined" in the mythical realities of the Seneca, and artifactual representations of these "panther/fire-dragon/great serpent man-beings" were possible manifestations of personal guardian spirits to guard against war, famine, and disease (Hamell 1998:265, 272, 276). Serpents occupy one end of the continuum of long-tailed and long-bodied animal man-beings, which also include salamanders, lizards, weasels, mink, fishers, martens, otters, and mountain lions/panthers. According to Hamell, these beings are closely identified with both "socially constructive" and "socially destructive" medicine (1987:78, 1998:258, 264, 269; Hamell and Fox 2005).

The fine engravings consist of linear, circular, and geometric designs located on the bodies of the animal figures. The only engraving on the human figure consists of a few generally horizontal lines at the waist or "belt" area. Designs on the creatures' bodies include modified hourglass or star designs (Wray 1963:45–46) as along with two circles, one with six and the other with eight radial spokes. The short comb base, between the teeth and the top of the handle (Wray 1963:36), also features fine engraving on both faces. These consist of a series of criss-crossed lines bordered by two horizontal lines, covering the entire width of the comb. This patterning is reminiscent of snakeskin as well as etching lines used on birch-bark scrolls (see Rajnovich 1994:29 for an example of a Midewiwin birch-bark scroll).

Lines, such as the ones radiating from the hourglass motifs, are often described by researchers as power lines and can be found on pictographs, Midewiwin scrolls (Rajnovich 1994:142), and the early artwork of Norval Morrisseau, many of whose early career pieces appear to have been inspired by northern Ontario rock art.

Unlike the power line and the hourglass and star/thunderbird motifs, the incised circles with spokes are rare. One similar example has been found on picture writing from northern Minnesota and northern Wisconsin (Rajnovich 1994:88, 91, Figure 72b). There, the circle with inside "spokes" was interpreted as a drum, which is the means of communication of Kitche Manitou, and an affirmation of the medicine given to the people.

The other almost complete Teiaiagon comb (Figure 10.8) was found by Historic Horizon Inc. with the remains of a woman in her twenties, who was laid in an extended position with her head to the west and her left arm placed across her chest. The interment was accompanied by five artifacts: a brass finger ring that was recovered from soil disturbed by the backhoe and was assumed to have been worn on her right hand; two additional brass rings found in situ on the fingers of her left hand; a small, fragmentary brass kettle containing a fragment of a fur pelt found on the right side of the body; and a finely made antler comb recovered from disturbed soils (Historic Horizon 2001:11).

The antler comb features a carved openwork motif of three human figures wearing European-style frock coats, with plaiting in the middle evident on at least one figure and perhaps a Dutch-style collar evident on the middle figure. The two outside figures are wearing European wide-brim hats. All of them have eyes and mouths etched.

At least four other partial combs were recovered from nineteenth-century explorations of the site, one of which likely, given the general design and number

Figure 10.8. Comb from the Teiaiagon site, found by Historic Horizon Inc.
Source: Photo of resin replica by Archaeological Services Inc. with digital enhancement by John Howarth.

and size of the teeth (Figure 10.9: upper left), predates the Seneca occupation, and two of which have been formed into rectangular shapes (Figure 10.9: upper middle and right). One of the rectangular combs was abandoned during manufacture as the teeth were not completed (Figure 10.9: upper middle).

Figure 10.9. Combs from the Teiaiagon site.
Source: Top row, collection of Royal Ontario Museum; *bottom left,* Canadian Museum of History; *bottom right,* from the Kirkwood site, Rochester Museum & Science Center; illustrations by Savannah Parent.

An effigy fragment (Figure 10.9: lower left), recovered by Charles Hirschfelder (see Robertson, this volume) is of a wolf or panther. If a wolf, it may be a piece from a Wolf clan doorkeeper comb similar to one documented and discussed by Hamell and Dean-John (1987) from the Seneca Kirkwood village (Figure 10.9: lower right) or the one from Rochester Junction/Tiotohatton discussed above. They argue that the Wolf clan were the last Seneca chiefs to agree to join the Confederacy and that, in return for their assent, they were appointed the Confederacy's western doorkeepers. A wolf image on a comb from Teiaiagon, where the flow of furs through the western door would be controlled, would be consistent with that interpretation.

1.2. Ganatsekwyagon-Bead Hill

An antler effigy comb (Figure 10.10) was recovered by Walter Kenyon in 1964 at Ganatsekwyagon-Bead Hill, with a semi-flexed interment of a single young adult female (see Poulton, this volume). Grave goods included at least fifty-three glass trade beads; a small wampum belt; ten long, tubular shell beads; fragments of a copper or brass kettle or small cup; a leather pouch containing an iron clasp knife; and a complete antler comb. Kenyon never wrote a report on this excavation. He retained the artifacts from the burial and reinterred the skeletal remains elsewhere on the property. The artifacts recovered from the burial are held at the Royal Ontario Museum.

The comb depicts three European figures in knee breeches and European-style hats. As Hill (2012) and others have noted, small dots are used to depict buttons and facial features. European explorers and missionaries were known to have been present at both Teiaiagon and Ganatsekwyagon, and although Haudenosaunee Peoples, and their adoptees, would have been exposed to Europeans for more than sixty years by that time, their increasing presence and impacts seem to have warranted comment in this art form. Bergseth (2008:18) argues these combs depicted trends or events that were changing Indigenous lives, such as the visits of Europeans and their animals, such as horses, to their villages. She suggests that Indigenous Peoples synchronized Indigenous and European symbols in an effort to make "sense of the Europeans in the context of their own artistic expressions" (Bergseth 2008:18).

1.3. Kenté

Six combs can be directly related to the site of Kenté, provided its probable location at Smokes Point and Bald Head Island in Wellers Bay is correct (see von Bitter et al., this volume). One other does not have a recorded provenience. Four of the Kenté combs were donated to the precursor of the Royal Ontario Museum in 1889 as part of the G. J. Chadd Collection (Orr 1922:119; see Harris 2020), along with a Middle Woodland comb. Two combs were found that the excavators concluded were likely associated with burials at the Hilton site at Smokes Point (Northeastern Archaeological Associates 2010).

The comb illustrated in Figure 10.11 was recovered by Chadd at Smokes Point and features a European man in striped breeches and a toque,

Iroquois du Nord Decorated Antler Combs 229

Figure 10.10. Comb from Ganatsekwyagon.
Source: Collection of Parks Canada, illustration by Savannah Parent.

accompanied by a dog, which is attached to his right hand. Engraved on the triangular arbour, perhaps reminiscent of a European roof, and on the chest of the individual, are elaborate stars (or suns) seen on other Seneca combs, as documented by Wray (1963:Figure 2c and v) (Figure 10.11).

Figure 10.11. Comb from Smokes Point.
Source: Chadd Collection, Royal Ontario Museum, illustration by Savannah Parent.

Bergseth (2008:19–22), in describing a comb from the Seneca town of Ganondagan (Kroup et al. 1986) that depicts a European in breeches and tricornered hat with a dog and musket, suggests on the basis of the squared muzzle that the dog could be a medium-sized hunting terrier. The height of the dog on the Kenté comb, from the front foot to the topline above its shoulder or from the hind foot to the topline at the lumbosacral area, suggests it, too, was medium-sized, likely reaching in height about mid-calf on the man. This, along with the short, floppy ears (which are unlike the long, floppy ears of a hound) and the square muzzle, similarly suggests a hunting terrier. It appears as if it is being fed from the hand, with its gaze directed either at the hand or perhaps up at its master, as in the dog on the Ganondagan comb.

Indigenous dogs were smaller than European dogs, more resembling foxes, with short, pointy ears and thick fur. The Jesuit Father Louis Nicolas, who lived with Algonquians in the 1660s and early 1670s, described them as having a different temperament than those of the French, melancholic like the savages. Bergseth (2008:22) suggests that the term "melancholy" was used to explain the calm and reserved behaviour of both Indigenous people and their dogs toward one another. An Indigenous dog would probably not jump up on its master. According to European observers, although Indigenous hunters valued their dogs, they did not pet or play with them.

European animals, such as goats, hogs, horses, cows, and sheep, were also introduced to the Haudenosaunee and other Indigenous Peoples during the IDN period; they would have been viewed at first as strange animals. In the case of horses, Bergseth (2008:21) points to the journal of Wentworth Greenhalgh, who wrote about his 1677 trip to the Seneca villages: "Here ye Indyans were very desirous to see us ride our horses, which wee did." No combs with images of horses have yet been recovered from IDN sites.

Bergseth also comments on the Indigenous reaction to European clothing, noting that Indigenous Peoples were fascinated with English clothing, especially buttons, so much so that colonists at Roanoke were told that the Indigenous name for the region was Wingandacoa, which was translated by Sir Walter Raleigh to "you weare good clothes, or gay clothes." Roger Williams reported that the Narraganset word for Europeans translates as "Coat-men, or clothed" (Bergseth 2008:22–23; Kupperman 2000:53). The incorporation of these images into Seneca cultural tradition and artistic expression suggests to Bergseth that these combs reflect a native fascination with the strangely clothed people and animals that visited their villages (see also Hill 2012:3–5).

A comb recovered from Bald Head Island (Figure 10.12: left), possibly from a cemetery associated with the village, features two opposing bears or panthers joined in their snouts and forelimbs and using negative circular spaces to create the image of hind limbs. The base above the teeth features two parallel engraved horizontal lines.

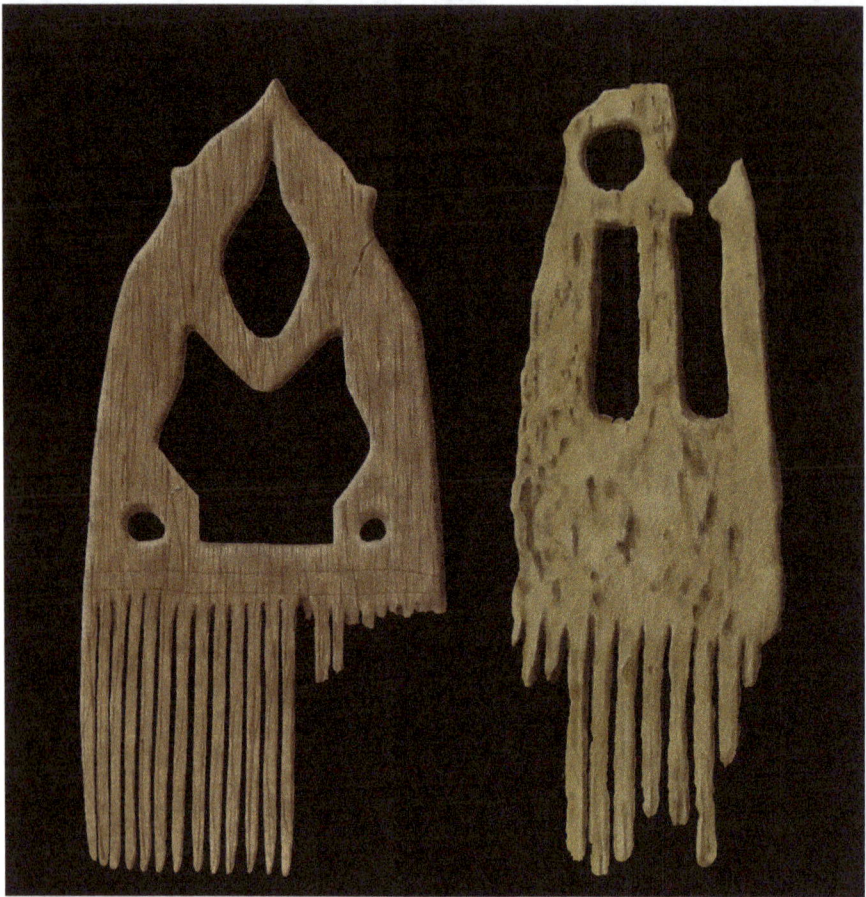

Figure 10.12. Combs from Bald Head Island and Smokes Point.
Source: Chadd Collection, Royal Ontario Museum, illustration by Savannah Parent.

Another comb from Smokes Point (Figure 10.12: right) is difficult to interpret, although central posts on combs are common. It is weathered and fragmentary, and likely represents two animals on either side of a post.

These combs and one of two others found at the Hilton site (Northeastern Archaeological Associates 2010:42), an Indigenous cemetery at Smokes Point containing between eighteen and thirty-three individuals (Northeastern Archaeological Associates 2010:78), feature common iconography for late seventeenth-century Haudenosaunee combs. They are symmetrical with opposing animals. The one from the Hilton site, which is very similar to the combs shown in Figure 10.13, features two opposing panthers attached to a central post, with their limbs positioned to create two hourglasses out of negative spaces. Interestingly, they are not quite symmetrical, with one animal larger than the other, a relatively rare occurrence in our experience, generally, although the

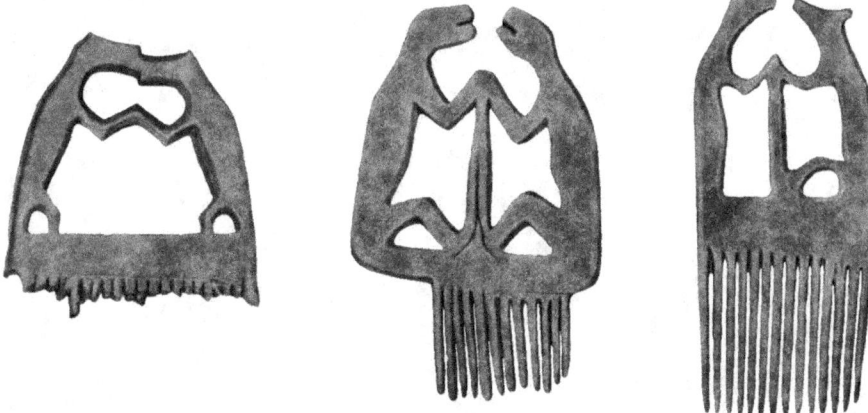

Figure 10.13. Three combs with asymmetrical panther, from the Dann site (*left, right*), Rochester Museum & Science Center; Silverheels site (*middle*), New York State Museum.
Source: Illustration by Savannah Parent.

same is true of the panthers in Figure 10.13 (left and right) and many additional examples of central post panther effigies. The teeth are missing and worn on the Smokes Point comb, suggesting it had been curated and placed in the grave despite it no longer serving a prosaic use.

Comparing the Smokes Point comb to one from Boughton Hill, we note that the latter features dots along the back of the panther creatures and edging the central hourglass, as seen in Figure 10.14 (left). Such dots are also present on at least one of the Smokes Point Hilton site comb panthers. It is interesting to note how distinctly these symbols are expressed. Many combs have dots outlining the animals and power lines extending along the centre of their bodies (Figure 10.14: right); only rarely are they interchangeable.

The other Smokes Point Hilton site comb seems to show an Indigenous man holding two animals near the back of their necks, which are positioned facing outward and attached to an outside frame. The man is standing on the top of the base of the comb. The teeth are highly fragmented. This, too, is a common comb design on Haudenosaunee sites in the homeland.

Another comb from the Chadd Collection (Figure 10.15: left), found in the vicinity of Carrying Place, is fragmented, but given the nature of the teeth, it seems that it may date to the late seventeenth century. The holes likely served as decoration or as starting points for more elaborate carvings. The other comb (Figure 10.15: right) is from the Chadd Collection; its provenience is unknown, but it is likely to be from the same area. It features a fragment, perhaps one half of a comb, with a rare human-like figure and face in profile, facing outward. In symmetrical form, it would have featured two opposing humans facing outwards in profile; opposing animal figures in profile facing outward are relatively rare.

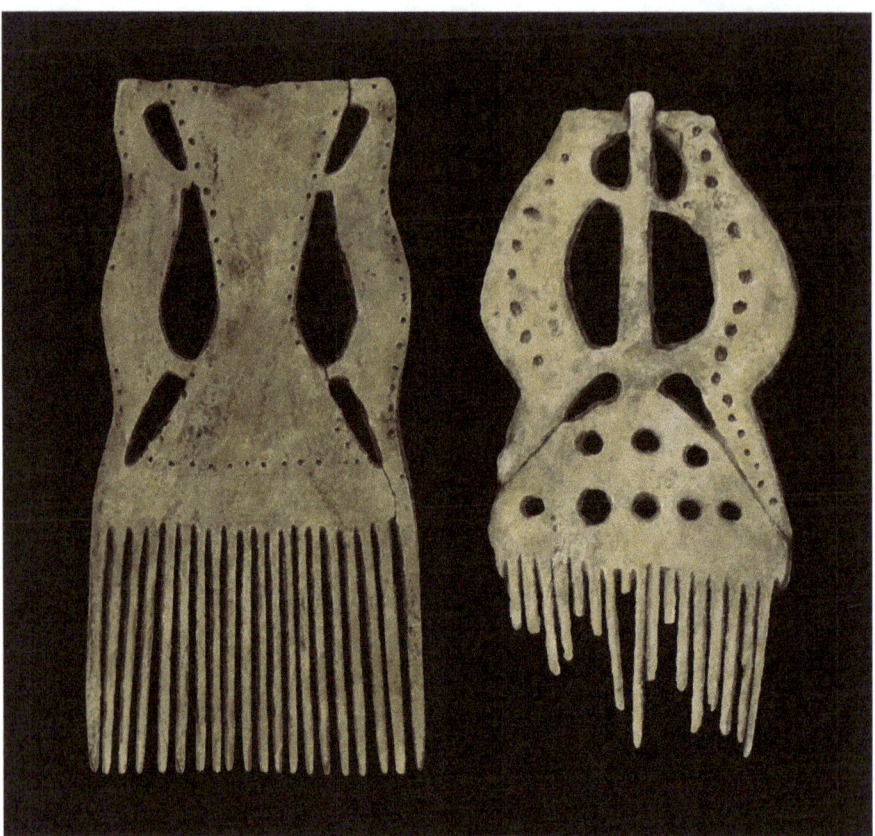

Figure 10.14. Two combs illustrating use of dots, from Boughton Hill site (*left*) and Ontario County (*right*). *Source*: Collection of Rochester Museum & Science Center, illustrations by Savannah Parent.

2. Discussion

In summary, the IDN combs are generally consistent with Haudenosaunee combs found in their homeland. The mortuary contexts of their discovery along the north shore of Lake Ontario are also likely similar.

With respect to the designs and decoration on these combs, Eldon Yellowhorn (2006) has argued that traditional narratives are important interpretive tools for creating a truly Indigenous archaeology. In this way, answers to the search for meaning of decorated material culture lie in traditional narratives and art, both accessible and inaccessible. Although we can never know the original intent of the artists who fashioned these combs or altered them throughout the objects' lives, we can look for parallel interpretations in the symbols that were routinely manipulated in other contexts where art was employed (e.g., rock art, body art, bark scrolls, other forms of material culture, and oral histories). This is what Rick Hill and George Hamell have done previously, and we have attempted to draw upon their experience and wisdom.

Iroquois du Nord Decorated Antler Combs 235

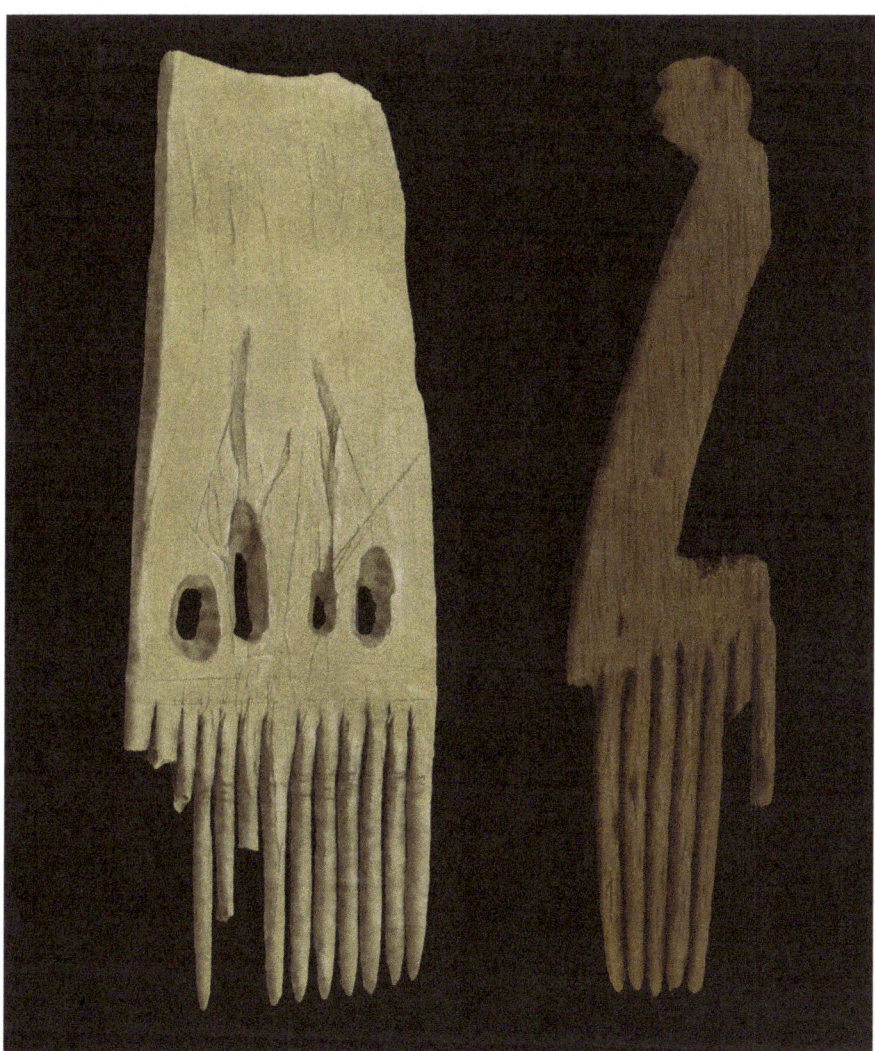

Figure 10.15. Comb from Carrying Place, and comb with unknown provenience. *Source:* Chadd Collection, Royal Ontario Museum; illustrations by Savannah Parent.

Combs were and are both profane and sacred objects, with stories to tell of past lives lived. They are also reflective of light, energy, and power. Bradley (2020:475) has noted that "rays and auras had long been used in the Eastern Woodlands to depict animacy and spiritual power, often in association with shamanism." They are present, for example, on a stone platform pipe from more than a thousand years ago (Bradley 2020:475, Figure 9.33), on a probable St. Lawrence Iroquoian or Anishinaabe stone pendant (Cooper 2005:69), a skull rattle from the early sixteenth-century Clearville site (Williamson and Veilleux 2005:3) and on various rock art sites throughout the Northeast as sun figures with circular heads and projecting rays (Vastokas and Vastokas 1973:59–65). The Vastokas (1973:55) relate these figures to the Kitchi Manitou (Great Spirit) in its manifestation as the sun, noting that Copway (1851:159), the Anisihinaabeg historian, wrote that "the sun is the wigwam of the Great Spirit and it is as the abode of this being that the Indians view that luminary." Such sun figures are not confined to northeastern North America but are a cross-cultural phenomena (e.g., Vastokas and Vastokas 1973:59–61, Figure 6) in the Americas.

Yet, we need look no further than nature (Figure 10.16) to see the interplay between the Sky World and our own. The sun, exploding hourglasses, rays, and power lines express themselves clearly where the sky meets water, and we need to open our eyes to these experiences, as did the ancestors. As Bradley suggested (2020:474), "the use of rays to depict spiritual power was intuitive" and does not require detailed explanation on our part.

Figure 10.16. Sun reflected in water.
Source: Photograph by Yuma Hori with digital enhancement.

Acknowledgements

Many individuals assisted or contributed to our work with the Iroquois du Nord combs. These include Andrea Carnevale, Martin Cooper, William A. Fox, George Hamell, April Hawkins, Dana Poulton, David Robertson, Stephen Cox Thomas, and Annie Veilleux. Expert comment regarding dog breeds was provided by Janet Steiss and Ed Aycock. We would like to thank Elizabeth Pietrzykowski and Kathryn Murano of the Rochester Museum & Science Center for their assistance with the Museum collections, Savannah Parent for her excellent illustrations of many of the combs and John Howarth for his digital enhancement of many of the other images.

11

IROQUOIS DU NORD CERAMIC VESSELS AND PIPES

William E. Engelbrecht and Ronald F. Williamson

Fragments of Indigenous ceramic vessels and pipes exist in collections made by avocational and professional archaeologists from and in the vicinity of Iroquois du Nord sites. In this chapter, we discuss the ceramic pottery and pipes recovered by avocational and professional archaeologists from three of the Iroquois du Nord sites situated on the north shore of Lake Ontario and occupied between the mid-1660s and the 1680s: Bald Head Island and Smokes Point, in Prince Edward County, argued by von Bitter et al. to be the site of Kenté (see von Bitter et al., this volume) and immediate environs; Bead Hill, identified as the village of Ganatsekwyagon (see Poulton, this volume); and Teiaiagon (also known as Baby Point) (see Robertson, this volume) (Figures 1.2 and 1.3). The ceramics we are dealing with lack stratigraphic context and were not recorded in archaeological contexts that could be dated, except for some of the material culture from Ganatsekwyagon. Therefore, we rely on ceramic styles known to be common in the seventeenth century in both Ontario and New York to identify whether these specimens could possibly date to mid- to late seventeenth-century Haudenosaunee settlement.

We consider these ceramic objects in the context of a survey of mid-seventeenth-century Haudenosaunee homeland sites that indicates Indigenous ceramic pipes and vessels were still being used in the 1660s (and later), though European-made kettles had largely replaced ceramic pots by this time and European-made pipes had also been introduced. We discuss possible reasons for the retention of these Indigenous-made objects into the second half of the seventeenth century.

First, however, we examine ceramic trends in the late sixteenth and seventeenth centuries and the inclination toward abandonment of Indigenous ceramic technology in favour of brass vessels and white clay pipes.

1. Late Ceramic Vessel Trends Among Northern Iroquoians

It seems that by the mid-seventeenth century, the size of Haudenosaunee ceramic pots decreased. This trend may relate to a combination of factors, including smaller family size as a result of increased mortality (Strauss 2000:151–152) and the use of large metal kettles for public use and smaller ceramic vessels for private use (Lauria 2019:91; Strauss 2000:104–105). Except for some very small, crudely made pots that may have been made by children and some very small, better made pots used for pigment or medicines, Iroquoian ceramic vessels are assumed to have been used for cooking. Smaller pots tend to be found in mortuary contexts, implying personal use (Strauss 2000:141, 144–145). The Onondaga had separate terms for large and small pots (Waugh 1973:57), suggesting that a size difference in pots was culturally meaningful.

In a detailed study of Wendat ceramic vessels of the historic period, Holly Martelle (2002:214) noted that rather than just small and large categories, historic Wendat pots were made in a variety of sizes. She identified tiny, cup-sized, small (1.5 L), medium (4–5 L), and large (7.5 L or more) vessels, the latter three classes all being used for various forms of cooking (Martelle 2002:233–234). These observations were possible because of the large samples she was able to examine, including vessels from the completely excavated early seventeenth-century Ball site. Martelle also noted the importance of larger vessels, citing Elisabeth Tooker (1964:70), who argued that some events employed thirty to forty larger vessels at a time. Although Martelle's work stresses that historic Wendat assemblages embodied a wide variety of vessel sizes and shapes, she also noted some general trends regarding vessel sizes and decorative attributes (Martelle 2002:426–427).

For Haudenosaunee vessels, it has been observed that collar height decreases during the sixteenth and early seventeenth centuries and that there is an increase in simple motifs on the collar, such as incised parallel oblique or vertical lines. The incidence of horizontal lines decreases in frequency over this same period. By way of comparison, we note that a precipitous decrease in horizontal lines on collars occurs in the fifteenth century for the Wendat sequences on the north shore of Lake Ontario (Williamson and Ramsden 2019). The bases of collars become plainer (fewer notches, punctates, and gashes) and there is little decoration below the collar or on the lip interior. Effigies decrease in frequency but continue to be placed under castellations. Among the Susquehannock, Cayuga, Seneca, Erie, Neutral, and Wendat, appliqué collared (frilled or lobed) ceramics become common around the 1620s. In the case of the Wendat, there was also a "deterioration in quality of design and all other aspects of manufacture design" (Martelle 2002:288–289), as observed by Martelle in the assemblage of the 1630s Thompson-Walker site, even though ceramic vessels were still being made in large quantities. The decline in quality of vessels may be consistent with other trends in Wendat society; for example, the increased role of maize in diet

(Pfeiffer et al. 2016) and the shortening of weaning periods (Pfeiffer et al. 2017), all perhaps attributable to the stress caused by heightened warfare between the Wendat and their allies and the Haudenosaunee.

Most Northern Iroquoian pots made after the mid-fourteenth century were collared, but non-collared ceramic vessels were also made, and this practice continued into the seventeenth century. It is not known why this dichotomy persisted over time and through space. Non-collared pots typically lack interior food encrustation, suggesting their use in brewing tea or perhaps boiling plant fibre. Residue analysis could be used to address possible functional differences between non-collared and collared pots. For a detailed discussion of ceramic trends in specific areas of Iroquoia, see the following: Seneca and Cayuga (Niemczycki 1984:40), Onondaga (Bradley 1987:121–122), Mohawk (Kuhn 1994:33), northern New York Iroquoians (Engelbrecht 1995:40–46), Wendat (Martelle 2002; Ramsden 1990:366, 368), Neutral (Lennox and Fitzgerald 1990:415), and Susquehannock (Lauria 2012, 2019).

2. Timing of the Decline of Indigenous-Made Ceramic Vessels and Pipes on Haudenosaunee Sites

During the mid-seventeenth century, the Wendat, Tionontaté, and Neutral confederacies and their traditional Algonquian allies, as well as the Erie, were defeated by the Haudenosaunee and ceased to inhabit their traditional homelands. Consequently, there is no evidence of sustained Indigenous ceramic production in the former's homeland areas after mid-century. On the other hand, Neal Trubowitz (1992) has argued that Indigenous-made stone and ceramic pipes are preferred by Great Lakes–Riverine groups in the early eighteenth century. To gain an understanding of how long Indigenous pottery vessels and pipes were produced among the Haudenosaunee, we briefly survey ceramic artifacts recovered from mid- to late seventeenth-century Seneca, Cayuga, Onondaga, Oneida, Mohawk, and Susquehannock sites (see Figures 11.1 and 11.2 for site locations).

2.1. Seneca

Charles Wray (1973:12, 27) was perhaps the first to assert that the Seneca began to replace ceramic pots with brass kettles by 1650, noting that ceramic vessels were scarce by 1670 and were no longer being made by 1700.

Martha Sempowski (personal communication 2019) has recently provided more detail to this trend, noting that the incidence of ceramic vessels begins to decline at the Power House and Steele sites (circa 1640–1660). This trend continues at the Dann and Marsh sites (circa 1660–1670), and by the time the Ganondagan (also known as Gannagaro or Boughton Hill; Jordan and Gerard-Little 2019:56) and Rochester Junction sites are occupied (circa 1670–1687), ceramic vessels are rare, although it should be noted that the data concerning

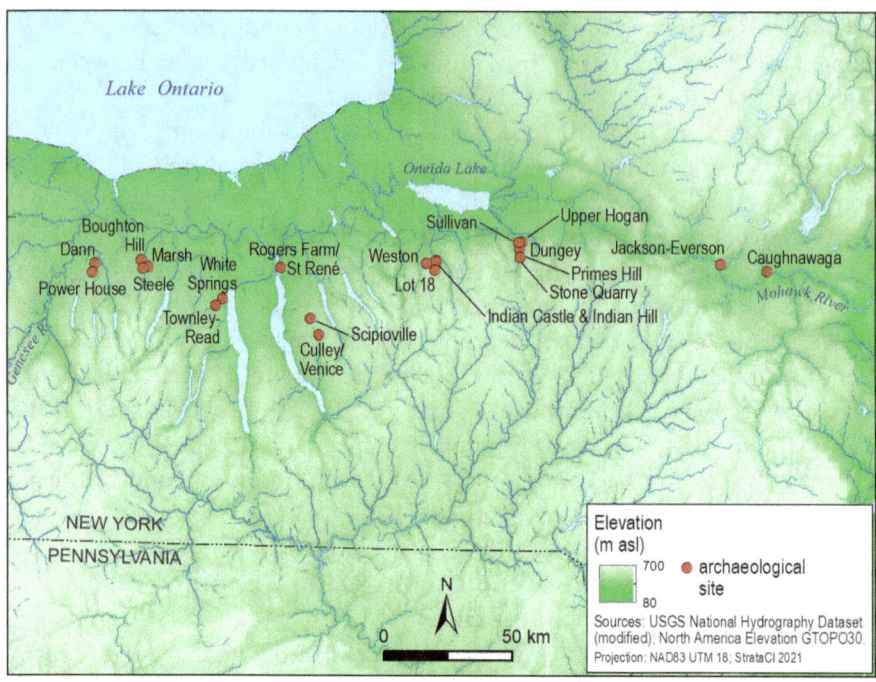

Figure 11.1. Map showing locations of select mid- to late seventeenth-century Seneca, Cayuga, Onondaga, Oneida, and Mohawk sites.
Source: Map by William Engelbrecht and Ron Williamson.

ceramics are primarily derived from mortuary contexts. Houghton (1912:452) believed Indigenous-made pots continued to be placed in graves after they were no longer being used in the household. Charles Wray and Robert Graham (1985), however, list twenty-seven rims recovered from a refuse area at Ganondagan. Robert Dean (1984:55) found that for the 1983 excavations, Indigenous-made pipe fragments ($n = 573$) outnumbered Native vessel sherds ($n = 210$) in domestic contexts; most of the 162 bowl fragments were Iroquois ring barrel types. Dean also reports the recovery of at least five European-made pipes of the Iroquois du Nord (IDN) period. No sherds from Indigenous-made vessels were recovered from excavations in domestic contexts at the circa 1688–1715 White Springs site (Kurt Jordan, personal communication 2020).

Much better data are available on trends regarding the use of Indigenous-made pipes (Jordan and Gerard-Little 2019). In a comparison of the Ganondagan (1670–1687) and White Springs (1688–1715) sites, Kurt Jordan and Peregrine Gerard-Little document a clear trend between the two sites, with a figure of 6.31 Indigenous-made pipe fragments per square metre at the former site and 1.51 at the latter, and 1.39 European pipe fragments per square metre at the former site and 6.54 at the latter. Indigenous pipes make up 81.9 percent of the pipe assemblage at Ganondagan and 18.8 percent at White Springs.

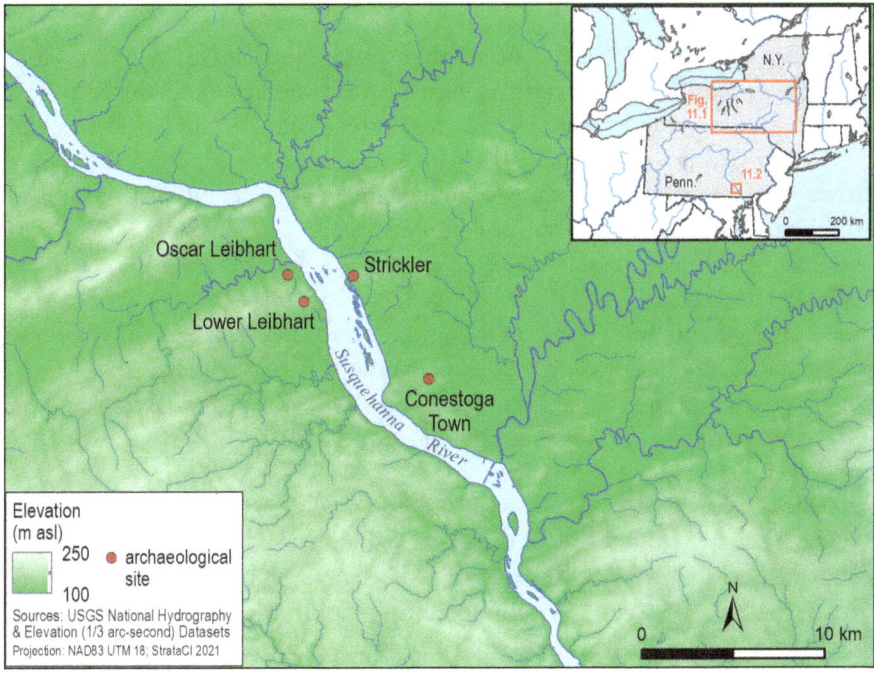

Figure 11.2. Map showing locations of select mid- to late seventeenth-century Susquehannock sites. *Source:* Map by William Engelbrecht and Ron Williamson.

At Townley-Read (1715–1754), they document only 13 Indigenous-made pipes, compared with 146 European pipes (91.8 percent of the assemblage) (Jordan and Gerard-Little 2019:49–51).

2.2. Cayuga

Adrian Mandzy (1990) has argued that the French Jesuit mission of St. René (1668–1684) is represented by the Rogers Farm site, a site known since the 1890s and collected on during the first half of the twentieth century. In addition to European material dating to this period, three pipes were discovered, two of which are of Indigenous manufacture. The University of Pittsburgh excavations on the site in 2000 recovered Indigenous ceramics, but these appear to relate to a pre-contact component (Williams-Shuker 2009; Kimberly Williams-Shuker personal communication 2020). Mandzy (1994:143, 150) notes a single vessel from a burial at the Venice (Culley) site, occupied prior to Rogers Farm. After that, Indigenous sherds are rarely encountered on Cayuga sites (Mandzy 1994:143).

2.3. Onondaga

James Bradley (1987:174) was previously of the opinion that copper kettles largely replaced Indigenous ceramic vessels by the mid-seventeenth century, as relatively little ceramic material was recovered from the Indian Castle and Lot 18 sites dating to this time (James Bradley, personal communication 2020). However, there is a substantial presence of Indigenous ceramics at the Indian Hill site (circa 1662–1683). "Most common were collared vessels with incised opposed—triangular or oblique—line motifs, notched collar bases, and plain necks and bodies" (Bradley 2020:326). Non-collared vessels, along with vessels from other ceramic traditions (mid-continent or Chesapeake Bay), were also present at Indian Hill (Bradley 2020:326). At the Weston site (circa 1677–1682), which largely follows Indian Hill, there is no evidence of Indigenous pottery (Gregory Sohrweide, personal communication 2019).

2.4. Oneida

Monte Bennett (1984:9–11, 31) notes that Indigenous-made pottery was in sharp decline at the Stone Quarry site, dated by Sempowski (2004:8–9) to between 1650 and 1660. The Indigenous ceramics recovered were from a mortuary context. At the Dungey site, dated to between 1655 and 1670 (Sempowski 2004:9–10), 99 percent of the material recovered is of European origin (Hosbach 2004:194; Hosbach et al. 2007:27; Neill et al. 2006). Pipes, of both Indigenous and European manufacture, along with a few Indigenous-made pottery sherds, were recovered from a domestic context (Hosbach et al. 2006:38, 2007:6). At the slightly later Sullivan site, 1665–1676 (Bennett 1983:55–56; Bennett and Wonderley, 2022), Indigenous-made pottery had been almost totally replaced (Bennett 1973:18). The same is true of the Upper Hogan site, 1677–1696 (Bennett and Cole 1974:10; Bennett and Wonderley, 2022), although the material from this site is poorly documented (Clark and Owen 1976). No Indigenous-made ceramics were recovered from the early eighteenth-century Primes Hill site (Bennett 1988:4, 7–8).

2.5. Mohawk

Kuhn (1994:34) suggests that southeastern Ontario potters were assimilated into Mohawk villages, influencing seventeenth-century Mohawk ceramics. Indigenous-made pottery is common on sites on the south side of the Mohawk River that were burned by the De Tracey expedition of 1666 (Wayne Lenig, personal communication 2019). However, Lenig cautions that some of these sites are multi-component. After 1666, Mohawk sites were established on the north side of the river, and pottery tends to be sparse on these sites except for Jackson-Everson.

The Jackson-Everson site is believed to represent a village of displaced Wendat dating to between 1657 and 1679 (Kuhn 1986, 1994:33;

Snow 1995a:403–410). In 1983, the State University of New York at Albany partially excavated a midden, recovering thirty-seven rim sherds representing seventeen vessels (Snow 1995a:406). "Twelve of the vessels could be identified as belonging to three Wendat types, Warminster Crossed, Huron Incised, and Warminster Horizontal" (Snow 1995a:406). Snow (1995a:406) states that three other vessels were of traditional Mohawk types—Wagoner Incised, Otstungo Notched, and Kelso Corded—and that the remaining two vessels could not be typed. The ceramics are less carefully executed than traditional ceramics (Kuhn 1986:866). Jordan (2018b:22–23) illustrates rim sherds from the site. Portions of five Indigenous-made pipes were also recovered from these excavations, one being a Wendat type (Snow 1995a:406).

Despite extensive excavations at the Caughnawaga site (circa 1683–1693), there is no mention of any ceramic vessels having been recovered (Snow 1995a:431–443), and Wayne Lenig states that after 1690, Indigenous-made vessels disappear (personal communication 2019).

2.6. Susquehannock

Kinsey (1959:94–95) recorded twenty-one Indigenous-made ceramic vessels from the Oscar Leibhart site, which is dated to 1665–1674 (Lauria 2019:99). However, no Indigenous-made pottery was found at Conestoga Town dating to after the 1690s; that is, after the Susquehannock defeat and dispersal (Kent 1984:145, 389; Kinsey 1959:98).

Effigy pipes similar to those found on Seneca sites are well known for the Stickler phase (1640 to mid-1660s) and are still present in low numbers at the Leibhart sites (Oscar Leibhart and Lower Leibhart). Tulip pipes apparently derived from ring bowl types are similarly popular in the Stickler phase (70 percent), many with painted red or black spirals on their stems. They are less common at the Leibhart sites. The ratio of Indigenous-made pipes to European ones falls from 10:1 at Strickler to 2:1 at the Lower Leibhart site. The European-made pipes at the Oscar and Bert (Byrd) Leibhart sites featured pipemaker's marks, including Tudor Rose, fleur-de-lys, and goblet forms (Omwake 1969:129–134). No Indigenous-made pipes were found at Conestoga Town (Kent 1984:145–151).

3. Significance, Persistence and Eventual Cessation of Indigenous Ceramic and Pipe Manufacture

European-made pipes were slow to be adopted and are rare on seventeenth-century Wendat sites (Creese 2017:72). One of the first whole white clay pipes in Iroquoia was recovered from the early seventeenth-century Wendat Warminster site (Cahiagué), visited by Samuel de Champlain in 1615. The Bayesian (68.2%) highest probability density estimates lie between 1585 and 1624 (Manning et al. 2018; see also Manning et al. 2019). European-made pipes broke more easily than Indigenous-made pipes, and the latter also likely possessed greater emotional, social, and spiritual value (Creese 2017; see also Braun 2012, 2015). European-made pipes appear to be less often included in graves than Indigenous ones (Jordan 2008:128–130) and may have been used by women in everyday contexts (Jordan 2014). Among the Haudenosaunee, Indigenous-made pipes persist in the archaeological record longer than Indigenous cooking vessels. This may be due, in part, to the fact that Indigenous pipes had a longer use life than pots, as the former are less breakable and more portable. Typically, ceramic cooking vessels have a use life of between six months and three years (Allen 1992; Schiffer 1987:49; Warrick 1988:30), making the existence of "heirloom" pots unlikely.

Copper kettles were traded early in the Northeast, but they, too, were slow to replace their Indigenous counterpart, being used instead as a source of copper to manufacture objects that were valued for spiritual or practical reasons (Bradley 1987:69; Howey 2011, 2017; Turgeon 1997). Creese (2017:76) suggests that they were not seen initially as superior cooking vessels, although Lisa Lauria (2019:109) enumerates several advantages of metal pots over ceramic pots for cooking. However, Saunders (1996:35) notes that cooking food in metal pots can lead to hemolytic anemia. Archaeologists commonly relegate Indigenous pottery vessels to a mundane, insignificant ideological realm as opposed to shiny trade kettles. However, the persistence of Iroquoian ceramic manufacturing traditions into the second half of the seventeenth century, when metal kettles were readily available, raises questions about that relegation.

In southern New England, Julie Woods (2013:106) notes the absence of metal kettles on a mid-seventeenth-century Pocumtuck site, in the middle Connecticut River Valley, and suggests that the inhabitants resisted the adoption of European containers for cooking, even while they adopted other European items. This echoes Robert Goodby's (1998:177–178) suggestion that the production of Indigenous pottery in seventeenth-century southeastern New England was a way of expressing and defending traditional identity and culture. Although not abundant, Indigenous ceramics were manufactured in southeastern New England until the onset of King Philip's War, in 1675 (Goodby 1998:178). Unlike seventeenth-century Iroquoian pottery decoration, which became simpler, Indigenous pottery decoration in seventeenth-century southern New England became more elaborate (Goodby 1998:171).

We propose that the decision to use Indigenous ceramic vessels or metal kettles was made by Iroquoian women and their families based on both individual economic situations and personal preferences. For some, the need for cloth, tools, firearms, alcohol, or some other commodity may have outweighed the need for metal kettles. For others, the slowness to adopt metal kettles for a cooking function may have related to the social, emotional, and spiritual value that Indigenous ceramic vessels held. They were, after all, made from clay originating from mother earth. Anthony Wonderley (2002:39) notes that, among the Haudenosaunee, ceramic vessels likely possessed social and spiritual value. Care was typically taken in their construction and decoration. Lauria (2019:91) argues that continuities in decoration style on Susquehannock sites reflect a persistence of Indigenous values and symbolic systems. Although pipes tend to be viewed as having had greater spiritual value, Indigenous pots were also likely imbued with some degree of animacy or power.

The clearest argument for the emotional and symbolic importance of Indigenous ceramics lies in their frequent inclusion in mortuary contexts well into the seventeenth century (Houghton 1912:452; Strauss 2000). A special form, the double-mouth pot, appears in mortuary contexts in the seventeenth century—examples are known from the Neutral Grimsby site, circa 1640–1650 (Kenyon 1982:15, 51, 71, 215), and from the Oneida Thurston site, circa 1630–1650 (Pratt 1976:224). The symbolic meaning of this form remains unknown. One possibility is that it relates to the important function of moieties during burial rituals, a function that continues to this day. Walter Kenyon (1982:234) remarked on the bilateral symmetry of both double-mouth pots and some antler combs and related these to dualities in Iroquoian life. It is also possible that bilaterally symmetrical objects referenced use in the afterlife, which reflected life on earth (see Williamson and von Bitter, this volume).

Wonderley (2002) has advanced a compelling argument that effigies under vessel castellations depict corn, specifically corn husk people and that the effigies are a visual way of giving thanks. In his discussion, he points out the central role of women in making pottery, growing crops, and preparing food. Engelbrecht further suggests that the frilled or lobed pottery that occurs throughout the Northeast in the seventeenth century (Engelbrecht 2007; Hawkins 2001:33) reflects stylized breasts. These could reference "Corn Mother" or "Corn Maiden," prominent in the Southeast. Pots, made from mother earth, provide nourishment. In the Haudenosaunee creation story it is the earth that gave life to humans (Hewitt 1928:498; Hill 2017:22).

Although the ceramic sequence comes to a halt in Ontario with the defeat and dispersal of Iroquoian people, ceramics continue to be made in New York, albeit in limited quantities. However, recent excavations at the village site of Notre-Dame-de-Lorette, established by the Wendat in 1673 and abandoned in 1697, have yielded a few fragments of Indigenous-made pottery, indicating that the traditions from historic Wendake, in Ontario, were carried on into the 1670s in Quebec (Louis Lesage, personal communication 2018).

4. The Iroquois du Nord Sample

The above consideration of Indigenous pottery production among the Haudenosaunee indicates that pottery was still produced in the 1650s and 1660s, although it was becoming increasingly uncommon.

The sample with which we worked is small. In the case of Kenté and environs, the examined material includes the artifacts collected by G. J. Chadd, the Trenton-based avocational collector who was active for a half-century in Prince Edward County. The ceramic material, held at the Royal Ontario Museum, includes 146 ceramic vessel fragments, 22 ceramic pipe fragments, and 3 stone pipes found on Bald Head Island; however, the collection from the island also includes artifacts from a wide time range preceding IDN settlement.

Significant quantities of ceramic material were also collected by Chadd throughout Prince Edward County, especially from Picton, Wellington, Ameliasburgh, and Murray Townships, along with Carrying Place and Indian Island. Situated on the Bay of Quinte, near the terminal end of the Carrying Place, Indian Island yielded seventy-three pipe fragments and more than fifty clay vessel fragments. The Chadd ceramic assemblage from these locales includes Transitional Woodland, Saint Lawrence Iroquoian, and ancestral Wendat types.

Professional excavations of the Hilton site, an Indigenous cemetery at Smokes Point, across from Bald Head Island, containing between eighteen and thirty-two individuals (Northeastern Archaeological Associates 2010:18), yielded numerous glass beads and antler combs that feature iconography commonly seen on late seventeenth-century Haudenosaunee combs (see Williamson and von Bitter, this volume). Although no ceramic artifacts were found by Chadd at Smokes Point, two fragments of an Iroquois conical ring pipe were found by Northeastern Archaeological Associates at the Hilton site (2010:42–43).

Scant ceramic material has been recovered from Ganatsekwyagon over the past few decades of periodic investigations (see Poulton, this volume). A small pot was found with the 1964 burial of an adult, and a juvenile rim, fragmentary sherds, and lumps of fired clay were found by Poulton in his investigations. Two incomplete pipes were also recovered from the site, including an effigy pipe and a collared ring pipe. A complete specimen and several fragments of pipes were also recovered from Teiaiagon along with a white clay pipe (see Robertson, this volume).

While most of these ceramics lack a precise archaeological context, the material recovered from Ganatsekwyagon and Teiaiagon is more likely to be from the period in question. It is, nevertheless, possible that there were earlier components in both cases.

Thus, our strategy was to choose specimens that appeared most likely to date to the mid- to late seventeenth century based on their attributes, and these are reported here. By the time the IDN sites are abandoned and the Mississauga occupied some of these same areas, Indigenous ceramics were no longer being manufactured.

4.1. Kenté

Given the mixed nature of the ceramic collection available for this study and the lack of a precise site location for Kenté, we cannot be certain that all the ceramics discussed in this section came from or are associated with the site. Nevertheless, we identified those sherds that are rims and that have enough attributes to ascertain that they may have been made in the last half of the seventeenth century (Figures 11.3–11.5; Table 11.1). The remainder are small, unidentifiable sherds. Lawson and/or Huron Incised as well as Warminster Crossed were included given their discovery at the Jackson-Everson site in the homeland, which is thought to be the result of the incorporation of individuals previously belonging to Wendat communities.

One caveat to our method is that some of these vessels, for example from the vicinity of the Carrying Place, may date to before the establishment of Kenté, as the region, and likely this access point into the interior, was travelled through in the first half of the seventeenth century by Haudenosaunee war parties and likely also in the 1650s and early 1660s (see Williamson, this volume).

We also examined the pieces from the following collecting locales in the Chadd Collection: Indian Island (one sherd of Lawson or Huron Incised

Figure 11.3. a) Effigy castellation, b) Hocker type pipe, G. J. Chadd Collection.
Source: Courtesy of the Royal Ontario Museum, photo by William Fox; digital enhancement by John Howarth.

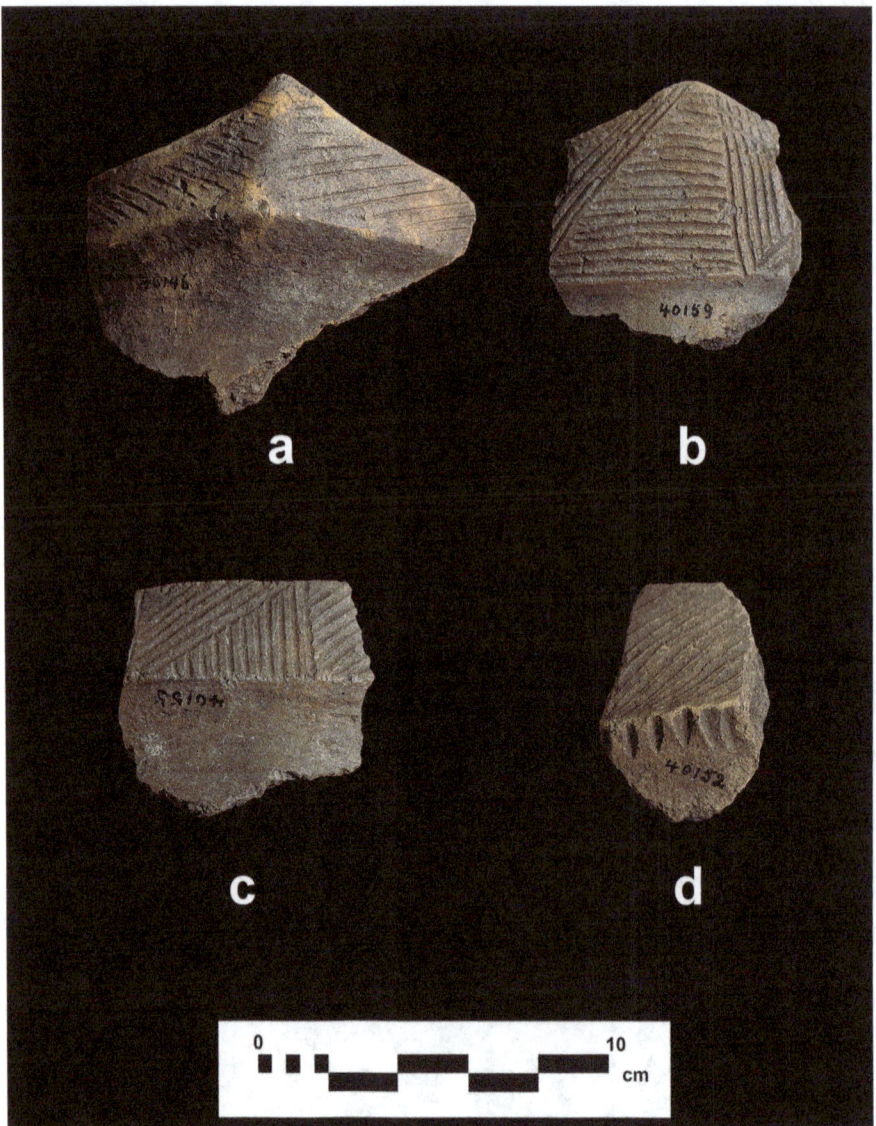

Figure 11.4. Ceramic vessel rim sherds from Bald Head Island, G. J. Chadd Collection: a) Lawson or Huron Incised, b) Cayuga Horizontal, c) Syracuse Incised, and d) Wagoner Incised.
Source: Courtesy of the Royal Ontario Museum, photographs by Robert von Bitter; digital enhancement by John Howarth.

[40450]); Wellington Beach (one sherd of Lawson or Huron Incised [40448]); Ameliasburgh (one castellation with effigy [39704]; Figure 11.3a); and Hillier Township (two sherds of Lawson and/or Huron Incised [(2) 40446]). There are also four sherds in the Chadd Collection with no catalogue numbers that are Lawson and/or Huron Incised or variants thereof. Many of these Lawson

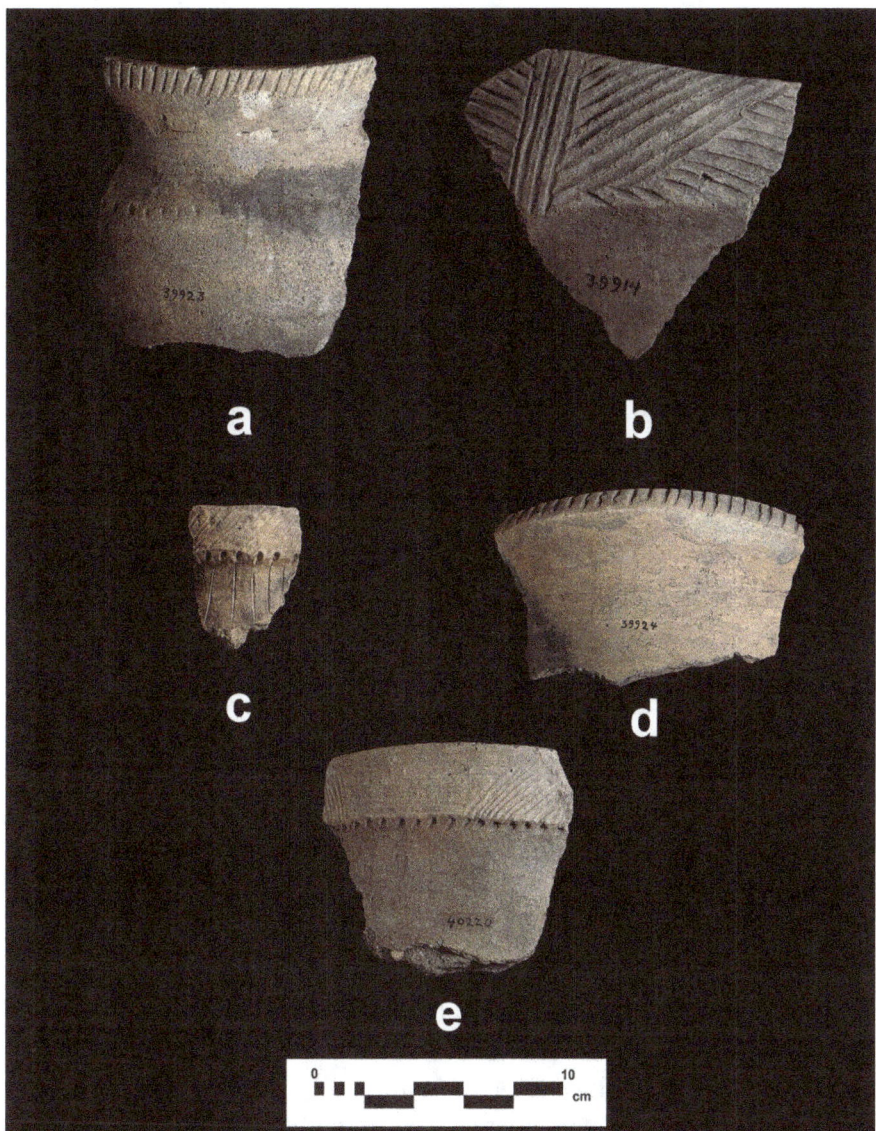

Figure 11.5. Ceramic vessel sherds from Wellers Bay (a, b, d); Prince Edward County (e); and Carrying Place (c), G. J. Chadd Collection, a) Lawson or Huron Incised, b) Syracuse Incised, c) Wagoner Incised, d) Rice Diagonal, and e) Cayuga Horizontal.
Source: Courtesy of the Royal Ontario Museum, photographs by Robert von Bitter; digital enhancement by John Howarth.

or Huron Incised vessel fragments may also date to the period between AD 1400 and 1600, when ancestral Wendat, perhaps combined with population segments from Jefferson County (Abel et al. 2019), occupied or travelled through the eastern north-shore area of Lake Ontario, including Prince Edward County

Table 11.1. Ceramic vessel fragments from the Kenté region

Site Name and Pottery Type	Quantity	Catalogue Numbers
Bald Head Island (N = 10)		
Variant of Lawson and/or Huron Incised	3	40138, 40149, 40198
Warminster Crossed	3	40119, 40131, 40143
Cayuga Horizontal	1	40159 (Figure 11.4b)
Lawson and/or Huron Incised	1	40146 (Figure 11.4a)
Syracuse Incised	1	40155 (Figure 11.4c)
Wagoner Incised	1	40152 (Figure 11.4d)
Wellers Bay (N = 8)		
Lawson–Huron Incised	2	39923 (Figure 11.5a), 39927
Warminster Crossed	2	39934, 39935
Lawson Opposed	1	39928
Variant of Lawson and/or Huron Incised	1	39920
Rice Diagonal	1	39924 (Figure 11.5d)
Syracuse Incised	1	39914 (Figure 11.5b)
Prince Edward County (N = 6)		
Syracuse Incised	2	40234, 40235
Warminster Crossed	2	40221, 40242
Cayuga Horizontal	1	40220 (Figure 11.5e)
Variant of Lawson and/or Huron Incised	1	40217
Carrying Place (N = 1)		
Wagoner Incised	1	40440 (Figure 11.5c)

Source: William Engelbrecht.

(e.g., Williamson 2014:27–28, Figure 3). Ancestral Wendat presence has been documented even farther east, at the early fifteenth-century Arbor Ridge site, in what is now Kingston, Ontario (Adams 2003), where both Huron Incised and Lawson Incised vessels were found.

The Ameliasburgh effigy (39704; Figure 11.3a) is very similar to more than a dozen effigy faces found on the late sixteenth-century Mantle (Jean-Baptiste Lainé) site vessels typed as Cayadutta-Otstungo Incised and Chance Incised, which are consistent themselves with effigies found on sixteenth-century Oneida, Onondaga, and Seneca site vessels (Birch and Williamson 2013:134–136; Wonderley 2002). Mantle is approximately 130 km northwest of Kenté in the Town of Whitchurch-Stouffville. Kuhn (1994:33) states that castellations decline in frequency during the seventeenth century in the Mohawk area but are still present. Wayne Lenig provided us with a photo of a figure effigy under a castellation from the Jackson-Everson site, although it is less detailed than the Mantle examples. Three seventeenth-century Wendat castellation effigies were found at the Auger site, and five were recovered from the Ball site (Curtis and Latta 2000), though judging by the one illustrated by Jenneth Curtis and Marti Latta (2000:8, Figure 6), these are not modelled in the same fashion and are cruder in form than the Mantle and Haudenosaunee examples.

Several effigy pipes were examined, including a hocker type (39243; Figure 11.3b), first illustrated by Orr in the Annual Archaeological Report for Ontario (AARO) for 1921–1922, that was found near Wellington, Ontario, about 25 km from Wellers Bay. Hocker-doorkeeper-type effigies were examined by George Hamell (1979) and linked to the notion of the Seneca being "western doorkeepers." The Wellington example differs from many of those effigies in that the face seems less humanoid than the typical examples on combs (see Williamson and von Bitter, this volume). It is singular and not connected to any other figure. There is a portion that may be a tail, or it may constitute a slip of the ceramicist's stylus. There are also two (perhaps three originally) unusual "panels" adjacent to the effigy that seem to exhibit a corn ear-type motif or perhaps a ladder to the underworld. Smoking is an activity related to transformation and the hocker figure is halfway between a reptile and a human. George Hamell has alternatively suggested it may be a tree frog motif, one commonly carved on Indigenous wooden objects in the North American northwest. Hamell notes that in tribal art worldwide, salamanders and lizards and frogs and toads are illustrated in hocker position, which is a "'natural' position for them"; he links this with the natural pose of a baby lying on its stomach and sees a possible analogy between the metamorphosis of a frog and that of the life history of an infant (personal communication 2020). If the portion that looks like a tail is intentional, it may signify the transition from tadpole to frog. Hamell also noted that a very similar effigy is known from the wooden handle of an unsheathed knife found on the mid-seventeenth-century Seneca Steele site that would have been suspended from a cord around a person's neck (personal communication 2020). Similarly suspended knives were also found during the IDN period, as documented by Jacques-René de Brisay de Denonville in 1687 (O'Callaghan 1853–1887).

Figure 11.6 illustrates five additional effigy pipes. The two effigy pipes illustrated in Figure 11.6a and b were found in Ameliasburgh Township, in which the Carrying Place Trail and Smokes Point are situated, at its western boundary. The eye on the right effigy has a small, white crystal emplaced, and the fragment includes more of the bowl below the effigy, with incised decoration.

We suspect that these specimens, as well as two from Ganatsekwyagon, are bear representations, given the shortened snout and the shape of the ear. They all have a striking resemblance with the bear effigy ring barrel pipes of the Onondaga Indian Castle site (Bradley 2020:236–237). According to Hamell (personal communication 2020), cougars, wolves, and bears can be confused, especially if only the animal's head is represented. He describes "cougars as

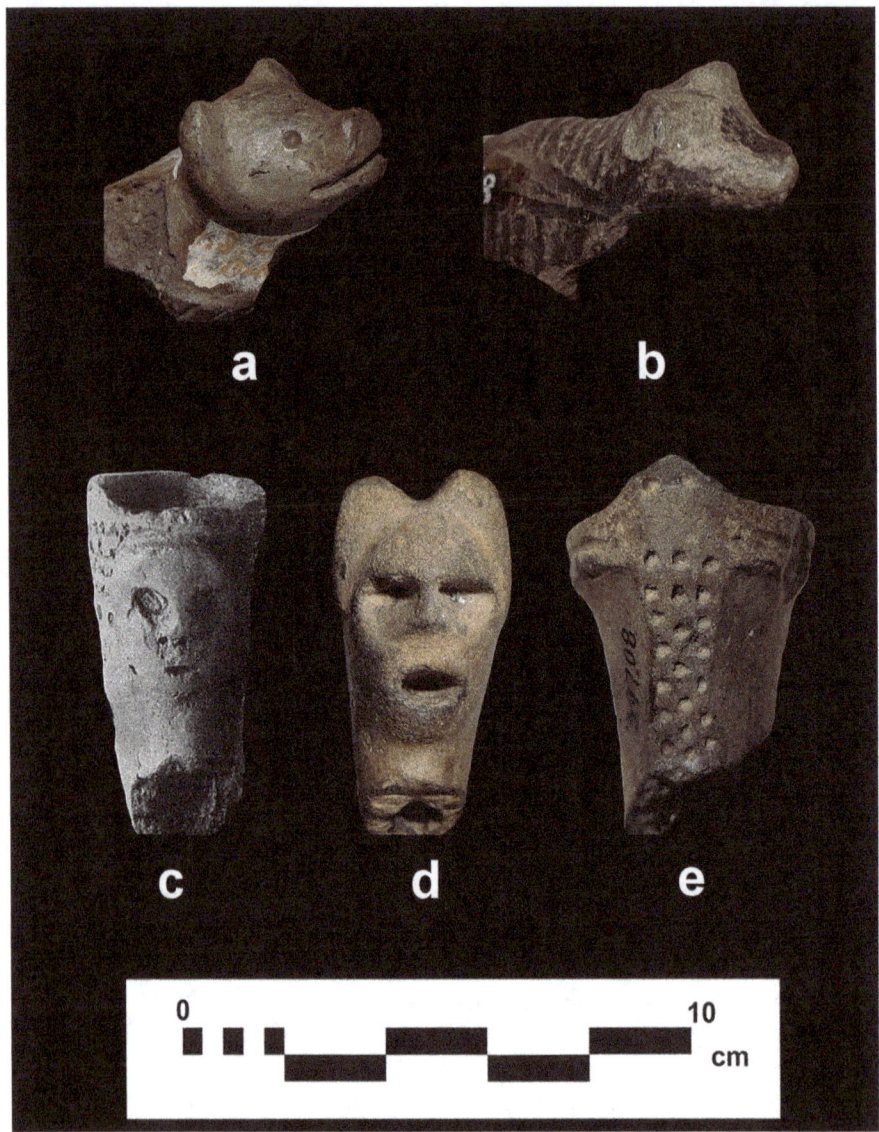

Figure 11.6. Effigy pipes found in Ameliasburgh Township (a, b, and e), Wellington (c), and Indian Island (d), G. J. Chadd Collection.
Source: Courtesy of the Royal Ontario Museum, photographs by Robert von Bitter (a, b, d, e) and from Orr (c) (1921–1922:112); digital enhancement by John Howarth.

having in addition to very long tails, short, 'rounded' ears and a relatively flat face, as do the other feline species of the region. Both the bear and wolf have pointed muzzles, the wolf more so than the bear and more pointed ears," and he also notes that "all three are 'medicine animals' and among the Seneca are participants in the animal medicine society. Bears are known to be helpers and are often associated with [herbal] medicine" (George Hamell, personal communication 2020). He believes that mother bears are identified with the adoption of abandoned human children and that the Bear clan's role is to adopt and incorporate outsiders.

Figure 11.6 illustrates three other bowl effigies, all of which were first illustrated by Orr in the AARO for 1921–1922. The pipe shown in Figure 11.6c is from Wellington; the eared effigy in Figure 11.6d is from Indian Island; and the pipe in Figure 11.6e is from Ameliasburgh Township. The eared pipe has four horizontal lines and a bordering row of annular punctates on the back of the bowl. The pipe in Figure 11.6c has a modelled face on the bowl, joined by a horizontal band of dentate-stamped lines. This pipe may predate the IDN period, although both it and the pipe bowl with an eared effigy are consistent with historic-period Seneca pipes (Wray 1973:13). The pipe illustrated in Figure 11.6e is an unusual, castellated type decorated with an annular punctate panel, interrupted horizontal lines below the lip, and two annular punctate eyes on the castellation (39708); punctates were also employed to represent facial features and create designs on antler combs (see Williamson and von Bitter, this volume). Pipes somewhat like this one with punctate panels were found on the Boughton Hill site (Ganondagan) (e.g., Rutsch 1973:Figure 167) and on the late Cayuga site of Scipioville (Rutsch 1973:Figure 146).

Figure 11.7 illustrates three complete pipes, two of which (Figures 11.7a and c) were first illustrated by Orr in the AARO for 1921–1922 and are from Wellington. The collared ring pipe (Figure 11.7b), which is from Bald Head, features seven incised rings and a short stem. The near-complete pipe on the bottom right (Figure 11.7c) is similar to the Seneca "helmeted" form described by Martha Sempowski and Lorraine Saunders (2001:243). Figure 11.7a is of a form described by Wray (1973) as one of the distinctive pipes of the early historic period. It is a ring bowl pipe with a bulbous, "acorn"-shaped bowl decorated with seven incised rings and a plain undecorated stem. Pipes such as these are usually short-stemmed, and it is not certain to us that the stem really goes with the bowl—collectors used to complete their pipes by attaching random stems to bowls.

Two fragments of an Iroquois conical ring pipe were found by Northeastern Archaeological Associates at the Hilton site (2010:42–43), on Smokes Point. The pipe is described as having an incised ring bowl 39 mm high, with a diameter of 30 mm across its bowl.

Other pipes of the Iroquois ring variety in the Chadd Collection were recovered from Bald Head (e.g., 39531, 39857), Murray Township (e.g., 40581), Hillier Township (e.g., 40412), and Ameliasburgh Township (e.g., 39706).

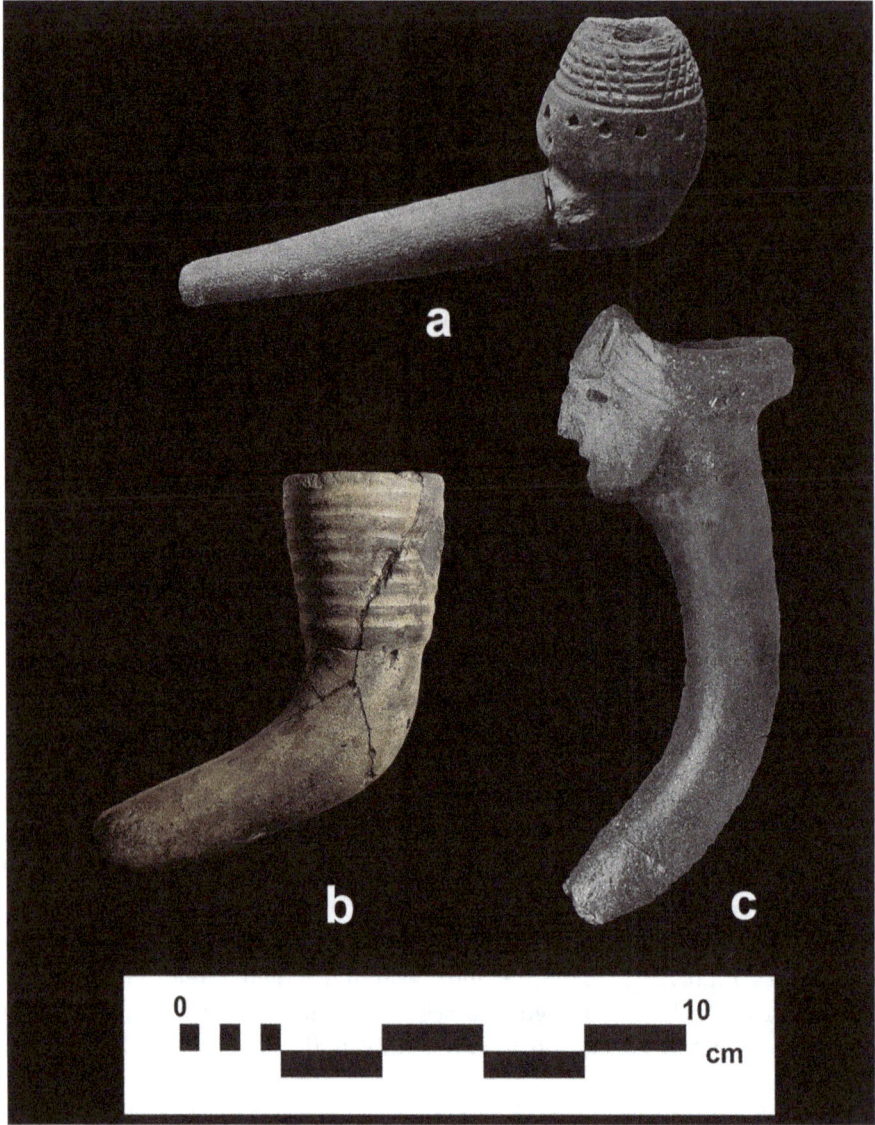

Figure 11.7. Three complete pipes, two from Wellington (a, c) and one from Bald Head Island (b), G. J. Chadd Collection.
Source: Courtesy of the Royal Ontario Museum, photographs from Orr (a, c) (1921–22:112) and by Robert von Bitter (b); digital enhancement by John Howarth.

4.2. Ganatsekwyagon

Figure 11.8 illustrates two pipe fragments recovered from Bead Hill. One is a probable bear effigy from a pipe bowl, apparently like another specimen also recovered from the site, while the other is a collared conical ring pipe with eight broad trailed channels creating eight ring ridges.

Figure 11.8. Two pipe bowl fragments from Ganatsekwyagon.
Source: Left, photograph by Parks Canada, digital enhancement by John Howarth; *right*, photograph by Dana Poulton, digital enhancement by John Howarth.

A single juvenile rim, fragmentary sherds, and lumps of fired clay were also recovered from the site.

4.3. Teiaiagon

David Boyle's 1888 AARO reproduces two Middle Archaic (Laurentian) ground stone gouges (Boyle 1888:Figures 65 and 66) that had been donated to the Royal Canadian Institute by James Kirkwood, "an enthusiastic collector" (Boyle 1888:40; see Robertson, this volume). The next year, Boyle published an illustration of a finely made conical ring type ceramic smoking pipe recovered from Baby Point (Boyle 1889:Figure 15), which had also been found by Kirkwood. It is almost complete and weakly collared, and it features seven finely incised rings.

A complete conical ring pipe and three other pipe bowls were recovered from the site by Charles A. Hirschfelder, in the early 1880s. Hirschfelder was an avocational archaeologist from Toronto who wrote and lectured on Ontario archaeology and sold a major collection from his activities in Ontario to the Geological Survey of Canada in 1884. A major promoter of a national archaeological museum, his gift now represents an important part of the archaeological collections of the Canadian Museum of History (Kapches 2013:214–218; see also Robertson, this volume). The complete pipe is a short-stemmed, collared ring pipe with five broad trailed rings (Figure 11.9a). The other fragments include a complete bowl that also has five broad trailed rings (Figure 11.9b), a half bowl that has seven incised lines (Figure 11.9c), and another that is too difficult to interpret.

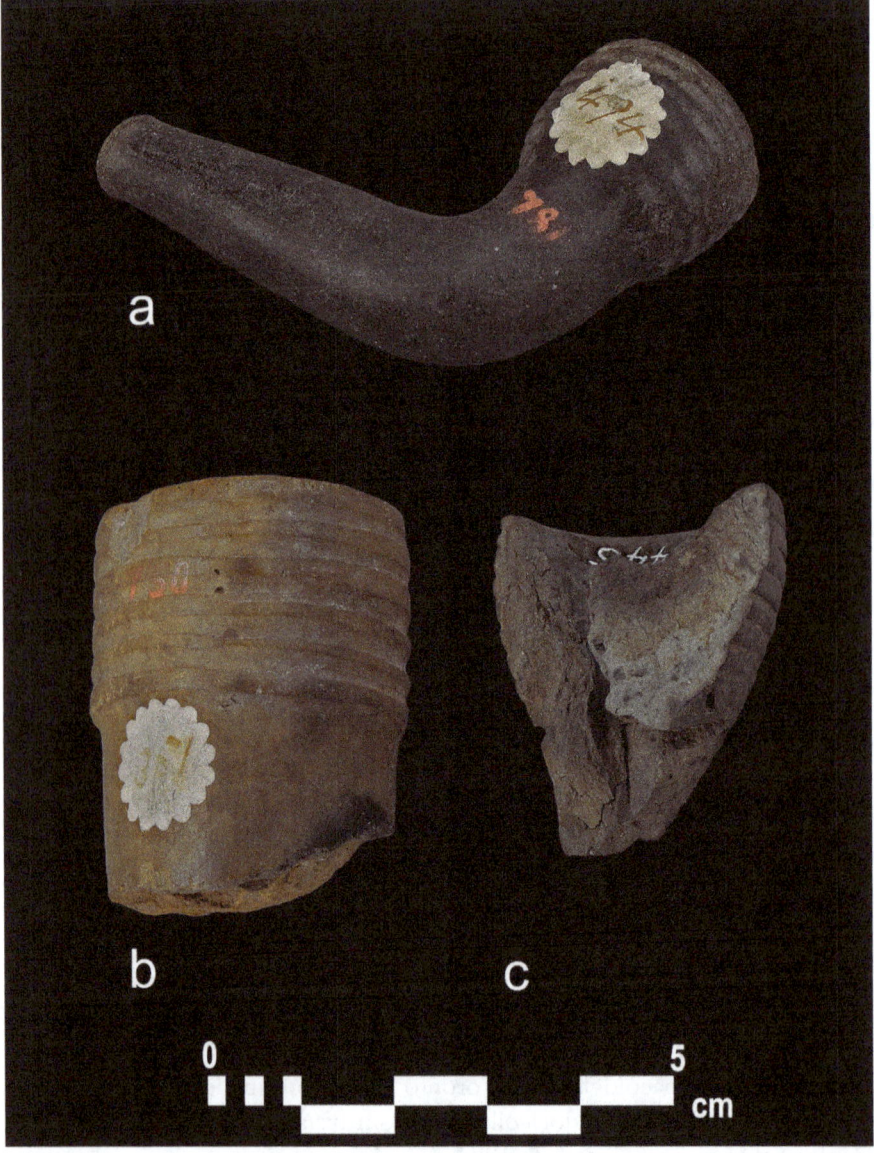

Figure 11.9. Three pipes from Teiaiagon.
Source: Canadian Museum of History, Charles A. Hirschfelder Collection, CMH photo archives; photographs digitally enhanced by John Howarth.

Two "pipe heads" and a pipe stem were recovered in Lambton Mills, perhaps on the Baby farm, and donated to the precursor of the Royal Ontario Museum by Wardie and Ottie White (Boyle 1889:97). Also recovered on Baby Farm by Kirkwood was a white clay pipe stem with two "lozenge-shaped" figures, quartered, each quarter containing a fleur-de-lys decoration typical of the mid-seventeenth century (Boyle 1889:50).

5. Discussion and Conclusion

The quantity of ceramic vessel fragments interpreted here as associated with the Iroquois du Nord sites would indicate that vessels were also rare on these sites, despite the sites' construction and occupation beginning in the mid- to late 1660s. In the Haudenosaunee homeland, these vessels became very rare by the late 1670s and 1680s. Dana Poulton (personal communication 2020) has noted that the occupants of these Iroquois du Nord villages may have belonged to the last adult generation to manufacture traditional ceramic vessels.

If the Ameliasburgh face effigy was indeed associated with Kenté, it would indicate the persistence of a shared Iroquoian belief system. Haudenosaunee ceramic vessels have long been a symbol of family and hospitality (Fenton 1978:303), and Alicia Hawkins (2004) discusses ceramic style as an assertion of identity—a way of "recreating home."

Indeed, Ontario Iroquoians adopted by the New York Haudenosaunee likely retained aspects of their original identity. The ceramic assemblage from the Jackson-Everson site, in Mohawk Territory, suggests that the Wendat who moved to the Mohawk Territory continued to manufacture ceramics in their traditional fashion, although not as carefully as previously. It is possible that some former Ontario Iroquoians and their descendants migrated from New York to the north shore and west of Lake Ontario (Ferris 2009:118, Ferris, this volume; Fox 2009:70). If they manufactured Indigenous pottery there, it may have been similar to that manufactured in Ontario during the first half of the seventeenth century and earlier.

The pipes are also consistent with Haudenosaunee homeland pipes (e.g., Boughton Hill). Their recovery almost exclusively from cemeteries speaks to a form of spiritual significance that contributed to their persistence in the record. The majority are ring bowl types that Sempowski and Saunders (2001:245, Figure 3.188) have proposed form "a continuum from realistic to highly stylized representations of snake effigies with ring bowl pipes constituting the ultimate abstraction."

During the contact period, Haudenosaunee sites reflect a selectivity in terms of the adoption of items of European manufacture. Indigenous ceramic vessels and pipes are among the last items of Native manufacture to be replaced. This is seen on both IDN sites and sites in the homeland. Iroquois du Nord sites also reflect adoption of individuals from other groups, signalling the Haudenosaunee's mobility and their detailed knowledge of geography. These practices were part of an adaptive strategy that led to Haudenosaunee survival to the present day.

Acknowledgements

We are grateful to the following individuals for their counsel on the timing of the cessation of ceramic production on the part of the Haudenosaunee: Martha Sempowski and Kurt Jordan (Seneca), Kimberly Williams-Shuker (Cayuga), Gregory Sohrweide and James Bradley (Onondaga), Anthony Wonderley (Oneida), and Wayne Lenig (Mohawk). Kurt Jordan also provided helpful comments on earlier versions of this manuscript, as did Suzanne Needs-Howarth. We would also like to acknowledge the assistance of William Fox, George Hamell, April Hawkins, Louis Lesage, Dana Poulton, and Robert von Bitter.

SECTION 4
THE ANISHINAABE OCCUPATION

12

AFTER THE HAUDENOSAUNEE

The Mississauga Occupation of the North Shore of Lake Ontario

GARY WARRICK AND RONALD F. WILLIAMSON

This chapter addresses the Mississauga occupation of southern Ontario and some of the Iroquois du Nord (IDN) settlements after the departure of the Haudenosaunee. By 1700, southern Ontario was inhabited permanently by Algonquian-speaking peoples, the Haudenosaunee having abandoned their north shore of Lake Ontario settlements by 1688 (Konrad 1981:139–142) and returned to their homeland in New York State. They were not to return permanently until 1784, when close to two thousand Haudenosaunee (mostly Mohawk, Cayuga, Onondaga, and Delaware) secured land rights on the Grand River (Haldimand Tract) and the Bay of Quinte (Tyendinaga) for their loyalty to the Crown in the American Revolution (Hill 2017:133–155).

The terms used by Europeans for the cultural affinities of these Algonquian groups changed through time. In the late 1640s, the French Jesuit priest and missionary Father Paul Ragueneau identified various tribes on the northern and eastern shores of Lake Huron, including the Michisaguek (Mississauga; Chippewa) and Paouitagoung (Chippewa) (Thwaites 1896–1901:33:149–151). Later, the French generally used the terms "Ottawa," "Mississauga," and "Saulteur" to refer to Algonquian-speaking peoples, but tribal terminology shifted with the British victory in the Seven Years' War (Smith 1975b:216, 221–222; Surtees 1985:20–21). In the Great Lakes area of Ontario, for example, the word "Saulteux" was gradually substituted with the word "Chippewa." One exception was the north shore of Lake Ontario, where groups continued to be known as Mississauga, although some observers, such as John Graves Simcoe, described them as a branch of the Chippewa, and the two terms were often used as synonyms. The nineteenth-century Mississauga also called themselves Ojibwa, especially when dealing with the English (Jones 1861:31).

By the twentieth century, the Canadian Department of Indian Affairs had divided these peoples into three different tribes. Based on the final British land purchases and treaties, the bands at Beausoleil Island, Cape Croker, Christian

Island, Georgina and Snake Islands, Rama, Sarnia, Saugeen, the Thames, and Walpole became known as Chippewa; the bands at Alderville, New Credit, Mud Lake (Curve Lake), Rice Lake, and Scugog were recorded and subsequently known as Mississauga; and northern groups on Lakes Huron and Superior, who signed the Robinson Treaty in 1850, remained known as "Ojibbewas" (Smith 1975b:222).

According to Rogers (1978:768), the terms "Chippewa" and "Ojibwa" are variant English renderings of the self-designation *ocipwe*. Although the root meaning of *ocipwe* is uncertain, it is generally believed to come from the name "Outchibous," relating to a seventeenth-century band who had united with the People of the Sault and two other bands by 1670 (Lovisek 1991:xviii; Rogers 1978:769). One explanation for the root meaning of the word *ocipwe* is "puckered up" or "gathering," referencing the general form of Ojibwa moccasins (Rogers 1978:769).

Regardless of these "outsider" naming practices over the past few centuries, it is most important to note that the Indigenous Peoples in question referred, and continue to refer, to themselves as Anishinaabeg, "an Indigenous term of identity, a collective noun that connects people who speak closely related dialects of the same language: Anishinaabemowin" (Bohaker 2006:2).

For the summary of the history of Mississauga occupation of southern Ontario in this chapter, we have employed the writings of early explorers, missionaries, fur traders, administrators, and surveyors to provide primary information on the Great Lakes region prior to large-scale European settlement, but we also acknowledge issues regarding the usefulness of European documents for describing non-European societies. It is clear that in some cases, the ethnographic data found in early European sources reveal "as much or more about the preoccupations of their authors than the people being observed" (Bohaker 2006:133). It is also clear that such documents require careful deconstruction and contextualization (e.g., Trigger 1976, 1985) and an examination of who was recording the information, for what purposes, and when; who was the intended audience; which people were being observed; and so forth. Used in this manner, these sources provide a wealth of information concerning the geography of the region and the Indigenous individuals and groups with whom Europeans interacted and about whom they heard.

We also reviewed a wide range of secondary sources, including unpublished theses and dissertations and published scholarly works from a variety of fields, as they are useful for evaluating the consensus of opinion regarding interpretations of primary material and other data.

This chapter also refers to previously published and/or previously recorded Indigenous oral traditions and histories. They include accounts recorded and published in the mid- to late nineteenth century and a few recorded and published earlier. Although the greater part of the historiography of Indigenous

Peoples of the Great Lakes area has been a chronicle of their interactions with Europeans, based on documentary sources, Indigenous oral histories and traditions represent an independent reference "that both complements and balances" that chronicle (MacLeod 1992:195). Indigenous versions of seventeenth- and eighteenth-century events have been orally transmitted from one generation to the next until some of them were recorded in print, many in the nineteenth century, and these can provide us with an Indigenous perspective of past events.

According to Peter MacLeod (1992:200–204), the main themes found in Anishinaabe oral history of the seventeenth and eighteenth centuries generally relate to military engagements and associated population movements by the Anishinaabeg, including their wars with the Haudenosaunee in southern Ontario that seem to have facilitated Anishinaabe expansion into that area. Bruce Trigger (1985:167) noted that George Copway's (1850) oral history of the Anishinaabe conquest of the Haudenosaunee contains important data corroborated by seventeenth-century historical documents (see more on this below). As MacLeod argues, the history provided in these kinds of narratives is valuable both for the comparative insight on contemporary European documents and as an independent record of the past from Indigenous perspectives. Even critics of the use of oral tradition, such as Ronald Mason (2006), argue that despite oral testimony not being critically reflexive, nor consistent with evidence-bound Western discourse, consideration of data provided by the archaeological, ethnographic, biological anthropological, and linguistic records, together with oral histories and traditions, can be mutually complementary ways of understanding the past (Mason 2006:27–28; also, Vansina 1985; von Gernet 2006).

1. History of the Mississauga Occupation

By the 1690s, tensions between the Haudenosaunee and the Anishinaabeg, the French, and their other Indigenous allies were considerable. Early in the winter of 1694–1695, a party of two hundred Seneca and Cayuga were reported to have gone on an expedition against the Miami, allies of the French. There was a Haudenosaunee attack at the Lake of Two Mountains, during which Sieur Jacques Chauvin de Charleville was killed. In retaliation, Louis-Hector de Callière sent about 120 men, Indigenous and French alike, in search of the enemy. Around this time, it was reported that "all our allies, with the exception of the Wendat, were constantly occupied in harassing the Haudenosaunee, and that they had actually nine hundred men in the field" (O'Callaghan 1856–1887:9:601–603). The Ottawa and Pottawatomi attacked a group of Haudenosaunee traders who had been hunting and wintering with the Wendat at Detroit. They brought back thirty scalps and thirty-two prisoners (men, women, and children) to Michilimackinac. They also plundered four hundred to five hundred beaver skins as well as English trade goods. It was reported that this last blow destroyed any chance of peace between the Haudenosaunee and the upper allied nations (O'Callaghan 1856–1887:9:646).

The main complaint of the Haudenosaunee near the end of the seventeenth century was that the Anishinaabeg were encroaching on their beaver hunting lands, which was the cause for all the warring. In 1699, the Seneca complained to the English that they were being attacked by the "far Indians" or the Dowaganhae (allies of the French), while out hunting, despite the peace. The English urged them not to trust the French and not to enter in any treaty with them (O'Callaghan 1856–1887:4:597–598). They claimed in 1701 that a remnant of one of the Ottawa tribes, which had earlier been driven off, returned, which "disturbed our beaver hunting" (O'Callaghan 1856–1887:4:905–909, cited in Trelease 1962:47). In June 1701, the chief sachem of the Onondaga complained to the French:

> the Wagannes take our land from us, where wee hunt beaver, let them hunt upon their own land else wee shall kill one another for the beavers when wee meet together. Wee doe suspect that some have been kill'd already by this meanes, therefore desire that the Waganhaes may make a little room that wee may finde out who knocks one another in the head— let us have no controversies for that place where the beaver keep. [O'Callaghan 1856–1887:4:891]

By this time, however, most of the beaver was being hunted to the west, rather than north of Lake Ontario (von Gernet 2002:8). As the governor of New York, Richard Coote, the Earl of Bellomont, reported in 1700: "The only good Beaver hunting lyes in that part of the country where the Dowaganhas and those other Nations live, and thither our 5 Nations are forc'd to goe a beaver-hunting, which is one reason of that perpetual war between those Nations and ours [...]" (O'Callaghan 1856–1887:4:796).

Brian Dunnigan (2001:4, 12) argues that in addition to being linked to fighting over beaver territories and trade alliances, war during this time was greatly influenced by military campaigns in Europe, specifically between France and England. For a while, the Haudenosaunee, relying on the support of the English in New York, were able to conduct attacks on New France. Near the end of the century, however, the Five Nations were effectively abandoned by the English; weakened by disease and famine, they were incapable of defending themselves against their enemies (von Gernet 2002:8).

Tensions between the Anishinaabeg and the Haudenosaunee culminated in a series of fierce battles between the two groups that form part of the oral tradition of different Anishinaabe nations throughout the Great Lakes region. As Leroy V. Eid (1979:299) explains, "These traditional accounts all tell the same story: the Ojibwa and their allies around the turn of the 17th century utterly crushed the Iroquois of the Five Nations." It must be mentioned, however, that except for some vague references in Haudenosaunee oral tradition to conflict with Anishinaabe groups in the west, there is no detailed Haudenosaunee oral history of these battles (Eid 1979). While there is a historic account of the Haudenosaunee complaining to the English of being harassed and attacked by Anishinaabe groups west of Lake Ontario in the 1690s (Eid 1979:309), there are no eighteenth-century accounts from the French or British that explicitly document a series of battles or a conquest of the Iroquois du Nord by the Anishinaabeg (i.e., Mississaugas and allies). Nonetheless, in 1793, the Anishinaabe community of Walpole Island told the British that their ancestors had fought the Haudenosaunee (Seneca) and "totally vanquished" them (Jacobs and Lytwyn 2020:191). Similar stories of Anishinaabe-Haudenosaunee conflict and victories were recorded by a number of Anishinaabeg communities and were written down and published in the nineteenth century (Eid 1979).

Reports of these battles were recorded by nineteenth-century Indigenous and non-Indigenous writers. As Eid (1979:301) explains, "while the various accounts generally emphasize just one aspect of the campaign, the total picture adds up to a description of a complicated strategy in which attackers subdivide to assault different areas and then reunite to continue the war."

George Copway and Francis Assikinack describe some of these battles. Copway[1] provided the following account:

> Tradition informs us that seven hundred canoes met at Kewetawahonning, one party of whom was to take the route to Mahamooseebee, the second towards Wahweyagahmah, (now Lake Simcoe), the third was to take the route towards the river St. Clair, and meet the southern Hurons [Wyandot].
>
> The warriors who took the Mahamooseebee, had several engagements with them, but outnumbering them, they easily routed the Iroquois. Those who had gone to St. Clair had likewise a fierce battle at the mouth of a river called by the Algonquins, Sahgeeng, and afterwards, being joined by the southern Hurons, overran the whole of the south of the peninsula.
>
> The bloodiest battles were fought on Lake Simcoe, at a place called Ramma, at Mud Lake, Pigeon Lake, and Rice lake: the last that was fought took place at the mouth of the river Trent. [Copway 1850:87–88]

---

1. George Copway, or Kahgegagahbowh, was born among the Mississauga in 1818 and followed a traditional lifestyle until his family converted to Christianity. He became a Methodist missionary in Canada and the United States and, later, a popular author and lecturer (MacLeod 1992:197; Smith 2000).

Copway then continues with more detailed descriptions of the latter battles.

According to artist Paul Kane, there was still evidence of one of these battles on the landscape near Saugeen in 1845:

> The Indian village of Saugeen, meaning "the Mouth of a River," contains about 200 inhabitants (Ojibbeways). It is the site of a former battleground between the Ojibbeways, as usually pronounced, or Chippawas, and the Mohawks. Of this, the mounds erected over the slain afford abundant evidence in the protrusion of the bones through the surface of the ground. [Kane 1859:3]

Assikinack[2] (1858:308–309) provides details on a battle that occurred near the Blue Mountains, which Eid (1979:298) identifies as one of the first battles of the war:

> The Odahwahs were also at war with the Nahdowag or Iroquois during their stay at Manitoulin Island, and the Nahdowag in their hostile expedition against the Islanders, used to go out into Lake Huron or Georgian Bay, by the Nahdowa Sahgi-River [also known as the Nottawasaga; a name translated by Assikinack as place where the Nahdowag, viz., the Mohawks or Iroquois, used to come out], until they got two or three severe defeats in the vicinity of the Blue Mountains, by Sahgimah [c. 1646–1721], the most celebrated warrior of the Odahwahs at that time. Instead of waiting for the Mohawks at the Island, he used to come and meet them at the Blue Mountains, hence that place is called to this very day, *Sahgimah Odahkahwahbewin*, viz., Sahgimah's watching place. The last time he met the enemy there he found them occupying his watching place. In the evening he went to view their camp alone, he saw their arms piled about the camp as if they suspected no danger, whilst their warriors were feasting and dancing. He then went for his men, and on his return, he found the Mohawks had retired to rest. Having placed his men in order, ready for attack, he entered the camp alone, and removed the arms of the slumbering enemy. The Mohawks being without arms were, of course, slaughtered, except a few who were spared on purpose. The Odahwahs cut off the heads of the slain, and fixed them on poles, with the faces turned towards the Lake. Sahgimah then selected a canoe, which he loaded with goods, provisions, and ammunition, put the survivors in and told them to

---

2. Francis Assikinack (b. 1824) was an Ojibwa of Manitoulin Island. He enrolled at Upper Canada College when he was sixteen, and after graduation he worked for the Indian Department as an interpreter, clerk, and teacher. He is said to have displayed deep pride in his heritage (MacLeod 1992:197).

go home and never to come there again; he also desired them to say when they got home that they had met Sahgimah on the top of the Blue Mountains, where he fixed the heads of their companions on poles, with the faces turned toward the Lake, and that he declared his determination to fix in a similar manner, the head of every Mohawk that he might fall in with in that quarter. [Assikinack 1858:308–309]

According to Peter S. Schmalz (1984:336, 1991:23–24), oral traditions of the Cape Croker and Chippawa Hill reserves (Saugeen-Nawash) relate that a number of other battles occurred in and around the Bruce Peninsula and surrounding territory. These took place on the clay banks of Walkerton; on Indian Hill near the Teeswater River; at Owen Sound; on White Cloud Island in Colpoy's Bay; on Griffith Island; at Cabot's Head; in the Fishing Islands; and at Red Bay in Albemarle Township. The latter is said to have received its name from the bloody waters following the defeat of the Mohawk at that location. Robert W. Reid (1997:78) also reported on the tradition of a brutal battle at Red Bay. Many interviews were conducted between 1975 and 2006 with individuals living in, or associated with, the Saugeen-Nawash regarding these battles with the Haudenosaunee. The interviewees related stories about the strategy of the Anishinaabe offensive and particular battles at Saugeen, Skull Mound, Red Bay, and other places. They indicated that they had heard about this fighting from their parents and grandparents (e.g., interviews with James Mason, Indian History Film Project, 1983; Pauline Ritchie, for Nnookmis Tabaajimawin of Saugeen, Grandmother Is Telling a Story [Nashkewa and George 2003:96]; John Nadjiwon, March 30, 2006; Elgin Mandawoub, Experience '81 Project, 1981; Perline Elliot, Saugeen Ojibway Nations Oral History Project, 1998).

Similarly, Robert Paudash[3] (1905:7–9) provides details passed on through generations of his family of the party that fought at Lake Simcoe and down the Trent-Severn Waterway:

---

3. Robert Paudash (1905) presented a history of the Mississauga people at a meeting of the Ontario Historical Society in June 1904. His history included a chronicle of their migration from the north shore of Lake Huron and military encounters with the Haudenosaunee that led to their occupation of southern Ontario. He noted that his history did not come from his reading of other sources or in any other way other "than from the mouth of Paudash, my father, who died aged 75 in the year 1893, the last hereditary chief of the tribe of Mississaugas situate at Rice Lake; and from the mouth of Cheneebeesh my grandfather, who died in 1869, at the age of 104, the last Sachem, or Head chief of all the Mississaugas, who had learned according to the Indian custom what Gemoaghenassee, his father, had heard from his father, and so on."

It being a matter of life and death to the Mississauga, they held a great council of war, and decided to attack the Mohawks, and, if possible, to drive them away. A party of Mohawks was entrenched at an island in lower Georgian Bay, afterwards known as Pequahkoondebaminis, or the Island of Skulls. The Mississagas surrounded and made great slaughter of them, the island taking its name from this circumstance. The remainder of the Mohawks were compelled to retreat eventually but being a fierce and warlike tribe, they resisted stubbornly. The Mississagas then advanced up what is now the Severn River to Shunyung, or Lake Simcoe, stopping at Mchickning, which means Fish Fence, at the narrows between Lake Simcoe and Lake Couchiching in order to get a supply of food. Parts of the fence remain to this day. There they received reinforcements, and making preparations for a campaign, divided into two parties. The main body proceeded along the portage, now called Portage Road, to Balsam Lake; the other party went south to Toronto.

Paudash goes on to describe the various battles and their locations along the Trent River, all the way down to Lake Ontario, and notes that the party that had gone to Toronto joined them during the course of these battles.

William Warren gives a very brief account of the same general tradition:[4]

Their anxiety to open the road to the white traders, in order to procure firearms and their much-coveted commodities, induced the Ojibways, Ottaways, Pottawatomies, Osaukies, and Wyandots to enter into a firm alliance. They sent their united forces against the Iroquois, and fighting severe and bloody battles, they eventually forced them to retire from Canada. [Warren 1984:146]

Peter Jones presented the following version:[5]

These brutal acts called forth the vengeance of the great Ojebway nation. A general council was called. [...] The first attack they made was on an island on the south shore of Lake Huron. There they fell on a large body

---

4. William Whipple Warren (b.1825) was the son of an American trader and a French–Ojibwa woman. He worked as an interpreter for the American government until 1850 and was then elected to the Minnesota House of Representatives (MacLeod 1992:198). His account was first published in 1885, by the Minnesota Historical Society.
5. Peter Jones, or Kahkewaquonaby, was born in 1802 to Mississauga and Welsh parents. He was raised by his mother among the Mississauga until his father sent him to school. He became a leading Methodist minister and a Mississauga chief (MacLeod 1992:197).

of the Nahdoways, who had been dancing and feasting for several nights, and were so exhausted as to have sunk into a profound sleep the night on which they were killed. The island is called Pequahkoondebaymenis, that is, skull island, from the number of skulls left on it. [...] From this island they extended their conquests to Lakes Simcoe, Ontario, Erie, St. Clair, and the interior parts of the country: wherever they went they conquered, destroying villages, and leaving dead bodies in heaps. [...] the Ojebways spared a few of their enemies, whom they suffered to depart in peace, that they might go and tell their brethren on the south side of Lake Ontario the fate of their nation—that all the country between the waters of the Ontario, Erie, St. Clair, and Huron, was now surrendered into the hands of the Ojebways. [Jones 1861:111–113]

Narratives of the Haudenosaunee being pushed out of Ontario are not limited to Anishinaabe oral histories. For example, Henry Schoolcraft (1848:93–94) provided a Wyandot tradition of one of the battles on Lake Erie, and Leroy V. Eid (1979:319–320) presented a later Wyandot oral history, as recorded by Peter Clarke (1870:39, 62–66), that supports this victory and details the subsequent peace treaty. Eid (1979:316) also cites an Onondaga version of the Iroquois Book of Rites, which was written in the couple of decades following the 1701 peace treaty, as supportive evidence of the Ojibwa oral tradition.

In addition to oral tradition, an Ojibwa victory over the Haudenosaunee has been depicted on material culture. For example, a birch-bark box decorated with undyed porcupine quill in the Royal Ontario Museum collection depicts two Ojibwa, one of whom is attacking a Mohawk with a club. The other Ojibwa is holding a musket. This interpretation was provided by Mesaquab (Jonathan Yorke of Rama), who was the creator of the box. According to the artist, the lid is an imitation of a rock painting on Lake Couchiching that had fallen into the lake a few years previous (Boyle 1904:14; see Schmalz 1984:344).

This Anishinaabeg version of the past, what Eid called the "Ojibwa Thesis," was initially rejected by many mainstream historians (but see Rogers 1978:762). One of the main reasons for this is that Anishinaabe accounts of their victories contrasted with previous colonialist historians' views concerning the power of the Haudenosaunee. According to MacLeod, this changed with the work of Eid and Schmalz, who used the oral tradition in conjunction with historical evidence to reconstruct the series of successful battles that forced the Haudenosaunee out of southern Ontario. In so doing, they introduced a revision of some long-standing opinions regarding the Haudenosaunee and the Anishinaabeg in the history of Ontario (Eid 1979; MacLeod 1992:208; Schmalz 1984). That the Haudenosaunee were considerably weakened by hostilities and disease by the end of the century is not in question (Havard 2001:61–66).

Moreover, von Gernet has noted (2002:8–9, n25) that many modern scholars now accept that, by the end of the seventeenth century, the southeastern Anishinaabeg from the north shores of Lake Huron and Lake Superior and their allies defeated the Haudenosaunee and drove them out of southern Ontario. He cites the following scholars: Dickason 1997:123, 129; Eid 1979:297–321; Fenton 1998:330, 345, 357; Jennings 1984:13, 207, n58, 212; Norton 1974:11–19; Richter 1992:195, 209; Rogers 1978:761–762; Schmalz 1991:18–33; Smith 1975a:i, 20–25, 1975b:215, 1981:68–69, 1987:19; Surtees 1994:94; Tanner 1987:31–35; Trigger 1985:288. Some readers may wonder how the Anishinaabeg could have organized a sufficient number of warriors to defeat the Iroquois du Nord. It must be remembered that in the late 1600s the Anishinaabeg, who lived on the north shore of Lake Huron (referred to as the Southeastern Ojibwa), were a group of allied nations (e.g., Saulteaux, Mississauga, Amikwa, Nikkouek) numbering seven hundred to eight hundred people with a warrior complement of 150 men (Rogers 1978:762). Most IDN villages were small, comprising one hundred people (in the case of Outinaouatoua) to five hundred to eight hundred people, although Quintio was smaller (Konrad 1981:138). The Anishinaabe oral tradition speaks of strategic coordinated attacks by warriors from several nations over Haudenosaunee war or trading parties away from their villages.

Some scholars, however, reject the "Ojibwa Thesis" (Brandão 1997:123; Brandão and Starna 1996:237, n59; Konrad 1981:142) or are equivocal (Osborn and Ripmeester 1997). Jon Parmenter (2010:244) argued, "In reality, the fighting between the Iroquois and the pays d'en haut nations during the 1690s was not only more balanced than oral tradition would indicate, it was also punctuated by repeated efforts to negotiate a peaceful conclusion prior to 1701."

It has been suggested that perhaps the best evidence of a successful Anishinaabe military campaign is that, as David Boyle famously stated (1895:14), "it is well known that when Canada became British all the Indians with whom the imperial and provincial governments had to deal in what is now Ontario, were Algonkians." Yet, that would have been the case regardless of how the transfer of the north-shore settlements occurred, whether that be by voluntary abandonment by the Haudenosaunee on account of hostilities in the homeland (Konrad 1981) or hostilities with the Mississauga, or both, the latter being the most likely.

It should be noted that during this tumultuous period, peace negotiations were held between the Anishinaabeg and their allies and the Haudenosaunee, starting as early as 1688. Such negotiations were held at various times throughout the 1690s, without the involvement of the French and English, much to their dismay (Lytwyn 1997:215–216; Richter 1983:544). By 1701, three separate treaties were settled: among the French, the Haudenosaunee, and the Anishinaabeg and their allies (known as the Great Peace of 1701); between the

English and the Haudenosaunee (known as the Nanfan Treaty, 1701); and between the Anishinaabeg and the Haudenosaunee without the involvement of the English and the French (1700).

A peace conference was held in July 1700, at Montréal, that included the French (Chevalier de Callière), the Haudenosaunee, and the Anishinaabe nations from around the Great Lakes and their allies (i.e., Wendat-Tionontaté). In the summer of 1701, more than one thousand people representing more than thirty nations met at Montréal to ratify the resultant peace treaty, the Great Peace of 1701. It was the largest gathering ever recorded by Europeans in the St. Lawrence River valley and Great Lakes region (Lytwyn 1997:217; for more information on the 1701 treaty, see Havard 2001).

Almost simultaneous with the Montréal proceedings, delegates from all the Five Nations were meeting separately with English colonial officials at Albany, New York. The English were represented by the Lieutenant Governor of the Province of New York, John Nanfan. On July 19, 1701, the Five Nations and the English agreed to a treaty, which is sometimes called the "Beaver Hunting Treaty" or the "Nanfan Treaty" (Lytwyn 1997:218). With this treaty, the Five Nations proclaimed: "Wee doe give and render up all that land where the Beaver hunting is which wee won with the sword eighty years ago to Coraghkoo our great King and pray that he may be our protector and defender there […]" (O'Callaghan 1856–1887:4:905). The Five Nations had thus achieved agreements with both colonial powers that guaranteed hunting and fishing rights to generally the same territory (Lytwyn 1997:218).

A map of the Nanfan deed created by Samuel Clowes shows the generalized boundaries of the territory "claimed by conquest and 'given' to the English," which is a large area, covering the southwestern part of the Canadian province of Ontario west of a dotted line between approximately present-day Etobicoke and Collingwood (von Gernet 2002:30, Figures 1 and 2) and parts of what are now the U.S. states of New York, Ohio, and Michigan.

Von Gernet, however, argued, that the southeastern Ojibway had a much better claim on the territory, as they and their allies had driven the Haudenosaunee out of southern Ontario by the end of the seventeenth century. The Haudenosaunee could not "surrender these lands to the English, because they did not have them to give up in the first place" (von Gernet 2002:59–60). As Eid (1979:315) explains: "By every standard the most historical proof would be that […] after the American Revolution, the British government had to buy the land in modern Ontario from the Mississauga in order to relocate the Iroquois loyal to the crown."

In the winter of 1700, separate peace talks were also held between delegates of the upper Algonquian and the Five Nations in their hunting grounds. This was followed by a meeting at Onondaga, in June 1700, where a delegation of "Dowaganhaes" (Mississauga) said:

> Wee are come to acquaint you that wee are settled on ye North side of Cadarachqui Lake near Tchojachiage [likely Teiaiagon] where wee plant a tree of peace and open a path for all people, quite to Corlaer's house, where wee desire to have free liberty of trade; wee make a firme league with ye Five Nations and Corlaer and desire to be united in ye Covenant Chain, our hunting places to be one, and to boile in one kettle, eat out of one dish, & with one spoon, and so be one; and because the path to Corlaers house may be open & clear, doe give a drest elke skin to cover ye path to walke upon. [O'Callaghan 1856–1887:4:694–695]

The Five Nations gave the following response: "Wee are glad to see you in our country and doe accept of you to be our friends and allies and doe give you a Belt of Wampum as a token thereof that there may be a perpetual peace and friendship between us and our young Indians to hunt together in all love and amity" (O'Callaghan 1856–1887:4:694–695).

It is clear in this record that by 1700, some of the "Dowaganhaes or far Nations" had moved to the north shore of Lake Ontario, occupying some of the villages that had been abandoned by the Haudenosaunee.

The Mississauga occupation persisted until treaties were settled with the British Crown. According to the "Enumeration" of 1736 (O'Callaghan 1856–1887:9:1052–1058), the "Mississagués" were dispersed on the north shore of Lake Ontario to Frontenac. Approximately 150 warriors were located at Kenté, at the River Toronto, and at the Head-of-the-Lake, where "there are no more Iroquois settled," the principal tribe was that of the Crane. By 1763, the Anishinaabeg had divided central and southwestern Ontario into fairly distinct and large hunting territories (Surtees 1985:22–26), including, among others, Mississauga in the Kingston–Bay of Quinte region, the Kawarthas, the shore of Lake Simcoe, Lake Couchiching, Matchedash Bay and the Penetanguishene peninsula, and the Toronto area, where camps were occupied along the Humber River (e.g., at the site of Teiaiagon) (see also Alexander Henry [1809], who described Mississauga villages in 1764 by the Humber and Rouge Rivers).

In the following section, we discuss the rather meagre archaeological record of the Mississauga occupation of the IDN settlements.

2. Archaeology of the Mississauga Occupation

Archaeological knowledge about Indigenous Peoples in southern Ontario between 1650 and 1784 is sparse because of a long-held, false perception by archaeologists that Indigenous Peoples generally abandoned the region in 1651 after attacks from the Haudenosaunee, and because of the relative archaeological invisibility of Anishinaabeg in colonial times (Ferris 2009:40–41). Except for information gained from some archaeological interest in Iroquois du Nord village sites of the late seventeenth century (Adams 1986; Konrad 1981; Poulton, this volume; Robertson, this volume) and test excavations of a few late eighteenth- and early nineteenth-century Haudenosaunee and Anishinaabe sites (Beaudoin 2019; Ferris 2009; Ferris et al. 1985; Kenyon and Ferris 1984; Archaeological Assessments Ltd. 2003; Triggs 2004; Warrick 2004, 2005, 2006), we still have an underdeveloped archaeological understanding of the daily life of Indigenous Peoples in southern Ontario from 1650 to 1800.

In order to predict the location of Mississauga sites that would leave a visible archaeological footprint, it is important to reconstruct regional population size and distribution and the seasonal movement of Mississauga families, using historical and anthropological information. As we mentioned above, portions of Anishinaabe nations from the north shore of Lake Huron moved into southern Ontario sometime after 1690, creating two main territorial groups: the western group's territory extended from east of Toronto to the Grand River, the Niagara Peninsula, and the north shore of Lake Erie (Credit Mississauga-Eagle Clan Michi Saagiig); and the eastern group's territory encompassed lands east of Toronto, to the eastern end of Lake Ontario and north to Rice Lake (Bay of Quinte Mississauga-Crane Clan Michi Saagiig) (Smith 2013b:30; Williams 2018:62–63). Although it is difficult to estimate population numbers for the Anishinaabeg of southern Ontario in 1700, historical records from the mid- to late eighteenth century indicate that both the western and eastern groups comprised about five hundred people each, for a total of one thousand Anishinaabeg (the generic name Mississauga was applied to all Anishinaabe groups on the north shore of Lake Ontario by the British in the mid-1700s) (Smith 1987:30). The eastern and western Mississauga groups were likely composed of smaller territorial communities. Historical records for the Anishinaabeg of southwestern Ontario (Chippewa) indicate that they were organized into four to six "territorial communities" of 150–300 people each (Ferris 2009:36–39). If we extrapolate from this, it is conceivable that the Mississauga were arranged in about four to six territorial communities, stretching from the Grand River to Prince Edward County. The territories would have been organized around major river drainages and their headwaters in the interior, fronting on Lake Ontario.

The late eighteenth-century Mississauga subsisted by hunting-fishing-collecting-sugaring and by planting maize and other crops on river flats (in the early nineteenth century they also planted beans and potatoes [Good 1998]). This subsistence regime demanded at least five seasonal moves for individual families of five to fifteen members each. The Mississauga, like their Chippewa relations in southwestern Ontario, would have observed the following annual cycle within a defined territory: In early spring, family groups would have gathered at selected maple sugar stands for the production of maple syrup. Later in spring, after sugaring season had finished, family groups would have moved to a large aggregation camp at the mouth of major rivers to capture spring-spawning fish. In May, they would have re-established summer villages on high ground overlooking river flats, where they planted maize and possibly beans and squash (individuals and families would have left the village periodically to set up temporary small hunting, fishing, and berrying camps). In fall, while still living at the village, they would have harvested their crop plants and then wild rice. In late fall, deer hunting season would have taken teams of hunters and families away from the summer village. At the end of the hunt, the summer camp was abandoned, and separate families would have dispersed into the interior for the winter.

The sugaring camps, spring fishing camps, and summer village would have been reoccupied, but smaller hunting, fishing, and collecting camps would probably not have been reoccupied (Ferris 2009:45–48; Good 1998:153–155, 157; Rogers 1994:138–140; Smith 2013b:38–40). Archaeologically, small, ephemeral camps would be almost invisible—perhaps only a single cooking hearth, some animal bones, and a few artifacts covering an area less than 150 m^2. In contrast, sugaring camps, spring fishing camps, and summer villages, which would have been reused annually, possibly for decades, would have resulted in a substantial archaeological footprint. For example, both the Beasley Landing site (late eighteenth-century Mississauga summer camp) and the Bellamy site (late eighteenth- to early nineteenth-century Chippewa summer camp) produced house floors, pit features, and scattered refuse deposits containing one hundred to over one thousand glass embroidery beads, lead shot, fragmented animal bones, and a variety of other European-made artifacts (e.g., gunflints, trade silver jewellery, brass and iron scrap, gun parts, tobacco pipe fragments) (Ferris 2009:48–56; Ferris et al. 1985; Triggs 2004). The Davisville 3 site (early nineteenth-century Mississauga camp), interpreted as a single-family occupation of less than a year's duration (summer-fall-winter), produced few European-made items (mostly lead shot ranging in size from 0.09 to 0.14 inches, with the most common sizes 0.11–0.12 and 0.09 inches, and glass embroidery beads), but more than twenty-two thousand animal bone fragments, most of them highly charred or calcined (Warrick 2005).

Archaeological signatures of eighteenth-century Anishinaabe sites should be similar to those of the excavated Mississauga (Beasley Landing and Davisville 3) and Chippewa (Bellamy) sites in southern Ontario and to colonial-period sites in northern Ontario (Pilon 1987). Artifact assemblages are dominated by glass beads (embroidery seed beads) and ammunition (lead shot). In addition, large quantities of highly fragmented burned and calcined bone dominate zooarchaeological assemblages (Triggs 2004:162) and can exceed 90 percent of all zooarchaeological remains (e.g., Davisville 3 [Warrick 2005]) (see Figures 12.1 and 12.2). In addition to glass beads and ammunition, assemblages also include brass scrap, gunflints and flakes, trade silver, and European white clay pipe fragments. It must be mentioned that

Figure 12.1. Davisville 2 (AgHb-242), East Locus, artifacts from 299E 300N 20–25 cm DBS: a) fragmentary sherds; b) lead shot; c) drill tip, Onondaga chert; d) chert debitage, Onondaga chert; e) zooarchaeological remains (charred and calcined animal bone).
Source: Photograph by Gary Warrick; digitally enhanced by John Howarth.

European-manufactured items on colonial Anishinaabe sites occur in low density (typically two to six items per square metre outside of middens and pit features), and that most items would not be recovered using standard ¼ inch (6.4 mm) or even ⅛ inch (3.2 mm) mesh (the most common artifacts on Mississauga sites are seed beads and lead shot smaller than 3 mm in diameter). In other words, in a standard test pit survey at a 5 m interval (the norm for research and cultural resource management archaeological work in Ontario), it would be possible to test pit an Anishinaabe camp site and miss it entirely. Deposits of zooarchaeological remains are ubiquitous in Anishinaabe sites, however, and a shovel test pit survey should find concentrations of burned and calcined bone, but this may be the only archaeological material found.[6] Given that Mississauga sites often overlap earlier, pre-colonial Indigenous occupations, in the absence of European-made artifacts, an

---

6. The discovery of the Davisville 3 Mississauga encampment, on the Grand River, in northwestern Brantford, was made during a shovel test survey at 5 m interval, using ¼ inch mesh. One shovel test pit contained 112 pieces of heat-altered bone. In that same survey, six other shovel test pits produced more than 10 pieces of burned/calcined bone each, and two of these produced more than 100 pieces each—Davisville 2 East Locus and Davisville 5 (Warrick 2005).

Figure 12.2. Davisville 3 (AgHb-243) artifacts: a) iron disk, 200E198N 33 cm DBS; b) brass plaque fragment, 200E200N 30–40 cm DBS; c) blue edge (pearlware) ceramic, 201E202N 34–35 cm DBS; d) blue edge (pearlware) ceramic, 201E202N 30–35 cm DBS; e) glass seed beads (orange, 201E200N 36–37 cm DBS; black and white, 201E200N 38–39 cm DBS; robin's egg blue and yellow, 199E201N 30–31 cm DBS); f) shell wampum bead (machine-drilled hole), 199E202N 40–41 cm; g) lead shot, 200E204N.
Source: Photograph by Gary Warrick; digitally enhanced by John Howarth.

archaeologist could misinterpret the mix of calcined bone and pre-colonial artifacts as a pre-colonial site.

The possibility that late eighteenth-century Mississauga were making domestic pottery and flaked stone tools has been inferred from finds at the Beasley Landing site (Triggs 2004). Although the stratigraphic association of colonial-period artifacts and pottery and chert debitage and tools at this site is beyond question, it may be that the pottery and debitage are pre-colonial in age and have become intermixed with the colonial occupation. Soil formation in forested environments in southern Ontario is exceedingly slow. Middle Woodland–period cord-marked pottery and flaked stone were found on the living floor of the Mohawk cabin at the Davisville 1 site and were found intermixed with Mississauga artifacts at the Davisville 3 site (identical to the Beasley Landing site). Other suspected Mississauga sites (Bead Hill [Poulton, this volume], Teiaiagon [Robertson, this volume], Kenté [von Bitter et al., this volume], and RBG [Scott Martin, personal communication 2020]), are intermixed with earlier Indigenous occupations. This being said, it is highly likely that some of the rough-stone artifacts (e.g., abraders and notched cobble net sinkers) found on eighteenth-century Indigenous sites in Ontario date to the colonial period, but it would be difficult to identify these as colonial in age on Mississauga sites with pre-colonial components. At the Bead Hill site (the location of the Seneca village of Ganatsekwyagon), pottery is rare and the abundant chert debitage was intermixed with European trade items and is interpreted as predating the seventeenth-century Seneca occupation (Poulton, this volume). Late eighteenth- and early nineteenth-century Kickapoo and Potawatomi sites in Illinois typically produce abundant flaked stone debitage and tools, which are generally interpreted as stratigraphic admixture of contact and pre-contact components. Illinois archaeologists have raised the possibility, however, that some triangular chert points in these sites were manufactured by the historic Indigenous Peoples who occupied these sites (Wagner 2006).

Perhaps a key identifying feature of a late eighteenth- to early nineteenth-century Mississauga site is large amounts of highly fragmented or comminuted burned and calcined bone (Triggs 2004; Warrick 2005), with average fragment size of 6–8 mm (see Figure 12.3). Highly fragmented mammal bone is a by-product of bone grease processing (Outram 2001), and bone grease was an important food of temperate latitude and Arctic and Subarctic hunter-gatherer-fishers (Baker 2009; Prince 2007; Vehik 1977). Bone grease production could therefore explain the presence of abundant tiny fragments of generally large mammal bone (e.g., deer) in contact-period Anishinaabe sites. But why are these fragments also commonly burned and calcined? Large quantities of burned/calcined bone fragments could be the result of rituals associated with feasting or simply sanitary cleanup of a campsite. Dense concentrations of calcined bone mash found on Subarctic (Cree, Innu, Beothuk) sites in Quebec, Labrador, and Newfoundland have been interpreted as by-products of ritual burning of food bones, perhaps associated with *makushan* feasts (Holly 2019:1445–1447). Another explanation could be the simple disposal of smelly bone grease residue to reduce odours and at the same time to discourage unwanted animal predators from wandering into camp. Considering that the Mississauga share many cultural features and even population history in certain cases (Bishop 1981) with the Anishinaabeg and the Cree of northern/Subarctic Ontario (Rogers 1978, 1994; Rogers and Taylor 1981), we suggest that the Mississauga engaged in bone grease production and incineration of the tiny bone fragments after rendering the grease, and that they continued to do so after moving to southern Ontario in the early eighteenth century. It is highly intriguing that Dana Poulton's excavation of the Bead Hill site (this volume) produced abundant burned and calcined animal bone fragments, primarily from the surface deposits of the village. Given that, according to historical and cartographic data (Poulton, this volume), Bead Hill was most certainly reoccupied by the Mississauga in the

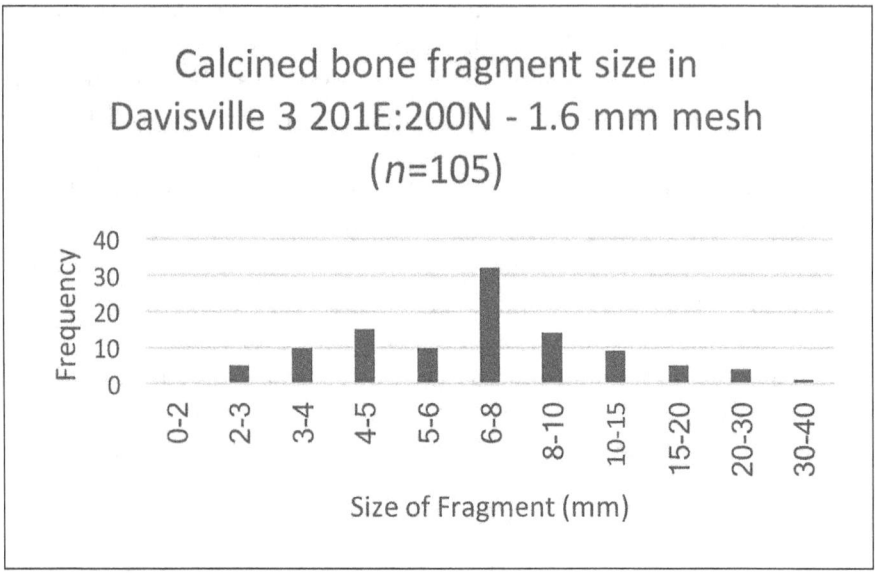

Figure 12.3. Size distribution of calcined bone from an excavation unit of Davisville 3 (AgHb-243). *Source:* Gary Warrick.

early eighteenth century, it seems likely that some of the burned and calcined bone is attributable to the Mississauga, not the Seneca.[7]

In summary, identification of Mississauga encampments at any of the Iroquois du Nord village sites could be difficult, particularly if the Mississauga occupied the former villages shortly after their abandonment by the Haudenosaunee. Later eighteenth-century Mississauga occupations could be differentiated from the Iroquois du Nord occupation by temporally diagnostic artifacts, such as trade silver jewellery, glass beads, gun parts, and coins (we note that at Bead Hill, an early eighteenth-century gun barrel was reported to have been found in the nineteenth century [Poulton, this volume]). It is interesting that Ganatsekwyagon was reoccupied by the Mississauga as early as 1700 and that they were using the lower Rouge River close to the Ganatsekwyagon in the late eighteenth and early nineteenth century, suggesting long-term occupation and use of this area that began in the early eighteenth century.

Although there is no definitive archaeological evidence, the Credit Mississauga also settled near Teiaiagon (on the lower Humber River), as

---

7. Although the eighteenth-century Seneca did render bone grease (Watson and Thomas 2013), no more than 25 percent of the zooarchaeological assemblage at Seneca sites in New York is charred or calcined. At Bead Hill, almost all recovered zooarchaeological remains are charred or calcined, and only 0.27 percent of the remains are identifiable to species (Poulton, this volume), similar to the Mississauga encampment of Davisville 3 (Warrick 2005).

evidenced in the records of a council meeting held in 1700 between the Haudenosaunee and the English at Albany and a 1736 French report on Indigenous settlement on the Humber River (Robertson, this volume).

There is provisional evidence that eastern Mississauga also occupied Kenté, as suggested by early nineteenth-century stories of a family who lived on the second concession of Ameliasburgh, on Lot 111. They had neighbours "who came from the Indian village in the fields on Smokes Point" and "would trade woven baskets and beads for bread smothered in butter and honey" (Calnan et al. 1987:192). A silver crucifix and silver armlet recovered from Bald Head Island have been identified as almost certainly related to Mississauga occupation of the region, as they are late eighteenth century in origin (Cooper, this volume).

3. Conclusion

There is clear documentary evidence for Mississauga occupation of some of the IDN settlements by 1700, as well as archaeological evidence at Ganatsekwyagon, which is consistent with their abandonment by the Haudenosaunee a decade or so earlier. There is a rich Anishinaabe oral tradition of a number of battles with the Haudenosaunee at this time, which many scholars now accept, and it is not unreasonable to assume that the enmity between the Haudenosaunee and the allied nations contributed to the physical abandonment of the area even if the Haudenosaunee continued to diplomatically claim an interest in lands along the north shore. Land treaties were signed later in the eighteenth century between Anishinaabe Peoples and the British, including one to provide land for Haudenosaunee who had fought with the British in the American War of Independence.

We also suspect that the Bay of Quinte Mississauga frequented the other, eastern Iroquois du Nord villages of Ganneious (Napanee), Quintio (Rice Lake), and Ganaraské (Port Hope). The Iroquois du Nord village sites possess all the geographical characteristics preferred by the Mississauga for their summer villages (location at the mouth of major rivers or on lakeshores, with fertile agricultural land on nearby river flats or terraces) (Adams 1986; Konrad 1981). We hope that, once the locations of these sites have been verified, archaeological investigations will reveal evidence similar to that outlined above.

Acknowledgements

Ron Williamson would like to gratefully acknowledge that the history outlined in this chapter was drawn largely from research and summaries provided by Annie Veilleux of Archaeological Services Inc. We also thank Bill Fox, Kurt Jordan, and Dana Poulton for their helpful comments on an earlier version of this chapter.

SECTION 5
DISCUSSION AND CONCLUSIONS AND THE HAUDENOSAUNEE VIEW

13 THE "IROQUOIS DU NORD" OF THE LATE SEVENTEENTH CENTURY

Revisiting the Haudenosaunee on the North Shore of Lake Ontario

VICTOR KONRAD

1. Archaeology, Geography, History, and Memory

On Saturday, November 2, 2019, I enjoyed the privilege of participating in an all-day session on the "Iroquois du Nord" (IDN) at the annual meeting of the Ontario Archaeological Society. My original intention was only to listen and learn about a research interest that had engaged me during the 1970s and 1980s. When I arrived, session co-organizer Ron Williamson asked me to say a few words at the end of the day, so I gathered my thoughts and offered initial comments on the papers. Recently, I have had an opportunity to read every paper that emerged from the conference, and I am pleased to share this revisit with the Haudenosaunee on the north shore of Lake Ontario.

My approach is shaped by an engagement not only with aspects of the archaeology, geography, and history of the late seventeenth-century north shore of Lake Ontario, but also with the role that memory plays in the revisitation and reconstruction. And in part, this relates to my memory. Clearly, it has been decades since I focused on this topic, and my memory is incomplete and formed from recollections of past research, set in print from the 1980s. Yet, there are aspects of an Indigenous memory that, in my estimation, need to be examined carefully, and likely more directly, in the cross-disciplinary and cross-cultural effort to unravel how, where, when, and why the IDN settled on the north shore of Lake Ontario. These aspects of memory lie in the traditions and articulated cultural expressions of the Haudenosaunee and their constituent nations, as revealed through archaeology, documented ethnohistory, and oral history. Also, memory is central in the oral history of the Mississauga and other Anishinaabe Peoples who replaced the IDN in the territory north of Lake

Ontario, and in most of the north-shore villages (MacLeod 1992; Smith 2013a, 2013b; Warrick and Williamson, this volume). Although the importance of this collective and integrated Indigenous memory is now acknowledged by scholars, the European documented memory remains privileged in our interpretations of the IDN. And although the shortcomings and biases of explorers, missionaries, and officials are known, sifting the facts remains a challenge, but also provides an opportunity, as illustrated by Neal Ferris's analysis of Outinaouatoua (this volume). Rather than indicate that there is just not sufficient data to form insights and conclusions, or to abrogate because we believe that we have exhausted the sources of information, we need to innovate approaches to integrating information from all possible sources, and particularly to re-evaluate information with the advance of exploratory technologies. This approach is forwarded in all the chapters in this book. Yet, I am convinced that new components of memory will unfold not only through advances in remote sensing technology and other novel approaches, but also through more effective synthesis. In a sense, the IDN conundrum lies at the edge of memory, yet this is a live edge, where notions of public and collective memory meet and collide, and where past and present populations mobilize memory to connect and detach from place (Shackel 2001). New information and insights will extend understanding of where the villages were located, who lived in the settlements, what the occupants' life was like, how ways of life were shaped, and why the Haudenosaunee came to various places on the north shore and then left.

The chapters in this volume draw on the accumulated historical and geographical understanding of the IDN, and they advance, substantially, the archaeology of the north shore of Lake Ontario in the late seventeenth century. Until recently, and before the contemporary explorations in IDN archaeology reported here, the narrative of Haudenosaunee migration to the north shore of Lake Ontario was relatively consistent, although divergent interpretations were offered in a substantial literature focused on their return to the region south of the Lake. Now we have evidence of a more complex and nuanced establishment of Haudenosaunee settlement north of Lake Ontario, and a suggestion that the Haudenosaunee return to the area south of Lake Ontario was likely due to a combination of voluntary abandonment and Anishinaabe victory, rather than an exclusive and decisive "Ojibwa Thesis" or "Iroquois Thesis" conceived through Eurocentric visions of territory (Warrick and Williamson, this volume). The key to a more balanced, detailed, and explanatory interpretation of the IDN story lies in effective deployment of exhaustive cross-disciplinary analysis and synthesis. All the contributors to this volume engage in this approach. It may have been useful that several decades ago detailed consideration of map documents added to the historical evidence and expanded the aperture for understanding (Konrad 1981). Furthermore, by acknowledging previously discounted Mississauga recollections (MacLeod 1992; Smith 2013a), it became possible to provide a more expansive and balanced account than had been available previously from historical records. The addition of new evidence to expand the narrative depended on finding, substantiating, and in some instances rediscovering the locations of the sites of the IDN settlements. Moreover, an explanatory dividend has occurred because researchers have added new archaeological evidence and re-evaluated the narrative in the context of new theories, insights, and data.

In addition to reviewing the findings of each chapter in turn, I construct my commentary around what I see as prominent themes and questions related to the archaeology, geography, and history of the IDN. I will not review the durable European account or the revised narrative informed largely by new archaeological evidence and synthesis; they are both well established in the introduction by Ron Williamson and referred to in each chapter. The introduction is an extensive contextual account, not only of the IDN story, but also of scholarship in the fields of archaeology, geography, and history related to the interacting worlds of the Indigenous Peoples in the Great Lakes region, as well as of the Europeans who entered and altered their dynamic territories during the seventeenth century. By the middle of the seventeenth century, territorial dynamics in the region changed, with the dispersal of the Attawandaron (the Wendat name for the Neutral), Wendat (Huron), and Tionontaté (Petun) by the Haudenosaunee, and a decidedly more powerful and unprecedented economic and political advantage was available to the Haudenosaunee. One outcome of this advantage was Haudenosaunee settlement expansion both to the south and to the north of Lake Ontario.

Our goal, then, is to understand to the greatest extent possible the nature of the growth that led to the establishment of the IDN villages on the north shore of Lake Ontario. With this advanced understanding, we may analyze the characteristics of the broadened settlement system and its spatial relations. We may additionally examine the Haudenosaunee expansion within a theoretical framework of borders, bordering, and re-bordering to gain additional insights regarding the expansion and contraction process. Finally, we may now populate the IDN villages based on previous knowledge and new insights from the archaeological and historical record, in order to enlarge understanding of the transformation into IDN settlements, the precarity and the prosperity of life on the north shore, and a sense of IDN becoming within the nations of the Haudenosaunee confederacy and of the overall League.

2. Confirmations of Site Locations

One of the major constraints to comprehensive interpretation of the IDN has been a lack of adequate and balanced archaeological confirmation of the settlements identified in the written documents and the historical maps. One objective of this volume is to rectify this situation by reviewing all the historical information in the context of the archaeological record, as well as new clues about where the settlements were located. Section 2 of this volume addresses the locations of all the IDN villages identified in the historical record, from Ganneious and Kenté in the east; Ganaraské and Quintio in the mid-north shore area; Ganatsekwyagon and Teiaiagon, on the two major branches of the Toronto Carrying Place; to Outinaouatoua, on the path between the western end of Lake Ontario and the Grand River. The following brief discussion is a summary of the current consensus emerging on where the villages were located.

Chris Menary and Rob von Bitter (this volume) integrate landscape analysis with reinterpretation of the historical record to establish approximate locations for Ganneious, Ganaraské, and Quintio, all sites without available and definitive archaeological evidence. LiDAR (light detection and ranging) remote sensing is then used in an effort to refine potential locations. The results of this integrative approach suggest the following sites. Ganneious remains unconfirmed, but the village appears to have been situated on the north shore of Hay Bay, east of the mouth of Little Creek, below a limestone ridge. A postulated secondary cabin acting as a tollgate was likely located on the bank of the Napanee River, at the end of a short portage, and in the vicinity of Middle Woodland mounds that served as a location marker for the portage (Menary and von Bitter, this volume). A more prominent example of this village-and-satellite settlement relationship appears evident for Ganaraské and Quintio. Ganaraské likely occupied the east or west bank rise in the prominent westward bend of the Ganaraska River near its mouth, although exact position through archaeological confirmation has not been possible. Remote sensing techniques and landscape analysis have been utilized effectively to define the portage route to Rice Lake, although confirmation of Quintio also remains elusive, perhaps because the IDN village has become covered by the town of Bewdley or drowned when the Hastings Dam raised the level of Rice Lake during construction of the Trent-Severn Waterway (Menary and von Bitter, this volume). LiDAR data have proven useful in identifying mounds in all these locations, and although they may be of Middle Woodland origin, they could have served as navigational and sacred sites within the IDN landscape.

Three village site locations are supported by evidence from historical documents and confirmed through contemporary archaeological excavation and previous artifact collections: Kenté, Ganatsekwyagon, and Teiaiagon. Rob von Bitter, Chris Menary, and Nick Gromoff (this volume) argue convincingly that Kenté was situated at Smokes Point and/or on Bald Island, on Wellers Bay. Although several potential targets are evident from the LiDAR data, landowner permission will be required for archaeological confirmation. However, the Squire site, at Consecon, has now been removed from the official archaeological record, and the Chadd Collection, originating from the Wellers Bay vicinity, has been associated with Kenté and environs. Dana Poulton (this volume) confirms that the Bead Hill site, on the west side of the Rouge River, is the best candidate for Ganatsekwyagon based on extensive historical information, landscape analysis, and archaeological confirmation. Similarly, based on integrated historical, geographical, and archaeological evidence, Baby Point, on the western, or Humber River, arm of the Toronto Carrying Place, is confirmed as the location of Teiaiagon (Robertson, this volume).

The location of Outinaouatoua, according to Neal Ferris (this volume), remains an enigma in part because we know approximately where it is from historical accounts (two days' travel from Cootes Paradise, near Dundas, and three days' travel from the Grand River on a trail between Lake Ontario and the Grand). Also, at least four sites dating from before 1650 have been found in the vicinity and at one time were considered candidates for Outinaouatoua. Finally, an enticing find of possible post-1650 artifacts was revealed briefly to Ferris by a collector, but efforts to explore the prospect were stymied by the elusiveness of the collector. However, although Ferris is not able to help us mark the definitive location of the village on a map, his essay compels us to examine more closely issues of IDN village systems and networks; the nature of Haudenosaunee settlement expansion; the transformation of Indigenous societies in the region; and the spatial, temporal, and cultural borderlands of being Haudenosaunee in the late seventeenth century. These issues comprise the focus of the following commentary.

3. East–West Regionalization and South–North Expansion of the Settlement System

History records that the Haudenosaunee expanded their settlement system after 1650, and that a component of this expansion was to create new settlements near to either the south or the north shore of Lake Ontario (Konrad 1981; Jordan, this volume). Furthermore, these villages were initiated and grouped according to alignment of traditional Haudenosaunee settlement territories: Seneca in the west, Cayuga in the middle, and Oneida in the east. The Onondaga did not settle on the north shore of Lake Ontario. The Mohawk were active in the region, although their attempt at settlement expansion may have been limited to a short-lived settlement on the St. Lawrence River, due to the establishment, in 1673, of Fort Frontenac, at the eastern end of Lake Ontario. The apparent east–west regionalization on the north shore, generated by south-to-north expansion of the settlement system, has led scholars to project an orderly, consistent, and durable Haudenosaunee settlement initiative on the north shore. Yet, as contributors to this volume have expressed, the system was not merely a duplicate but rather a transformation, because, in part, the functions of the settlements were different from both the homeland and the expansion settlements to the south of Lake Ontario. Furthermore, the settlements appeared and disappeared at different times in a shifting and mobile, systematic framework incentivized by the fur trade and other resource exploitation, and by territorial control.

Accordingly, we may view the IDN settlements as exchange locations, tollgates, strategic points, and places invested with power and control. But the main north-shore settlements were also villages where most inhabitants engaged in agriculture, gathering, fishing, and/or hunting. Some villages, Outinaouatoua, for example, may have been located more directly to enable access to deer and bear food resources than any strategic route control function (Ferris, this volume). Other settlements, Quintio, for example, likely functioned primarily as tollgates in the broader fur trade regulation system portrayed in the unique spatial positioning of the IDN villages. Whereas Quintio may have served a more limited set of functions, nearby Ganaraské was both an agricultural settlement and a strategic access point to the north-shore hinterland (Menary and von Bitter, this volume). The establishment of Fort Frontenac may have shifted Seneca use of the Toronto Carrying Place from the east arm to the west arm, and consequently Ganatsekwyagon may have lost prominence to Teiaiagon as a strategic access point on the north shore. However, a great deal of importance is attributed to this apparent shift, and as Ron Williamson has suggested (personal communication 2021), we may be missing some valuable information in confirming the reason(s) for the shift. Meanwhile, missionary activity on the north shore became more focused on attracting potential converts east, toward the environs of Fort Frontenac and Montréal, thus adding a new dynamic to the shifts.

As Kurt Jordan argues (this volume), the decisions to establish a Haudenosaunee presence on the north shore of Lake Ontario were decidedly plural, consisting of choices by separate nations and the League. The reasons for the expansion were also plural, and they were complex. In addition to the major reason given in the literature—expansion and control of the fur trade—were broader influences of European presence, and of more specific demographic forces. The dynamics of population fission and fusion, according to Jordan, were linked to the dynamics of territorial expansion (and then contraction) in several ways. Most evident is the expansion of villages during the peak power of the Haudenosaunee, between 1650 and 1680. Important, however, is the growing acknowledgement among scholars that village growth may have been accelerated by incorporation of individuals and groups from other nations into these new settlements. Archaeological evidence from satellite settlements to the south of Lake Ontario confirms cultural diversity due to incorporation. Some of the IDN settlements may have been even more diverse in their population characteristics due to the flow-through nature of these communities. On the other hand, Neal Ferris (this volume) makes a strong case for designating Outinaouatoua as a settlement largely inhabited by incorporated Neutral in the process of becoming Haudenosaunee. North-shore villages were likely diverse along many demographic planes and not expressly defined by their Seneca, Cayuga, or Oneida affiliation.

In order to expand our understanding of the settlement system of the IDN, it is useful to place the loosely aggregated system of the Iroquois du Nord in the context of Kurt Jordan's conceptualization of Haudenosaunee territorial space. Local space is the immediate village and environs; regional space is within 20 to 80 km, or two days' travel; and extra-regional space is beyond 80 km from the village. By this measure, the satellite or expansion villages to the south of Lake Ontario can be considered within regional space, whereas the IDN villages are in extra-regional space, implying perhaps a "different kind" of Haudenosaunee settlement as well as a spatially distanced settlement. On the other hand, canoe travel around the ends of the lake may have expedited access to the north shore and, in a sense, brought these villages into a space between regional and extra-regional. The conceptualization of Haudenosaunee territorial space is, in my estimation, very useful and promising as a theoretical construct for further exploration and refinement. The explication of territorial space also raises the question of borders.

4. Iroquois du Nord Territory as Borderlands and the Advancement of Border Theory

Another theoretical framework to be considered is border theory. The field of border studies has grown rapidly since the 1980s, as scholars in the social sciences and the humanities have moved beyond state-based conceptions of territory to the acknowledgement and understanding of hybrid and liminal spaces at boundaries (Paasi 1996; Newman and Paasi 1998). Although border studies gained incentive and prominence in addressing the shifts brought about through globalization and its attendant de-territorialization and a-territorialization, historical and pre-historical research has also benefited from the application of border theory (Konrad and Brunet-Jailly 2019). Richard White's (1991) conceptualization of "middle ground" established a borderlands perspective on the Great Lakes region during the period 1650 to 1815. In Ontario archaeology, the notion of borderlands has been applied to conceptualizing Late Woodland settlement shifts and integration in southwestern Ontario. Amy St. John and Neal Ferris (2019:48) illustrate: "In this Late Woodland world of shifting, multi-scalar fluid borders, a spatial transition zone across a broader material cline of expression, or archaeological borderland, would have encompassed people expressing deep generational traditions of lifeways and material culture." The authors go on to explain how these borderlands people were engaging robustly with innovation at the intersection of Western Basin Tradition and Ontario Iroquoian Tradition space, and how complex, overlapping identities were articulated within and beyond material expression. The concept of borderlands enables understanding beyond the normative constructs of ethnicity and culture.

In the 1970s and 1980s, I did not envision or acknowledge this promise in adopting a borderlands approach. At the time, contemporaries in research on issues in Great Lakes prehistory maintained bordered conceptions of archaeological traditions, although this belief in the integrity and consistency of these traditions was being questioned. At the time, for example, William C. Noble and I conducted soil chemical research on the Walker site to establish the considerable plurality and diversity in historic Neutral settlement patterns and illustrate the malleability of bordered conceptions of archaeological traditions (Konrad and Noble 1986). During the 1980s, archaeological research in Ontario was already offering extensive evidence of how fluid and malleable boundaries had become (or always were) between Indigenous Peoples in the Great Lakes region. Recent "linguistic and genetic evidence around shifting identities is that, like happened in the Neolithic transition in Europe with grains, maize was introduced to resident Algonquian-speaking populations in Ontario who adopted not only farming but the language and farming culture of those who introduced it and there was about a 700-year-long acculturation process of becoming Iroquoian in Ontario" (Ron Williamson, personal communication 2021; see also Beales 2013).

During the presentations at the Ontario Archaeological Society conference in 2019, and again when reading the chapters assembled in this volume, I was struck by the vocabulary of transition, transformation, motion, emergence, and becoming that resonates within contemporary issues and debates in border studies. Although Neal Ferris, Amy St. John, Ron Williamson, and others engaged in Ontario archaeology are exploring the application and advancement of border theory in their work, my suggestion is that there is more scope for employing this theoretical context. Given the confluence of archaeological and historical information available for the IDN, as well as the availability of substantial geographical knowledge about the IDN settlement system and its relationship to the Haudenosaunee village and territorial network, it is enticing to view this settlement dynamic with a borderlands lens.

A borderlands approach to the study of the IDN would enable extensive theoretical framing of the spatial and temporal context of the Haudenosaunee move to the north shore of Lake Ontario and the retreat to the homeland. The nature of boundaries could be articulated within an established conceptual framework of frontiers, borders, zones, border regions, borderlands, and, most recently, "borderscapes" (Brambilla 2015). Processes of bordering, de-bordering, and re-bordering could be situated within the framework. Territorial practices could be differentiated from a-territorial aspects of bordering associated with social class, gender, age, and other societal characteristics. Transition could be differentiated from transformation in spatial and temporal contexts by applying such concepts as liminality, parallelism, and parallax to articulate and calibrate the shifts that occur in borderlands. Additionally, border theory has acknowledged and integrated the "motion turn" in the social sciences to enable more explicit analysis of temporal shifts (Konrad 2015; Nail 2016). Kurt Jordan's conceptualization of Haudenosaunee space already contains the components of a borderlands framing. In my estimation, a borderlands framing would advance a more complete understanding of how the IDN fit into the Haudenosaunee mobilization of their frontiers (in the widest sense of the term), and the theoretical insights from such a framing could be applied to a comparative and better understanding of frontiers in formative Woodland and Iroquoian traditions in the Great Lakes region. Moreover, the application of the borderlands approach in this regard has the potential to advance border theory in general, drawing from the "long-term archaeological gaze" to inform border studies more widely (St. John and Ferris 2019:54). The growing and deepening interdisciplinary dialogue on borders and bordering is a primary contributor to advancing theory in border studies (Newman 2006).

5. A Re-populated North Shore: Transformation, Prosperity, Precarity, and Becoming Iroquois du Nord

Although the archaeology of the IDN remains constrained by limited in situ evidence of the most extensive north-shore settlements, uncertainties about the location of the remaining villages, and lack of access to possible sites, the synthesis of historical and geographical information with the archaeological evidence that is available allows us to populate the north-shore villages. I will review the evidence for each settlement, from west to east, in order to construct a composite of IDN occupation of the north shore. The composite draws on the confirmation, and to a certain extent the postulation, of assessments forwarded in the comprehensive studies of the IDN villages offered in this book. This is not a concluding statement but rather an interim assessment and a call for more research.

Outinaouatoua remains an enigma, but Neal Ferris (this volume) makes a compelling case for populating the small village with people of Neutral lineage in the process of becoming Haudenosaunee. He offers a strong argument for describing them as hunters occupying a locale with ample deer and bear, within a wider region that was familiar to them from prior and perhaps continual occupation. Ferris argues for a deeper preservation of Indigenous heritage across the landscape, and he argues against the notion that Outinaouatoua, like Teiaiagon and Ganatsekwyagon, maintained a route control function simply because the village was located on a path from the head of Lake Ontario to the Grand River. Ferris also underlines the point in the evidence from René de Bréhant de Galinée's record that the people in the village were becoming Haudenosaunee, and not Seneca. The population of Outinaouatoua was in transition and transformation in regard to their group identity, and their settlement may have been transitory as well, perhaps even seasonal given its primary function as a hunting location. Neal Ferris's essay compels the reader to view all the IDN settlements with a perspective that is more critical of the documentary evidence based upon French preoccupations of the time and to see these villages and their inhabitants as both engaged and caught in processes of transformation and becoming. I would suggest that these frontier places were also sites of fluctuating prosperity and precarity, and that perhaps this vacillation was most indicative of becoming IDN.

Whereas Outinaouatoua and the Van Son site, on Grand Island, in the Niagara River (Cooper, this volume), both appear to have been populated by Neutral under Seneca control as extra-regional satellites, the nature of their inclusion with Teiaiagon and Ganatsekwyagon as a part of an extra-regional domain under Seneca coordination remains to be clarified. Were there other settlements in this extra-regional domain? Should they be designated as part of the IDN settlement system, or are they a part of another Seneca extra-regional domain? Is our definition of IDN settlement too constraining if it is based on a fur trade route-and-point system? The contributions to this book have helped us to engage with some of these issues, but they remain to be resolved. Given the proximity of the Neutral ancestral territory to both the Seneca homeland and the north shore of Lake Ontario, one may anticipate a complex and diverse array of interactions among people in the space of becoming Haudenosaunee.

The synthesis of information about Ganatsekwyagon and Teiaiagon, in the light of historical evidence and ongoing if limited archaeological exploration of both sites, confirms that these settlements were autonomous yet associated "towns" in a western pole of the IDN settlement system, as well as northern outposts in the Seneca extra-regional domain. Ganatsekwyagon, according to Dana Poulton (this volume), exhibits material culture remains consistent with the Seneca settlements in the homeland, so the Seneca lived there. Yet after 1665, when the settlement was established, the site was also occupied by Haudenosaunee adoptees and other Indigenous Peoples and was visited by English, Dutch, and French traders and missionaries. There is evidence of agriculture, fishing, and hunting as well as trade. Population estimates suggest that perhaps eight hundred or more people occupied the settlement (Poulton, this volume). Although Teiaiagon may have been established around the same time as Ganatsekwyagon, this settlement on the western arm of the Toronto Carrying Place did not gain prominence as a strategic trade route gateway until after Fort Frontenac was constructed, in 1673, to monitor Haudenosaunee travel from their homeland around the eastern end of Lake Ontario. Teiaiagon then emerged as the most important Haudenosaunee settlement on the north shore, as well as the central Seneca presence in their extra-regional domain. Meanwhile, the now-favoured western end route around Lake Ontario must have been assured by Haudenosaunee and adoptee presence in the Niagara and Hamilton region. David Robertson (this volume) enlarges our understanding of who lived in and frequented Teiaiagon during the 1670s, and it appears that it may have been an even more diverse frontier "town" than Ganatsekwyagon. No archaeological or historical data are available to support population estimates, but it may be inferred that Teiaiagon had at least as many inhabitants as Ganatsekwyagon at its peak population. Recent excavations at the Baby Point site have provided a wider range of artifacts than those available from historical collections of the twentieth century to expand understanding of life at Teiaiagon during its brief decade of prominence.

Both Seneca settlements have produced diagnostic material culture in archaeological collections assembled in the nineteenth and twentieth centuries and during more recent excavations. The assemblages of glass, stone, shell, and bone beads recovered from both Teiaiagon and Ganatsekwyagon confirm that these settlements were associated with the Seneca (Fox et al., this volume). Although both settlements provide vestiges of pottery, ceramic pots were uncommon after 1650, and they appear to have been contextual choices by women. That is, ceramic pots "persist in some contexts and certainly in cemetery contexts perhaps because of their symbolic importance, although they occur in fewer numbers" (Ron Williamson personal communication 2021; see also Engelbrecht and Williamson, this volume). These formerly sensitive diagnostic aspects of material culture were replaced by metal vessels. The metal kettles and components of vessels dating to the late seventeenth century are found in both the homeland sites of the Seneca and their settlements on the north shore (Cooper, this volume). Another ceramic manufacture of the Haudenosaunee prevails more extensively during the late seventeenth century. Englebrecht and Williamson (this volume) provide an analysis of ceramic smoking pipes with inscribed effigies associated with the IDN settlements of Teiaiagon, Ganatsekwyagon, and Kenté, but these "legacy" ceramics "which follow people rather than denote broader culture" are not as useful as beads to confirm Seneca and Cayuga affiliation, and the west–east dichotomy of settlements on the north shore (Fox et al., this volume). In fact, William Fox, April Hawkins, and David Harris (this volume) suggest that the bead evidence illustrates several important shifts in Haudenosaunee settlement. First, there is the shift from homeland or local space to regional space. Next, there is the shift to extra-regional space, with settlements established on the north shore. Moreover, there are two more shifts evident. One is the diffusion from primary IDN sites to fishing, hunting, and tollgate locations, and the other is the shift of the settlement focus and presence from east to west along the north shore. The bead assemblages appear to be sensitive markers of spatial and temporal change in the IDN and greater Haudenosaunee settlement system, and they may prove useful as well in identifying more subtle differences among and within settlements.

Although we do not know the exact locations of Kenté, Ganaraské, Quintio, and Ganneious, we do know enough from historical accounts and collections of artifacts associated with some of the settlements to characterize these short-lived IDN villages. Kenté, the primary Cayuga village on the north shore, was the hub of a multi-settlement, diverse system. It commanded the major thoroughfare along the north shore by being situated on the only portage. The Cayuga could manage the traffic of Haudenosaunee and other Indigenous groups on Lake Ontario as long as they used the eastern route around the lake. Accordingly, Kenté was selected as the site of the Sulpician mission, although the Sulpicians soon learned that they needed to follow the potential converts not only to Ganaraské but to smaller outposts, such as Quintio, as well. It was a system of satellite settlements. We can infer how this worked in the case of Kenté, Ganaraské, and Quintio, but the relationship between Kenté and Ganneious is not as evident. Ganneious is documented as Oneida and apparently commanded the base of the portage from Hay Bay to the Napanee River, thereby suggesting a separate and definitive role for the Oneida on the north shore. The question remains, however: How did the Oneida fit into the north-shore settlement system? Was the population of Ganneious largely of Oneida origin or perhaps more likely constituted of adoptees and some Cayuga as well? Unfortunately, we do not have enough material to answer these questions for Ganneious, nor a similar set of questions for Ganaraské. Populating Kenté, on the other hand, is possible to an extent from the information contained in the Chadd Collection. Bead analysis confirms Kenté as a Cayuga settlement (Fox et al., this volume). Kenté has metal assemblages consistent with those found on other IDN sites and in the Cayuga homeland (Cooper, this volume). Without stratigraphic context for artifacts from Kenté, it is difficult to convey more about the inhabitants of the village. Consequently, the character of Kenté and the other eastern villages of the Cayuga and Oneida remains uncertain except for the few glimpses offered by the Sulpicians, and comparative information available from homeland settlements and their satellites to the south of Lake Ontario. Whereas the former source is finite, the promise for greater inference lies in Haudenosaunee archaeology.

Indeed, reading and understanding the settlement of the north shore of Lake Ontario during the last half of the seventeenth century will depend as much on comparative analysis of "north–south" archaeology, history, and geography as on the chances of obtaining more evidence from a rapidly disappearing archaeological record of largely ephemeral sites on the north shore. Yet, there is some promise for expanding knowledge of the IDN from the meagre archaeological record. In their analysis of antler combs from Kenté, Ganatsekwyagon (Bead Hill), and Teiaiagon, Ron Williamson and Rob von Bitter (this volume) confirm the similarity of combs found on the north-shore sites with those originating in the Haudenosaunee homeland. Furthermore, many of the combs depict the origins and nature of the Haudenosaunee confederacy, therefore corroborating League allegiance and Haudenosaunee ideology among the IDN. The antler combs are objects of transformation, signifying the bilateralism of the real and the spiritual world. Also, the combs were prized possessions in life and in death, and they remain as symbolic objects to confirm the antiquity of Haudenosaunee ideology and memory. Williamson and von Bitter quote Rick Hill as portraying the combs as media for recording cultural change. It remains to be seen what more may be learned from the antler combs, and from other archaeological evidence that may emerge.

6. An Anishinaabe North Shore

It is somewhat intriguing and perhaps inevitable that the Anishinaabe occupation of the north shore of Lake Ontario is manifested in a western and an eastern Mississauga grouping of settlements. As Gary Warrick and Ron Williamson (this volume) relate in the final part of the book, the Anishinaabeg moved to the north shore in what initially manifested as an occupation of recent Haudenosaunee settlements. It was in part a replication of the settlement pattern because former Haudenosaunee space was incorporated into Anishinaabe space, including settlement sites, fields, and hunting and fishing locations. But the settlement pattern diverged and developed in a direction consistent with Anishinaabe seasonal activities, which increasingly had less to do with the fur trade in the immediate region. In the summer, the Anishinaabeg reoccupied the former Haudenosaunee settlements on the north shore of Lake Ontario, and at other times of the year they were on the move in a round of hunting, fishing, collecting, and sugaring activities in specific locales and extensive areas north of the lake. Yet, the summer villages predominated, thus adding validity and confirmation to the Anishinaabe takeover of the north shore. Meanwhile, the Haudenosaunee used their former hunting and fishing territories north of the lake through treaties made with the French and the English, and with the Mississauga (Konrad 1981:142; Warrick and Williamson, this volume). Clearly, the spatial imaginary of territory, borders, and spaces of resource utilization differed between Europeans and Indigenous Peoples in the Great Lakes region. Furthermore, these spatial imaginaries differed between the Haudenosaunee and the Anishinaabe, and this difference in territorial conception and spatial organization needs to be understood more thoroughly.

Unfortunately, as Warrick and Williamson (this volume) portray in their analysis, the relative limited archaeological visibility of the Anishinaabeg in colonial times makes it difficult to assemble comparative information. There is a marked absence of European artifacts on Anishinaabe sites before the eighteenth century, and the sites are most readily identified by large amounts of highly fragmented burned and calcined bone from bone grease production. The current composite understanding of Anishinaabe occupation of the north shore at the beginning of the eighteenth century is four to six territorial communities of Mississauga focused on major drainages fronting on Lake Ontario between the Grand River and what is now Prince Edward County. Although the progressive alienation of these territorial communities is a matter of record (Smith 2013a, 2013b), their formation and perseverance at the turn of the eighteenth century remain to be understood.

7. Prospective

Although the contributions to this book advance significantly our understanding of the IDN presence on the north shore of Lake Ontario, it seems that for every clarification gained we encounter more uncertainties about this relatively short-lived yet intriguing period of encounter and change among Indigenous and European protagonists in our part of the world. Perhaps this territorial affinity makes the event even more important to us. A portion of southern Ontario was altered and reformulated in this shifting of territories and borders, not only between Indigenous and European communities but also between different Indigenous communities. We are obliged to see the encounter through Indigenous perspectives, and that is a good thing. We are compelled to engage with a more nuanced and detailed deconstruction of transformation, and this enables a more comprehensive understanding of the process. One aspect of this is the process of becoming, and the revision of identities, often ossified in our designations of groups and cultures. Also, as the contributions to this book demonstrate, we need to re-engage with conceptions of scale, duration, and regionalization in order to understand more fully the IDN move to the north shore. Framing the study within a theory of borders helps to distinguish and reveal aspects of frontiers, territories, and borderlands. In addition to exploring the IDN experience within a border theory framework, our comprehension is also broadened through the application of remote sensing technologies for site location and confirmation. All these conceptualizations and applications advance our knowledge of the IDN and promise greater understanding as new archaeological evidence emerges.

Several notions continue to resonate as I consider where we may wish to look more closely in order to continue our study of the IDN. One lens that could be used more effectively is the perspective of traditional Indigenous knowledge. Rick Hill (this volume) comments on this direction. Also, as Kurt Jordan reminds us, we need to view the Haudenosaunee in the context of their considerable uncertainty during this time. Clearly, these were precarious times, and Lake Ontario's environs were precarious spaces, where a vortex of considerable change was engaging all nations and communities in the region. Neal Ferris captures the essence as "a borderland of becoming between pasts, presents, and futures that scholarship still seeks to know beyond distant French preoccupations of the time" (Ferris, this volume). As Ron Williamson points out in his extensive contextual account and introduction (this volume), we need to question the over-reliance on an explanatory template of economic exchange and strategic advantage, and we need to question the familiarity we have developed with notions of power, intrigue, and well-worn pathways. My concluding assessment is that the chapters in this book assemble, as completely as possible, what we know and understand about the IDN, and illustrate the pivotal and durable impact of Indigenous relations on the history and geography of the lower Great Lakes region.

14

VIEW FROM THE NORTH SHORE
Indigenous Imaginations, Then and Now

RICK HILL

The north shore of Lake Ontario has held many Indigenous footprints over the centuries. Indigenous Peoples have been travelling through the region, stopping to hunt, fish, or gather medicines, or to erect settlements. They made peace, made war, and made peace again. Many languages were heard by the waterways and forests of the region—Haudenosaunee and Anishinaabe languages. It was massive stretch of fertile land yet became a no man's land of sorts.

For the Haudenosaunee, who generally settled in upstate New York, there was an ancestral connection to the First People of this region—the Huron-Wendat, who lived a similar lifestyle, spoke a similar language, and shared a common love of the land. They were cousins to each other.

That love did not always transfer to political and economic relations. In the seventeenth century, the Haudenosaunee warriors, in defence of their economic interests, often raided and devastated the Huron-Wendat. The emerging fur trade and divided loyalties between the French and English crowns caused my ancestors to disrupt the peace and harmony that was meant to be perpetual through the original Dish with One Spoon Treaty. The concurrent loss of Haudenosaunee populations due to disease likely motivated the adoption of many other peoples into Haudenosaunee society. Like the Borg of *Star Trek* fame, resistance was futile, and Haudenosaunee identity and consciousness was slowly enculturated into the prisoners of war.

No one knows the exact origin of this first intra-Indigenous treaty, an agreement that the Haudenosaunee and Anishinaabe-speaking nations would not fight over the resources provided by the Great Dish—Our Mother, the Earth. It was a beautiful arrangement, whereby this region in particular was part of the shared Dish, where families could come to harvest the foods and medicines they needed, without fear of harm by others. It was the ultimate sign of respect—to share life sustainers.

The principle of respectful sharing was lost during the era of colonization and the subsequent competitive fur trade. This region became stained with blood, rage, and death, to the point where, except for the Mohawks at the Bay of Quinte who settled in the eighteenth century at the far eastern end of Lake Ontario, the Haudenosaunee settlements along the north shore disappeared.

Like ants at a picnic, archaeologists, both professional and amateur, began to scour the landscape, seeking evidence of the First People of this land. In the beginning, it was not the kind of systematic archaeology practised today. Almost haphazardly, evidence began to surface. First by the farmer's plow, then by the construction of buildings and roads. Finally, professional archaeologists moved in, to salvage as much as possible of the material evidence held by the earth that was threatened by progress.

Unfortunately, that also meant the uncovering of Indigenous burials. All I can say is that in former days, there was a real lust to possess the bones of the First People, particularly the skulls. Like Hamlet, archaeologists felt those skulls were speaking through them. The voice, songs, beliefs, even the jokes of those skulls were gone, but archaeologists speculated on what kind of thinking went on within the brain cavity of the skull.

Graves represented a great mystery, especially ossuaries, where a mass of human remains led to all kinds of speculation about why they were buried thusly. Speculation became fact. Fact fuelled more research. Further research elaborated or disproved the "facts." Our collective understanding of the past changes with each generation. Archaeology on the north shore is a great intellectual challenge. It is an ongoing Indigenous question. What happened to the people who used to live here?

Predicting Indigenous behaviours is risky business for archaeologists. It is one thing to examine a site for what the relationships of objects might tell you. Archaeologists seek patterns of culture in what was found and where it was found. It is another thing to look at historical factors that might have impacted on the material culture, village patterns, and the occurrence of death. Archaeologists seek to put together the puzzle of historical influence on cultural change.

Speculation on how the Indigenous people used to think is another matter altogether. My fine art training was predicated on the history of the evolution of artistic expression. In art history courses, we examined the philosophy behind the various art practices through time. Artistic movements and innovations were defined, redefined, and categorized. Art historians sought universal definitions of visual art. Their conclusions influenced the way I learned about art, in the 1960s. But the conclusions have changed dramatically since then.

Artists began to rebel against those definitions. The canon of fine art was dismantled, and a free-for-all has taken place. What this generation considers art would be quite startling to Rembrandt or Michelangelo. At times, it startles me!

The same might be said about contemporary Indigenous art. When you compare what the earth has revealed from the sixteenth, seventeenth, and eighteenth centuries to what is shown in art galleries by contemporary Indigenous artists, the difference is almost insurmountable.

In my former curatorial days, I used to argue that threads of continuity in concept, vision, and execution could still be evident in modern art. Then, I argued that creativity was our tradition, and that change is not always about assimilation. It is *indigenuity*. The vitality of a culture is reflected by the creativity of their arts.

I first had to think of what messages my ancestors were sending in the work that they created, as evidenced by the objects uncovered at a seventeenth-century village site named Gannagaro, or Ganondagan, near Victor, New York. I was part of a team to develop an interpretive plan for the historic site, and I had a specific task to write and design two books on the site—one on the art produced by Seneca inhabitants of the massive village of about five thousand people, and another on the destruction of the village during an attack by the French, led by Jacques-René de Brisay de Denonville, in 1687. The Senecas, to thwart the French advance, burned their own village to the ground. The Seneca, along with the Cayugas and Oneidas, had been involved in establishing settlements on the north shore of Lake Ontario between 1665 and 1670. The Haudenosaunee had become familiar with the region through their hunting and raiding parties trying to control the flow of furs in the first half of the seventeenth century. Other authors of chapters in this volume explain the history and nature of those settlements. Ironically, the Haudenosaunee in those communities held lucrative trade with the French until the Haudenosaunee interests were turned over to the Anishinaabeg and Algonquian Peoples. If these communities were meant to be an early-warning defence network, their ability to do so was greatly reduced by the time of the Denonville expedition.

My artist-trained eyes found a mysterious beauty in the reshaping of bone, antler, and shell by the ancestral artists from that village. It was amazing what they could produce given the technology of the times. My father, Stan Hill, had become a bone carver, and despite my encouragement, showing him photos of the antler hair combs in the hope that he would carve one, he was reluctant to do so.

"Those designs belong to them," he said. "It was their way of expressing themselves. I'm not them. I can't take it from them and make it mine. I did not live their lives."

That was not the only lesson the untrained artist father taught the art school–trained son. It taught me to be careful about projecting back onto the art of the past the hopes of the present. Yet, the hair combs did speak to me, and what I "heard" from them changed the way I thought about the past—past longhouse village life, the fur trade, and coping with change. All from a series of antler carvings.

However, while I was falling in love with the delicate carvings and the imagined artists who had produced them, our Haudenosaunee advisory committee, which was helping plan the interpretation of Ganondagan, threw a serious wrench into my love affair. Most of the most visually stunning hair combs were recovered from graves. The older members of this committee, including Corbett Sundown, Tonawanda Seneca Chief; Huron Miller, Onondaga ritualist; and Chief Oren Lyons, Onondaga nationalist and artist, did not feel it was morally right to publish these images.

It was a perfect Haudenosaunee storm. How could I not share the most significant pieces of art that have affected my own vision of myself? How could we put back into the ground some of the most beautiful examples of creativity and artistic excellence of our ancestors? It took some time and a lot of discussion with my mentors and within myself. We finally compromised. In the essay that accompanied the photos of the combs, I wrote:

> We do not doubt the artistic merits of these works, but are troubled by the important ethical question about how the works were acquired. [...] Regardless of their historical and artistic importance, the removal of the objects from burials is a serious violation of the cultural and spiritual values of the Haudenosaunee. [...] We believe the removal of such objects is a theft from the dead. [...] It is a testament to the significance of the burial ritual. It is a demonstration of the humanity of the people who produced the art and wanted their deceased relatives to carry these objects into the spiritual world. [...] Together we must honor our ancestors and demonstrate to future generations our respect for the dignity of all our relatives. [Hill 1986b:8]

After my father developed cancer, he changed his thinking about the hair combs and began to carve his versions of hair combs. I think that he felt closer to those ancestors as he faced his own demise. It also spoke to the comfort and connection created by making and sharing such works of art. We can only wonder what the people who used or wore these combs felt as the teeth of the comb slid into their hair.

All this came rushing back to me when I saw the PowerPoints and read the essays by the archaeologists for this publication. Especially when I saw the hair comb from Teiaiagon (Theyagon). This comb at first looks mysterious. A man emerging from the back of a long-tailed creature. The likely panther also seems to be emerging out of his own body, and if the comb followed Seneca artistic convention of the time, it likely had a second panther head meeting above the head of the human figure, as recreated in the text by Ron Williamson and Robert von Bitter.

At first, we tend to think of the Anishinaabe underwater panther, especially since this panther's body mimics known Anishinaabe depictions of it. As George Hamell has shown, the Haudenosaunee also have a panther in our oral and artistic legacy. It intrigues me how the artist who made this comb uses both positive and negative spaces to bring the figures into relationship. The human figure, represented by an hourglass form with arms and head, recalls the ways that humans are depicted in wampum belts as a symbol of unity, with the arms interlocked with the creature. This represents the sharing of power and spirit.

My wife, Chandra Maracle, has been intensely studying the Haudenosaunee Creation Story as collected by J. N. B. Hewitt, my great-uncle on my mother's side of the family. In one version of the story, a Sky Panther is a Trickster figure who transforms into a young, handsome, athletic lacrosse player, trying to win the heart of the soon-to-be Sky Woman. In talking to him, even though she rejected his advances, she gets cast from the Sky World by her jealous, older "husband."

The Sky Panther then tries to make it up to her as she is falling through space and gives her things that she will need to survive on the soon-to-be-made Turtle Island. These "gifts" were a corn seed to plant, a corn pounder to process the corn, a bundle of kindling to make a fire to cook the corn, and a clay pot in which to cook it. This is what I think about when I look at this comb. Not a panther as a life taker, whose tail creates waves to upset canoes and drowns humans whom he likes to devour, but a panther as a life giver. A human is in the moment of transformation from the panther. But that is my speculation on meaning. It is what I need to draw from this at this moment in my life.

Teiaiagon was strategically placed to watch over movements on the lake, and to guard the mouth of the Humber River, the Toronto Carrying Place, which had been in use for centuries. My ancestors wanted an early-warning system in case the French attempted an end run to invade our territory or bypass our commercial trade routes, upon which we were the toll takers. The other hair combs from those communities show intimate connections to their homelands to the south, thus showing that they carried their worldview with them to the north.

We do not know how they were impacted by their experiences there, which only lasted for a generation or two. However, the few objects that they left behind that have resurfaced speak across the generations. The artistic intention and the science of archaeology have combined to give us a chance to reflect on meaning. For that I am thankful.

References Cited

7th Town Historical Society
1984 7th Town/Ameliasburgh Township: Past and Present. County Magazine Printshop, Bloomfield, Ontario.

Abel, Timothy J.
2019 New Radiocarbon Dates for the Iroquoian Occupation of Northern New York. Archaeology of Eastern North America 47:23–28.

Abel, Timothy J., Jessica L. Vavrasek, and John P. Hart
2019 Radiocarbon Dating the Iroquoian Occupation of Northern New York. American Antiquity 84:748–761.

Adams, Nicholas
1986 Iroquois Settlement at Fort Frontenac in the Seventeenth and Early Eighteenth Centuries. Ontario Archaeology 46:5–20.
2003 The Arbor Ridge Site: A Study in Settlement Dynamics and Population Movement During the Fifteenth Century at the Eastern End of Lake Ontario. Master's thesis, School of Archaeology and Ancient History, University of Leicester, U.K.

Allen, Kathleen
1992 Iroquois Ceramic Production: A Case Study of Household-Level Organization. In *Ceramic Production and Distribution: An Integrated Approach*, edited by George J. Bey III and Christopher A. Pool, pp. 133–154. Westview Press, Boulder, Colorado.

Anciens Élèves du Collège de Montréal
1930 Une mission éphémère, Kenté. *Bulletin de l'Association des Anciens Élèves du Collège de Montréal* 20:1–50.

Aquila, Richard
1983 *The Iroquois Restoration: Iroquois Diplomacy on the Colonial Frontier, 1701–1754*. Wayne State University Press, Detroit, Michigan.

Archaeological Assessments Ltd.
2003 Report on the 1991 Ministry of Transportation Stage 4 Excavation of the Dewar Site (AgHa-55), Highway 54, Seneca Township, Regional Municipality of Haldimand-Norfolk. Report on file at the Ontario Ministry of Heritage, Sport, Tourism and Culture Industries, Toronto, Ontario.

Archaeological Services Inc. (ASI)
2006 *Archaeological Monitoring of Natural Gas Laterals Installation/Repair and Associated Works and Stage 4 Archaeological Investigation of Burial 1 at 23 Baby Point Crescent, within the Archaeologically Sensitive Area of Baby Point (AjGu-6), in the City of Toronto*. Submitted to City of Toronto, Culture Division, Heritage Preservation Services.
2007 *Archaeological Monitoring of Natural Gas Laterals Installation/Repair and Associated Works and Stage 4 Archaeological Investigation of Burial 1 at 23 Baby Point Crescent, within the Archaeologically Sensitive Area of Baby Point (AjGu-6), in the City of*

Toronto. Report on file at the Ontario Ministry of Heritage, Sport, Tourism and Culture Industries, Toronto, Ontario.

2009 *Southeast Collector Recreational Enhancements, East Branch of the Toronto Carrying Place: An Historical Overview*. Report on file at the Ontario Ministry of Heritage, Sport, Tourism and Culture Industries, Toronto, Ontario.

2016 *City of Toronto Archaeological Management Plan Background Research Report: The Archaeology and History of Teiaiagon, Baby Point*. Manuscript on file, Archaeological Services Inc., Toronto, Ontario.

Archéotec

2007 *Île-aux-Tourtes: BiFl-5 Site: Archaeological Intervention of 2006*. Report on file at the ministère de la Culture et des Communications, Québec.

Archives du Séminaire de Saint-Sulpice de Montréal

1679 C133 86 Dossier 4, 5 October 1679. Bail . . . entre Mathieu Ranuyer, p.s.s. économe du séminaire de Montréal et Pierre Chartier, François Tardival et Abraham Botté de la terre et l'habitation de Quenté en Ontario. Copie collationée par Antoine Adhémar et Pierre Raimbault, le 18 juillet 1702.

Assikinack, Francis

1858 Social and Warlike Customs of the Odahwah Indians. *Canadian Journal of Industry, Science and Art* 3:297–309.

Austin, Shaun J.

1995 The Toronto Carrying-Place Trail Today. *Profile* 14(1):1–12.

Baker, Jonathan D.

2009 Prehistoric Bone Grease Production in Wisconsin's Driftless Area: A Review of the Evidence and Its Implications. Master's thesis, Department of Anthropology, University of Tennessee, Knoxville, Tennessee.

Bathurst, Rhonda

2008 *Bead Hill: Osteological Analysis Report*. Manuscript on file, Department of Anthropology, University of Toronto, Toronto, Ontario.

Beales, Eric

2013 A Critical Analysis of the Adoption of Maize in Southern Ontario and Its Spatial, Demographic, and Ecological Signatures. Master's thesis, Department of Anthropology, Trent University, Peterborough, Ontario.

Beauchamp, William M.

1901 *Wampum and Shell Articles Used by the New York Indians*. The New York State Museum Bulletin Vol. 8, No. 41. University of the State of New York, Albany.

1903 *Metallic Ornaments of the New York Indians*. The New York State Museum Bulletin Vol. 55. University of the State of New York, Albany, New York.

Beaudoin, Matthew

2019 *Challenging Colonial Narratives: Nineteenth-Century Great Lakes Archaeology*. University of Arizona Press, Tucson, Arizona.

Benn, Carl

2018 Fort Rouillé an Outpost of French Diplomacy and Trade. *The Fife and Drum* 22(1):1–2, 10–13.

Bennett, Monte R.
1973 The Moot Site (Sullivans), OND 3–4. *Bulletin of the Chenango Chapter of the New York State Archaeological Association* 14(1):1–20.
1982 A Salvage Burial Excavation on the Lanz-Hogan Site, OND 2–4. *Bulletin of the Chenango Chapter of the New York State Archaeological Association* 19(4): 1–25.
1983 Glass Trade Beads from Central New York. In *Proceedings of the 1982 Glass Trade Bead Conference*, edited by Charles F. Hayes III, pp. 51–58. Research Records No. 16. Rochester Museum & Science Center, Rochester, New York.
1984 The Stone Quarry Site (MSV 4–2): A Mid-Seventeenth Century Oneida Iroquois Station in Central New York. *Bulletin of the Chenango Chapter of the New York State Archaeological Association* 21(2): 1–35.
1988 The Primes Hill Site, MSV 5–2: An Eighteenth-Century Oneida Station. *Bulletin of the Chenango Chapter of the New York State Archaeological Association* 22(4):1–21.

Bennett, Monte R., and Richard Cole
1974 The Upper Hogan Site, OND 5–4. *Bulletin of the Chenango Chapter of the New York State Archaeological Association* 15(2):1–24.

Bennett, Monte R., and Anthony Wonderley
forth- An Overview of Oneida Archaeology. In *The Archaeology of New York State,*
coming *Revisited,* edited by Susan Maguire and Lisa Anselmi. New York State Museum Bulletin. New York State Museum, Albany.

Bergseth, Amy Dianne
2008 "Reversing the Gaze" with Early Native American Visual Imagery. Undergraduate thesis, Department of History, Miami University, Oxford, Ohio.

Bernou, Claude
1680 Carte des Grands Lacs. https://mdl.library.utoronto.ca/collections/scanned-maps/carte-des-grands-lacs.

Biggar, Henry P. (editor)
1922– *The Works of Samuel de Champlain.* 6 vols. Champlain Society, Toronto,
1936   Ontario.

Birch, Jennifer
2015 Current Research on the Historical Development of Northern Iroquoian Societies. *Journal of Archaeological Research* 23(3):263–323.

Birch, Jennifer, and John P. Hart
2018 Social Networks and Northern Iroquoian Confederacy Dynamics. *American Antiquity* 83:13–33.

Birch, Jennifer, Sturt W. Manning, Samantha Sanft, and Megan Anne Conger
2021 Refined Radiocarbon Chronologies for Northern Iroquoian Site Sequences: Implications for Coalescence, Conflict, and the Reception of European Goods. *American Antiquity* 86:61–89.

Birch, Jennifer, and Ronald F. Williamson
2013 *The Mantle Site: An Archaeological History of an Ancestral Wendat Community.* AltaMira Press, Lanham, Maryland.

2015 Navigating Ancestral Landscapes in the Northern Iroquoian World. *Journal of Anthropological Archaeology* 39:139–150.

2018 Initial Northern Iroquoian Coalescence. In *The Archaeology of Villages in Eastern North America*, edited by Jennifer Birch and Victor Thompson, pp. 89–105. University Press of Florida, Gainesville, Florida.

Birmingham, Robert A., and Carol I. Mason

2017 Iconographic ("Jesuit") and Other Rings. In *La Belle: The Archaeology of a Seventeenth-Century Ship of New World Colonization*, edited by James E. Bruseth, Amy A. Borgens, Bradford M. Jones, and Eric Ray, pp. 531–541. Texas A&M Press, College Station, Texas.

Bishop, Charles A.

1981 Territorial Groups Before 1821: Cree and Ojibwa. In *Subarctic*, edited by June Helm, pp. 158–160. Handbook of North American Indians, Vol. 6, William C. Sturtevant, general editor, Smithsonian Institution, Washington, D.C.

Blair, Emma Helen (editor)

1911 *The Indian Tribes of the Upper Mississippi Valley and Region of the Great Lake.* 2 vols. A. H. Clark, Cleveland, Ohio.

Bohaker, Heidi

2006 Nindoodemag: Anishinaabe Identities in the Eastern Great Lakes Region, 1600 to 1900. PhD dissertation, Department of History, University of Toronto, Toronto, Ontario.

Bouchette, J., and W. Faden (cartographers)

1815 Composite of Map of the Provinces of Upper and Lower Canada with the Adjacent parts of the United States of America. David Rumsey Map Collection, Image No. 4431014—MU 2041, Archives of Ontario, North York, Ontario.

Boyle, David

1888 Archaeological Report. In *Annual Report of the Canadian Institute, Session 1886–87: Being Part of Appendix to the Report of the Minister of Education, Ontario, 1887.* Warwick and Sons, Toronto, Ontario.

1889 Archaeological Report. In *Annual Report of the Canadian Institute, Session, 1888–9: Being Part of Appendix to the Report of the Minister of Education, Ontario, 1888.* Warwick and Sons, Toronto, Ontario.

1891 Archaeological Report. In *Fourth Annual Report of the Canadian Institute (Session 1890–91): Being Part of Appendix to the Report of the Minister of Education, Ontario*, pp. 57–58. Warwick and Sons, Toronto, Ontario.

1895 *Notes on Primitive Man in Ontario, Being an Appendix to the Report of the Minister of Education for Ontario.* Warwick Bros. and Rutter, Toronto, Ontario.

1897 *Annual Archaeological Report 1896–97: Being Part of the Report of the Minister of Education Ontario*, p. 48. Warwick Bros. and Rutter, Toronto, Ontario.

1898 *Archaeological Report 1898: Being Part of Appendix to the Report of the Minister of Education Ontario*, pp. 5–43. Warwick Bros. and Rutter, Toronto, Ontario.

1904 *Annual Archaeological Report 1903: Being Part of Appendix to the Report of the Minister of Education Ontario*, pp. 87–88. L. K. Cameron, Toronto, Ontario.

1908   *Annual Archaeological Report, 1907: Being Part of Appendix to the Report of the Minister of Education, Ontario, 1908.* Legislative Assembly of Ontario, Toronto, Ontario.

Boyle, David (editor)
1896   *The Township of Scarboro 1796–1896.* William Briggs, Toronto, Ontario.

Bradley, James W.
1987   *Evolution of the Onondaga Iroquois: Accommodating Change 1500–1655.* Syracuse University Press, Syracuse, New York.
2011   Re-visiting Wampum and Other Seventeenth-Century Shell Games. *Archaeology of Eastern North America* 39:25–51.
2020   *Onondaga and Empire: An Iroquoian People in an Imperial Era.* New York State Museum Bulletin No. 514. New York State Museum, Albany, New York.

Brambilla, Chiara
2015   Exploring the Critical Potential of the Borderscapes Concept. *Geopolitics* 20(1):14–34.

Brandão, José A.
1997   *"Your Fyres Shall Burn No More": Iroquois Policy Toward New France and Its Native Allies to 1701.* University of Nebraska Press, Lincoln, Nebraska.
2020   Competing Pasts: Narratives of Haudenosaunee Warfare in Ontario During the 1600s. *The Fife and Drum* [newsletter of The Friends of Fort York and Garrison Common] 24(2):1–8.

Brandão, José A., and William A. Starna
1996   The Treaties of 1701: A Triumph of Iroquois Diplomacy. *Ethnohistory* 43(2):209–244.

Braun, Gregory Vincent
2012   Petrography as a Technique for Investigating Iroquoian Smoking Rituals. *Journal of Archaeological Science* 39(1):1–10.
2015   Ritual, Materiality, and Memory in an Iroquoian Village. PhD dissertation, Department of Anthropology, University of Toronto, Toronto, Ontario.

Breithaupt, William H.
1920   President's Message. In *Eighth Annual Report of the Waterloo Historical Society*, pp. 108–111.

Bridges, Dusti C.
2020   Investigation of the Palisade Locus, White Springs Site (1688–1715), Geneva, N.Y. Manuscript on file, Department of Anthropology, Cornell University, Ithaca, New York.

Bridges, Dusti C., and Kurt A. Jordan
2019   Toward a Household Archaeology of the Onöndowa'ga:' (Seneca Iroquois) White Springs Site, circa 1688–1715 CE. Paper presented at the 84th Annual Meeting of the Society for American Archaeology, Albuquerque, New Mexico.

Brouwer, Joachim
2018   Speculations on the Seneca Outpost of Tinawatawa. *Ontario Professional Surveyor* 61(2):28–30.

Brown, D.
1983   *Fort Rouillé Excavation, Summer 1982.* Learnxs Press, Toronto, Ontario.

Brown, William
1849   *America: A Four Years' Residence in the United States and Canada.* Kemplay and Boland, Leeds, U.K.

Browne, John O. (cartographer)
1851   Map of the Township of York. Series 443, File 40. City of Toronto Archives, Toronto, Ontario.

Calnan, Marion Mikel, Peggy Dymond Leavey, and Julia Rowe Sager
1987   *Gunshot and Gleanings of the Historic Carrying Place, Bay of Quinte.* 7th Town Historical Society, Ameliasburgh, Ontario.

Cameron, Catherine M., Paul Kelton, and Alan C. Swedlund (editors)
2015   *Beyond Germs: Native Depopulation in North America.* University of Arizona Press, Tucson, Arizona.

Canniff, William
1869   *History of the Settlement of Upper Canada (Ontario,) with Special Reference to the Bay of Quinte District.* Dudley & Burns, Toronto, Ontario.

Carruthers, Peter J.
2014   Preliminary Excavations at Sainte Marie II. *Ontario Archaeology* 94:114–141.

Ceci, Lynn
1988   Tracing Wampum's Origins: Shell Bead Evidence from Archaeological Sites in Western and Coastal New York. In *Proceedings of the Shell Bead Conference*, edited by Charles Hayes III and Lynn Ceci, pp. 63–80. Research Records No. 20. Rochester Museum & Science Center, Rochester, New York.

Census of Canada
1881   Statistics Canada Fonds, Record Group 31-C-1. LAC microfilm C-13162 to C-13286. Library and Archives Canada, Ottawa. http://www.bac-lac.gc.ca/eng/census/1881/Pages/About-census.aspxl.

Chartrand, René
2005   *French Fortresses in North America 1535–1763.* Osprey Publishing, Oxford, U.K.

Chaussegros de Léry, Gaspard Joseph
1726   Carte du Lac Ontario et de la Rivière jusques au-delà de L'Isle de Montréal. Département Cartes et plans, Bibliothèque nationale de France, Paris. http://gallica.bnf.fr/ark:/12148/btv1b59689479?rk=21459;2.

Clark, Arthur J.
1916   Archaeological fieldnotes. A. J. Clark papers, National Museum of History, Gatineau, Québec.

Clark, Douglas, and Allen Owen
1976   Excavations on the Cody Site. *Bulletin of the Chenango Chapter of the New York State Archaeological Association* 16(3):1–7.

Clark, John
2003 Baby, James. *Dictionary of Canadian Biography*, Vol. 6. University of Toronto/ Université Laval, http://www.biographi.ca/en/bio/baby_james_6E.html, accessed February 11, 2020.

Clarke, Peter Doyentate
1870 *Origin and Traditional History of the Wyandotts and Sketches of Other Indian Tribes of North America*. Hunter, Rose & Co., Toronto, Ontario.

Cleland, Charles E.
1992 *Rites of Conquest: The History and Culture of Michigan's Native Americans*. University of Michigan Press, Ann Arbor, Michigan.

Cleland, Charles E. (editor)
1971 *The Lasanen Site: An Historic Burial Locality in Mackinac County, Michigan*. Anthropological Series Vol. 1, No. 1. Michigan State University Museum, East Lansing, Michigan.

Connors, Dennis J., Gordon C. DeAngelo, and Peter P. Pratt
1980 *The Search for the Jesuit Mission of Ste. Marie de Gannentaha*. Manuscript on file, Office of Museums and Historic Sites, County of Onondaga Department of Parks and Recreation, Liverpool, New York.

Cooper, John Irwin
1978 *Ontario's First Century 1610–1713*. The Lawrence Lande Foundation, McGill University, Montréal, Québec.

Cooper, Martin S.
2007 *Pickering Burials*. Manuscript on file, Archaeological Services Inc., Toronto, and D. R. Poulton & Associates Inc., London, Ontario.
2020 Neutrals on the Frontier: History and Ecology of the Lake Erie Hatiwendaronk. PhD dissertation, Department of Anthropology, University of Toronto, Toronto, Ontario.

Copway, George
1850 *The Traditional History and Characteristic Sketches of the Ojibway Nation*. Charles Gilpin, London, U.K.

Cottam, S. Barry
2003 White, Aubrey. *Dictionary of Canadian Biography*, Vol. 14. University of Toronto/ Université Laval, http://www.biographi.ca/en/bio/white_aubrey_14E.html, accessed March 11, 2020.

Cowin, Verna L.
2000 Shell Ornaments from Cayuga County, New York. *Archaeology of Eastern North America* 28:1–14.

Coyne, James (translator and editor)
1903 *Exploration of the Great Lakes 1669–1670 by Dollier de Casson and De Bréhant de Galinée: Galinée's Narrative and Map*. Ontario Historical Society Papers and Records, Vol. 4. Ontario Historical Society, Toronto, Ontario.

Creese, John L.
2017 Beyond Representation: Indigenous Economies of Affect in the Northeast Woodlands. In *Foreign Objects: Rethinking Indigenous Consumption in American Archaeology*, edited by Craig N. Cipolla, pp. 59–79. University of Arizona Press, Tucson, Arizona.

Curtis, Jenneth E., and Martha A. Latta
2000 Ceramics as Reflectors of Social Relationship: The Auger Site and Ball Site Castellations. *Ontario Archaeology* 70:1–15.

Cushman, David
1986 A Description and Analysis of the Jackson-Everson Excavations. In *The Mohawk Valley Project: 1983 Jackson-Everson*, edited by Robert D. Kuhn and Dean R. Snow, pp. 67–74. Institute for Northeast Anthropology, State University of New York, Albany.

D'Allemtejo, Rafaella
2003 Historical Paternosters and Rosaries. https://docplayer.net/29176303-Historical-paternosters-and-rosaries-by-mestra-rafaella-d-allemtejo-ol-november-a-s-xxxviii-2003.html, accessed January 13, 2020.

Davis, Nancy
1988 Conservation of Archaeological Shell Artifacts. In *Proceedings of the 1986 Shell Bead Conference*, edited by Charles F. Hayes and Lynn Ceci, pp. 13–16. Research Records No. 20. Rochester Museum & Science Center, Rochester, New York.

de Belmont, François V.
1840 *Histoire de l'eau-de-vie en Canada*. Quebec Library and Historical Society, Québec.

de Casson, François Dollier
1871 *Histoire du Montréal, 1640–1672*. Eusebe Senécal, Montréal, Québec.
1928 *A History of Montreal: 1640–1672*, translated by Ralph Flenley. J. M. Dent & Sons, Toronto, Ontario.

de Denonville, Marquis
1855 Expedition of M. de Denonville Against the Senecas. Memoir of the Voyage
[1687] and Expedition of the Marquis de Denonville, pursuant to the King's orders, against the Senecas, enemies of the Colony; By the same M. de Denonville. October. In *Documents Relative to the Colonial History of the State of New-York: Procured in Holland, England and France*, Vol. 9, edited by Edmund B. O'Callaghan, pp. 358–369. Weed, Parsons and Company, Albany, New York.

Dean, Robert L.
1984 *Archaeological Investigations at Gannagaro State Historic Site, Victor, Ontario County, New York 1983–1984*. Submitted to New York State Office of Parks, Recreation and Historic Preservation by Dean and Barbour Associates, Environmental and Archaeological Services, Buffalo, New York.

Delisle, Guillaume (cartographer)
1703   Percy Robinson fond, F 1080—MU 2431, Archives of Ontario, Copy of manuscript from Public Archives of Canada, Map Division (July 6, 1938), Plle JJ75, Pièce 202, Public Archives of Canada, Map Division, Ottawa, Ontario.

Dening, Greg
1994   The Theatricality of Observing and Being Observed: Eighteenth-Century Europe "Discovers" the ? Century "Pacific." In *Implicit Understandings Observing, Reporting, and Reflecting on the Encounters between Europeans and Other Peoples in the Early Modern Era*, edited by Stuart Schwartz, pp. 451–483. Cambridge University Press, New York.
1997   Introduction: In Search of a Metaphor, Histories of Self. In *Through a Glass Darkly: Reflections on Personal Identity in Early America*, edited by Ronald Hoffman, Mechal Sobel, and Fredrika Teute, pp. 1–12. University of North Carolina Press, Chapel Hill, North Carolina.

DeOrio, Robert N.
1978   A Preliminary Sequence of the Historic Cayuga Nation within the Traditional Area, 1600–1740. *Beauchamp Chapter Newsletter* [New York State Archaeological Association] 9(4).

Dickason, Olive P.
1997   *Canada's First Nations: A History of Founding Peoples from Earliest Times*. 2nd ed. Oxford University Press, Oxford, U.K.

Disotell, Samuel R.
2021   An Analysis of Faunal Materials from the White Springs Site, a 17th–18th Century Seneca Town in Upstate New York. Master's thesis, Archaeology Program, Cornell University, Ithaca, New York.

Donaldson, William S., and Stanley Wortner
1995   The Hind Site and the Glacial Kame Burial Complex. *Ontario Archaeology* 59:5–95.

Dunnigan, Brian Leigh
2001   *A Frontier Metropolis: Picturing Early Detroit, 1701–1838*. Wayne State University Press, Detroit, Michigan.

Eastly, Sarah A.
2012   A Question of Faith: Jesuit Missions to the Seneca Iroquois as Viewed through Archaeological and Textual Records. Master's thesis, Archaeology Program, Cornell University, Ithaca, New York.

Eid, Leroy V.
1979   The Ojibwa-Iroquois War: The War the Five Nations Did Not Win. *Ethnohistory* 26(4):297–324.

Ellis, Chris J., Ian Kenyon, and Michael Spence
1990   The Archaic. In *The Archaeology of Southern Ontario to A.D. 1650*, edited by Chris J. Ellis and Neal Ferris, pp. 65–124. Occasional Publication No. 5. London Chapter, Ontario Archaeological Society, London, Ontario.

Engelbrecht, William
1995 The Case of the Disappearing Iroquoians: Early Contact Period Superpower Politics. *Northeast Anthropology* 50:35–59.
2003 *Iroquoia: Development of a Native World*. Syracuse University Press, Syracuse, New York.
2007 Iroquois Ceramics with Appliqué Collar. Manuscript on file, Archaeological Services Inc., Toronto, Ontario.

Esarey, Duane E.
2013 Another Kind of Beads: A Forgotten Industry of the North American Colonial Period. PhD dissertation, Department of Anthropology, University of North Carolina, Chapel Hill, North Carolina.

Fenton, William N.
1978 Northern Iroquoian Culture Patterns. In *Northeast*, edited by Bruce G. Trigger, pp. 296–321. Handbook of North American Indians, Vol. 15, William C. Sturtevant, general editor, Smithsonian Institution, Washington, D.C.
1998 *The Great Law and the Longhouse: A Political History of the Iroquois Confederacy*. University of Oklahoma Press, Norman, Oklahoma.

Ferris, Neal
1986 Beyond the Frontier: An Early Historic Trade Axe from Kent County. *Kewa* [newsletter of the London Chapter of the Ontario Archaeological Society] 86(7):19–23.
2006 In Their Time: Archaeological Histories of Native-Lived Contacts and Colonialisms in Southwestern Ontario AD 1400–1900. PhD dissertation, Department of Anthropology, McMaster University, Hamilton, Ontario.
2009 *The Archaeology of Native-Lived Colonialism: Challenging History in the Great Lakes*. University of Arizona Press, Tucson, Arizona.
2014 Being Iroquoian, Being Iroquois: A Thousand Year Heritage of Becoming. In *Rethinking Colonial Pasts through Archaeology*, edited by Neal Ferris, Rodney Harrison, and Michael Wilcox, pp. 371–395. Oxford University Press, Oxford, U.K.

Ferris, Neal, William Fox, and Carl Murphy
1990 A Late Wolf Phase Occupation at the Libby-Miller Site, Wallaceburg, Ontario. *Kewa* [newsletter of the London Chapter of the Ontario Archaeological Society] 90(3):3–9.

Ferris, Neal, Ian Kenyon, Rosemary Prevec, and Carl Murphy
1985 Bellamy: A Late Historic Ojibwa Habitation. *Ontario Archaeology* 44:3–22.

Ferris, Neal, and Michael Spence
1995 The Woodland Traditions of Southern Ontario. *Revista de Arqueología Americana* 9:83–138.

Finlayson, William
1998 *Iroquoian Peoples of the Land of Rocks and Water, A.D. 1000–1650: A Study in Settlement Archaeology*. 4 vols. London Museum of Archaeology Special Publication No. 1. University of Western Ontario, London, Ontario.

Fisher, Sidney T.
1985   *The Merchant Millers of the Humber Valley: A Study of the Early Economy of Canada.* N.C. Press, Toronto, Ontario.

Fitzgerald, William R.
1982   *Lest the Beaver Run Loose: The Early 17th Century Christianson Site and Trends in Historic Neutral Archaeology.* Mercury Series, Archaeological Survey of Canada Paper No. 111. National Museum of Man, Ottawa, Ontario.
1983   Further Comments on the Neutral Glass Bead Sequence. *Arch Notes* [newsletter of the Ontario Archaeological Society] 83(1):17–25.
1990   Chronology to Culture Process: Lower Great Lakes Archaeology, 1500–1650. PhD dissertation, Department of Anthropology, McGill University, Montréal, Québec.

Fitzgerald, William R., Dean H. Knight, and Paul A. Lennox
1994   Catholic Devotional Items from 17th Century Ontario Archaeological Sites. *Arch Notes* [newsletter of the Ontario Archaeological Society] 94(2):9–19.

Fitzgerald, William R., and Peter G. Ramsden
1988   Copper Based Metal Testing as an Aid to Understanding Early European-Amerindian Interaction: Scratching the Surface. *Canadian Journal of Archaeology / Journal canadien d'archéologie* 12:153–161.

Foster, Gary
1990   *The Wolfe Creek Site AcHm-3: A Prehistoric Neutral Frontier Community in Southwestern Ontario.* Monographs in Ontario Archaeology No. 3. Ontario Archaeological Society, Toronto, Ontario.

Fox, William A.
1971   A French Gunflint from an Historic Petun site. Manuscript on file, Archaeological Services Inc., Toronto, Ontario.
1980   Miskwo Sinnee Munnidominug. *Archaeology of Eastern North America* 8:88–98.
1992   Odawa Lithic Procurement and Exchange: A History Carved in Stone. *Archeologiques* 6:52–58.
2002   Thaniba Wakondagi Among the Ontario Iroquois. *Canadian Journal of Archaeology / Journal canadien d'archéologie* 26(2):130–151.
2009   Events as Seen from the North: The Iroquois and Colonial Slavery. In *Mapping the Mississippian Shatter Zone: The Colonial Indian Slave Trade and Regional Instability in the American South,* edited by Robbie Ethridge and Sheri M. Shuck-Hall, pp. 63–80. University of Nebraska Press, Lincoln, Nebraska.
2013a   The Old Sites Project: An Update. *Kewa* [newsletter of the London Chapter of the Ontario Archaeological Society] (1):1–8.
2013b   The Old Sites Project. *Arch Notes* [newsletter of the Ontario Archaeological Society] 18(3):7–10.
2014   Lithics of the Ball Site. Manuscript on file, Department of Anthropology, Trent University, Peterborough, Toronto.
2020   Shell Beads Among the Neutral and Their Ancestors. *Kewa* [newsletter of the London Chapter of the Ontario Archaeological Society] 20 (1–3):2–12.

Fox, William A., and Charles Garrad
2004   Hurons in an Algonquian Land. *Ontario Archaeology* 77–78:121–134.

Fox, William A., Stan Wortner, Keith Henderson, and Neal Ferris
2018   Sixteenth Century Chatham, Ontario. Paper presented at the 45th Annual Symposium of the Ontario Archaeological Society, Chatham, Ontario.

Frost, Leslie M.
1973   *Forgotten Pathways of the Trent*. Burns & MacEachern, Don Mills, Ontario.

Galinée, René de Bréhant (cartographer)
1670a Carte du Lac Ontario et des habitations qui l'environnent ensemble le pays que M.M. Dollier et Galinée, missionnaires du Séminaire Saint-Sulpice ont parcouru. Reproduced as Map I.14 in R. Louis Gentilcore and C. Grant Head (editors), 1984, *Ontario's History in Maps*. University of Toronto Press, Toronto, Ontario.
1670b Untitled map. Percy Robinson fond, F1080—MU 2041, Archives of Ontario. Copy from Plle JJ75, Public Archives of Canada, Map Division, Ottawa, Ontario.

Garrad, Charles
1994   Three Jesuit Rings and a Medallion from Petunia. *Arch Notes* [newsletter of the Ontario Archaeological Society] 94(1):23–27.
2014   *Petun to Wyandot: The Ontario Petun from the Sixteenth Century*, edited by Jean-Luc Pilon and William A. Fox. Mercury Series No. 174. Canadian Museum of History, Gatineau, Canada, and University of Ottawa Press, Ottawa, Ontario.

Garrad, Charles, Tom Abler, and Larry Hancks
2003   On the Survival of the Neutrals. *Arch Notes* [newsletter of the Ontario Archaeological Society] 8(2):12–21.

Gehring, Charles, and William Starna (editors)
1988   *A Journey into Mohawk and Oneida Country, 1634–1635: The Journal of Harmen Meyndertsz van den Bogaert*. Syracuse University Press, Syracuse, New York.

Gentilcore, R. Louis, and C. Grant Head (editors)
1984   *Ontario's History in Maps*. University of Toronto Press, Toronto, Ontario.

Gerard-Little, Peregrine A.
2017   "A Pleasure Garden in the Desert, to Which I Know No Comparison in This Country": Seneca Iroquois Landscape Stewardship in the 17th and 18th Centuries. PhD dissertation, Department of Anthropology, Cornell University, Ithaca, New York.

Golder Associates Ltd.
2017   Revised Report: Stage 2 Archaeological Assessment, TransCanada Eastern Mainline Project MLV 134B to MLV 138A, Newcastle to Trenton. Report on file at the Ontario Ministry of Heritage, Sport, Tourism and Culture Industries, Toronto, Ontario.

Good, E. Reginald
1998   Colonizing a People: Mennonite Settlement in Waterloo Township. In *Earth, Water, Air and Fire: Studies in Canadian Ethnohistory*, edited by David T. McNab, pp. 145–180. Wilfrid Laurier University Press, Waterloo, Ontario.

Goodby, Robert G.
1998 Technical Patterning and Social Boundaries: Ceramic Variability in Southern New England, A.D. 1000–1675. In *The Archaeology of Social Boundaries*, edited by Miriam T. Stark, pp. 161–181. Smithsonian Institution Press, Washington, D.C.

Guillet, Edwin C.
1933 *Early Life in Upper Canada*. University of Toronto Press, Toronto, Ontario.

Hakas, D.
1967 Trent Valley Archaeological Survey. Manuscript on file, Department of Anthropology, Trent University, Peterborough, Ontario.

Hall, Robert
1997 *An Archaeology of the Soul: North American Indian Belief and Ritual*. University of Illinois Press, Chicago, Illinois.

Hamell, George R.
1979 Of Hockers, Diamonds and Hourglasses: Some Interpretations of Seneca Archaeological Art. Paper presented at the Conference on Iroquois Research, Albany, New York.
1980 Gannagaro State Historic Site: A Current Perspective. In *Studies on Iroquois Culture*, edited by Nancy Bonvillain, pp. 91–108. Occasional Publications in Northeastern Anthropology No. 6. Department of Anthropology, Franklin Pierce College, Rindge, New Hampshire.
1998 Long-Tail: The Panther in Huron-Wyandot and Seneca Myth, Ritual, and Material Culture. In *Icons of Power: Feline Symbolism in the Americas*, edited by Nicholas J. Saunders, pp. 258–291. Routledge, London and New York.
2012 Lord of the Manor: The American Indian Surveying His Domain. [Revised from 2003 original in February 2012.] Manuscript on file, Rochester Museum & Science Center, Rochester, New York.

Hamell, George R., and William A. Fox
2005 Rattlesnake Tales. *Ontario Archaeology* 79–80:127–149.

Hamell, George R., and Hazel Dean John
1987 Ethnology, Archeology, History and "Seneca Origins." Paper presented at the Conference on Iroquois Research, Rennselaerville, New York.

Hamilton, Michelle A.
2010 *Collections and Objections: Aboriginal Material Culture in Southern Ontario*. McGill-Queen's University Press, Kingston and Montréal, Canada.

Hancock, Ron G. V.
2013 European Glass Trade Beads in Northeastern North America. In *Modern Methods for Analysing Archaeological and Historical Glass*, edited by Koen Janssens, pp. 457–469. John Wiley & Sons, Chichester, U.K.

Hancock, Ron G. V., and Susan Aufreiter
1995 *Chemical Analysis of White Glass Trade Beads*. Manuscript on file, Ontario Heritage Trust, Toronto, Ontario.

Hancock, Ron G. V., A. Chafe, and Ian Kenyon
1994 Neutron Activation Analysis of Sixteenth- and Seventeenth-Century European Blue Glass Trade Beads from the Eastern Great Lakes Area of North America. *Archaeometry* 36(2):253–266.

Hancock, Ron G. V., Jon McKechnie, Susan Aufreiter, Karlis Karklins, Mima Kapches, Martha Sempowski, Jean-François Moreau, and Ian Kenyon
2000 Non-Destructive Analysis of European Cobalt Blue Glass Trade Beads. *Journal of Radioanalytical and Nuclear Chemistry* 244:567–573.

Harris, Cole R., and Geoffrey J. Matthews
1987 *Historical Atlas of Canada: I. From the Beginning to 1800*. University of Toronto Press, Toronto, Ontario.

Harris, David
2020 "It Will Enlighten the Public and Create a Greater Interest in Pre-historic Finds": The Life, Collection, and Museums of G. J. Chadd. *Ontario Archaeology* 100:102–118.

Havard, Gilles
2001 *The Great Peace of Montreal of 1701: French-Native Diplomacy in the Seventeenth Century*. Translated by Phyllis Aronoff and Howard Scott. McGill-Queen's University Press, Kingston and Montréal, Canada.

Hawkins, Alicia L.
2001 Genoa Frilled Pottery and the Problem of the Identification of the Wenro in Huronia. *Ontario Archaeology* 72:15–37.
2004 Recreating Home? A Consideration of Refugees, Microstyles and Frilled Pottery in Huronia. *Ontario Archaeology* 77–78:62–80.

Hawley, Charles
1879 *The Sulpitian Mission at Quinte Bay in Cayuga History: Jesuit Missions in Goi-O-Gouen, 1656–1684. Also an account of the Sulpitian Mission Among the Emigrant Cayugas About Quinte Bay in 1668*. Auburn, New York.

Hayes, Charles F., III
1980 An Overview of the Current Status of Seneca Ceramics. In *Proceedings of the 1979 Iroquois Pottery Conference*, edited by Charles F. Hayes III, George R. Hamell, and Barbara M. Koenig, pp. 87–93. Research Records No. 13. Rochester Museum & Science Center, Rochester, New York.
1988 An Introduction to the Shell and Shell Artifact Collection at the Rochester Museum & Science Center. In *Proceedings of the 1986 Shell Bead Conference*, edited by Charles F. Hayes and Lynn Ceci, pp. 37–43. Research Records No. 20. Rochester Museum & Science Center, Rochester, New York.

Hayes, Charles F., III, Daniel M. Barber, and George R. Hamell
1978 An Archaeological Survey of Gannagaro State Historic Site, Ontario County, New York: Archaeological Site Report. Rochester Museum & Science Center, Rochester, New York. Submitted to New York State Parks and Recreation Division for Historic Preservation.

Heidenreich, Conrad
1971 Huronia: A History and Geography of the Huron Indians, 1600–1650. McClelland and Stewart, Toronto, Ontario.
1978 Seventeenth-Century Maps of the Great Lakes: An Overview and Procedures for Analysis. *Archivaria* 6:83–112.
1980 Mapping the Great Lakes / The Period of Exploration, 1603–1700. *Cartographica* 17(3):32–64.
1987 French Exploration. In *Historical Atlas of Canada: I. From the Beginning to 1800*, edited by R. Cole Harris, Plate 36. University of Toronto Press, Toronto.
1988 An Analysis of the 17th Century Map "Nouvelle France." *Cartographica* 25(3):67–111.
1990 History of the St. Lawrence–Great Lakes Area to A.D. 1650. In *The Archaeology of Southern Ontario to A.D. 1650*, edited by Chris J. Ellis and Neal Ferris, pp. 475–492. Occasional Publication No. 5. London Chapter, Ontario Archaeological Society, London, Ontario.

Henderson, Robert
2005 *Every Trail Has a Story: Heritage Travel in Canada*. Dundurn Press, Toronto, Ontario.

Henderson, Robert, and James Bandow
2009 Watch Your Step: Where Was Tinawatawa? *Ontario Professional Surveyor* Summer:14–15.

Henry, Alexander
1969 *Travels and Adventures in Canada in the Indian Territories Between the Years 1760 and 1776*. Burt Franklin, New York.

Herrington, Walter S.
1913 *History of the County of Lennox and Addington*. MacMillan, Toronto, Ontario.

Hewitt, J. N. B.
1928 *Iroquoian Cosmology, Part 2*. Bureau of American Ethnology Annual Report No. 43, 1925/26. Smithsonian Institution, Washington, D.C.

Hill, Richard
1986a Seneca Art in Transition. *Turtle Quarterly* 1(1):4–6.
1986b Theft from the Dead. In *Art from Ganondagan, the Village of Peace*, edited by Ben Kroup, pp. 8. New York State Office of Parks, Recreation and Historic Preservation, Bureau of Historic Sites, Waterford.
2012 Hodinohso: ni Art Lesson 1. Manuscript on file, Deyohahá: ge: Indigenous Knowledge Centre, Six Nations of the Grand River, Brantford, Ontario.

Hill, Susan M.
2017 *The Clay We Are Made Of: Haudenosaunee Land Tenure on the Grand River*. University of Manitoba Press, Winnipeg, Manitoba.

Historic Horizon Inc. (HHI)
1999 Archaeological Assessment Report 49 Baby Point Crescent, Toronto, Ontario. Report on file at the City of Toronto Heritage Preservation Services and

Ontario Ministry of Heritage, Sport, Tourism and Culture Industries, Toronto, Ontario.
2001 Archaeological Mitigation Report, Baby Point IV Burial Site (AjGu-40), Toronto, Ontario. Report on file at the City of Toronto Heritage Preservation Services and Ontario Ministry of Heritage, Sport, Tourism and Culture Industries, Toronto, Ontario.

Holly, Donald H., Jr.
2019 Toward a Social Archaeology of Food for Hunters and Gatherers in Marginal Environments: A Case Study from the Eastern Subarctic of North America. *Journal of Archaeological Method and Theory* 26:1439–1469.

Home Smith and Co.
1914 The Humber Valley Surveys: Building Restrictions. Fonds 200, Series 724, Item 401v. City of Toronto Archives, Toronto, Ontario.

Hosbach, Richard E.
2004 Carlo I and Carlo II Coins Found on Two New York Iroquois Sites. In *A Passion for the Past: Papers in Honour of James F. Pendergast*, edited by James V. Wright and Jean-Luc Pilon, pp. 193–204. Mercury Series Archaeology Paper No. 164. Canadian Museum of Civilization, Gatineau, Québec.

Hosbach, Richard E., Stanford Gibson, Alexander Neill, Francis J. Hailey, and Gordon Ginther
2007 Firearms and Gun Accessories of the Oneida Dungey Site (MSV-6) with a Comparison of Similar Material on Other Mid-seventeenth Century Oneida and Iroquois Sites. *Bulletin of the Chenango Chapter of the New York State Archaeological Association* 30 (10A):1–40.

Hosbach, Richard E., Alexander B. Neill, Francis J. Hailey, Gerald L. Hayes, and Daryl E. Wonderly
2006 The Dungey Site (MSV-6): An Historic Oneida Village—A Short Longhouse. *Bulletin of the Chenango Chapter of the New York State Archaeological Association* 29(1):37–71.

Houghton, Frederick
1909 Report on Neuter Cemetery, Grand Island, N.Y. *Bulletin of the Buffalo Society of Natural Sciences* 9(3):376–385.
1912 The Seneca Nation from 1655 to 1687. *Bulletin of the Buffalo Society of Natural Sciences* 10(2):363–464.
1922 The Archaeology of the Genesee Country. *Researches and Transactions of the New York State Archaeological Association* 3(2):39–66.

Howey, Megan C. L.
2011 Colonial Encounters, European Kettles, and the Magic of Mimesis in the Late Sixteenth Century Indigenous Northeast and Great Lakes. *International Journal of Historical Archaeology* 15:329–357.
2017 Sympathetic Magic and Indigenous Consumption of Kettles During Early Colonial Encounters in the Northeast. In *Foreign Objects: Rethinking Indigenous*

Consumption in American Archaeology, edited by Craig N. Cipolla, pp. 162–183. University of Arizona Press, Tucson, Arizona.

Hunt, George T.
1940 The Wars of the Iroquois: A Study in Intertribal Trade Relations. University of Wisconsin Press, Madison, Wisconsin.

Hunter, J. Howard
1882 Central Ontario. In Picturesque Canada: The Country as It Was and Is, Vol. 2, edited by Monroe G. Grant, pp. 621–654. Belden Bros., Toronto, Ontario.

Hunter, James
1985 The Implications of Firearms Remains from Sainte-Marie Among the Hurons A.D. 1639–1649. In Proceedings of the 1984 Trade Gun Conference, Part II, edited by Charles F. Hayes III, pp. 1–7. Research Record No. 18. Rochester Museum & Science Center, Rochester, New York.

Ionico, Daniel
2018 The Products of Turbulent Times: Continuities and Change of 17th Century Neutral Iroquoian Ceramic Technology. Master's thesis, Department of Anthropology, McMaster University, Hamilton, Ontario.

Irwin, John
1978 Ontario's First Century: 1610–1713. Lawrence Lande Foundation, McGill University, Montréal, Québec.

Jackes, Mary
2008 The Mid Seventeenth Century Collapse of Iroquoian Ontario: Examining the Last Burial Place of the Neutral Nation. In Towards an Anthropology of Disasters, Proceedings of the 9th Valbonne Anthropology Days, edited by Luc Buchet, Catherine Rigeade, Isabelle Séguy, and Michel Signoli, pp. 347–373. APDCA, Antibes, France.

Jackson, Lawrence
1976 An Archaeological Survey of the Western Rice Lake Basin. Manuscript on file, Department of Anthropology, Trent University, Peterborough, Ontario.

Jacobs, Dean M., and Victor P. Lytwyn
2020 Naagan ge bezbig emkwaan: A Dish with One Spoon Reconsidered. Ontario History 112 (2):191–210.

Jaenen, Cornelius J. (editor)
1996 The French Regime in the Upper Country of Canada During the 17th Century. Champlain Society, Toronto, Ontario.

Jamison, Thomas R.
1998 Group Identity and Cluster Analysis: The Pen Site Cemetery, Jamesville, New York. Paper presented at the 38th Annual Meeting of the Northeastern Anthropological Association, Orono, Maine.

Jenkins, Tara
2016 Contexts, Needs and Social Messaging: Situating Iroquoian Human Bone Artifacts in Southern Ontario, Canada. In Theoretical Approaches to Analysis and

Interpretation of Commingled Human Remains, edited by Anna Osterholtz, pp. 139–184. Springer, New York.

Jennings, Francis
1984 *The Ambiguous Iroquois Empire: The Covenant Chain Confederation of Indian Tribes with English Colonies from Its Beginnings to the Lancaster Treaty of 1744*. W. W. Norton, New York.

Jezierski, John V.
1970 A 1751 Journal of Abbé François Picquet. *New York Historical Society Quarterly* 54:361–381.

Johnson, Leo A.
1973 *History of the County of Ontario, 1615–1875*. Hunter, Rose & Co., Toronto.

Johnston, Richard B., and Lawrence J. Jackson
1980 Settlement Pattern at the Le Caron Site, a 17th Century Huron Village. *Journal of Field Archaeology* 7(2):173–199.

Jolliet, Louis (?) (cartographer)
1673? Untitled map. 4044 B: No. 43, Service Hydrographique Bibliothèque, Paris. Reproduced in Percy Robinson, 1933, *Toronto During the French Regime*. Ryerson Press, Toronto, Ontario.
1674? Carte du Lac Ontario ou de Frontenac. GESH18PF124DIV9P12. Bibliothèque nationale de France, Département Cartes et plans, Paris, https://gallica.bnf.fr/ark:/12148/btv1b53016904s.

Jones, Eric E., and Sharon N. DeWitte
2012 Using Spatial Analysis to Estimate Depopulation for Native American Populations in Northeastern North America, AD 1616–1645. *Journal of Anthropological Archaeology* 31(1):83–92.

Jones, Peter
1860 *Life and Journals of Kah-ke-wa-quo-na-by: (Rev. Peter Jones), Wesleyan Missionary*. Wesleyan Printing Establishment, Toronto, Ontario, Ontario.
1861 History of the Ojebway Indians with Especial Reference to Their Conversion to Christianity. A.W. Bennett, London, U.K.

Jordan, Kurt A.
2004 Seneca Settlement Pattern, Community Structure, and Housing, 1677–1779. *Northeast Anthropology* 67:23–60.
2008 *The Seneca Restoration, 1715–1754: An Iroquois Local Political Economy*. University Press of Florida and Society for Historical Archaeology, Gainesville, Florida.
2009 Regional Diversity and Colonialism in Eighteenth Century Iroquoia. In *Iroquoian Archaeology and Analytic Scale*, edited by Laurie E. Miroff and Timothy D. Knapp, pp. 215–230. University of Tennessee Press, Knoxville, Tennessee.
2013 Incorporation and Colonization: Postcolumbian Iroquois Satellite Communities and Processes of Indigenous Autonomy. *American Anthropologist* 115(1):29–43.

2014 Enacting Gender and Kinship Around a Large Outdoor Fire Pit at the Seneca Iroquois Townley-Read Site, 1715–1754. *Historical Archaeology* 48(2):61–90.

2016 Categories in Motion: Emerging Perspectives in the Archaeology of Postcolumbian Indigenous Communities. *Historical Archaeology* 50(3):62–80.

2018a From Nucleated Villages to Dispersed Networks: Transformations in Seneca Haudenosaunee (Iroquois) Community Structure, circa AD 1669–1779. In *The Archaeology of Villages in Eastern North America*, edited by Jennifer Birch and Victor D. Thompson, pp. 174–191. University Press of Florida, Gainesville, Florida.

2018b Markers of Difference or Makers of Difference? Atypical Practices at Haudenosaunee (Iroquois) Satellite Sites, ca. 1650–1700. *Historical Archaeology* 52(1):12–29.

2022 Small and Under-Recorded Sites as Evidence for Gayogǫhó:nǫʔ (Cayuga) and Onöndowa'ga:' (Seneca) Regional Settlement Expansion, circa 1640–1690. In *Archaeologies of Indigenous Presence*, edited by Tsim D. Schneider and Lee M. Panich, pp. 242–264. University Press of Florida, Gainesville, Florida.

Jordan, Kurt A., and Peregrine A. Gerard-Little
2019 Neither Contact nor Colonial: Seneca Iroquois Local Political Economies, 1670–1754. In *Indigenous Persistence in the Colonized Americas: Material and Documentary Perspectives on Entanglement*, edited by Heather Law Pezzarossi and Russell N. Sheptak, pp. 39–56. University of New Mexico Press, Albuquerque, New Mexico.

Kane, Paul
1859 *Wanderings of an Artist Among the Indians of North America*. Charles E. Tuttle, Rutland, Vermont.

Kapches, Mima
1983 What the People Said: An Archaeological Exchange Revisited (98 Years Later). *Royal Ontario Museum Archaeological Newsletter* 213:1–4.
2013 Charles Augustus Hirschfelder (1857–1946): An Antiquarian from Toronto. *Ontario Archaeology* 93:214–218.

Karklins, Karlis
1974 Seventeenth Century Dutch Beads. *Historical Archaeology* 8(1):64–82.
1992 Facsimile of email 28 April 1992 to Dana R. Poulton, subject line entitled *Re: Bead Hill Artifact Update*. Manuscript on file, Parks Canada Service, Cornwall, and D. R. Poulton & Associates Inc., London, Ontario.
2012 Guide to the Description and Classification of Glass Beads Found in the Americas. *Beads: Journal of the Society of Bead Researchers* 24:62–90.

Karklins, Karlis, and Adelphine Bonneau
2019 Evidence of Early 17th-Century Glass Beadmaking in and Around Rouen, France. *Beads: Journal of the Society of Bead Researchers* 31:3–8.

Karklins, Karlis, Laure Dussubieux, and Ron G. V. Hancock
2015 A 17th-Century Glass Bead Factory at Hammersmith Embankment, London, England. *Beads: Journal of the Society of Bead Researchers* 27:16–24.

Kent, Barry C.
1984   *Susquehanna's Indians*. Anthropological Series No. 6. Pennsylvania Historical and Museum Commission, Harrisburg, Pennsylvania.

Kent, Donald H.
1974   *Iroquois Indians II: Historical Report on the Niagara River and the Niagara River Strip to 1759: Commission Findings of the Indian Claims Commission*. Garland Publishing, New York and London, U.K.

Kenyon, Ian T.
1985   A Preliminary Report on the Misner Cemetery Glass Beads. *Kewa* [newsletter of the London Chapter of the Ontario Archaeological Society] 85(5):14–20.

Kenyon, Ian T., and Neal Ferris
1984   Investigations at Mohawk Village, 1983. *Arch Notes* [newsletter of the Ontario Archaeological Society] 84(1):19–49.

Kenyon, Ian T., and William A. Fox
1982   The Grimsby Cemetery: A Second Look. *Kewa* [newsletter of the London Chapter of the Ontario Archaeological Society] 82(9):3–16.

Kenyon, Ian T., R. G. V. Hancock, and S. Aufreiter
1995   Neutron Activation Analysis of A.D. 1660–1930 European Copper-Colored Blue Glass Trade Beads from Ontario, Canada. *Archaeometry* 37(2):323–337.

Kenyon, Ian T., and Tim Kenyon
1983   Comments on Seventeenth Century Glass Trade Beads from Ontario. In *Proceedings of the 1982 Glass Trade Bead Conference*, edited by Charles F. Hayes III, pp. 59–74. Research Records No. 16. Rochester Museum & Science Center, Rochester, New York.

Kenyon, Walter A.
1977   Some Bones of Contention. *Rotunda* [newsletter of the Royal Ontario Museum] 10(3):4–13.
1982   *The Grimsby Site: A Historic Neutral Cemetery*. Royal Ontario Museum, Toronto, Ontario.
1986   *Mounds of Sacred Earth: Burial Mounds in Ontario*. Royal Ontario Museum, Toronto, Ontario.

Kidd, Kenneth E.
1949   *The Excavation of Ste Marie I*. University of Toronto Press, Toronto, Ontario.

Kidd, Kenneth E., and Martha A. Kidd
1970   A Classification System for Glass Beads for the Use of Field Archaeologists. In *Canadian Historic Sites Occasional Papers in Archaeology and History* No. 1, pp. 45–89, Ottawa, Ontario.

Killan, Gerald
1993   *Protected Places: A History of Ontario's Provincial Park System*. Dundurn Press, Toronto, Ontario.
2003   Kirkwood, Alexander. *Dictionary of Canadian Biography*, Vol. 13. University of Toronto / Université Laval, http://www.biographi.ca/en/bio/kirkwood_alexander_13E.html, accessed February 11, 2020.

Kinsey, W. Fred, III
1959   Historic Susquehannock Pottery. In *Susquehannock Miscellany,* edited by John Witthoft and W. Fred Kinsey, pp. 61–98. Pennsylvania Historical and Museum Commission, Harrisburg, Pennsylvania.

Konrad, Victor A.
1973   *The Archaeological Resources of the Metropolitan Toronto Planning Area: Inventory and Prospect.* Discussion Paper No. 10. Department of Geography, York University, Toronto, Ontario.
1974   Iroquois Villages on the North Shore of Lake Ontario 1665–1687. Paper presented at a Meeting of Ontario Historical Geographers, Ottawa, Ontario.
1981   An Iroquois Frontier: The North Shore of Lake Ontario During the Late Seventeenth Century. *Journal of Historical Geography* 7(2):129–144.
1987   The Iroquois Return to Their Homeland: Military Retreat or Cultural Adjustment. In *A Cultural Geography of North American Indians,* edited by Thomas Ross and Tyrel Moore, pp. 191–211. Westview Press, Boulder, Colorado.
2015   Toward a Theory of Borders in Motion. *Journal of Borderlands Studies* 30(1):1–18.

Konrad, Victor, and Emmanuel Brunet-Jailly
2019   Approaching Borders, Creating Borderland Spaces, and Exploring the Evolving Border between Canada and the United States. *The Canadian Geographer / Le Géographe canadien* 63(1):4–10.

Konrad, Victor, and William C. Noble
1986   Residual Soil Stain Definition of Historic Neutral House Plans. *The Canadian Geographer / Le Géographe canadien* 30(1):82–85.

Konrad, Victor, and William A. Ross
1980   An Archaeological Survey for the North Pickering Project. In *Three Heritage Studies,* edited by David Skene Melvin, pp. 65–107. Heritage Planning Study No. 5, Archaeological Research Report No. 14. Heritage Planning and Research Branch, Ontario Ministry of Culture and Recreation, Toronto, Ontario.

Krohn, Mathew R.
2010   Innovation and Identity in Seneca Iroquoian Lithic Debitage: Analysis of Stone Tools from the White Springs and Townley-Read Sites, circa 1688–1754. Master's thesis, Archaeology Program, Cornell University, Ithaca, New York.

Kroup, Ben A., Robert L. Dean, and Richard Hill
1986   *Art from Ganondagan: "The Village of Peace."* New York State Office of Parks, Recreation and Historic Preservation, Waterford, New York.

Kuhn, Robert D.
1986   Indications of Interaction and Acculturation through Ceramic Analysis. In *The Mohawk Valley Project: 1983 Jackson-Everson Excavations,* edited by Robert D. Kuhn and Dean R. Snow, pp. 75–92. Institute for Northeast Anthropology, State University of New York, Albany, New York.

1994 The Cromwell Site (NYSM 1121): Including a Brief Treatise on Early Seventeenth-Century Mohawk Pottery Trends. *The Bulletin* [journal of the New York State Archaeological Association] 108:29–38.

Kupfer, Carl, and David Buisseret
2019 Seventeenth-Century Jesuit Explorers' Maps of the Great Lakes and Their Influence on Subsequent Cartography of the Region. *Journal of Jesuit Studies* 6(1):57–70.

Kupperman, Karen Ordahl
2000 *Indians and English: Facing Off in Early America*. Cornell University Press, Ithaca, New York.

LaGrasta, Kaitlin R.
2021 "Binding the People Together": Onöndowa'ga:' (Seneca) Glass Beads, Aesthetics, and Economy, 1670–1754. Master's thesis, Archaeology Program, Cornell University, Ithaca, New York.

Lajeunesse, Ernest
1960 *The Windsor Border Region: Canada's Southernmost Frontier*. Champlain Society, Toronto, Ontario.

Lamontagne, Leopold
1958 The Quinte Mission. In *Royal Fort Frontenac*, edited and translated by Richard Preston and Leopold Lamontagne, pp. 3–16. Champlain Society, Toronto, Ontario.

Landon, Fred
1944 Lake Huron. In *The American Lake Series*, edited by Milo M. Quaife. Bobbs-Merril, New York.

Laprairie, Rick
2018 Toronto's Cartographic Birth Certificate Hiding in Plain Sight for 350 Years. *Ontario History* 110 (2):152–175.

Lauria, Lisa M.
2012 Defining Susquehannock: People and Ceramics in the Lower Susquehanna River Valley, AD 1575 to 1690. PhD dissertation, Department of Anthropology, University of Virginia, Charlottesville, Virginia.
2019 Public Kettles, Private Pots. In *The Susquehannocks: New Perspectives on Settlement and Cultural Identity*, edited by Paul Raber, pp. 91–115. Pennsylvania State University Press, University Park, Pennsylvania.

Lenig, Wayne
2020 Mohawk Community Relationships 1666–1779: An Archaeological Framework. Manuscript on file, Department of Anthropology, Cornell University, Ithaca, New York.

Lennox, Paul A.
1981 *The Hamilton Site: A Late Historic Neutral Town*. Mercury Series, Archaeological Survey of Canada Paper No. 103, pp. 211–403. National Museum of Man, Ottawa, Ontario.

1984 *The Hood Site: A Historic Neutral Town of 1640 A.D.* Mercury Series No. 121. National Museum of Man, Ottawa, Ontario.

Lennox, Paul A., and William R. Fitzgerald
1990 The Culture History and Archaeology of the Neutral Iroquoians. In *The Archaeology of Southern Ontario to A.D. 1650*, edited by Chris J. Ellis and Neal Ferris, pp. 405–456. Occasional Publication No. 5. London Chapter, Ontario Archaeological Society, London, Ontario.

Léouffre, Delphine, Tiziana Gallo, Chloe Lee-Hone, and Brad Loewen
2019 From Beads to Buttons: The Evolution of Worked Bone at Pointe-à-Callière, Montréal, 1642–1912. Poster presented at the 13th International Conference of the International Council for Archaeozoology, Ankara, Turkey.

Lesage, Louis, and Ronald F. Williamson
2020 When and Where Did the St. Lawrence Iroquoians and the North Shore of Lake Ontario Iroquoians Go and Why? The Huron-Wendat Perspective. *Ontario Archaeology* 100:34–61.

Lewis, Evan (cartographer)
1755 A General Map of the Middle British Colonies in America, viz Virginia, Mariland, Delaware, Pensilvania, New-Jersey, New-York, Connecticut and Rhode Island, of Aquanishuonigy, the Country of the Confederate Indians Comprehending Aquanishuonigy Proper, Their Place of Residence, Ohio and Tiiuxsoxruntie, Their Deer-Hunting Countries, Couxsaxrage and Skaniadarade, Their Beaver-Hunting Countries, of the Lakes Erie, Ontario and Champlain, and of Part of New-France, Wherein Is also Shewn the Antient and Present Seats of the Indian Nations. Bibliothèque nationale de France, Département Arsenal, EST-1504 (29).

Lizars, Kathleen M.
1913 *The Valley of the Humber, 1615–1913*. William Briggs, Toronto, Ontario.

Loewen, Brad
2019 Glass and Enamel Beadmaking in Normandy, 1590–1635. *Beads: Journal of the Society of Bead Researchers* 31:9–20.

Lovisek, Joan A. M.
1991 Ethnohistory of the Algonkian Speaking People of Georgian Bay: Precontact to 1850. PhD dissertation, Department of Anthropology, McMaster University, Hamilton, Ontario.

Lynch, James
1985 The Iroquois Confederacy and the Adoption and Administration of Non-Iroquoian Individuals and Groups Prior to 1756. *Man in the Northeast* 30:83–99.

Lytwyn, Victor P.
1997 A Dish with One Spoon: The Shared Hunting Grounds Agreement in the Great Lakes and St. Lawrence Valley Region. In *Papers of the 28th Algonquian Conference*, edited by D. Pentland, pp. 210–227. University of Manitoba, Winnipeg, Manitoba.

MacDonald, John
1991 The Neutral Freelton Village Site. *Kewa* [newsletter of the London Chapter of the Ontario Archaeological Society] 91(3):2–23.

MacLeod, D. Peter
1992 The Anishinabeg Point of View: The History of the Great Lakes Region to 1800 in Nineteenth Century Mississauga, Odawa and Ojibwa Historiography. *Canadian Historical Review* 73(2):194–210.

MacNeish, Richard S.
1952 *Iroquois Pottery Types: A Technique for the Study of Iroquois Prehistory*. Bulletin No. 124. National Museum of Canada, Ottawa, Ontario.

Mandzy, Adrian Oleh
1990 The Rogers Farm Site: A Seventeenth-Century Cayuga Site. *The Bulletin* [journal of the New York State Archaeological Association] 100:18–25.
1992 History of Cayuga Acculturation: An Examination of the 17th-century Cayuga Iroquois Archaeological Data. Master's thesis, Department of Anthropology, Michigan State University, East Lansing, Michigan.
1994 The Results of Interaction: Change in Cayuga Society During the Seventeenth Century. In *Proceedings of the 1992 People to People Conference*, edited by Charles F. Hayes III, Connie Cox Bodner, and Lorraine P. Saunders, pp. 133–156. Rochester Museum & Science Center, Rochester, New York.

Manning, Sturt W., Jennifer Birch, Megan Anne Conger, Michael W. Dee, Carol Griggs, and Carla S. Hadden
2019 Contact-Era Chronology-Building in Iroquoia: Age Estimates for Arendarhonon Sites and Implications for Identifying Champlain's Cahiagué. *American Antiquity* 84:684–707.

Manning, Sturt W., Jennifer Birch, Megan Anne Conger, Michael W. Dee, Carol Griggs, Carla S. Hadden, Alan G. Hogg, Christopher Bronk Ramsey, Samantha Sanft, Peter Steier, and Eva M. Wild
2018 Radiocarbon Re-dating of Contact-Era Iroquoian History in Northeastern North America. *Science Advances* 4(12): https://www.science.org/doi/10.1126/sciadv.aav0280.

Manning, Sturt W., and John P. Hart
2019 Radiocarbon, Bayesian Chronological Modeling and Early European Metal Circulation in the Sixteenth-Century AD Mohawk River Valley, U. S. A. *PLoS ONE* 14(12): https://journals.plos.org/plosone/article?id=10.1371/journal.pone.0226334.

Margry, Pierre (editor)
1879 *Découvertes et établissements des français dans l'ouest et dans le sud de l'Amérique Septentrionale 1614–1698,* Vol. 1. Maisonneuve, Paris, France.

Martelle, Holly
2002 Huron Potters and Archaeological Constructs: Researching Ceramic Micro-stylistics. PhD dissertation, Department of Anthropology, University of Toronto, Toronto, Ontario.

Mason, Carol I.
2003 Jesuit Rings, Jesuits, and Chronology. *Midcontinental Journal of Archaeology* 28(2):233–257.
2009 Iconographic ("Jesuit") Rings: A Case Study in Chronological Placement. In *Painting the Past with a Broad Brush: Papers in Honour of James Valliere Wright*, edited by David L. Keenlyside and Jean-Luc Pilon, pp. 371–391. Mercury Series No. 170. Canadian Museum of Civilization, Gatineau, Québec, and University of Ottawa Press, Ottawa, Ontario.
2010 Reading the Rings: Decoding Iconographic ("Jesuit") Rings. *Historical Archaeology* 44(2):8–13.

Mason, Carol I., and Kathleen Ehrhardt
2009 Iconographic (Jesuit) Rings in European/Native Exchange. *French Colonial History* 10:55–73.

Mason, Ronald J.
2006 *Inconsistent Companions: Archaeology and North American Indian Oral Traditions*. University of Alabama Press, Tuscaloosa, Alabama.

Mayer, Pihl, Poulton and Associates Inc. (MPPA)
1988 *The Archaeological Facility Master Plan Study of the Northeast Scarborough Study Area*. Report on file at the Ontario Ministry of Heritage, Sport, Tourism and Culture Industries, Toronto, Ontario.

Mayer, Poulton and Associates Inc. (MPA)
1991 *Report on the 1991 Excavations of the Bead Hill Site, City of Scarborough, Ontario*. Report on file at Canadian Parks Service, Cornwall and the Ontario Ministry of Heritage, Sport, Tourism and Culture Industries, Toronto, Ontario.

McIlwraith, Thomas F.
1998 *Looking for Old Ontario*. University of Toronto Press, Toronto, Ontario.

McKay, William A.
1961 *The Pickering Story*. The Township of Pickering Historical Society, Pickering, Ontario.

Mercier, Caroline
2011 "Jesuit" Rings in Trade Exchanges between France and New France: Contribution of a Technological Typology to Identifying Supply and Distributional Networks. *Northeast Historical Archaeology* 40(1):21–42.

Mohr, Thomas
1998 The Gandy Project: Locating the Historic Seneca Village of Gandatsketiagon. Manuscript on file, Toronto Region Conservation Authority, Toronto, Ontario.

Morgan, Lewis Henry
1962 *League of the Iroquois*. Citadel Press, Secaucus, New Jersey. Originally published
[1851] as *League of the Ho-De'-No-Sau-Nee or Iroquois*. Sage and Brother, Rochester, New York.

Morton, Ann
2010 Honeoye Falls #6 Road over Spring Brook, Monroe County, New York DOT PIN #4753.88, BIN #3317760: Phase IB Cultural Resource Survey. Fisher Associates. Submitted to Monroe County Department of Transportation, New York.

Nail, Thomas
2016 *Theory of the Border.* Oxford University Press, Oxford, U.K.

Nasmith Ramsden, Carol
1989 The Kirche Site: A 16th Century Huron Village in the Upper Trent Valley. Occasional Papers in Northeastern Archaeology No. 1. Copetown Press, Dundas, Ontario.

National Parks of Canada
1934 *The Lake Erie Cross Port Dover, Ontario.* National Parks of Canada, Historic Sites, Ottawa, Ontario.

Needs-Howarth, Suzanne
2008 Appendix A: Faunal Analysis: Analysis of Zooarchaeological Remains from the 2006 and 2007 Stage 4 Excavations at Fort Frontenac (Bbgc-8), Kingston, Ontario. In *Stage 4 Archaeological Mitigation Fort Frontenac Street Upgrading*, edited by Helen Sheldon, pp. 39–62. Report on file at the Ontario Ministry of Heritage, Sport, Tourism and Culture Industries, Toronto, Ontario.

Neill, Alexander B., Richard E. Hosbach, Francis J. Hailey, Gerald L. Hayes, and Daryl E. Wonderly
2006 The Dungey Site (MSV-6): An Historic Oneida Village—Iron Knives and Trade Axes. *Bulletin of the Chenango Chapter of the New York State Archaeological Association* 29(1):73–77.

New York State Division of Military and Naval Affairs
2012 Forts. https://dmna.ny.gov/forts/fortsindex.htm, accessed August 29, 2020.

Newman, David
2006 Borders and Bordering: Towards an Interdisciplinary Dialogue. *European Journal of Social Theory* 9(2):171–186.

Newman, David, and Annsi Paasi
1998 Fences and Neighbours in the Postmodern World: Boundary Narratives in Political Geography. *Progress in Human Geography* 22(2):186–207.

Nichols, John D.
1995 *The Ojibwe Peoples Dictionary.* University of Minnesota Department of American Indian Studies and University Libraries and the Minnesota Historical Society, https://ojibwe.lib.umn.edu/, accessed on May 5, 2020.

Niemczycki, Mary Ann Palmer
1984 *The Origin and Development of the Seneca and Cayuga Tribes of New York State.* Research Records No. 17. Rochester Museum & Science Center, Rochester, New York.

Noble, William
1978 The Neutral Indians. In *Essays in Northeastern Anthropology in Memory of Marian E. White*, edited by William E. Engelbrecht and Donald K. Grayson, pp. 152–164. Occasional Publications in Northeastern Anthropology No. 5. Department of Anthropology, Franklin Pierce College, Rindge, New Hampshire.
1984 Historic Neutral Iroquois Settlement Patterns. *Canadian Journal of Archaeology / Journal canadien d'archéologie* 8(1):3–27.
1985 Tsouharissen's Chiefdom: An Early Historic 17th Century Neutral Iroquoian Ranked Society. *Canadian Journal of Archaeology / Journal canadien d'archéologie* 9(2):131–146.

Northeastern Archaeological Associates
2010 Registrar's Special Investigation of Dr. Jack Hilton's House Foundation, Part Lot 1, Concession SECP, Ameliasburgh Township, Prince Edward County, Ontario RP 47R 760, Parts 1–5. Report on file at the Ontario Ministry of Heritage, Sport, Tourism and Culture Industries, Toronto, Ontario.

Norton, Thomas E.
1974 *The Fur Trade in Colonial New York, 1686–1776*. University of Wisconsin Press, Madison, Wisconsin.

O'Callaghan, Edmund B.
1850– *The Documentary History of the State of New York*, Vol. 1. Weed, Parsons and
1851 Company, Albany, New York.

O'Callaghan, Edmund B. (editor)
1853– *Documents Relative to the Colonial History of the State of New-York: Procured in*
1887 *Holland, England and France*. 15 vols. Weed, Parsons and Company, Albany, New York.

Omwake, H. Grieger
1969 White Kaolin Pipes from the Oscar Liebhart Site. In *Susquehannock Miscellany*, edited by John Witthoft and W. Fred Kinsey III, pp. 126–135. 2nd ed. The Pennsylvania Historical and Museum Commission, Harrisburg, Pennsylvania.

Ontario
1819 Otonabee Township Patent Map. Government of Ontario Record RG 1-100-0-0-1852. Archives of Ontario, Toronto, Ontario.

Orr, Rowland B.
1913 Additions to the Museum. In *Annual Archaeological Report, 1913: Being Part of Appendix to the Report of the Minister of Education, Ontario, 1913*, pp. 94–96. William Briggs, Toronto, Ontario.
1922 New Accessions to Museum, New Material. In *Thirty-Third Annual Archaeological Report 1921–22: Being Part of Appendix to the Report of the Minister of Education Ontario*, pp. 102–132. Clarkson W. James, Toronto, Ontario.
1925 New Materials. In *Thirty-Fifth Annual Archaeological Report 1924–1925: Being Part of Appendix to the Report of the Minister of Education Ontario*, pp. 114–123. The United Press Limited, Toronto, Ontario.
1928 Accessions to the Archaeological Collections. In *Thirty-Sixth Annual Archaeological Report, 1928, including 1926–1927: Being Part of Appendix to the Minister of*

Education, Ontario, 1928, pp. 78–79. The United Press Limited, Toronto, Ontario.

Osborne, Brian, and Michael Ripmeester
1997 The Mississaugas between Two Worlds: Strategic Adjustments to Changing Landscapes of Power. *Canadian Journal of Native Studies* 17(2):259–291.

Outram, Alan K.
2001 A New Approach to Identifying Bone Marrow and Grease Exploitation: Why the "Indeterminate" Fragments Should not Be Ignored. *Journal of Archaeological Science* 28:401–410.

Paasi, Annsi
1996 *Territories, Boundaries and Consciousness: The Changing Geographies of the Finnish–Russian Border.* Wiley-Blackwell, New York.

Parker, Arthur C.
1922 *The Archaeological History of New York.* 2 vols. New York State Museum Bulletin, Albany, New York.

Parkman, Francis
1905 *France and England in North America, Count Frontenac and New France Under Louis XIV,* Vol. 2. Little, Brown and Company, Boston, Massachusetts.

Parmenter, Jon William
2010 *The Edge of the Woods: Iroquoia, 1534–1701.* Michigan State University Press, East Lansing, Michigan.

Paudash, Robert
1905 The Coming of the Mississagas. *Ontario Historical Society Papers and Records* 6:190.

Pfeiffer, Susan, Judith C. Sealy, Ronald F. Williamson, Crystal Forrest, and Louis Lesage
2017 Patterns of Weaning Among Ancestral Huron-Wendat Communities, Determined from Nitrogen Isotopes. *American Antiquity* 82:244–261.

Pfeiffer, Susan, Judith C. Sealy, Ronald F. Williamson, Suzanne Needs-Howarth, and Louis Lesage
2016 Maize, Fish, and Deer: Investigating Dietary Staples Among Ancestral Huron-Wendat Villages, as Documented from Tooth Samples. *American Antiquity* 81:515–532.

Pilon, Jean-Luc
1987 Washahoe Inninou Dahtsuounoaou: Ecological and Cultural Adaptation Along the Severn River in the Hudson Bay Lowlands of Ontario. Ontario Ministry of Citizenship and Culture Conservation Archaeology Report 10, Northwestern Region. Ontario Ministry of Citizenship and Culture, Kenora, Ontario.

Pratt, Peter P.
1961 *Oneida Iroquois Glass Trade Bead Sequence, 1585–1745.* Indian Glass Trade Beads, Colour Guide Series No. 1. Fort Stanwix Museum, Rome, New York.
1976 *Archaeology of the Oneida Iroquois,* Vol. 1. Occasional Publications in Northeastern Anthropology. Man in the Northeast, George's Mills, New Hampshire.

Preston, Richard A., and Leopold Lamontagne
1958   *Royal Fort Frontenac*. Champlain Society, Toronto.

Prince, Paul
2007   Determinants and Implications of Bone Grease Rendering: A Pacific Northwest Example. *North American Archaeologist* 28:1–28.

Pritchard, James S.
1973a   For the Glory of God: The Quinte Mission, 1668–80. *Ontario History* 65:131–148.
1973b   *Journey of My Lord Count Frontenac to Lake Ontario*. Downtown Kingston Business Association, Kingston, Ontario.

Raffeix, Pierre (cartographer)
1688   Le Lac Ontario avec les Lieux circonvoisins & particulièrement les cinq nations Iroquoise. H3902. Service historique de la Marine, Bibliothèque, Paris. Reproduced as Map I.15 in R. Louis Gentilcore and C. Grant Head (editors), 1984, *Ontario's History in Maps*. University of Toronto Press, Toronto, Ontario.

Rajnovich, Grace
1994   *Reading Rock Art: The Indian Rock Paintings of the Canadian Shield*. Natural Heritage/Natural History, Toronto, Ontario.

Ramsden, Peter G.
1977   *A Refinement of Some Aspects of Huron Ceramic Analysis*. Mercury Series Archaeology Paper No. 63. National Museum of Man, Ottawa, Ontario.
1990   The Hurons: Archaeology and Culture History. In *The Archaeology of Southern Ontario to A.D. 1650*, edited by Chris J. Ellis and Neal Ferris, pp. 361–384. Occasional Publication No. 5. London Chapter, Ontario Archaeological Society, London, Ontario.

Reeve, Harold
1967   *The History of the Township of Hope*. [self-published] Peterborough, Ontario.
1991   The Rice Lake Gravel Road. Unknown newspaper, article on file, Cobourg Library, Cobourg, Ontario.

Reid, Robert
1997   "Striking the War Post": North American Indian Warfare in What Is Now Bruce County. *Bruce County Historical Society Annual Yearbook*, pp. 66–80.

Revel, Elizabeth
1982   Translation of Letter Written by Father Pierre Joseph-Marie Chaumonot, August 1641. *Kewa* [newsletter of the London Chapter of the Ontario Archaeological Society] 82(2):4–7.

Richter, Daniel K.
1983   War and Culture: The Iroquois Experience. *William and Mary Quarterly* 40:528–559.
1992   *The Ordeal of the Longhouse: The Peoples of the Iroquois League in the Era of European Colonization*. University of North Carolina Press, Chapel Hill, and Omohundro Institute of Early American History and Culture, Williamsburg, Virginia.

Rick, Anne M.
1992   *Bone Remains from the Bead Hill Site: An Historic Seneca Village at Scarborough, Ontario.* Zooarchaeological Program, Canadian Museum of Nature, Ottawa, Ontario.

Ridley, Frank
1961   *Archaeology of the Neutral Indians.* Etobicoke Historical Society, Etobicoke, Ontario.

Ritchie, William A.
1944   *The Pre-Iroquoian Occupation of New York State.* Rochester Museum of Arts and Sciences Memoir No. 1. Rochester, New York.
1965   *The Archaeology of New York State.* Natural History Press, New York.

Roberts, Arthur C. B.
1978   An Archaeological Survey in Selected Townships along the North Shore of Lake Ontario. Report on file at the Ontario Ministry of Heritage, Sport, Tourism and Culture Industries, Toronto, Ontario.

Roberts, David, and Josiah C. Roberts
2003   Smith, Robert Home. *Dictionary of Canadian Biography*, Vol. 16. University of Toronto/Université Laval, http://www.biographi.ca/en/bio/smith_robert_home_16E.html, accessed February 17, 2020.

Robinson, C. Blackett
1884   *History of the County of Peterborough, Ontario.* C. Blackett Robinson, Toronto, Ontario.
1885   *History of Toronto and the County of York Ontario,* Vol. 1. C. Blackett Robinson, Toronto, Ontario.

Robinson, Percy J.
1933   *Toronto During the French Régime: A History of the Toronto Region from Brûlé to Simcoe, 1615–1793.* Ryerson Press, Toronto, Ontario, and University of Chicago Press, Chicago, Illinois.
1939   Gandatsekiagon and the Rouge Trail. *St. Andrews College Review* midsummer:17–19.

Roets, Michael, William Engelbrecht, and John Holland
2014   Gunflints and Musket Balls: Implications for the Occupational History of the Eaton Site and the Niagara Frontier. *Northeast Historical Archaeology* 43:189–205.

Rogers, Edward S.
1978   Southeastern Ojibwa. In *Northeast*, edited by Bruce G. Trigger, pp. 760–771. Handbook of North American Indians, Vol. 15, William C. Sturtevant, general editor, Smithsonian Institution, Washington, D.C.
1994   The Algonquian Farmers of Southern Ontario. In *Aboriginal Ontario,* edited by Edward S. Rogers and Donald B. Smith, pp. 122–166. Dundurn Press, Toronto, Ontario.

Rogers, Edward S., and J. Garth Taylor
1981   Northern Ojibwa. In *Subarctic*, edited by June Helm, pp. 231–243. Handbook of North American Indians, Vol. 6, William C. Sturtevant, general editor, Smithsonian Institution, Washington, D.C.

Rubertone, Patricia E.
2000   The Historical Archaeology of Native Americans. *Annual Review of Anthropology* 29:425–446.

Rutsch, Edward, S.
1973   *Smoking Technology of the Aborigines of the Iroquois Area of New York State*. Fairleigh Dickinson University Press, Madison, New Jersey.

Ryan, Beth, and Adam G. Dewbury
2010   The Eugene Frost Collection: Artifacts from the Seneca Iroquois Dann Site, Circa 1655–1675. Cornell University Archaeological Collections Documentation Project Report No. 1. Manuscript on file, Division of Rare and Manuscript Collections, Cornell University Library, Ithaca, New York.

Sanft, Samantha M.
2013   Beads and Pendants from Indian Fort Road: An Analysis of a Sixteenth-Century Cayuga Site in Tompkins County, New York. Master's thesis, Archaeology Program, Cornell University, Ithaca, New York.

Saunders, Lorraine P.
1996   Orbital Pitting: Diet or Cooking Utensil? *Journal of Middle Atlantic Archaeology* 12:35–41.

Schiffer, Michael B.
1987   *Formation Processes of the Archaeological Record*. University of New Mexico Press, Albuquerque, New Mexico.

Schillaci, Michael, Craig Kopris, Søren Wichmann, and Genevieve Dewar
2017   Linguistic Clues to Iroquoian Prehistory. *Journal of Anthropological Research* 73(3):448–485. https://doi.org/10.1086/693055.

Schlesier, Karl H.
1976   Epidemics and Indian Middlemen: Rethinking the Wars of the Iroquois, 1609–1653. *Ethnohistory* 23(2):129–145.

Schmalz, Peter
1984   The Role of the Ojibwa in the Conquest of Southern Ontario, 1650–1701. *Ontario History* 76(4):326–352.
1991   *The Ojibwa of Southern Ontario*. University of Toronto Press, Toronto, Ontario, Ontario.

Schoff, Harry L.
1949   "Black Robes" Among the Seneca and Cayuga. *Pennsylvania Archaeologist* 19(1–2):18–26.

Schoolcraft, Henry R.
1848   *The Indian in His Wigwam, or, Characteristics of the Red Race of America*. Derby & Hewson, Buffalo, New York.

1851   *Historical and Statistical Information Respecting the History, Condition, and Prospects of the Indian Tribes of the United States.* Lippincott, Grambo, Philadelphia, Pennsylvania.

Scott, Patricia Kay
1998   Historic Contact Archaeological Deposits within the Old Fort Niagara National Historic Landmark. *The Bulletin* [journal of the New York State Archaeological Association] 114:45–57.

Sempowski, Martha L.
1988   Fluctuations through Time in the Use of Marine Shell at Seneca Iroquois Sites. In *Proceedings of the 1986 Shell Bead Conference,* edited by Charles F. Hayes and Lynn Ceci, pp. 81–96. Research Records No. 20. Rochester Museum & Science Center, Rochester, New York.
2004   Glass Bead Classification and Analysis. Report submitted to History Section, Legal Department, Oneida Indian Nation, Oneida, New York.

Sempowski, Martha L., A. Nohe, R. Hancock, J.-F. Moreau, F. Kwok, S. Aufreiter, K. Karklins, J. Baart, C. Garrad, and I. Kenyon
2001   Chemical Analysis of 17th-Century Red Glass Trade Beads from Northeastern North America and Amsterdam. *Archaeometry* 43(4):503–515.

Sempowski, Martha L., and Lorraine P. Saunders
2001   *Dutch Hollow and Factory Hollow: The Advent of Dutch Trade Among the Seneca.* 3 vols. Charles F. Wray Series in Seneca Archaeology No. 3, Research Record No. 24. Rochester Museum & Science Center, Rochester, New York.

Shackel, Paul A.
2001   Public Memory and the Search for Power in American Historical Archaeology. *American Anthropologist* 103 (3):655–670.

How, Shu-wu
1971   Catlinite. In *The Lasanen Site: An Historic Burial Locality in Mackinac County, Michigan,* edited by Charles E. Cleland, pp. 41–52. Anthropological Series Vol. 1, No. 1. Michigan State University Museum, East Lansing, Michigan.

Silliman, Stephen
2005   Culture Contact or Colonialism? Challenges in the Archaeology of Native North America. *American Antiquity* 70:55–74.

Skinner, Alanson
1921   *Notes on Iroquois Archeology.* Indian Notes and Monographs No. 18. Museum of the American Indian, Heye Foundation, New York.

Smith, Donald B.
1975a   The Mississauga, Peter Jones, and the White Man: The Algonkians' Adjustment to the Europeans on the North Shore of Lake Ontario to 1860. PhD dissertation, Department of History, University of Toronto, Toronto, Ontario.
1975b   Who Are the Mississauga? *Ontario History* 67(4):211–222.
1981   The Dispossession of the Mississauga Indians: A Missing Chapter in the Early History of Upper Canada. *Ontario History* 73(2):67–87.

1987 *Sacred Feathers: The Reverend Peter Jones (Kahkewaquonaby) and the Mississauga Indians.* University of Toronto Press, Toronto, Ontario.
2013a *Sacred Feathers: The Reverend Peter Jones (Kahkewaquonaby) and the Mississauga Indians.* 2nd ed. University of Toronto Press, Toronto, Ontario.
2013b *Mississauga Portraits: Ojibwe Voices from Nineteenth-Century Canada.* University of Toronto Press, Toronto, Ontario.

Snow, Dean R.
1994 *The Iroquois.* Blackwell, Cambridge, Massachusetts.
1995a *Mohawk Valley Archaeology: The Sites.* Institute for Archaeological Studies, State University of New York, Albany, New York.
1995b *Mohawk Valley Archaeology: The Collections.* Occasional Papers in Anthropology No. 23. Matson Museum of Anthropology, Pennsylvania State University, University Park, Pennsylvania.
1996 *The Iroquois.* [paperback edition] Blackwell, Cambridge, Massachusetts.

Snow, Dean R., Charles T. Gehring, and William A. Starna (editors)
1996 *In Mohawk Country: Early Narratives About a Native People.* Syracuse University Press, Syracuse, New York.

Snow, Dean R., and Kim M. Lanphear
1988 European Contact and Indian Depopulation in the Northeast: The Timing of the First Epidemics. *Ethnohistory* 35(1):15–33.

Sohrweide, A. Gregory
2001 Onondaga Longhouses in the Late Seventeenth Century on the Weston Site. *The Bulletin* [journal of the New York State Archaeological Association] 117:1–24.

Squire, Rev. Bowen P.
1958a The Squire Site, Consecon. *Ontario Archaeology* 4:4–17.
1958b The Indian Site at Consecon. *Historic Kingston* 7:53–63.
1959 Rediscovery of the Kenté Region. *New Pages of Prehistory* (reprinted from *Ontario History*) 1959:4–8.

St. John, Amy, and Neal Ferris
2019 Unravelling Identities on Archaeological Borderlands: Late Woodland Western Basin and Ontario Iroquoian Traditions in the Lower Great Lakes Region. *The Canadian Geographer / Le Géographe canadien* 63(1):43–56.

Starna, William A.
1994 Concerning the Extent of "Free Hunting" Territory under Treaty of 1701 between the Five Nations Confederacy and the British Sovereign, and the Harvesting Activities Protected under that Treaty. Submitted to Ontario Native Affairs Secretariat, Toronto, Ontario.

Starna, William A., and Ralph Watkins
1991 Northern Iroquoian Slavery. *Ethnohistory* 38(1):34–57.

Stone, Lyle M.
1971 Rosary and Glass Beads. In *The Lasanen Site: An Historic Burial Locality in Mackinac County, Michigan*, edited by Charles E. Cleland, pp. 74–85.

Anthropological Series Vol. 1, No. 1. Michigan State University Museum, East Lansing, Michigan.

1974   Rosary Beads. *Fort Michilimackinac 1715–1781: An Archaeological Perspective on the Revolutionary Frontier*: 114–117. The Museum, Michigan State University, East Lansing, in cooperation with Mackinac Island State Park Commission, Michigan.

Stone, Lyle M., and Donald Chaput

1978   History of the Upper Great Lakes Area. In *Northeast*, edited by Bruce G. Trigger, pp. 602–609. *Handbook of North American Indians*, Vol. 15, William C. Sturtevant, general editor, Smithsonian Institution, Washington, D.C.

Stothers, David

1981   Indian Hills (33-WO-4): A Protohistoric Assistaeronon Village in the Maumee River Valley of Northwestern Ohio. *Ontario Archaeology* 36:47–56.

Strauss, Alisa N.

2000   Iroquoian Food Techniques and Technologies: An Examination of Susquehannock Vessel Form and Function. PhD dissertation, Department of Anthropology, Pennsylvania State University, Pennsylvania.

Sullivan, J. (editor)

1921   *The Papers of Sir William Johnson*, Vol. 3. University of the State of New York, Albany, New York.

Surtees, Robert

1985   *A Cartographic Analysis of Indian Settlements and Reserves in Southern Ontario and Southern Quebec, 1763–1867*. Research Branch, Indian and Northern Affairs Canada, Ottawa, Ontario.

1994   Land Cessions, 1763–1830. In *Aboriginal Ontario: Historical Perspectives on the First Nations*, edited by Edward S. Rogers and Donald B. Smith, pp. 92–121. Dundurn Press, Toronto, Ontario.

Swayze, Kenneth

1973   Archaeological Research in Prince Edward County: January to March 1973. Report on file at the Ontario Ministry of Heritage, Sport, Tourism and Culture Industries, Toronto, Ontario.

1976   Inventory of Prince Edward County: Conservation Archaeology Report. Submitted to Ontario Ministry of Culture and Recreation, Toronto.

Tailhan, R. P. J. (editor)

1864   *Mémoire sur les mœurs, coustumes et religion des sauvages de l'Amérique Septentrionale par Nicolas Perrot*. A. Franck, Leipzig and Paris. https://gallica.bnf.fr/ark:/12148/bpt6k110266c.texteImage.

Tanner, Helen H. (editor)

1987   *Atlas of the Great Lakes Indian History*. Oklahoma University Press, Norman, Oklahoma.

Taschereau, Sylvie, and Robert Lagassé

2015   Lachine. *The Canadian Encyclopedia*. Historica Canada, https://www.thecanadianencyclopedia.ca/en/article/lachine, accessed April 1, 2020.

Taylor, David
1968 *The Kenté Mission: 1668 to 1680.* Prince Edward County Historical Society, Wellington, Ontario.

The Globe [Toronto]
1920 Indian Bones Are Unearthed. August 7:9. Toronto, Ontario.

Thwaites, Reuben G. (editor)
1896– *The Jesuit Relations and Allied Documents.* 73 vols. Burrows Brothers, Cleveland,
1901 Ohio.
1903 *A New Discovery of a Vast Country in America by Father Louis Hennepin.* 2 vols. A. C. McClurg, Chicago, Illinois.
1905 *New Voyages to North America by Baron de Lahontan.* A. C. McClurg, Chicago, Illinois.

Tooker, Elisabeth
1964 *An Ethnography of the Huron Indians, 1615–1649.* Bureau of American Ethnology Bulletin No. 190. Smithsonian Institution, Washington, D.C.

Trelease, Allen W.
1962 The Iroquois and the Western Fur Trade: A Problem in Interpretation. *Mississippi Valley Historical Review* 49:32–51.

Trigger, Bruce G.
1976 *The Children of Aataentsic: A History of the Huron People to 1660.* 2 vols. McGill-Queen's University Press, Kingston and Montréal, Canada.
1985 *Natives and Newcomers: Canada's "Heroic Age" Reconsidered.* McGill-Queen's University Press, Kingston and Montréal, Canada.

Triggs, John R.
2004 The Mississauga at the Head-of-the-Lake: Examining Responses to Cultural Upheaval at the Close of the Fur Trade. *Northeast Historical Archaeology* 33:153–176.

Trouvé, Claude
1871 Abrégé de la Mission de Kenté. In *Histoire du Montréal, 1640–1672,* by François Dollier de Casson, pp. 119–128. Eusèbe Senécal, Montréal, Québec.

Trubowitz, Neal L.
1992 Thanks, but We Prefer to Smoke our Own: Pipes in the Great Lakes-Riverine Region During the Eighteenth Century. In *Proceedings of the 1989 Smoking Pipe Conference,* edited by Charles Hayes, Connie Box Bodner, and Martha L. Sempowski, pp. 97–112. Research Records No. 22. Rochester Museum & Science Center, Rochester, New York.

Tuck, James A.
1971 *Onondaga Iroquois Prehistory: A Study in Settlement Archaeology.* Syracuse University Press, Syracuse, New York.

Turgeon, Laurier
1997 The Tale of the Kettle. *Ethnohistory* 44(1):1–29.
2001 French Beads in France and Northeastern North America During the Sixteenth and Seventeenth Centuries. *Historical Archaeology* 35(4):58–81.

Turkon, Paula
2010   White Springs Macrobotanical Report: 2007 and 2008 Field Seasons. Manuscript on file, Department of Anthropology, Cornell University, Ithaca, New York.

Upper, Boyd
1956   Consecon Farm Yields Many Historical Relics of Laurentian Period. *Globe and Mail* 21 June:29–30. Toronto, Ontario.

Vandrei, Charles E.
1987   Observations on Seneca Settlements in the Early Historic Period. *The Bulletin* [journal of the New York State Archaeological Association] 95:8–17.

Vansina, Jan
1985   *Oral Tradition as History*. University of Wisconsin Press, Madison, Wisconsin.

Vasey, April
1991   Seneca Hair Combs as Material Culture: A Study. Master's thesis, Arts and Sciences College of William & Mary, Williamsburg, Virginia. https://dx.doi.org/doi:10.21220/s2-kbb7-qm19.

Vastokas, Joan M., and Romas K. Vastokas
1972   *Sacred Art of the Algonkians: A Study of the Peterborough Petroglyphs*. Mansard Press, Peterborough, Ontario.

Vehik, Susan C.
1977   Bone Fragments and Bone Grease Manufacturing: A Review of Their Archaeological Use and Potential. *Plains Anthropologist* 22:169–182.

von Gernet, Alexander
2002   "Within the Prick'd Line": The Historical Context of the 1701 Deed from the Iroquois to the King of England of a Vast Tract of Land. Submitted to Province of Ontario.
2006   The Influence of Bruce Trigger on the Forensic Reconstruction of Aboriginal History. In *The Archaeology of Bruce Trigger: Theoretical Empiricism*, edited by Ronald F. Williamson and Michael Bisson, pp. 174–193. McGill-Queen's University Press, Kingston and Montréal, Canada.

Wagner, Mark J.
2006   "He Is Worst Than the [Shawnee] Prophet": The Archaeology of Nativism Among the Early Nineteenth Century Potawatomi of Illinois. *Midcontinental Journal of Archaeology* 31:89–116.

Walder, Heather
2013   Stylistic and Chemical Investigation of Turquoise Blue Glass Artifacts from the Contact Era of Wisconsin. *Midcontinental Journal of Archaeology* 38(1):119–142.
2018   Small Beads, Big Picture: Assessing Chronology, Exchange, and Population Movement through Compositional Analyses of Blue Glass Beads from the Upper Great Lakes. *Historical Archaeology* 52(1). doi:10.1007/s41636-018-0100-4.

Warren, William W.
1984   *History of the Ojibway People*. Minnesota Historical Society Press, St. Paul, Minnesota.

Warrick, Gary A.
1983   A Report on the Archaeology of the Cooper Sites (AgHb-18, AgHb-19). Manuscript on file, Ontario Heritage Trust, Toronto, Ontario.
1988   Estimating Ontario Iroquoian Village Duration. Man in the Northeast 36:21–60.
2004   Archaeological Investigation of the Davisville Community, City of Brantford, Brant County: Results of the 2002 Test Pit Survey, Test Excavation of Davisville 7 Site (AgHb-253) and Partial Excavation of Davisville 2 Site (AgHb-242). Report on file at the Ontario Ministry of Heritage, Sport, Tourism and Culture Industries, Toronto, Ontario.
2005   The Archaeological Visibility of Post-contact Hunter-Gatherers. Paper presented at the 38th Annual Meeting of the Canadian Archaeological Association, Nanaimo, B.C.
2006   Davisville 2 Site: Archaeological Test Excavation of an Early 19th Century Mohawk Cabin on the Grand River. Annual Archaeological Report, Ontario 13 (N.S.): 53–57.
2008   A Population History of the Huron-Petun, A.D. 500–1650. Cambridge University Press, Cambridge, U.K.

Waterman, Kees-Jan
2008   "To Do Justice to Him and Myself": Evert Wendell's Account Book of the Fur Trade with Indians in Albany. American Philosophical Society, Philadelphia, Pennsylvania.

Watson, Adam S., and Stephen Cox Thomas
2013   The Lower Great Lakes Fur Trade, Local Economic Sustainability, and the Bone Grease Buffer: Vertebrate Faunal Remains from the Eighteenth-Century Seneca Iroquois Townley-Read Site. Northeast Anthropology 79–80:82–123.

Waugh, Frederick W.
1973   Iroquois Foods and Food Preparation. Anthropological Series No. 12, Memoirs of the Canadian Geological Survey No. 86. Government Printing Bureau, Ottawa. Originally published 1916, Department of Mines, Ottawa, Ontario.

Weiskotten, Daniel
2000   Patterns of Iroquois Burial. http://freepages.rootsweb.com/~nc99usgw/history/BurialPatterns.html, accessed August 27, 2020.

Weisshuhnat, Karine
2004   Les peignes amérindiens dans le Nord-Est américain. Master's thesis, Anthropology Department, University of Montréal, Montréal, Québec.

Wheeler, Robert C., Walter A. Kenyon, Allan R. Woolworth, and Douglas A. Birk
1975   Voices from the Rapids: An Underwater Search for Fur Trade Artifacts 1960–73. Minnesota Historical Society Press Series No. 3. St. Paul, Minnesota.

White, Marian E.
1968   A Reexamination of the Historic Iroquois Van Son Cemetery on Grand Island. Bulletin of the Buffalo Society of Natural Sciences 24:7–48.

1972   On Delineating the Neutral Iroquois of the Eastern Niagara Peninsula of Ontario. *Ontario Archaeology* 17:62–74.

1978   Neutral and Wenro. In *Northeast*, edited by Bruce Trigger, pp. 407–411. *Handbook of North American Indians*, Vol. 15, William C. Sturtevant, general editor, Smithsonian Institution, Washington, D.C.

White, Richard

1991   *The Middle Ground: Indians, Empires, and Republics in the Great Lakes Region, 1650–1815*. Cambridge University Press, New York.

Williams, Doug (Gidigaa Migizi)

2018   *Michi Saagiig Nishnaabeg: This Is Our Territory*. ARP Books, Winnipeg, Manitoba.

Williamson, Christine

2004   Contact Archaeology and the Writing of Aboriginal History. In *The Archaeology of Contact in Settler Societies*, edited by Tim Murray, pp. 176–199. Cambridge University Press, Cambridge, U.K.

Williamson, Ronald F.

2007   "Ontinontsiskiaj Ondaon" ("The House of Cut-Off Heads"): The History and Archaeology of Northern Iroquoian Trophy Taking. In *The Taking and Displaying of Human Body Parts as Trophies by Amerindians*, edited by Richard J. Chacon and David H. Dye, pp. 190–221. Springer, New York.

2014   The Archaeological History of the Wendat to A.D. 1651: An Overview. *Ontario Archaeology* 94:3–65.

Williamson, Ronald F., and Peter Ramsden

2019   Time, Space and Ceramic Attributes—the Ontario Iroquoian Case. Paper presented at the 84th Annual Meeting of the Society for American Archaeology, Albuquerque, New Mexico.

Williamson, Ronald F., David A. Robertson, and Susan Hughes

2017   Archaeological Resource Management in Toronto: Planning, Preservation and Interpretation. In *Urban Archaeology, Municipal Government and Local Planning: Preserving Heritage within the Commonwealth of Nations and the United States*, edited by Sherene Baugher, Douglas R. Appler, and William Moss, pp. 69–90. Springer, New York.

Williamson, Ronald F., and Annie Veilleux

2005   A Review of Northern Iroquoian Decorated Bone and Antler Artifacts: A Search for Meaning. *Ontario Archaeology* 79–80:3–37.

Williams-Shuker, Kimberly L.

2009   "Bottom-Up" Perspectives of the Contact Period: A View from the Rogers Farm Site. In *Iroquoian Archaeology and Analytic Scale*, edited by Timothy D. Knapp and Laurie E. Miroff, pp. 189–213. University of Tennessee Press, Knoxville, Tennessee.

Wintemberg, William J.

1908   The Use of Shells by the Ontario Indians. In *Annual Archaeological Report, 1907: Being Part of Appendix to the Report of the Minister of Education, Ontario*, pp. 38–90. L. K. Cameron, Toronto, Ontario.

1939 *Lawson Prehistoric Village Site, Middlesex County, Ontario.* Bulletin No. 94. National Museum of Canada, Ottawa, Ontario.

Wonderley, Anthony
2002 Oneida Ceramic Effigies: A Question of Meaning. *Northeast Anthropology* 63:23–48.
2005 Effigy Pipes, Diplomacy, and Myth: Exploring Interaction between St. Lawrence Iroquoians and Eastern Iroquois in New York State. *American Antiquity* 70:211–240.
2020 Epic of the Oneida Iroquois: 550 Years in Upstate New York. Manuscript on file, Department of Anthropology, Cornell University, Ithaca, New York.

Wonderley, Anthony, and Martha L. Sempowski
2019 *Origins of the Iroquois League.* Syracuse University Press, Syracuse, New York.

Wood, Alice S.
1974 A Catalogue of Jesuit and Ornamental Rings from Western New York. *Historical Archaeology* 7:83–104.

Wood, William R.
1911 *Past Years in Pickering.* William Briggs, Toronto, Ontario.

Woodhouse, Roy
1969 La Salle's Probable Route to Tinawatawa. *Wentworth Bygones: From the Papers and Records of the Head-of-the-Lake Historical Society* 8:2–5.

Woods, Julie
2013 Response and Resistance: A Comparison of Middle Connecticut River Valley Ceramics from the Late Woodland Period to the Seventeenth Century. Master's thesis, Department of Anthropology, University of Massachusetts, Amherst, Massachusetts.

Wray, Charles F.
1963 Ornamental Hair Combs of the Seneca. *Pennsylvania Archaeologist* 33 (1–2):35–50.
1973 *A Manual for Seneca Iroquois Archeology.* Cultures Primitive, Honeoye Falls, New York.
1983 Seneca Glass Trade Beads c. A.D. 1550–1820. In *Glass Bead Conference*, edited by C. Hayes III, pp. 41–49. Research Records Vol. 16. Rochester Museum & Science Center, Rochester, New York.
1985 The Volume of Dutch Trade Goods Received by the Seneca Iroquois, 1600–1687 AD. *Bulletin KNOB* [newsletter of the Koninklijke Nederlandse Oudheidkundige Bond] 84(2):100–112.

Wray, Charles F., and Robert J. Graham
1960 New Discoveries on an Old Site: The Bunce Site. *The Bulletin* [journal of the New York State Archaeological Association] 18:1–4.
1985 The Boughton Hill Site, Victor, New York. Originally published 1966. *The Iroquoian* [newsletter of the Morgan Chapter, New York State Archaeological Association] 10:2–66.

Wray, Charles F., and Harry L. Schoff
1953   A Preliminary Report on the Seneca Sequence in Western New York, 1550–1687. *Pennsylvania Archaeologist* 23:53–63.

Wray, Charles F., Martha L. Sempowski, Lorraine P. Saunders,
and Gian Carlo Cervone
1987   *The Adams and Culbertson Sites*. Charles F. Wray Series in Seneca Archaeology Vol. 1, Rochester Museum & Science Center Research Records No. 19. Rochester Museum & Science Center, Rochester, New York.

Wright, Gordon
1963   *The Neutral Indians: A Source Book*. Occasional Papers of the New York State Archaeological Association No. 4. New York State Archaeological Association, Rochester, New York.

Wright, Jonathan
2004   *The Jesuits: Missions, Myth and Histories*. HarperCollins, London, U.K.

Yellowhorn, Eldon
2006   The Awakening of Internalist Archaeology in the Aboriginal World. In *The Archaeology of Bruce Trigger: Theoretical Empiricism*, edited by Ronald F. Williamson and Michael Bisson, pp. 194–209. McGill-Queen's University Press, Kingston and Montréal, Canada.

Index

A

Accelerator Mass Spectrometry (AMS), 33
Adams, Nick, 1, 78, 81, 88–89, 91, 98, 101, 104, 123, 142, 144, 153, 186, 252, 274, 281
Adolphus Reach, 89
Aenons, 14
Albany, 5, 89, 120, 129, 147, 185, 245, 273, 281
Alderville Community, 29, 264
Algonquin, 11–13, 16, 22, 35, 120, 132, 267
Algonquin Park, 132
Ameliasburgh, 66, 69, 71–72, 166, 180, 248, 250, 252–255, 259, 281
American Revolution, 51, 263, 273
Amikwa, 24, 272
Andastes (Andastogués), 5, 22, 146, 149
Anishinaabe, 5–6, 9, 21, 29, 78, 116, 120, 181, 235, 265–267, 269, 271–273, 275–277, 279, 281, 285–286, 297, 301, 305
Anishinaabeg-Haudenosaunee battles (Ojibwa Thesis), 271–272, 286
Annenraes, 17
Annual Archaeological Report for Ontario (AARO), 253
antler comb(s), 28, 71, 76, 111, 113, 136–137, 213–237, 247–248, 255, 296–298
Archaeologically Sensitive Area (ASA), 93, 119, 134, 137, 186, 189–191, 223–224, 226, 281
archaeological management plan, 136–137
Archaeological Services Inc. (ASI), 93, 119, 134, 137, 186, 189–191, 223–224, 226, 281
Arendarhonon (Wendat Rock nation), 12, 14, 17, 19
Assikinack, Francis, 267–269
Attignawantan (Wendat Bear nation), 14, 17
Attigneenongnahac (Wendat Cord nation), 14, 17–19

B

Baby family (farm, Point), 27, 99, 116, 125–126, 129–138, 187, 191, 239, 257, 259, 289, 295
Baie des Puants (Green Bay), 25–26
Bald Head Island (Bald Head, Bald Bluff), 28, 63, 75, 77, 187, 203–207, 212, 228, 231–232, 239, 248, 250, 252, 256, 281
bannerstones, 65, 67
barley, 50
barque(s), 74–75
Barthélemy, Michel, 58
Battle of Lake Champlain, 12
Bayesian modelling, 33
Bay of Quinte, 1, 72, 74, 82–85, 87, 89, 98, 165, 217, 248, 263, 274–275, 281, 302
Beasley Landing site, 276, 278
Beausoleil Island, 263
beaver(s), 5–6, 9, 11, 18, 21, 24, 35, 115–116, 185, 190, 220, 266
Bécancour, René Robinau de, 129
Bellamy site, 276
Bellomont, Richard Coote, the Earl of, 266
Belmont, François Vachon de, 24, 79–80, 82–84, 88–91, 128
Bennett, Monte, 37–38, 47–48, 50–51, 161–162, 244
Bergseth, Amy Dianne, 214, 228, 231
Bernou, Claude, Abbé, 6, 61–62, 84, 86, 104, 118
Beverly Swamp, 144, 154
Bewdley, 89, 94, 288
birdstone(s), 65, 67, 132
black bear, 115

Bloomfield, 167, 176
Blue Mountains, 268–269
Bohaker, Heidi, 6, 19, 264
bone bead(s), 27, 159, 178–180, 186, 295
border theory, 291–293, 298
Boyle, David, 28, 104, 117, 121, 131–133, 159, 162, 164, 175, 177, 181, 183, 191, 257, 259, 271–272
Bradley, James, 11, 36–38, 42, 44–51, 175–176, 191, 193, 195, 199, 235–236, 241, 244, 246, 253, 260
Brandão, José, 8, 11, 13, 145, 151, 153, 272
brass kettle(s), 41, 50, 69, 136, 187, 189, 193, 225, 228
brass ring(s), 41, 71, 136, 202, 225,
Brébeuf, Father Jean de, 5
Bretonvilliers, Abbé Alexandre Le Ragois de, 59
Bronte Creek, 155
Buffalo History Museum, 209, 212
Burlington Bay, 145, 147, 185

C

calcined bone, 276–280, 297
Callière, Louis-Hector de, 265, 273
Canadian Register of Historic Places, 99
Canniff, William, 63, 75, 90
Carheil, Father Étienne de, 35
Carrying Place, Town, 27, 62–63, 71–72, 125–126, 168, 187, 233, 248–249, 288–290, 294, 305
Carrying Place Trail (Toronto Passage, Le Passage du Toronto), 13, 17, 126
Casson, François Dollier de, 73, 78–79, 103, 141, 185
Cataraqui River, 24, 59, 62
Catherine Creek, 41
cattle, 50, 57

Cayuga, 3–5, 18, 22, 33, 35–39, 41, 45–47, 49, 51, 55–60, 69, 77–78, 91, 93, 98, 119, 122, 161–162, 182, 184–185, 187, 215, 240–243, 250–252, 255, 260, 263, 265, 289, 291, 295–296
Cayuga Lake, 41
ceramics, Indigenous, 28, 239, 241, 243, 248
Chadd, G. J., 28, 63, 70–73, 75, 159, 176–180, 182–185, 188–189, 193–194, 196–197, 199, 203, 206, 228, 230, 232–233, 235, 248–251, 254–256, 288, 296
Champlain, Samuel De, 8, 12–13, 34, 79, 82, 121, 245
Charleville, Sieur Jacques Chauvin de, 265
Chequamegon Bay, 21
Chesapeake Bay, 244
Chippewa, 129, 263–264, 275–276
Cicé, Abbé Louis-Armand Champion de, 58
Clark, A. J., 104–105, 129, 133–134, 244
Clowes, Samuel, 273
Coe Hill, 168, 180, 184
Colbert, Jean-Baptiste Antoine, Marquis de Seignelay, 25
Consecon, 27, 60, 62–65, 69–70, 72, 76, 288
Cootes Paradise, 142, 147–148, 289
Copway, George, 236, 265, 267–268
Cornell University, 49, 52, 186
Courcelle, Daniel de Rémy de, 145
Curve Lake Community, 29, 264

D

Davisville 1 site, 278
Davisville 2 site, 277
Davisville 3 site, 276–278, 280
Dean, Robert, 37–38, 43, 50, 109, 208, 221, 228, 242
Delaware River, 21

Denonville, Marquis Jacques René de Brisay de, 4, 25–26, 45–46, 60, 81, 86, 117, 119–122, 162, 221, 253, 303
Detroit, 21, 25, 265
Digital elevation model (DEM), 91
disease(s), epidemic(s), 11, 40, 43–44, 152, 224, 266, 271, 301
Dish with One Spoon Treaty, 301
dog(s), 113, 220, 229, 231, 237
doorkeeper(s), 221–222, 227–228, 253
Duffins Creek (West Duffins Creek), 101
Dunnigan, Brian, 266

E

Eid, Leroy V., 266–268, 271–273
Engelbrecht, William, 18, 28, 33, 70, 76, 109, 113, 115, 119, 131, 151, 153, 187, 189, 191, 217, 222, 239, 241–243, 247, 252, 295
Erie, Ehriehronnon (Cat), 22
Esarey, Duane, 41, 175–176
European coins, 207

F

Ferris, Neal, 3, 27, 40, 99, 123, 141, 144–146, 150–153, 185, 259, 274–276, 286, 289–294, 298
Finlan site, 66
firearm(s), 22, 40, 43, 121, 188, 198–200, 211, 246, 270
Fitzgerald, William, 117, 142–143, 150–152, 154–155, 160, 189, 198, 205, 207, 209, 241
Fort Conti, 42, 210
Fort de la Montagne, 58
Fort Denonville, 45, 120
Fort Frontenac, 3, 6, 24, 59, 81, 89, 91, 97–98, 103, 185–186, 289–290, 294
Fort Hennepin, 42
Fort Hunter, 50

fortification(s), palisade(s), 14, 36, 38, 44–46, 48, 58–59, 94, 116–119, 129, 133, 151
Fort LaSalle, 42
Fort Michilimackinac, 179–180
Fort Rouillé (Fort Toronto, Fort Saint-Victor), 129
Fothergill, Charles, 94
Franquelin, Jean-Baptiste-Louis, 79–80, 84–86, 88–89
Fredericksburg, 90
Fremin, Father Jacques, 153
French invasion of the Haudenosaunee homelands, 4
Frenchman's Bay, 118
Frontenac Island, 215–216, 218
Frontenac, Louis de Buade, Comte de, 23–25, 45, 59, 79, 88, 103, 185
fur brigades, 5, 11, 78, 103–104

G

Gahoendoe (Christian Island, St. Joseph Island), 19–20, 198, 202, 263
Galinée, René de Bréhant, 7, 27, 82–83, 102–103, 141–142, 144–150, 153–156, 293
Ganaraska River, 1, 27, 79, 86, 89, 91, 93–95, 288
Gardenville, 70
Garnier, Father Julien, 153
Geographical Information Systems (GIS), 35
Georgian Bay, 20, 83, 88, 131, 181, 268, 270
Glanmore House National Historic Site, 66
glass bead(s), 28, 41, 43, 48, 50, 69–71, 111, 118, 142–144, 154, 159–160, 162–174, 178, 180–181, 184, 186, 198, 248, 276, 280
Grand Island, 187, 208, 210–212, 294
Grand River, 1, 84, 105, 141–143, 149, 151–152, 263, 275, 277, 288–289, 293, 298
Great Peace of Montréal, 120–121

Greenhalgh, Wentworth, 36–39, 42, 47, 100, 117, 231
gunflin(t), 43, 109 111, 188, 200–201, 211, 276,

H

Haldimand Tract, 263
Halton Region, 18
Hamell, George, 63, 102, 107, 113, 123, 186, 214, 220–225, 228, 234, 237, 253, 255, 260, 305
Hamilton Township, 94, 98
Hancock, Ron, 159, 165, 186
Hare Island, 90
Hastings, 87, 94, 163, 288
Hatrick Point, 88
Haudenosaunee burial practices, 43
Haudenosaunee confederacy, 287, 296
Haudenosaunee (Five Nations Iroquois), 1, 33
Haudenosaunee village(s) (homeland), 4, 6, 9, 27–28, 33, 40, 55, 59, 74, 76, 85, 105, 117, 125, 128, 161–162, 165, 212, 259, 292, 296
  Alhart, 8
  Allen, 45, 47, 191
  Beal (Bunce Cemetery), 37, 39, 44–45
  Caughnawaga (Veeder), 44–46, 245
  Coye, 51
  Crouse, 45
  Dann, 35, 44, 50, 103, 113, 161–163, 165, 184, 199, 233, 241
  Dungey, 244
  Dutch Hollow, 162, 181–182, 193
  Eugene Frost, 41
  Factory Hollow, 162, 181–182, 193
  Fort Hill, 44–46
  Fox Farm, 37–38
  Freeman, 191
  Ganondagan (Boughton Hill, Canagorah, Gannagaro), 36–38, 43–45, 49–50, 99, 103, 105, 109, 112–113, 161–162, 164, 182, 184–186, 198–199, 202, 207, 209, 214, 221, 231, 233–234, 241–242, 255, 259, 303–304
  Huntoon, 51
  Indian Castle, 191, 199, 244, 253
  Indian Fort Road, 41
  Indian Hill, 37–38, 44, 191, 208, 244, 269
  Ithaca, 41
  Jackson-Everson, 37, 39, 109, 244, 249, 252, 259
  Jamesville, 47–50
  Keinte-he, 99, 117
  Kendaia, 48
  Lanz-Hogan, 51
  Leichner, 45
  Marsh, 103, 113, 161–162, 184, 191, 241
  Mead, 37
  Milton Smith, 47–48
  Pattington, 51
  Pen cemetery, 49
  Power House, 182, 191, 241
  Primes Hill, 47–50, 244
  René Ménard Bridge Hilltop (RMBH), 37
  Rogers Farm, 37–39, 184, 243
  Rumrill-Naylor, 191
  Scipioville, 255
  Steele, 182, 191, 241, 253
  Stone Quarry, 244
  Thurston, 247
  Tiotohatton (Rochester Junction), 37–38, 44–45, 99–100, 103, 112, 117, 162, 164, 184–186, 221–222, 228, 241
  Townley-Read, 34, 51–52, 109, 115, 243
  Upper Hogan, 37–38, 44–45, 244
  Weston, 37, 44–46, 48, 50, 244
  White Orchard, 37–38, 44–45
  White Springs, 34, 47–50, 52, 109, 115, 242
  Young Farm, 37, 47, 49

Hay Bay, 1, 81, 83–86, 88–91, 96–97, 288, 296
Heidenreich, Conrad, 5, 11, 14, 61, 79, 82–85, 97, 119, 142, 145, 151–153
Henderson, Heather, 136, 142
Henry, Alexander, 274
Heritage Conservation District (HCD), 138–139
heron, 220
Hewitt, J. N. B., 1, 102, 247, 305
Hiawatha Community, 29
Highway 28, 94–95
Hillier Township, 250, 255
Hill, Rick, 29, 301, 304
Hilton site, 76, 173, 177, 184, 186, 228, 232–233, 248, 255
Hirschfelder, Charles, 131–132, 227, 257–258
Historic Horizon Inc., 136, 189–190, 202, 225–226
Holland Landing, 126
Holland River, 102, 126
Hope Township, 89
horse(s), 105, 214, 220, 228, 231
Hostilities. *See* Iroquois Wars
hourglass motif(s), 220, 225
Hudson River valley, 13
human bone artifacts, 10
Humber River, 1, 27, 29, 99, 101, 125–127, 129, 133, 185, 187, 274, 280–281, 289, 305
Hunter, A. F., 116, 118, 133, 198
Huron-Wendat, 5, 14, 160, 188–189, 193, 195–196, 198, 202, 211–212, 215, 301
Huron-Wendat villages
  Angoutenc, 14
  Arbor Ridge, 252
  Auger, 253
  Aurora, 9
  Ball, 9, 181, 240, 253
  Contarea, 15–16
  Draper, 8
  Ekhiondastsaan, 18
  Ihonatiria, 13–14
  Jean-Baptiste Lainé (Mantle), 9, 94, 252–253
  Keffer, 8
  Lite, 8
  McKenzie-Woodbridge, 9
  Notre-Dame-de-Lorette, 247
  Ossossané, 13–14, 202
  Payne, 69
  Quackenbush, 8
  Quieunonascaran, 14
  Saint Jean-Baptiste, 21
  Saint Michel, 21
  Seed-Barker, 9, 94
  Skandatut, 9
  St. Joseph, 19
  St. Louis, 19
  St. Xavier, 15
  Taenhatentaron, 18–19
  Teanaostaiaé, 16, 18
  Tiondatsae (La Chaudière), 18
  Toanche, 13–14
  Warminster (Cahiagué), 245, 249, 252

I

Île aux Tourtes, Sulpician Mission, 58
Illinois, 24–26, 44, 279
Indian Island, 165–166, 248–249, 254–255
Indian River, 82, 88
iron knives, 41, 193, 197–198
iron trade axe(s), 69, 115, 135, 187
Iroquet, 12
Iroquois Book of Rites, 271
Iroquois du Nord village(s), 3–4, 58, 82, 86, 121, 128, 259, 274, 280–281
Ganaraské, 1, 3, 27, 58, 73–74, 77–79, 82–85, 88–89, 91, 93, 97–98, 184–185, 281, 288, 290, 295–296
Ganatsekwyagon (Bead Hill), 1–3, 6–7, 24, 27, 29, 58, 72–75, 77–79, 88, 93, 98–99, 101–104,

107, 117–122, 128, 137, 161, 163, 171, 173–175, 178, 183–185, 187–189, 192–195, 198–203, 208, 212, 223, 228–229, 239, 248, 253, 256–257, 279–281, 288–290, 293–296
Ganneious, 1, 3, 27, 74, 77, 79, 81, 83–86, 88–91, 96–98, 161, 185, 281, 288, 295–296
Kenté, 1, 3, 7, 18, 27–28, 55–60, 62–67, 69–70, 72–79, 81, 84–86, 88–89, 97–98, 102–103, 128, 184–188, 193, 203–205, 207, 209, 223, 228, 231, 239, 248–249, 252, 259, 274, 278, 281, 288, 295–296
Outinaouatoua, 1, 27, 99, 141–150, 153–156, 185, 272, 286, 288–290, 293–294
Quintio, 1, 3, 27, 74, 77–79, 82–88, 91, 93–95, 97–98, 184–185, 272, 281, 288, 290, 295–296
Tannouate, 73–74
Teiaiagon (Baby Point), 1–3, 6–7, 18, 27–29, 58, 72–75, 77, 88, 93, 98–99, 101–105, 116–117, 121, 125–131, 133, 135, 137, 139, 161, 163, 172–174, 177–178, 182–185, 187–200, 202, 205–206, 222–228, 239, 248, 257–258, 274, 278, 280, 288–290, 293–296, 304–305
Iroquois Wars, 1, 5, 8, 26
attacks and raids in Haudenosaunee homeland, 81
attacks and raids in Wendake, 13, 16–17

J

Jackson, Lawrence (Laurie), 94
Jesuits, 14–15, 19–20, 22–24, 39, 42, 55–56, 60, 153, 206
Jolliet, Adrien, 103, 141, 148
Jolliet, Louis, 60–62, 82, 84–85, 103, 141, 148–149

Jones, Peter, 263, 270–271
Jordan, Kurt, 3–5, 26, 29, 33–41, 43–48, 50–51, 78, 81, 89, 99–100, 103, 107, 109, 115, 117, 119, 123, 128, 145, 150–151, 186, 211, 241–243, 245–246, 260, 281, 289–291, 293, 298

K

Kalm, Pehr, 102
Kane, Paul, 268
Karklins, Karlis, 112, 123, 159, 165, 186
Kawartha Lakes, 83
Kenté mission, 56, 58, 64, 66, 69, 75, 78, 185–186
Kenyon, Ian, 113, 123, 142–143, 159–160, 175, 181, 193, 195, 275
Kenyon, Walter, 88, 93, 96, 98, 105, 228, 247
Kettle Burial site, 69, 70
Keweenaw Peninsula, 22
King Louis XIV, 55, 60
Kingston, 24, 65, 252, 274
Kingston Historical Society, 65
Kirkes family, 13
Kirkwood, James and family, 37, 44–45, 99, 117–118, 132–133, 199, 227–228, 257, 259
Kiskakon, 24
Kitche Manitou, 225
Konrad, Victor, 1, 3, 5–6, 23, 26, 29, 40, 46, 73–75, 78, 89, 93, 98, 101–102, 104–105, 116–118, 120, 123, 126–128, 135, 142, 144, 148, 153, 161, 183–185, 263, 272, 274, 281, 285–286, 289, 291–293, 297
Kuhn, Robert, 39, 241, 244–245, 252

L

La Barre, Governor Joseph Antoine Le Fèbvre de, 25, 44
Lajeunesse, Ernest, 142–143
Lake Champlain, 12, 34

Lake Consecon, 27, 60, 63–65, 69, 72
Lake Couchiching, 5, 270–271, 274
Lake Huron, 23, 26, 145, 263, 268–270, 272, 275
Lake Simcoe (Lac de Taronto), 2, 5–6, 17, 19, 24, 75, 82, 84, 131, 267, 269–270, 274
Lake Superior, 22, 24, 103, 272
Lalemant, Father Gabriel, 22, 152–153
Lambton Mills, 131–132, 135, 259
La Salle, René-Robert Cavelier de, 27, 79, 81–82, 84, 88, 103, 128, 141–142, 144–146, 148–149, 201, 210, 211
Lasanen site, 179–181
Laval, Bishop François de, 56–57, 161
least cost path analysis, 93–96
Le Jeune, Father Paul, 11
Lenig, Wayne, 34, 37, 44–45, 47, 51, 244–245, 252, 260
Léry, Chaussegros de, 86
LiDAR, 27, 76, 88, 91, 93, 95–97, 288
Little Creek, 97, 288
Logan, Brianna, 60, 76
Loups (Mohegans of Taracton), 6, 22, 24
Loyola, Saint Ignatius, 56, 201, 206
lynx, 220
Lyons, Onondaga nationalist and artist Oren, 304

M

Mackinac Island, 21
MacLeod, Peter, 265, 267–268, 270–271, 286
magasin royal, 129
Mahican, 13, 35
Mandzy, Adrian, 37, 39, 47, 49, 161–162, 184, 243
Manitoulin Island (Ekaentoton), 16, 19–20, 268
Mansell, William, 135
Mariet, Abbé Joseph, 7, 58, 128
Marquette, Jacques, 82, 84
Martelle, Holly, 240–241
Mason, Carol, 42, 201, 209, 212
Mason, Ronald, 265
Mayer, Poulton and Associates (MPA), 105, 107, 119, 192, 199, 200
McMaster University, 143
Melville Snackbar Burial, 66
Mercadier, Abbé Isadore, 58
Meyersburg, 87
Miami(s), 25, 44, 265
Michilimackinac (Missilimackinac), 24–26, 180, 265
Miller Mounds, 88
Miller, Onondaga Ritualist Huron, 304
Mississauga (Michi Saagiig), 22, 24, 26, 29, 51, 90, 99, 102, 116, 120–121, 128–129, 133, 207, 248, 263–265, 267, 269–270, 272–281, 285–286, 297
Mississippi River, 84
Mohawk(s), 9, 12–13, 15, 17–18, 22–23, 33–34, 36–40, 42–45, 47–51, 55, 109, 112, 115, 153, 191, 198, 223, 241–242, 244–245, 252, 259–260, 263, 268–271, 278, 289
Mohr, Tom, 118–119, 123
Montréal, 24–25, 34, 42, 55–59, 63, 78, 86, 98, 103, 120–121, 145, 149–150, 273, 290
Morrisseau, Norval, 225
Mothe-Fénelon, François de Salignac de la, 7, 56, 103, 209
Murray Canal, 63
Murray Township, 71–72, 170, 255
muskrat, 115

N

Nanfan Treaty, 273
Napanee River, 83–86, 88–89, 91, 96–98, 288, 296
Neutral (Attawandaron), 5, 35, 39, 143, 287
Neutral village(s), 17, 202
  Christianson, 142
  Clearville, 235

Freelton, 142, 207
Grimsby cemetery, 193, 215
Hood, 198, 200, 202
Lake Medad, 142, 160, 181
Lawson, 215, 218, 249–252
Pipeline, 200
Rattlesnake Point, 200
Van Ordt, 8
Walker, 142, 193, 240, 292
New Holland, 6, 23–24, 104
New Sweden, 20
Niagara, 4, 25–26, 42, 86, 120, 129, 143, 208–209, 211, 275, 294
Niagara Falls, 45, 149, 208, 210
Nicolas, Father Louis, 231
Nine Mile Rapids, 87
Nipissing, 11, 13, 20, 24, 35, 58
Northeastern Archaeological Associates, 75, 165, 173, 177, 200, 228, 232, 248, 255
Northumberland County, 91
Nottawasaga River, 19
Nouvel, Father Henri, 24
Nut Island, 90

O

Odawa, 8, 19, 21, 24, 35, 181
Ohio, 41, 51, 152, 273
Ohio River, 146
Old Portage Road, 72
Oneida(s), 3, 5, 12–13, 15, 17, 22, 33, 36–38, 44–45, 47–51, 55, 77, 90–91, 98, 112, 119, 153, 161–162, 185, 215, 241–242, 244, 247, 252, 260, 289, 291, 296, 303
Onondaga(s), 12, 17–18, 21–23, 25, 33, 36–39, 42, 44–51, 55, 59, 120, 153, 191, 193, 199–200, 211, 223, 240–242, 244, 252–253, 260, 263, 266, 271, 273, 277, 289, 304
Onontchataronon, 12
Ontario Archaeological Society, 1, 51, 65, 285, 292

Ontario Archaeology, Journal, 65
Ontario County, 103
Ontario Historical Society, 65, 269
Ontario Provincial Police (OPP), 105
Orr, Rowland, 5, 28, 133, 135, 176, 182–183, 228, 253–256
ossuary (ossuaries), 39, 189, 198, 202, 302
Otonabee River, 82, 88, 98
Ottawa valley, 8, 12
otter(s), 220, 225
Outaouas, 22–24, 26

P

panther(s), 137, 192, 215, 220–221, 223–225, 227, 231–233, 304–305
Paré, François, 60, 76
Parks Canada, 105, 122–123, 192, 200–201, 203, 208, 229, 257
Parmenter, Jon, 33, 35, 39–40, 42, 45, 145
Paudash, Robert, 269–270
peach(es), 50
Peel Region, 18
Pendergast, James, 66
Penetanguishene peninsula, 274
Pennsylvania, 41, 51, 213
Percy Portage, 87, 94
Perrot, Nicolas, 22, 26
Pickering Township, 103
Picquet, Abbé François, 63
Picton, 73, 169, 176, 248
pig, swine, 44, 50, 57
porcupine, 81, 103, 115, 271
Port Hope, 281
Poulain, Father Guillaume, 13
Presqu'ile, 60, 63
Prince Edward County, 27–28, 60, 63, 66, 70, 73–74, 90, 161, 183–185, 187, 222, 239, 248, 251–252, 275, 298
prisoner adoption, 9
projectile point(s), chert, 43, 89, 115, 187, 193–194, 209, 211

projectile point(s), metal, 43, 69, 115, 187–188, 193–194, 209, 211

Q
Queen Anne gun barrels, 104

R
rabbit (hare), 90, 115
Raffeix, Father Pierre, 2, 6, 75, 85, 88, 102, 118
Ragueneau, Father Paul, 5, 19, 263
Ranuyer, Abbé Mathieu, 58
rattlesnake, 137, 223
religious medallion(s), 186, 201–202 205–207, 212
Rice Lake Drive South, 94
Rice Lake (Lake Kentsio), 1, 27, 78–80, 82–89, 91–92, 94–95, 98, 125–126, 264, 269, 275, 281, 288
Richelieu river, 12
Richter, Daniel, 9–11, 33, 126, 214, 272
Ritchie, W. A., 66, 109, 216–217, 269
Robinson, Percy, 1, 102–104, 120–121, 126–129, 133, 135, 142, 144, 148
Rochester Museum & Science Center, 162–164, 186, 213, 221–222, 227, 234, 237
Roebuck site, 8
Rohario, Cayuga Chief, 55, 57
Rosemount, 94
Rouge National Urban Park, 99–100
Rouge River, 1, 27, 99, 101–102, 104, 107, 117–120, 125–126, 128, 185, 280, 289
Royal Ontario Museum, 28, 70, 75, 105, 162, 164, 173–176, 178–180, 182–183, 186, 189–190, 194–195, 197–199, 204–207, 212, 219, 221, 227–228, 230, 232, 235, 248–251, 254, 256, 259, 271

runtee(s) (marine shell disc), 41, 175–178

S
Sainte Marie de Gannentaha, 42, 55
Sainte-Marie I, Sainte-Marie II, 19–20, 34, 57, 196, 198, 202, 207
Saugeen-Nawash, 269
Sault, 23, 264
Saulteur, 22, 263
Saunders, Lorraine, 162, 246, 255, 259
Saut de St. Louys, 5
scalp(s), 11, 215, 265
scattered human bone, 9–10
Schenectady, 34, 42
Schmalz, Peter S., 269, 271–272
Schoolcraft, Henry, 271
Scugog Island Community, 29, 125–126, 264
Sempowski, Martha, 9, 51, 159, 162, 175, 181, 193, 223, 241, 244, 255, 259–260
Seneca(s), 3–5, 7, 9, 13, 15, 17, 18, 22, 24, 26, 33–39, 41–42, 44–52, 74, 91, 93, 98–99, 102–105, 107, 109, 112–113, 115–122, 126, 131, 136, 141, 143–144, 146–147, 149–150, 153–154, 159–162, 175, 181–182, 184, 187, 193, 199, 202, 207, 209–215, 220–224, 226, 228, 230–231, 240–242, 245, 252–255, 260, 265–267, 279–280, 289–291, 293–295, 303–304
Seneca Lake, 41, 48
Serpent Mounds, 93, 96
Seven Years' War, 129, 263
Shawnee, 39, 148
sheep, 50, 231
Simcoe, Lieutenant Governor John Graves, 129, 263
Sky World, 214, 236, 305
slave(s), 39, 148
Smith, Robert Home, 130–131, 133, 137–138

Smokes Point, 70, 72, 75, 77, 98, 165, 173, 184, 186–187, 200, 228, 230, 232–233, 239, 248, 253, 255, 281, 288
Smoking Pipe(s), European, 43
Smoking Pipe(s), Indigenous, 199, 239–260, 295
snipe, 220–221
Snow, Dean, 9, 11, 33–34, 36–38, 43–48, 117, 191, 198, 245
Sohrweide, Greg, 44–46, 51, 244, 260
Spencer Creek, 144, 154–155
Squire, Rev. Phillip Bowen, 27, 60, 63–67, 70, 75–76
Squire site, 27, 60, 65–66, 69–70, 72, 288
St. Lawrence Iroquoian, 215, 235
St. Lawrence valley, 13, 40
stone bead(s), 111, 180–183
Sturgeon valley, 18
Sulpicians, Society of the Priests of Saint Sulpice, 7, 23, 56–58, 60, 74, 185, 209, 212, 296
Sundown, Seneca Chief Corbett, 304
Susquehannock, 5, 11, 17, 35, 38–39, 146, 149, 240–241, 243, 245, 247
Susquehannock site(s), 241, 243, 247
  Bert (Byrd) Leibhart, 245
  Conestoga Town, 245
  Lower Leibhart, 245
  Oscar Leibhart, 245
Swayze, Ken, 60, 63, 66, 69–70, 75–76

T

Tahontaenrat (Wendat Deer nation), 14, 17
Talon, Jean, 56
Tangwaonronnon, 20
The Canadian Institute, 131–132, 135
The Griffon, 74
Thousand Islands, 82
thunderbird, 220, 225
Tionontaté (Petun), 5–6, 8, 11, 15, 17, 19, 21, 35, 101, 160, 181, 183, 189, 196, 198, 200, 202, 212, 241, 273, 287
Tionontaté villages
  Ehwae, 15, 175, 181
  Etharita, 19
  Hamilton-Lougheed, 175
  Kelly-Campbell, 202
  Plater-Martin, 200, 202
tollgate(s), 5, 78, 88–89, 91, 96, 288, 290, 295
Tooker, Elizabeth, 240
Tracy, Alexandre de, 23, 42
Treaty of Utrecht, 50
Trenton, 28, 66, 70, 72, 248
Trenton Mountain, 70
Trent River (Sagetewedgewam), 60, 62, 82, 84, 86–88, 125, 170, 177, 180, 182, 270
Trent valley, 7
Trigger, Bruce, 8–9, 11–20, 74, 150, 198, 264–265, 272
Trouvé, Abbé Claude, 7, 56, 58–59, 62, 73–74, 76, 185
Trubowitz, Nealturtle, 241
Twenty Years' War, 44, 46

U

University of Waterloo, 60, 76
Urfé, Abbé François-Saturnin Lascaris de, 58, 77–79, 89, 97

V

Van Son cemetery, 4, 187, 209–210, 212
Vasey, April, 213, 220
Vastokas, Joan and Ron, 236
Veilleux, Annie, 29, 137, 214–215, 220, 223, 235, 237, 281
von Bitter, Robert, 23, 60, 185, 250–251, 253–254, 256, 288
von Gernet, Alex, 26, 265–266, 272–273

W

Walder, Heather, 159

Walpole Island Community, 267
Wampum, 175, 274
Wappoose (Waupoos) Island, 90
Warren, William Whipple, 270
Weisshuhn, Karine, 213
Wellers Bay, 27–28, 60–63, 70, 72, 75–77, 84, 159, 165, 171, 173, 179–180, 183–187, 196, 228, 251–253, 288
Wellington, 73, 222, 248, 250, 253–256
Wendake, 5, 7, 9, 12, 19, 26, 34, 55, 57, 82, 87, 198, 247
wheat, 50, 60
Whitchurch-Stouffville, 252
whitefish, 115
White, Richard, 11, 21, 23, 25
White, Wardie and Ottie, 133, 259
Williamson, Ronald, 1, 3–4, 6–10, 18, 26, 28–29, 33, 39, 46, 51, 55, 70, 76–77, 90, 101, 109, 113, 115–116, 120, 123, 129, 131, 136–137, 139, 145, 163, 176, 186–187, 189, 212–215, 220, 222–223, 235, 239–240, 242–243, 247–249, 252–253, 255, 263, 281, 285–287, 290, 292, 295–298, 305
wolf, 220, 222, 227–228, 254
Wonderley, Anthony, 9, 48, 51, 223, 244, 247, 252, 260
Woods, Julie, 246
Wray, Charles, 35, 37, 39, 43–44, 103, 109, 113, 122, 143, 160–162, 184–185, 193–196, 207, 213, 215, 220, 225, 230, 241–242, 255
Wright, J. V., 56, 66
Wyandot, 21, 44, 181, 267, 271

Y

Yellowhorn, Eldon, 234
York, City of, 131
York Region, 17–18
York Township, 129, 132–133

MERCURY SERIES / LA COLLECTION MERCURE

The best resource on the history, archaeology, and culture of Canada is proudly published by the University of Ottawa Press and the Canadian Museum of History

Les Presses de l'Université d'Ottawa et le Musée canadien de l'histoire publient avec fierté la meilleure ressource en ce qui a trait à l'histoire, à l'archéologie et à la culture canadiennes

Series Editor/Direction de la collection: Pierre M. Desrosiers
Editorial Committee/Comité éditorial: Laura Sanchini, Janet Young
Managing Editor/Responsable de l'édition: Robyn Jeffrey
Coordination: Pascal Scallon-Chouinard

Strikingly Canadian and highly specialized, the *Mercury Series* presents works in the research domain of the Canadian Museum of History and benefits from the publishing expertise of the University of Ottawa Press. Created in 1972, the series is in line with the Canadian Museum of History's strategic directions. The *Mercury Series* consists of peer-reviewed academic research, and includes numerous landmark contributions in the disciplines of Canadian history, archaeology, culture, and ethnology. Books in the series are published in at least one of Canada's official languages, and may appear in other languages.

Remarquablement canadienne et hautement spécialisée, la *collection Mercure* réunit des ouvrages portant sur les domaines de recherches du Musée canadien de l'histoire et s'appuie sur le savoir-faire des Presses de l'Université d'Ottawa. Fondée en 1972, elle répond aux orientations stratégiques du Musée canadien de l'histoire. La *collection Mercure* propose des recherches scientifiques évaluées par les pairs et regroupe de nombreuses contributions majeures à l'histoire, à l'archéologie, à la culture et à l'ethnologie canadiennes. Les ouvrages sont publiés dans au moins une des langues officielles du Canada, avec possibilité de parution dans d'autres langues.

The Mercury Series / La collection Mercure

Frances M. Slaney, *Marius Barbeau's Vitalist Ethnology*, 2023.

Kenneth R. Holyoke and M. Gabriel Hrynick, eds., *The Far Northeast: 3000 BP to Contact*, 2022.

Stacey J. Barker, Krista Cooke, and Molly McCullough, *Material Traces of War: Stories of Canadian Women and Conflict, 1914–1945*, 2021.

Michael K. Hawes, Andrew C. Holman, and Christopher Kirkey, eds., *1968 in Canada: A Year and Its Legacies*, 2021.

Steven Schwinghamer and Jan Raska, *Pier 21: A History, 2020. / Steven Schwinghamer et Jan Raska, Quai 21 : une histoire*, 2020.

Robert Sweeny, ed., *Sharing Spaces: Essays in Honour of Sherry Olson*, 2020.

Matthew Betts, *Place-Making in the Pretty Harbour: The Archaeology of Port Joli*, Nova Scotia, 2019.

Lauriane Bourgeon, *Préhistoire béringienne : étude archéologique des Grottes du Poisson-Bleu (Yukon)*, 2018.

Jenny Ellison and Jennifer Anderson, eds., *Hockey: Challenging Canada's Game–Au-delà du sport national*, 2018.

Myron Momryk, *Mike Starr of Oshawa: A Political Biography*, 2018.

John Willis, ed., *Tu sais, mon vieux Jean-Pierre: Essays on the Archaeology and History of New France and Canadian Culture in Honour of Jean-Pierre Chrestien*, 2017.

Anna Kearney Guigne, *The Forgotten Songs of the Newfoundland Outports: As Taken from Kenneth Peacock's Newfoundland Field Collection, 1951–1961*, 2016.

Ian Dyck, *The Life and Work of W. B. Nickerson (1865–1926): Scientific Archaeology in Central North America*, 2016.

Brad Loewen and Claude Chapdelaine, eds., *Contact in the 16th Century: Networks Among Fishers, Foragers and Farmers*, 2016.

Mauro Peressini, *Choosing Buddhism*, 2016.

Pierre Bibeau, David Denton, and André Burroughs, eds., *Ce que la rivière nous procurait : archéologie et histoire du réservoir de l'Eastmain-1*, 2015.

Charles Garrad, *Petun to Wyandot: The Ontario Petun from the Sixteenth Century*, 2014.

For a complete list of the University of Ottawa Press titles, visit:
Pour une liste complète des titres des Presses de l'Université d'Ottawa, voir :
www.press.uOttawa.ca

www.ingramcontent.com/pod-product-compliance
Lightning Source LLC
Chambersburg PA
CBHW050301010526
44108CB00040B/1922